B-17 MEMORIES
FROM
MEMPHIS BELLE TO VICTORY

T/SGT. JAMES LEE HUTCHINSON, ED.S.

AuthorHouse™
1663 Liberty Drive
Bloomington, IN 47403
www.authorhouse.com
Phone: 1-800-839-8640

© 2014 T/Sgt. James Lee Hutchinson, Ed.S.. All rights reserved.

No part of this book may be reproduced, stored in a retrieval system, or transmitted by any means without the written permission of the author.

Used with permission from the Stars and Stripes. @ 2006 Stars and Stripes.
Cover photo credit: Memphis Belle by Scott Maher of Liberty Belle Foundation

Published by AuthorHouse   05/21/2014

ISBN: 978-1-4969-1135-3 (sc)
ISBN: 978-1-4969-1134-6 (e)

Library of Congress Control Number: 2014908588

Any people depicted in stock imagery provided by Thinkstock are models, and such images are being used for illustrative purposes only.
Certain stock imagery © Thinkstock.

This book is printed on acid-free paper.

Because of the dynamic nature of the Internet, any web addresses or links contained in this book may have changed since publication and may no longer be valid. The views expressed in this work are solely those of the author and do not necessarily reflect the views of the publisher, and the publisher hereby disclaims any responsibility for them.

Dedicated to my Family

Special thanks to Mike and Sherri Alexander, Don Lueking, Susan Hutchinson, Scott Maher, Debera Reed and Eric Swain, 490th Group Historian, and the two men who had the foresight to record our history and to all airmen who contributed their memories in the:
"History of the 490th Bombardment Group"
Lt. Col. Lawrence S. Lightner and T/Sgt. Frederick R. Holland
Oct. 1943 to October 1945

Contents

Chapter One 1
About the Author 1
Mission Alert 2
Here Comes the Draft! 3
Poor as Church Mice 5
Caught in the Draft 6
Air Cadet Basic Training in Texas 9
Sioux Falls Radio School 11
Earning my Wings at Yuma 14
Sioux City Combat Crew Training 19
Camp Kilmer and the Queen Mary 23
Flying the North Atlantic 24

Chapter Two 27
The Mighty Eighth 27
Bomber Group Assembly 30
Combat Box Formation 31
Flying Combat Missions 35
Flak - Airman's Nightmare 40
The Memphis Belle Story 43
The 95th Bomb Group 50
Lt. William "Ed" Charles 51
Shuttle Missions 52
    15th Air Force – 99th BG 53
    8th Air Force 95th BG 54
The "Bloody Hundredth" 56
Sweater Girl of the 100th BG 57
    Lt. Kenneth Barron-POW 58
    S/Sgt. "Ike" Wright- POW 58
Captain James R. Stout's Combat Log 63
War Department Telegrams 82
The Armored New Testament 83

Lt. John C. Walter, B-17 Pilot 84
Lt. Charles F. Miller, Bombardier 94

Chapter Three 98
490th Bomb Group (H) History 98
Lt. William E. Cranston, Co-Pilot 98
Bombardier Lt. Harry Lomicka 105
Sgt. Michael Walsh – POW 105
Lt. George B. Reeves 108
We Arrive at Eye 112
Hut # 29 – The Brome Dome 113
The Swan Pub 116
Merseburg Mission 117
T/Sgt Frank McKinley's Story 118
Visits to Diss 122
B-17G Flying Fortress 126
490th Bomb Group Bombers 130
S/Sgt. John Gann's Merseberg Mission 132
Hutch's Missions 139
   Hutch #1   Berlin   Dec. 5, 1944 139
   Hutch   Lutzkendorf (Aborted)   Dec. 6 146
Eyes of the Bomber 147
   Hutch #2   Hannover Dec. 15 148
   Hutch #3   Stuttgart Dec. 16 149

Chapter Four 151
   Hutch #4   Frankfort on Christmas Eve 151
General Castle's Medal of Honor 153
490th BG December Report: 154
Promoted to Lead Crew 156
   Hutch #5   Bad Kreuznack Jan. 2, 1945 158
   Hutch #6   Aschaffenberg Jan. 3 159
Mid-Air Collision   Jan. 5 160
   T/Sgt. Roger Coryell 161
Major Edward F. Blum's Bail Out 163
Lt. Joseph F. Tighe's Cologne Mission 165

Sgt. Richard L. Lynde, Ball Turret Gunner 167
S/Sgt. Richard T. Keough's Walk Out 168
   Hutch #7   Derben Jan. 14 171
Our Little Friends 174
Bandits and Bogies 176
   Hutch #8 - Augsburg Jan. 15 178
   Hutch #9   Sterkade-Rheine Jan. 20 179

Chapter Five 181
Streets of London 181
Templeton Crew Flak Casualty 186
T/Sgt. Howard Tuchin's Thirteenth Mission 188
   Hutch #11   Frankfort Feb. 17 191
   Hutch #12   Ansbach Feb. 22 192
Lt. Ron Cargill - A Tiny Piece of Flak 193
   Hutch #12 B   Ulm Mar. 1 196
T/Sgt. Howard Tuchin Bails Out 197
The Caterpillar Club 201

Chapter Six 204
Date With a Brit 204
Jet Fighter Attack 209
ME-109 Fighter Attack 211
   Hutch #17   Roudnice, Czech April 17 213
490th Black Thursday 214
   Lt. Lawrence J. Bellarts 215
   Lt. Buford E. Stovall 215
   Sgt. Dennis M. Richardson 216
   Maj. Joel R. Johnson (Ret.) 217
German SS Atrocity 218
   S/Sgt. Wilbur Lesh 219
   Sgt. Newton Parker 220
   Lt. Lorenzo G. Smith JR. 221
The 490th Monument in Czechoslovakia 223
   Hutch #18   Nauen April 20 223

Chapter Seven ... 225
The Twelfth and Fifteenth Air Forces ... 225
S/Sgt. Harold Plunkett ... 227
S/Sgt. James Allinder - Ploesti Oil Raid ... 237
Oxygen Mask Troubles ... 239
    T/Sgt. James S. Peters Sr. ... 240
    Lt. Jules F. Brendt ... 242
    T/Sgt. Howard Tuchin ... 243
    Lt. John C. Walter, B-17 ... 243
T/Sgt. James Peters Sr. ... 244
    RDX Bombs ... 246
    Friend or Foe? ... 247
Tuskegee Airmen – Red Tails ... 249

Chapter Eight ... 253
Salute to Ground Troops ... 253
Massacre at Oradour-Sur-Glane ... 253
Paratroops and Gliders ... 255
S/Sgt. Merrill St. John ... 258
D-Day, June 6, 1944 ... 260
Brig. Gen. Theodore Roosevelt, Jr. ... 262
Ninth Infantry Division World War II ... 265
John Hill's Story ... 266
    John's Story Begins ... 267
    The Battle of the Bulge ... 270
    The Ardennes Forest ... 275
    Remagen Bridge - John Hill ... 289
    German Counter-Attack ... 291
    Battle at Dessau ... 302
Sgt. Arlie Propes' Re-con Duty ... 307
Corporal Ermy Bartlett in Italy ... 309

Chapter Nine ... 314
Sgt. Arlie Propes' Story Continued ... 314
Ohrdruf Death Camp ... 314
Mauthausen Extermination Complex ... 317

The Holocaust 319
The Auschwitz Album 321
Mercy Missions 322
VE- Day — Victory in Europe 324
Victory Flight Tours 327
T/Sgt. Howard Tuchin's Repatriation Flight 327
Simon Wiesenthal 330
World War II Memorial 331
Willie and Joe 332
The Mighty Eighth Museum 335
Salute to WW II Veterans 337

Addenda 339
The Short Snorter 339
Britain Says "Thanks Yanks" 342
The Queen's Letter 344
The Boeing B-17G Specification 345
Eighth Air Force Bomb Groups in England 346
Hutch's WWII Books 347

Reader's Guide and Glossary

B-17 Flying Fortress – four motor heavy bomber – cost $276,000, ten man crew, thirteen .50 caliber machine guns– no heat, 40 below zero at 25,000 feet – not pressurized for high altitude – oxygen masks B-24 Liberator – four motored heavy much the same.

1. Fighter groups --- RAF Spitfire, Mosquito and Hurricane --- U.S. - P-51Mustang, P-47 Thunderbird and P-38 Lightning
2. Squadron - 12 to 18 bombers each with a crew of ten
3. Bomb Group - consisted of four squadrons
4. Wing – three to four Bomb Groups
5. Division – three or more wings –
6. Royal Air Force (RAF).
7. Flak – shrapnel from bursting shells
8. Flak happy - mental fatigue from combat
9. Chaff – aluminum coated paper dropped to foul up flak gun radar
10. Gestapo- Geheime Staats Polizei (German state secret police.)
11. Happy Valley or Flak Alley- heavily protected targets in the industrial Ruhr valley
12. Hardstand --- parking space for a bomber
13. Electrical Jammers- equipment to distort enemy's radio and radar
14. Ditching – emergency landing of a damaged bomber in the sea.
15. Electric suit – gloves and socks worn under heavy clothing and boots – plugged into outlet at each crew-member's position
16. Mae West – inflatable life preserver vest worn under the parachute harness.

17. Parachute –chest pack hooked to a harness – seat pack type for pilots
18. Flak jacket – Apron of sheets of steel covered with canvas to protect the torso front and back- weighed 45 pounds
19. Flak helmet - regular steel helmet - with flaps to cover headsets
20. Mess Hall – food (chow) for the base – we lined up cafeteria style with metal trays - officers mess was a separate section
21. Chowhound – a hungry GI
22. GI –government issue- slang for soldier, we were all GIs
23. Latrine – toilet and shower room
24. Lucky Bastards – men who did the required missions to go home
25. Turret – rotating machine gun position on bomber
26. Mission Alert – notice to fly a mission next morning
27. Red Alert - air raid ---- enemy bombers or buzz bombs
28. Milk Run – easy mission – not much flak
29. MACR – missing air crew report filed after bomber was lost
30. POW Prisoner of War
31. Purple Heart – medal awarded to wounded or killed
32. Purple Heart Corner, Coffin Corner or Tail-end Charlie – position of last planes flying in squadrons of bombing formation – an easy target for fighters
33. PX- post exchange (store) on the base
34. Air Medal awarded for every six missions
35. Prop Wash – air disturbance from propellers of planes flying ahead of you
36. Sack – cot or bunk bed
37. Sack time- sleep or rest - a good place to keep warm.
38. Sad Sack – a 'goof off 'or poor
39. Crew Chief – head mechanic assigned to maintain the plane
40. Bogey or Bandit – enemy fighter or unidentified aircraft
41. Scuttlebutt – rumor or gossip
42. AWOL – absent without leave
43. Piccadilly Commando - London prostitute
44. SS German national secret police (Shutzstaffle)

CHAPTER ONE

ABOUT THE AUTHOR

Photo - Bloomington IN, Herald Times

James Lee Hutchinson is the author of four books and a DVD interview on memories of his service in the 8th Army Air Corps over Germany in World War II. He writes to record sacrifices of some of the WW II boys in the B-17 Flying Fortress and/or their boyhood in the pre-war depression. He says, "WW II was the last war we won; it preserved our nation and constitution from those who would change it." February, 2008 the Indiana General Assembly passed a resolution by Sen. Brent Steele and Rep. Eric Koch honoring the author for his WW II service and his first book, "Through These Eyes." Hutch grew up in a small town in the hills of southern Indiana in the Great Depression. His boyhood was much the same as that of many of the sixteen million men and women who served in World War II.

At age eighty- nine, he continues telling stories by writing newspaper articles, speaking to schools, and civic groups. He presently volunteers as co-host of a History Project of the North Lawrence Community

Schools. The project's mission is to interview and preserve stories for the general public and school history classes. View at (Star Station on Vimeo)

Home from the war at age twenty, he attended Indiana University on the G.I. Bill. Degrees include: 1949, B.S. (History and Journalism); 1952, Masters, (elementary education); 1967, EdS (School Administration). He served thirty-seven years in public schools as an elementary teacher, Principal and Assistant Superintendent. Community service includes United Fund, American Legion, Rotary Club (Paul Harris Award), 50 year member of the Masonic Lodge and an elder in the Presbyterian Church.

Hutch says Google "Wings Over Europe My Smithville" to see my video interview with combat film footage. The DVD was directed by Rob Ramsey of the Smithville Phone Company after I wrote my first book, "Through These Eyes." the Smithville Telephone crew did an excellent job of weaving my stories into historic film footage of WW II bombing missions. I refer it to classes or audiences whenever I present a program, because it gives a very real picture of my teenage combat memories of life and death in the flak-filled skies over Germany. Seventy–one years ago our B-17 Bomber formations flew at 25,000 feet, we were on oxygen and wearing heavy clothing over electric suits, gloves and boots for protection from 40 degrees below zero.

Mission Alert

Mission alert, we're scheduled to fly
A day of combat; perhaps to die.
Early to bed for a restless night
We get the call before dawn's light.

Breakfast, briefing and out to our plane
We pray to survive combat again.
Loaded bombers soar into the sky
Airmen on both sides are going to die.

Many decades have passed
Since I heard mission alert last
But I remember those B-17 boys;
The deadly missions; the terrible noise.

Flak filled skies --- enemy fighters too
Waited for bombers in WW II.
Victory was won at a terrible cost
I salute the 26,000 who were lost.

Veteran WW II airmen share my tears
Our ranks grow thin with the passing years.
Generations must know of their days of glory
And so I write to tell our story.
by T/Sgt James Lee Hutchinson

Here Comes the Draft!

Sunday, December 7, 1941 the Empire of Japan made a sneak attack on Pearl Harbor while their envoys were in Washington discussing peace. The attack was truly, as President Roosevelt said, "A day of infamy." and ended all ideas of isolation and propelled our nation into World War II.

Six Japanese aircraft carriers launched 353 planes (167 carried bombs or torpedoes) to attack the U.S. Navy base at Pearl Harbor. The Jap bombers sank four battleships, damaged fifteen other and destroyed 188 aircraft. The approximate military casualty list was 2,400 dead and 12,000 wounded. Congress declared war on the Axis Powers of Japan, Germany and Italy the day after Pearl Harbor.

The terrific costs of World War I ruined the economies of most nations and a worldwide depression destroyed governments. Germany, Italy and Japan gave up on and chose dictators. Those countries recovered by building strong military forces and attacking their neighbors. The United States was slow to build defenses and our army and navy forces were very weak. The Air Corps was a small army unit with few planes. Pearl Harbor caught us by surprise. Our country needed to build military forces in a hurry. We were short of men and equipment. The bombing of Pearl Harbor found us in a bad depression and unprepared for war but, unemployment dropped from twenty-four to two percent as able-bodied men went to war and women went to work in factories. In the next three years sixteen million men went to war and American industries produced enough tanks, ships, and planes to fight and win a war in both Europe and the Pacific.

Congress had passed the Selective Service and Training Act in September of 1940 as war clouds gathered in Europe and the U.S. had a 24 % unemployment rate. The first "draft" for military service ever passed in peacetime required all men ages 18 to 35 to register with local Draft Boards. Remember Pearl Harbor became the nation's battle cry as all men registered and were classified to determine those best fit to serve. For instance:

1 A ---- healthy single men	3 A ---- man with wife and children
3 D -----extreme family hardship	4 F ---- physically or mentally unfit
4 A ---- too old	2 B --- workers in a war industry
2 C --- farmers, agricultural workers	
1 A-O Conscientious objector limited to non- combat service	

A lottery system was used to draw names of the draftees, nobody wanted to win that one. Suddenly, the "4 F syndrome" hit the neighborhood and several guys developed a weak heart or some other serious ailment to keep them from going. We always said they just didn't have the heart to go! A few others joined a church, suddenly became very religious and claimed to be "conscientious objectors" who didn't believe in fighting for their country. Local Draft Boards gave very few deferments and neither did the Army. Later when I was line at the induction center a buddy in front of me claimed he was a 1 A-O. They tried to convince him he wasn't, but he didn't give in. He ended up on an island in the pacific as an unarmed Medic. Parents had struggled to feed and protect their children during the hunger and trials of the world's greatest depression. They had high hopes for a better future for their children, only to have them jerked away and sent to war. Many young fathers left a wife and children to serve their country.

Poor as Church Mice

The economy was going well when I was born in 1925 in a farmhouse near Leesville, Indiana. Dad was a tenant farmer on a large farm owned by his uncle Emory who was also a schoolteacher. In those days, most births took place in the home. The doctor, when summoned, cranked up his Model "T" Ford and came to the house where he was assisted by family female relatives or friends. I guess the men-folk boiled lots of water or just sat around and whittled. I don't remember the details!

When I was four, Dad went to work in a Bedford limestone quarry and built a new house on Granddad Hutchinson's farm. We later moved to a house on a dairy farm on the outskirts of Bedford. Dad bought a four-room in the southeast edge of town, just before the great depression That four room house had no utilities, so we carried water from a neighbor, used kerosene lamps, cooked meals and heated with wood or coal stoves. The stock market had crashed in 1929, the national unemployment rate shot up to twenty-five percent and it was even higher in southern Indiana because all limestone quarries and mills were shut down. Many workers moved away when jobs became as scarce as hen's teeth and men were willing to work for a dollar a day. Later the WPA, a government work project, paid a dollar fifty a day. I was a "depression kid" all through school but so was nearly everyone else. We thought any kid who's Dad had steady job was a rich kid.

During the summer between grades four and five grade, my buddy, Chad and I made our first stab at earning money. We used my little red wagon to go into the junk business. We patrolled neighborhood alleys to collect metal, rags or paper we could sell at the junkyard. Of course we were competing with the push cart men who also searched the alleys, but their main source of income came from hauling trash from stores or businesses around the square.

Chad and I collected metals; iron, brass from light bulb bases, zinc from fruit jar lids and anything aluminum. The junkyard would also buy rags and paper. Our main goal that summer was to earn at least thirty cents, which was enough to buy us two bottles of Nehi pop and tickets to a Saturday matinee. Our weekend was a success when got to see a rip-roaring 'Shoot'em up" Western, B movie and serial at the Von Ritz theater. The Great Depression lasted until Pearl Harbor and World War II when young men went to war and women and older men labored in wartime factories to build President Roosevelt's "Arsenal of Defense."

I endured the exercise of "doing without" right up to the day I got may draft notice. I was a six foot teenager who weighed 150 pounds soaking wet. Obesity was not a problem for my pre-war generation, food was scarce and folks lived without the fattening fast food hamburgers and high fructose sodas served kids today. Mothers prepared three meals a day from "scratch" and most families had a large vegetable garden. As a teenager, I earned spending money with several part-time jobs which no longer exist. I could caddy at the golf course, set pins at the bowling alley, get a newspapers route or work at Bill's Auto Store until the start of WW II. Times were tough; I did all three and never earned more than .25 cents an hour!

Caught in the Draft

My Senior Class graduated in May, 1943 and the majority of the boys enlisted in order to join their favorite branch of service and avoid the draft. However, I was a mid-year senior because I failed second grade so I needed six more hours to graduate. I was planning to be the first in my Granddad's family to graduate and I wanted to beat my cousins. The Draft Board was taking everyone who was warm, but I decided to not enlist and take my chances on making it back to school in September. Well, I didn't make it! My selective service notice to register for the draft arrived June 13, 1943, the day after my eighteenth birthday!

My "Greetings" letter from my friends and neighbors came July 22 and I went before the draft Board to apply for a deferment to finish school, but said they were taking everyone. If you didn't have a deferment, you were in uniform. I never made it back to my last semester at Bedford High. There were some deferments for workers needed in agriculture or critical skills in the defense industry. Some tried for medical deferments and suddenly developed weak hearts, bad backs or sleepwalking problems, but they miraculously passed the army's medical and were rewarded with a brand new uniform. One guy in our neighborhood gave us a valuable less when he went AWOL (absent without leave) and came home. The M.P.s (military police) came and found him under his parents' front porch, hiding like a possum. They quickly dragged him out handcuffed him, shoved him in the Jeep and took him back to the guardhouse (jail). That incident was a stern lesson for all teenagers in the neighborhood. None of us wanted that treatment. My Granddad tried to console me about not graduating but it came out wrong when he said the Army was scrapping the bottom of the barrel when they drafted me. I hated to leave home, but looked forward to serving my country and three square meals a day in the Mess Hall.

I was inducted into the Army at the Armory in Louisville, Kentucky on August 4, 1943. So, on August 25th, a week before my fall semester of high school started, I was aboard a Greyhound bus with about fifteen other Lawrence County boys. It was ironic that the bus drove past Bedford High and the business of the draft board chairman as we pulled out of town. It was a sad day, but I had one consolation, I was not a "drop-out," I was a "pull-out." Little did I realize at the time, but that bus ride was the first step of a having a full scholarship provided my rich Uncle Sam! The bus was taking us away from homes and families and our future was to be determined by the Army at Fort Benjamin Harrison in Indianapolis. A ramrod straight corporal met our bus and immediately made it clear that we were in the Army now and we had better "shape up". He guided us to the supply room and we began the process of changing from draftees to Buck Privates. We were issued clothing; everything was "olive drab"; a wool dress uniform, two sets of work clothes (fatigues), underwear socks and heavy shoes. There were also tan shirts and trousers for summer dress. Finally, loaded with clothing, we marched to our barracks, picked out a bunk and put on the work fatigues. We had the option of shipping our "civies" home or tossing them in the trash barrel. Most of us chose the trash barrel before the Corporal marched us to the Mess Hall where we got in our first line. Little did we know that is was the first of many hours we would spend waiting in line. We had been introduced to the military "hurry up and wait" policy. Thirty minutes later, we picked up a compartmentalized steel tray and moved along the chow line as the guys on KP (Kitchen Police) slapped on gobs of food. We went back to the barracks after our first taste of Army food and the Corporal gave us free time until a six a six o'clock formation in front of the barracks next morning

At breakfast we were introduced to another Army tradition which was ham and gravy on toast, or better known as S____ on a shingle!

The rest of the morning was spent getting a G.I. burr haircut, medical exam and shots. That afternoon we were issued two aluminum ID tags on a chain. Imprinted on those "dogtags" was our name, serial number, religious preference and blood type. We were told to wear them around our necks as long as we were in the Army. The Corporal put it more clearly, "You have two dogtags so when you got killed they can take one for their records and leave the other to identify your body."

Boy, what an introduction to the Army!

I was in the Infantry at Ft. Benjamin Harrison in Indianapolis, waiting for assignment and dreading it. They kept us busy mopping floors, cleaning the latrine (restrooms) and laying sod around the parade ground. Rumors said we would be sent overseas as soon as we finished basic training. That bit of news did nothing to cheer me up! One hot August day we were taking a break on our work detail and the Corporal mentioned that the Army Air Corps was taking recruits for the Air Cadet program, but you had to volunteer to fly and pass a color-blind test before you could transfer. They say "never volunteer," but I made one of the greatest decisions of my life when I signed up immediately.

Two weeks in the infantry was enough for me and I was now a Volunteer Flight Trainee (VFT) and I carried that designation throughout my Air Force service. A few days later, several hundred eager VFTs boarded a troop train for Air Cadet basic training in Amarillo, Texas. We were eager beavers, planning to be pilots and soar through the air like the heroes in all the war movies. Troop trains were the main means of transportation in the states. It was a three-day trip with no bunks, so we slept in our seats or on our pile of duffel bags in the back of the car, for a thousand miles. It would be several weeks before I learned that the Air Corps had recruited VFT's from all branches of the Army, because what they really needed were gunners for heavy bombers crews!

Air Cadet Basic Training in Texas

Our barracks was designated Training Group 904, Tech School 409. I was an Air Cadet ready for training as a pilot, navigator or bombardier so I purchased a sterling silver Air Cadet ring. Buck privates were paid $50 a month, so I bought the ring for thirteen dollars, sent money home, and was broke the rest of the month. However, it became my lucky ring. I wore it on all my missions and I wear it yet today. That ring and my silver wings are great "attention getters" when I'm talking to students or peddling books.

Non-commissioned officers had almost as much authority as officers, in basic training and the Drill Corporals and Sergeants laid down the law. As the saying goes, when they said, jump we yelled, How high? Basic training was like a high school post-graduate course because the majority of us were fresh out of a Midwest High School. I never dreamed that someday the Congress would pass a G.I. Bill which would allow me to earn three degrees from Indiana University. Marching and singing helped build our lungs for high altitude flying (so we were told.) We sang all the old favorites from "I've Got Sixpence" to most of George M. Cohan's patriotic songs. The majority of us were from the mid-west so there were also the Wisconsin, Ohio State and Indiana fight songs.

I never realized that someday my rich Uncle Sam would pay my way through college.

Reveille was at 5:00 a.m. every weekday morning during basic training, but the Bugler didn't have to get up. They blasted a recording over the loudspeakers around the camp and sleepy-eyed rookies dressed and scrambled out of the barracks into to fall into line in the cold desert air for roll call. We were then led by a small band in a parade on a lane around the Company area. The jack rabbits and coyotes probably held their ears as the brass band and the singing of several hundred teenage buck privates shattered the darkness of the early Texas morning! That parade around the block in the cool desert morning was a great eye opener. We were allowed a short break before falling into formation again for a march to the Mess Hall, singing all the way. We were free to scoot back to the barracks and latrine until the next formation.

We all drew a turn at KP duty (kitchen police) in the Mess Hall. I usually ended up feeding dirty trays through the hot steamy dishwasher called the "China Clipper." I didn't mind doing KP duty once in a while because of all the food available. One day a cook chewed me out for eating too many pineapple slices. Several weeks on KP duty or a few days in the guardhouse was also used as punishment for goldbricks (goof offs) or AWOLS.

Six weeks later most of us were "washed out" of the Air Cadet program, only four of the forty guys in our barracks made the cut. The rest of us suddenly became gunners. Remember we had volunteered to fly! However, I wore my ring as a good luck charm on all my missions and it's still on my finger. I was a thousand miles from home a "pull out" and now a "wash out" completing my basic training.

Amarillo, Texas had a typical desert climate, cold at night and blazing hot by mid-afternoon. Yard-bird duty was tough. The corporal gave you a bag and a stick with a nail in the end and you walked around the squadron area for a few hours spearing cigarette butts and paper to put in the bag.

After day of drill or on the rifle range, we were always hot so we often walked into the showers fully clothed to cool off wash our dirty sweaty fatigues at the same time. They dried overnight and were ready for the next day. The boots took a little longer, but were ready a new coat of polish for Inspection. Those "fun in the sun" activities of drills, marches and trips to the rifle range created a greater appreciation of our indoor classes. Frequent wind and dust storms kept us busy at dusting and sweeping our barracks to keep it clean long enough to pass inspection on Saturday and earn a pass to town.

Somewhere I have the barracks group photo of the guys in my class. It helps me recall names of some of those guys like Bill Irk, Lloyd Carnahan and Don Goodfellow and the faces of several others. Many of them did not make a tech school but went directly to gunnery school, combat crew training and were in combat long before arrived at Eye. I later learned that some had already finished their tour of duty and others had been wounded or killed. Guys who had endured basic training in the very hot Texas temperatures of September through early November and qualified for radio school were glad to be going north, but the Air Force over-corrected. Three Pullman cars of future radio operators pulled out of Amarillo a few days before Thanksgiving and we waved goodbye to the hot dusty Texas Pan Handle. Three days later, we stepped off the train into six inches of snow and freezing temperatures. We had arrived at Sioux Falls, South Dakota, "The Meeting Place of the West."

Sioux Falls Radio School

We moved into our Radio Technical School barracks two days before Thanksgiving, 1943 and its three coal fed pot-bellied stoves were a welcome sight. Our thin blood had to adjust to a drop of 70 degrees in the three day trip from basic training in Amarillo, Texas. Our new address was Squadron 809, barracks 421. The barracks were one story un-insulated buildings designed for warmer climates, no better insulated than those we left in Texas. They were heated by three large pot bellied-stoves. One man had to miss class each day to be "barracks guard" and feed the stoves. He was truly the "keeper of the flame" and his duty was to keep the home fires burning! He carried coal from the bins out back, carried out the ashes and kept a gallon bucket of water on each stove top (our humidifiers.) The stoves were included in barracks inspection and had to be clean at all times. Worse still, our company latrine was out the back door and fifty yards down the alley. A furnace heated the latrine and we had hot water, but we had to be warmly dressed to make a visit.

Classes were seldom cancelled because of snow or frigid weather and we marched to and from classrooms five days a week. Dress uniforms, long johns, four- buckle boots knit caps and heavy winter overcoats were the order of the day! I recall wearing a gas mask to class in sub-zero temperatures. Luckily, our barracks was only a half mile from the classroom buildings. The winter dress code was strictly enforced to avoid flu and pneumonia cases. When we had a Saturday pass, we had to pass inspection by an MP (military Police) before boarding the bus. I spent a few days in the hospital with the flu in February, but managed to keep up with my class.

The radio school ran two shifts a day because radio operators were in high demand in both the European and Pacific air war. Our class drew the night shift from 3:00 to 11:00 pm. During the next five months, we studied radio mechanics and Morse code. We were students in radio mechanics class on equipment, frequencies and radio theory half of each class. The other half, we sat in a large, but quiet room of forty or so guys at desks wearing headsets to listen and write down Morse code messages at as specific speed level. The early training theory seemed to be, "it is better receive, than to send." We practiced hours on the sending key. We had to be able to send and receive sixteen words per minute to graduate with our class. There were monthly proficiency tests on the knowledge of radio mechanics and speed of sending and receiving code. Failing meant repeating that four week session. The final weeks, we practiced in mock-ups of a bomber radio room with a BC-375-E long range Liaison transmitter, BC-348-Q receiver, 274N pilot's command radio, and radio compass to give us the location of equipment and the feel of being a radio operator on a real bomber.

However, it would be months before I sat at B-17 desk in full dress for a four mile high mission at - 40 degrees wearing an electric suit, gloves and socks under all the regular clothing. An oxygen mask, flak helmet,

45 pound flak jacket and parachute harness mandatory. I would have to take off heavy gloves to send or write Morse code messages and if we were above 10,000 feet, I needed a portable oxygen bottle to leave that desk.

Voice messages would not travel long distances so the military used the International Morse code, for long range radio tramsmission. My sending key was attached to the desk to right of the receiver. A adjustable spring kept it from making contact with the base. I tapped it to send the Morse code alphabet in the secret "bomber code" of the day. The dot was a quick "dit" and I held down a second of a fraction longer for the dash or "dah." Crew members often referred to their radio operator as Sparky or the dit - dah guy!

Mastering the Morse code was accomplished by weeks of repetition in long practice sessions in aroom full of guys wearing headsets.

```
A ·-      J ·---    S ···     1 ·----
B -···    K -·-     T -       2 ··---
C -·-·    L ·-··    U ··-     3 ···--
D -··     M --      V ···-    4 ····-
E ·       N -·      W ·--     5 ·····
F ··-·    O ---     X -··-    6 -····
G --·     P ·--·    Y -·--    7 --···
H ····    Q --·-    Z --··    8 ---··
I ··      R ·-·               9 ----·
                              0 -----
```

Most of our radio instructors were combat veterans who knew the skills needed by a good bomb crew radio operator. They all had the same goal; the Air Corps needed radiomen overseas and they were determined to provide them! One of my instructors, Jim Guthrie, was from my home town. Sixty three years later, I met another former instructor, Harold Plunkett, who had finished 55 missions as B-17 ball turret gunner and/or radio operator in Africa and Italy early in the war. Harold's combat diary is included in "Bombs Away" and this book.

Our classroom training continued at this base to prepare each crew member for combat. Radio operators also used the Short Operation Signals (Q codes.) We were required to memorize the three dozen or more code signals used as short-cuts to eliminate transmitting long messages and avoid crowding the airwaves. The "Q signals" were especially useful to radio operators on a mission, because they could send one three letter signal with a lot of meaning to give or seek information quickly. Below is a list of the most frequently used Q signals:

QPZ --- Yes, QQZ --- No
QAM --- Request weather report.
QMF --- I need a frequency check.
QRJ ---- Did you receive my message?
QDM --- What is my magnetic course to reach you?
QTE --- What is your bearing?
QLF --- Your frequency is too high.
QRS --- Send message more slowly.
QTH --- What is your position?
QAA --- When will you arrive?

Earning my Wings at Yuma

Graduation from Radio School meant we had survived the below zero weather, passed all tests, especially code speed, and therefore qualified to attend Aerial Gunnery school. It was a three day troop train ride from the frozen north to Yuma Air Base in the southwest corner of Arizona. We stepped off the train into 98 degrees of dry desert heat with no trees, barren mountains and very high temperatures. Grass and trees grew only where they were watered regularly. One of the first things they issued us was a silver painted helmet liner, which we were required to wear to prevent heatstroke. We soon realized it was a blessing. We had been transported from frostbite to heat stroke!

Gunnery school in the desert was a lot like my days in Amarillo, only dryer. It was a drastic climate change from a winter in North Dakota. Training was in two parts: classes were outdoors each morning and indoors after the noon Mess Hall.

In the first phase of training, we endured hot outdoor classes of firing shotguns to hit clay pigeons. This skeet shooting exercise taught us to aim and hit a flying target and we destroyed thousands of them. Many had never fired a shotgun, my rabbit and squirrel hunting experience proved valuable and I scored well. Later, we moved to another range, an oval track around twelve trap shacks. Half of us took turns in one of those trap shacks to load and send the clay pigeons flying in the sky to provide targets for the guys with the shotguns. Later, gunners rode around the track in the back of a pick-up truck. The truck had special braces to support the student, the instructor and a shotgun mounted in an airplane type machine-gun frame. Guys in the trucks were to hit the flying clay pigeon while traveling 15 t0 20 miles per hour. The trick was to lead the target by aiming behind it to compensate for the speed of the truck. This imitated firing from a 150 MPH bomber and buckshot (bullets) would catch up with the target.

Indoor classes were concentrated on Aircraft Recognition and repairing the Browning fifty caliber machine gun which had approximately 150 parts. Mounted machine guns were set up at five work stations and each day instructors created various malfunctions in the guns. We worked in squads of five and our job was to find and repair the problem. We practiced taking apart and reassembling those guns for weeks. Our final test would be to take a machine gun apart and reassemble it in five minutes while blindfolded. We also spent many hours in instant recognition of enemy and U.S. planes. All instructions were important because these were skills that could save our lives.

Letter from Yuma - This letter, dated May 21, 1944, illustrates that I was a naïve teenage Hoosier, a product of the depression, who had been sent out into the world too soon. That world, seventy-one years ago, was a place vastly different than it is today.

"*Dear Mom,*

> *Well, we just had inspection and I got "gigged" The Lieutenant said my bunk and foot locker are was neat, but not arranged like it was supposed to be so I don't get a pass next weekend although that doesn't worry me. I had a pass yesterday and Keen Umbehr and I went into Yuma. Boy it is some town, just like the western town in the movies, but it's small, maybe*

only 6,000 people, about half the size of Bedford. We just ran up and down the main street. All the stores have porches out over the sidewalk so it's always shady. Their stores are full of souvenirs and novelties and there are plenty of them. Mexicans and Indians are as thick as fleas. The women had loud scarves over their long black hair and most of the men wore hats or bright rags around their head. We took in a show, "Four Jills and a Jeep" and it was a pretty good one. We saw lots of the townspeople in the theater, pretty little tow headed kids and high school kids. Everybody looked healthy and happy and on the whole the white people in town treated us OK. I got another roll of film, it's rationed but I can take a lot of pictures if I ever get a camera!

I agree with you, clipping the chickens' wings is a good idea. I'm sure it will keep them from flying out of the coop. I figure old man Smith's dogs will catch them if they get out.

No, the pressure chamber I told you about is not on a plane, it's a big metal airtight chamber that can seat about eight guys. They locked us in and drew the air out of the chamber until it was the same as it would be if we were really at high altitude. You get lighted headed when that happens. They wanted to check us out, and show us how you can pass out without oxygen. I did get to go up in a plane yesterday and it was really something! It was my first time in a big plane. My only other airplane ride was in a Piper Cub during my last week of training at Sioux Falls and I got sick on that flight. We went up in a brand new silver B-17G and flew up above the clouds. I looked down on all the mountains and the Colorado River. I think we flew over California for a while, since California is across the river and we crossed it! My first B-17 ride was a hoot. There were eight of us besides three instructors and the two pilots. They let us move all over the bomber and I got to ride in the bombardier seat in the glass nose for a while. It was like I was in a glass cage. I could see left, right, up and down. I had a clear view of the ground under me and could look back to see the motors and whirling propellers. Later, I was sitting on the floor in the radio man's compartment and looked up across the room and out of the small side window and saw the ground! The pilot had put the plane in a sharp bank and I didn't know it until I looked out!

> *We were up for over an hour and along toward the end of the ride some of the guys started getting airsick and two guys puked in the bomb-bay. They had to clean it out when we got down. Thanks for sending me Chad's V-mail letter, I had seen one before, but not one that had been written by candlelight in a foxhole. He must be leading a hell of a life over there in the infantry. Guess I'll close now and get this mailed. Today is Sunday so I have time to go swimming. Lots of Love ------"*

Note - *Chad, my best boyhood buddy, was killed in France in November, 1944 about the same time I arrived at Eye.*

Our class moved on to firing from a B-17 bomber in flight. We finally got to fly in B-17s and fire machine guns from the waist gunner position at targets on the ground. Last, we got down to the serious business of flying and air-to-air gunnery. The next two weeks we spent part of every day in a bomber firing the .50 caliber machine gun at a long cloth sleeve target towed on a very long cable by another plane flying beside and ahead of us. The waist gun was fed clusters of six-inch bullets painted different colors in a metal belt hanging from an overhead ammunition canister. Our gunnery instructor assigned a section of color to each of us. He said they would examine the target sleeve to see how many "hits" were made by each man. The chattering machine gun, sagging ammo belts and brass shell casings spewing onto the floor added realism to our training. I got a kick out of learning about the plane's radio room and sat at the radio operators's desk at the receiver and code key for a while. A long range transmitter and tuning units hung the bulkhead behind. The swivel chair allowed the radio operator to swivel around to change frequencies if notified to switch tuning units. He could see into the bomb-bay or turn and look back over the ball turret and see the gunners in the waist area. It was exciting to get get aquainted with my future position.

Eight of us were on each flight and we were allowed to roam through the plane from the tail-gun position to the plexiglass nose. The big thrill was to walk across the narrow catwalk through the bomb bay when the bomb bay doors were open! You could see the desert scenery rushing beneath you, several thousand feet below. It was especially exciting since we had no parachutes!

One final test was just five minutes. We had to take a .50 caliber machine gun, with approximately 150 parts, apart and reassemble it while blindfolded. There were many hours of aircraft recognition to gain the ability to recognize 'friend or foe' in an instant. Three days after we graduated, this article was in the newspaper, but I didn't write home about that event.

FIVE FLIERS DIE IN CRASH NEAR YUMA.

Yuma, June 29. -- (AP) -- Five Army airmen were killed instantly yesterday when a B-17 bomber crashed and exploded against the side of a lofty peak in the Gila Mountains, 18 miles east of the plane's base at Yuma Army airfield.
Col. Herbert W. Anderson, field commander, said all aboard the plane perished and identified the dead as ----

We finished gunnery school and our next destination was Lincoln, Nebraska to be assigned to for combat crew training. We had earned our sterling silver gunner wings and had Corporal's stripes on our sleeves! We were ready for the next challenge!

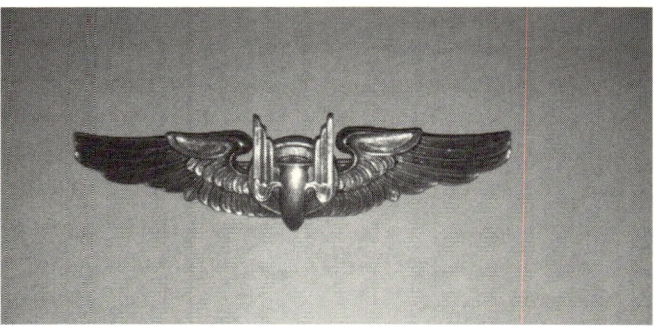

Photo by Mike Alexander

SIOUX CITY COMBAT CREW TRAINING

We left Yuma on a troop train to Lincoln, Nebraska for a few days of testing and reassignment. Late August 1944, I arrived at Sioux City, Iowa for aircrew training and was assigned to the crew of Lt. William D. Templeton on a B-17 Flying Fortress. It was all I had hoped for and I was completely satisfied with Uncle Sam. The guys on our new ten man crew soon became buddies and were eager to get into a bomber. We enlisted men all had experience in a B-17 in gunnery school, but now we would be training for missions at our combat stations. Pilot Bill Templeton and co-pilot Dale Rector were in the cockpit. Navigator, Bruno Conterato and bombardier Walter "Benny" Benedict had desks in their plexiglass nose section. Flight Engineer, Ewing "Rod" Roddy had a jump seat behind the pilot and could step up into his top twin-gun turret in few seconds. My radio room was just behind the bomb-bay. The other gunners had seats in the waist area. Ball turret gunner, Wilber Lesh, sat in the waist area where he could quickly open the ball turret hatch and slide under the twin guns in that ball hanging under the bomber. Waist gunners, Orville "Robby" Robinson and Bert Allinder, had benches at their gun positions at each window. Tail-gunner, Ralph Moore, had to crawl back past the rear landing tail wheel to his small seat behind the twin machine guns that provided an extra "stinger" for the bomber.

Our crew represented a cross-section of our country as not one of us was from the same state. We ranged from Connecticut to Oklahoma and received our training in many sections of the country. For example Bert Allinder completed armor school in Denver, Colorado, and gunnery school in Reno, Nevada. Ewing Roddy completed the aircraft mechanic school in Amarillo, Texas, and gunnery school in Kingman, Arizona. They were a bunch of well trained guys and we adjusted very well as a crew. I credit those guys for saving my life during those combat missions over Germany.

My radio area was snug with its small desk and window. I even had a sunroof, but they had removed the machine gun. At last, I had my own office with scads of radio equipment on a desk bolted to the bomb-bay bulkhead (wall) in front of me. The Liaison heavy-duty transmitter for long distance sending by Morse code messages were fastened to the waist bulkhead behind my swivel chair. The receiver and telegraph key were fastened to my desk. There was also a transmitter and receiver for long distance voice communication, an FM set for inter-squadron voice use by the pilot, an IFF (identification, friend or foe) transmitter a radio compass for use in navigation, and ten or more intercom stations for crew members. I also had an electrically-operated winch to reel out a trailing wire antenna for long range transmissions. We had three months of flight training to become a combat crew. The ground classroom training was important, but it was those hours of training missions in the plane flying over Iowa and South Dakota that we loved. We practiced take-offs and landings, bomb runs over specific targets the navigator had to locate. We also did night flights. Our final tests were cross country flights to "bomb" other air bases in Boise, Idaho or Dalhart, Texas. Our crew trained hard and enjoyed our weekend passes into town. Our favorite hangout was a place called the Town Pump. It was downtown just off the main drag, down an alley into a basement! It was a popular spot with enlisted men.

Aircrew training included "touch and go" practice landings by the pilot and co-pilot. Bombers took off, circled the field and came in for a landing and took off again after the wheels touched the runway. I remember one day Rod and I were down near the flight-line when a B-17 came in too fast and crashed into another plane before it took off. They collided and crashed into one of the base fire departments. Trainees on two crews and firemen died as other fire trucks rushed to the base. It was not an encouraging event! A few weeks later more of our training class died when one of our bombers was involved in a mid-air collision with a fighter. The Sioux City newspaper carried the story:

Six Perish Killed In Mid –Air Crash

Six men were killed, one missing and four parachuted to safety Friday when a P-47 fighter plane from the Bruning, Nebraska army air base and a B-17 bomber from the Sioux City base collided. The fighter pilot was killed, four men parachuted, two

> *with minor injuries, two had serious injuries but are expected to recover. The names of the dead are being withheld pending notification of the next of kin.*

We didn't know any of the guys on that crew, they were in a more advanced training class, but once again we were reminded of the dangers of flying. Things got even more serious during the last week of combat crew training. We were all scheduled for a private session at the Personal Affairs Office to complete insurance and legal papers before going overseas. My Corporal's pay wasn't much, but I was assured of making Buck Sergeant or better once I began flying combat missions. Before I left that office I had signed up for several payroll deductions to start in November. I agreed to: a $6.40 monthly premium for a $10,000 Government life insurance policy with my parents as beneficiary, a $40.00 a month payroll deduction for Mom to save and $7.50 a month for War Bonds. That experience really brought danger home. It was about like filling out your will. I walked out of there hoping the news about those automatic promotions to Sergeant was right!

Well they were true, once I began flying combat with the Mighty Eighth I received a promotion a month until I reached the rank of Tech Sergeant. That paper titled, AAF PERSONAL AFFAIRS STATEMENT was reviewed, updated and placed in my personnel folder at Drew Field, Florida August 5, 1945 when I returned from England. I was given my folder when I was discharged at Baer Field, Ft. Wayne, Indiana on November 16, 1945.

We completed our training in mid-October and learned we were to be combat replacement crews for the Eighth Air Force and our plane was waiting for us in England. Lo and behold, just before we completed training, I received a letter from the principal of Bedford High stating I could apply to graduate with the class of 1945. I filled out the application, mailed it back to my old High school and forgot it. After all, I had graduated from basic training and three of Uncle Sam's Technical schools and I had a job. I wasn't a pilot, navigator or bombardier, but I was an important crew member. I would just sitting in the radio room behind the bomb bay instead of in front of it!

T/Sgt. James Lee Hutchinson, Ed.S.

Radio operator desk with code key

2002 Photo by Susan Hutchinson

The original radio room with receivers, earphones and sending key on the desk and transmiters on the bulkhead behind me. My daughter and I were allowed to board the historic bomber when it was located at Mud Island in Memphis. Note the yellow oxygen tank above the ball turret.

Camp Kilmer and the Queen Mary

The highlight of my troop train ride to Camp Kilmer, New Jersey was the fact that someone stole all the money out of my billfold while I was asleep. I was going overseas just as I came into the army-- broke! Camp Kilmer was just across the harbor from New York City. I was really impressed with the harbor and that skyline full of skyscrapers so near and yet so far away. England's Queen Mary liner sat in the harbor, waiting to take another 16,000 troops to war. We were taking our ocean cruise in style, the Queen, once the top civilian ships, was now our largest and fastest troopship. They said Adolph Hitler had issued a standing offer of $250,000 and the Iron Cross for the U-Boat captain who sank her.

November 4, 1944, (my mother's birthday,) I lugged my duffel bag up the gangplank of the Queen Mary in New York harbor. The band was playing a rousing march—it was "Our Director" which was dear old Bedford High's school song! Talk about irony! We sailed past the Statue of Liberty into the North Atlantic and headed for the United Kingdom and the Eighth Army Air Corps. The Queen Mary was so fast she sailed alone in a zig-zag course without the protection of Navy ships in a convoy. The luxurious staterooms were stripped of furniture and eight of us slept in hammocks, we had only two poor meals a day on the entire cruise across the North Atlantic dodging icebergs and German submarines. Lifeboat drills were held every day, I don't know why because there weren't nearly enough boats for all of us! They launched depth bombs form the stern area several times during the trip, but we were never alerted for a submarine attack. Mickey Rooney and a USO Group were on board and he put on a great show for us on the fourth day. Dozens of guys were seasick during our on the first day, but it didn't hit me until the fourth day; I blamed it on all those Brussels sprouts they fed us.

On the sixth day, we sailed up the Firth of Clyde, (my Dad's name) landed in Greenock, Scotland where we had good meals and spent a couple of nights in cots instead of a hammock. We enjoyed the hospitality of the British Army and their warm brick barracks for two days before boarding a small train for a long trip to our airbase.

Flying the North Atlantic

Pilot's Diary - "Orders had come through, the B-17 bombers and crews were to leave our base at Grand Island, Nebraska and fly the northern route to England. It was September, 1943 and the Eighth Air Corps needed our help to destroy Hitler's war industries. We flew to Bangor, Maine to start the first leg of our journey to Goose Bay, Labrador. The next day we were over the ocean again. We saw a large convoy and several icebergs before we landed in Greenland. The next hop was to Iceland and we ran into bad weather before we landed. It was fall at home, but winter here in Iceland. The weather kept us grounded and we forced to lay over a day. Some of us started to hike down to a fishing village along the cold blue sea, but we "aborted" that chilly walk. Iceland was a cold, windy and barren place full of boulders. Someone later said that Icelanders sided with the Germans, so it was probably a good thing we turned back. Next day the weather eased up, but we weren't cleared for take-off until noon, several hours later we landed safely at Prestwick, Scotland. We had flown the northern route across the North Atlantic in about a week. Our next 400 mile trip was in a day coach on a small English train to temporary quarters at a training site for new arrivals north of London. The classrooms were cold Quonset huts. We had five days of survival classes on about everything from ditching a plane to how to escape if shot down over enemy territory. In our free time, we learned that English beer (bitters) was really bitter, Nazi "buzz bombs" could hit anytime, and there were four girls for every guy at the local dances. English blackouts were strictly enforced because German bombing raids were a constant threat. One night, they hit an airport about ten miles north of us. We heard the explosions and flashes of the exploding bombs lit up the night.

Two weeks later we finished the training classes and were assigned to a Bomb Group a few miles farther north of London. We packed our bags, boarded army trucks and moved out to our combat base. Now, we thought we were ready to take a bomber into combat, but we were wrong.

Mighty Eighth bombers were flying missions every day there was forecast for good weather over enemy targets. New aircrews were needed, but not until they were ready. Group commanders, mission leaders and every bomb crewman wanted to be sure the "replacements" were ready to fly in a combat formation. Nobody wanted a bunch of "greenhorns" flying close formation with them on a mission. Mid-air collisions were too frequent and too deadly! Therefore, new crews spent the next nine days in classes on the ground and in the air over England. It was great to get aboard a B-17 and back into the air. Ground instructors and those on the training flights made sure every man knew what to expect on long high altitude missions. We were warned to double-check all equipment, guns, ammo and to be especially alert over enemy territory. Heavily oiled guns tend to freeze up when its 40 below zero. Frostbite or worse and oxygen masks are dangers, too! Battling the sub-zero temperatures and oxygen loss (anoxia) was stressed. The airman is often not aware when his oxygen mask fails. Ice crystals in the mask or flak damage to an oxygen tank can cause failure and death. The pilot appoints someone, often the co-pilot, to make periodic intercom checks on every man during missions.

Our training did not keep us isolated from the realities of war. I suppose the same type of events were happening at our other forty-one heavy bomber bases in England, but it did seem like our base was extremely dangerous:

1. Loaded B-17 with 23,000 gallons of gas caught fire in the flight line and exploded killing a fireman and blowing the engines two blocks away.

2. Plane in the landing pattern ran out gas and crashed - no survivors.
3. Germans bombed the airbase east of us last night.
4. Gunner on the flight line accidently fired his .50 Caliber machine gun and killed a ground crew mechanic.
5. One night an RAF plane on fire, spun and crashed near the base.
6. Our "final exam:" a simulated mission of all three squadrons (fifty planes) out over the North Sea was a practice mission, so none of the bombers had machine guns. The lead navigator took us out too far and we ended up about twenty miles from the Holland coast and a German airbase at Schipol. We turned tail and ran for home, but three ME-109 fighters hit the rear squadron and shot down two B-17's before anyone knew they were there. One bomber exploded and the other managed to "ditch" in the North Sea. We lost two bombers and twenty men. Those fighters could have shot down everyone our unarmed planes! Somebody should be court-martialed for that fiasco!

"The deadly accident warning came true all too soon!"

Chapter Two

The Mighty Eighth

The Eighth Army Air Corps was activated January 28, 1942 in Savannah, Georgia and the first heavy bombers landed in England July 1, 1942. Thirty- two B-17E bombers arrived by the end of the month providing the 97th Bomb Group with four squadrons (340, 341, 342 and 414.) Our country mobilized for war and new planes rolled off the assembly lines as new airmen were trained sent overseas to join the air war. Eventually, there were forty-three U.S. heavy bomber airfields crowded into the East Anglia farmlands, many only five or ten miles apart. Southeast England also hosted US fighter and Royal Air Force (RAF) fields. The sky over the United Kingdom was filled with aircraft by the summer of 1943!

The stories in this book tell the experiences of the men (boys) who served in the U.S. Army's Eighth Air Force during World War II. The Eighth Army Air Corps was formed with three major units: Bomber Command, Fighter Command and Ground Forces. The Eighth under the leadership of General Ira Eaker and later General Jimmy Doolittle, grew into the largest air armada in history; the Mighty Eighth! By mid 1944, it had 200,000 members and could send out more than 2,000 four engine bombers and 1,000 fighters on a single mission against Third Reich targets. Heavy bombers of the 43 Bomb Groups in England flew 6,866 daylight bombing missions against Nazi occupied targets in Europe from May, 1942 until the Nazi surrender May 8, 1945.

By 1943 there were three divisions in the Eighth, the First, Second and Third. The First and Third consisted of B-17s and the Second Division flew B-24s. The B-24 was faster than the B-17, but the B-17 could fly higher so they could not fly in the same formation. Each heavy bomber airfield was stocked with fifty B-24 or B-17 heavy bombers and 2,500 men in airmen and ground crews to service or repair planes. An article in the March, 1945, Eighth AF Newsletter, Army Talks, said:

"For every heavy bomber there are thirty men on the base who never fly. Some service and maintain planes, others handle the bombs, bombsights, radar, machine guns, ammo, flying equipment or parachutes. Some are drivers and others man the Mess Halls. There are men who have little contact with the planes or flying, but are essential to the base and the success of missions."

In many towns, G.I. airmen outnumbered local citizens by a large margin because most young Englishmen were away in the armed forces. British people welcome the young Americans who had come to their rescue when their backs were to the wall. We literally invaded the country and were instructed to avoid rubbing the "locals" the wrong way. Problems did arise because of the millions of Americans in Great Britain prior to D-Day. The Brits had a saying about American GIs, "The trouble with the Yanks is, they're overpaid, oversexed and over here." Sometimes they added overfed and overbearing. Some locals resented the fact that GIs were paid three or four times better than British servicemen. U.S. soldiers showered the local girls with presents from the base PX and about 60,000 romances ended in marriage during the war years.

The expansion of the USAAF was a miracle of production and training by a nation determined to survive. December of 1939 the Air Corps consisted of 24,724 men and 2,400 aircraft. Those figures grew and by August, 1945 the USAAF was the world's largest air power with a total of 2,253,182 in uniform. In spite of WW II losses, the inventory of combat aircraft stood at 41,163.

Statistics report that a total of 350,000 men served in the Mighty Eighth during World War II. Approximately 120,000 were air crew members and only one crew in five completed their tour of duty. A total of 26,000 airmen were killed in action (KIA), thousands were wounded and 28,000 bailed out of disabled planes to be listed as MIA (missing in action.) Thousands of those guys served time in German prisoner of war (POW) camps, but many men were never located. The Eighth Air force had one of the highest casualty rates of any unit in the Armed Forces as our fighters overwhelmed Luftwaffe fighters and our bombers literally destroyed Hitler's Third Reich, leaving Germany in ruins.

Note - *After the war, General Eisenhower and other Allied commanders said the Allies could not have won the war without the Air Force heavy bombers. However, I would add, we might never have won without our long range fighters!*

Post-war reports stated that the heavy bombers dropped almost 700,000 tons of bombs and the Fighter Command had 566 aces and 11,200 victories in aerial combat. German leaders said that the bombing caused their defeat. However the impressive record of strategic bombing was achieved at a very high cost! The Mighty Eighth lost 6,866 heavy bombers, 3,695 fighters and suffered almost half of all losses of the WW II Air Forces. Almost three fourths of the graves in the American cemetery at Cambridge, England are Eighth Air Force airmen.

Medals awarded to Eighth airmen included:

A. 17 Medals of Honor, with scads of DFCs, Purple Hearts and 442,000 Air Medals

B. Bombers lost B-17 (4754) B-24 (2,112)
   Fighters lost:
   P- 47 (1,043) P- 38 (451) P-51 (2,201)

C. 440 missions, dropped 697,000 tons of bombs

D. 5,100 crashes (mid-air and ground)

Jan 27, 1943	first B-17 raid on Germany
Aril 8, 1943	P-47 begins escort duty
August 1, 1943	B-24 based in Libya first B-24 raids on Ploesti. Romania oil fields
Dec 5, 1943	P-47 and P-51 fighters, equipped with gasoline drop tanks, could now escort bombers to the target
March 4, 1944	8th AF flew the first daylight mission to Berlin
May 1, 1945	Germany asked for a truce (ceasefire)

T/Sgt. James Lee Hutchinson, Ed.S.

A Royal Air Force Compliment:

> *"The US Eighth Fighter and Bomber Commands in late 1943and 1944 performed the impossible. They did what we, in the Royal Air Force, had told them they could never do – what we, with our equipment, could never have done. What's more, the Luftwaffe generals – and indeed, the colonels who were actively mixing it in combat with the Fortresses and Liberators – had advised Hitler and Goering that it couldn't be done."*
>
> *Laddie Lucas, Royal Air Force, World War II*

Bomber Group Assembly

Early morning bomber assembly was very complicated because the sky over England was crowded with of hundreds of bombers in the air at the same time. The pre-mission formation required skilled pilots, mechanically perfect planes and good weather. Unfortunately, a high majority of mid-air collisions occurred because of the failure of one or more of those requirements. Many crews and bombers were lost in collisions in the early morning skies over England.

One of the most dangerous phases of a mission was the assembly of a Bomb Group's planes over England. It began when bombers took off from various air-fields and climbed to a specific assigned altitudes altitude to form into three squadrons around colored flares fired by their squadron's lead plane. Snow and fog made for poor flying conditions, and we often took off with only 500-600 yard visibility. Take–off, assembly and landings in bad weather caused many mid-air collisions, crashes and fatalities.

Flying blindly up through the thick fog was an eerie and dangerous experience. The pilot stayed on the radio beam from a radio transmitter called a "splasher" located near their base. Crewmembers sat near a window holding an inter-com mike, ready to warn the pilots for any other planes in the area. We were very aware of the possibility of a mid-air collision in the friendly skies over England!

The American cemetery at Cambridge has 3,812 graves the majority of which are American airmen lost in collisions or combat. Once pilots broke out into the clear, they searched for his squadron's flare colors of the day and united with their squadron. Numerous radio "splashers" located on or near airfields were used to send radio signals to guide pilots climbing through an overcast sky. The # 6 splasher near Eye was operated by the RAF out of a converted bus. Pilots jockeyed bombers into their assigned flight position in the "Low, Middle or High" squadron. Once assembled the three squadrons formed into a combat box formation and were ready to find their place in the bomber stream. Bomb Group formations joined the bomber stream on radio signals from a "buncher," a more powerful radio signal generally in a permanent location to start the mission. The group formations then soared out over the English Channel or North Sea gaining altitude before they reached enemy air space. Heavy bombers filled the sky, leaving contrails streaking across the horizon. Moisture particles in the engine exhausts froze at high altitude and the snow white contrail patterns of hundreds of bombers in the English skies was a beautiful sight. It was ironic that they were headed out to rain destruction on German military targets. In turn, the German anti-aircraft gunners and fighters loved those cloudless days, but I imagine the people at the target weren't too happy.

Combat Box Formation

Early in the air war Eighth Air Force bombers were not getting enough satisfactory bombing results and were suffering high loses to flak and the swarms of Luftwaffe fighters they faced on every mission. Germany's air superiority was based on hundreds of planes and veteran pilots who had fought in the Spainish civil war. High ranking generals were critics of the daylight bombing strategy and complaints were loud and clear by Christmas of 1942. Eighth heavy bomber pilots soon realized that bombers in loose formations were more exposed to fighter attacks. Luftwaffe fighters generally attacked loose formations first. Bomber gunners had only a few seconds to take aim and fire at an enemy fighter diving through their formation.

Major Curtis LeMay of the 305th Bomb Group was the Group Commander who devised the tight box formations for better protection against fighter attacks. He also used no "evasive action" in the flak during a bomb run. This tactic allowed the bombardier to hold the bomber steady to adjust his bombsight. Major LeMay proved his theory when his 305th BG began getting better strike results on their targets and gain maximum use of firepower from gunners. His combat box formation consisted of three levels of bombers stacked and staggered at High, Middle and Low levels (squadrons) to avoid collisions. Each level was built on six elements of three planes flying at the same altitude in a "vee" pattern with the planes on the left and right of the lead plane in each element flying approximately fifty feet behind the tail of their lead plane, they were to vary no more than fifty feet left of right of an imaginary line from the lead planes wing tips. Of course those distances would were subject to change because of air currents, visibility and the skill of the pilots. Each level's Lead bombers and "Tail-end Charlie" had the least protection.

The 8th AF Bomb Groups had used various formation schemes with some degree of success beginning in 1942, but the Box Formation had eventually become a standard for all 8th AF group formations.

The Combat Box Formation was made up of a number of basic airplane relationships. From the smallest to the largest, these formations were:

1. Element Formation: three planes
2. Squadron Formation: four Elements - twelve planes
3. Group Formation: three Squadrons – thirty-six planes
4. Wing Formation: three Groups – one hundred and eight planes

Element Formation - An Element of three planes was the basic unit in all formations. The Element lead was responsible for maintaining his Element's position relative to the Squadron lead at all times. One plane flew off his left wing and one off his right wing. Those flying the left and right wing positions were responsible for staying in "tight formation" with the Element lead at all times, but on the bombing run to the target in particular. The Element wing positions tried to maintain their positions about the same altitude, one wing length horizontally from and one wing length behind the Element lead.

This Basic Element Formation was really the most tedious and perhaps dangerous formation position to fly in the Squadron or Group formation, because of the close operating distances and the dependence on the "other guy" to do his job reasonably well. Usually the pilot/co-pilot took turns, perhaps fifteen minutes or so at a time, maintaining their plane's position with the Element lead. In a tight formation the vertical and horizontal distances between the Element leads might be only a few hundred feet.

The positions of the Elements in a Squadron formation were:

1. The Lead Element became the Squadron lead with the other three Elements flying positions oriented on his lead position.
2. The High Element flew above, to the right and behind the Squadron Lead.
3. The Low Element flew below, to the left and behind the lead the Squadron Lead.

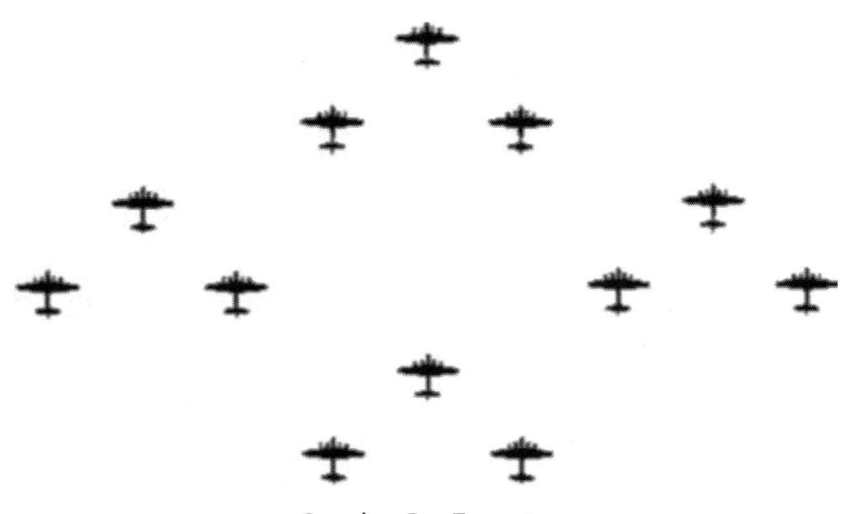

Squadron Box Formation

Tight formations resulted in much better bombing results and more efficient use of bomber guns to create larger cones of machinegun fire to protect against fighter attacks. The gunners on each bomber had only a few seconds to spot fighters slicing through the formation, take aim and get off a burst from their .50 caliber machine guns. However, it was still a one-sided battle for any formation without a fighter escort for protection.

Formation charts with individual bomber assignments were issued for each mission. Pilots knew their squadron and element positions for Assembly. It was also understood that if bombers were forced to drop out of the formation those behind were to move up to fill those slots to maintain the tight combat formation. We often flew so close that we could wave at guys in the bombers flying next to us. Pilots in the rear often had a difficult the time with turbulent air and "prop wash" of bombers ahead. Mid-air collisions were usually the result of violent air currents or pilot error. Tight formations also faced the possibility of a flack damaged plane crashing into others. The worst tragedy occurred if a bomber received a direct hit in the bomb-bay it exploded to took down or damage others in the formation. One of the most costly happened in this report:

"On the bomb run over the target, just prior to bomb release, one the low squadron B-17's was hit by an anti-aircraft shell. The direct hit in the open bomb-bay exploded the 5000 pound bomb-load. That explosion blew six bombers out of the sky and badly damaged three others. Nine of the twelve planes in the low squadron were lost to the bomb group while over the target."

In October 1943 the Eighth began using the Pathfinder (PFF) radar system (nicknamed 'Mickey') developed by the British and used by RAF bombers. It was installed on lead B-17s in place of the ball turret and could be raised or lowered in flight. The Mickey allowed aircraft to bomb through cloudy and overcast skies. Bombers leading each squadron carried a radar dome and a Command pilot, bombardier, navigator and a Mickey operator (his desk was across the aisle from mine in the radio room.)

B-17 MEMORIES

Lead crew squadrons and formations were led by specially picked Lead Crews. Staff officers served as command pilots and rode in the co-pilot seat. The crew's co-pilot rode in the tail gunner position to keep Command Pilot informed of what was happening in the formation behind. The Mission Commander rode in the Lead plane. Our Templeton crew made lead crew after four missions, it was a dubious honor, since squadron leaders were the first target of fighters and flak!

USAAF photo

Box formations of several Bomb Groups head for an enemy target

> *The first lesson is that you can't lose a war if you have command of the air, and you can't win a war if you haven't.*
> Gen. Jimmy Doolittle

FLYING COMBAT MISSIONS

The men (boys) who flew those daytime Eighth Air Force combat missions in WW II needed skill, nerves of steel and a faith that they would survive the hazards they faced in those deadly skies over Germany. A lot of thoughts go through your mind while you're plodding through the snow to a jeep or truck to take you out to your bomber. You've gone through briefing and you know the target. In a few hours you'll be soaring over the North Sea at 25,000 feet, at 40 below zero and on oxygen. You realize your life is going on the line and you may never see home again, but with the optimism of youth you believe you'll make it, but you say a prayer to ask God's protection. Then, you toss your equipment into the truck and yell to the rest of the crew, "Let's get this show on the road!"

The weatherman gives the OK, a flare is fired from the control tower and thirty or so loaded planes taxi out to the runway and line up for take-off every three minutes. The roar of those powerful motors wakes up every English citizen in the neighborhood, but they're glad the Yanks are here. You know every B-17 is loaded with the bombs and equipment needed for a mission to blow hell out of an Axis target. You also know the flak and enemy fighters will be waiting!

There was a constant mental stress on aircrew members. We worried most of the night on the eve of a bombing raid, and sweated out every mission from take-off until landing. Most airmen feared flak worst of all and there was always the reality of facing it over every target and unexpected locations. Briefing sessions before a mission always included information on the safest route to and from the target. Aircrews relied on their pilot and navigator to avoid those hot spots, but many anti-aircraft guns were mounted on railroad cars, boats and river barges. Those mobile guns could raise havoc with a bomber formation. Flak was terrifying because there was no way of knowing when the sky would be filled with deadly exploding shells, especially if the Nazi gunners were "tracking" us on the bomb-run! By the time we saw the puffs of black smoke from exploding shells, the sky around us was full of iron slugs. It was even worse when they concentrated fire into a barrage over the target and we saw a sky full of flak we had to fly into it to drop our bombs! Flak brought death and destruction to our bomber formation as we delivered the same to those below. There was no defense against the flak barrage. Flak shrapnel could wound or kill crew members and a direct hit by an anti-aircraft 88 shell meant disaster. Flak hit our plane many times on our eighteen combat missions. I remember one time a slug came zinging through my radio room over my head, over the Mickey operator's head and out the other side of the plane! The ground crew patched more than a hundred flak holes after our Hohenbudberg raid. Severe flak damage to a bomber meant dropping out of the protection of the formation. It also meant crewmembers might be busy tending to buddies with flak wounds or burns. There are many stories of boys striving to ease the pain or save a buddy's life with bandages, salve and morphine shots on the long voyage home. Ambulances, doctors and nurses waited at every airbase to aid the wounded or take away the dead.

Lone flak-crippled bombers became prime targets for lurking Luftwaffe fighters armed with machine guns, cannon and rockets. A crippled bomber's best chance of surviving was to be picked up and protected by some of our escort fighters until they could make it out of enemy territory.

Enemy fighters cannon fire and rockets could do great damage to a bomber and often sent an aircraft down in flames. Every combat mission was a test of endurance with every crew member doing the best job possible at his position. Aircrews often flew two or three days in a row. The odds of a B-17 bomber completing a safe mission depended on luck, teamwork, skill and the grace of God. There was no place for a crewman who was not in good mental condition. The crews on heavy bombers faced many hazards besides the actual mission. Examples include: crashes on take-off or landings, mid-air collisions, fire, engine or equipment failure, sub-zero temperature and anoxia (oxygen loss.) Combat fatigue was common and aircrew members sometimes "snapped" under the constant fear of death. Crews often flew missions two or three days in a row when the weather was clear. Men sometimes broke down. The common term was around the base was "flak happy," but we all sympathized, because we knew we might be the next victim of combat fatigue. Some crews endured unbelievable experiences in those dangerous skies of World War II. The crewman who said he was not afraid, was either crazy or lying!

In his recent book "No Man's Sky," author R.C. Cline writes the true story of a B-17 waist gunner who flew twenty-nine missions with the 490th Bomb Group.

T/Sgt. James Lee Hutchinson, Ed.S.

> *"For S/Sgt. J. Emerson Krieger, the youngest member of his crew; combat was not a romantic dash--or a magical moment of as he flew "off— into the wild blue yonder." He was too young to vote, but he was not too young to fight or die for his country. For James C. Cox his experiences in combat gave him memories that would last for the rest of his life. For Delbert Hesseltine, flying was a day to day job of hard work, details and team effort. For Arthur Struempler, flying was job that gave him friendships that would never fail him. Each man flew and fought as a team, defending liberty in a B-17G Flying Fortress. It was team work by all of the young airmen men who bombed Germany. "They shortened the war," concluded Edward Jablonski. "They were young men when the war began, and if they lived, they were old, when it ended." Sadly, some of the men who flew in combat paid the ultimate price for victory. Their bodies rest in graves marked on foreign shores."*

The Stars and Stripes, our army newspaper, printed daily reports on the war's progress. We could fly a mission and see the results of the Mighty Eighth's bombing and fighter raids the next day. After each off our missions, I clipped out stories of the previous day's bomber and fighter raids to paste in my diary. We were always faced with the brutal statistics of the air war. Bombers that went down carried nine or ten men, so it was easy to count the casualties. Usually, the men (boys) listed as MIA (missing in action) were either dead or prisoners of war. The Air Force recognized the fatigue problem and combat crews were given frequent three day passes to London or other recreational areas. Large R&R (rest and relaxation) centers were established in hotels or mansions for crews needing a week's vacation from the war! Airmen were keenly aware of the number of bombers and crews lost on each mission. Every airbase kept a special clean-up squad go to the barracks of crews that were shot down and move out all property and traces of boys who were missing. This "sanitizing" prevented looting, and preserved the missing men's personal property for relatives. Most of all, it helped surviving crews forget their unfortunate buddies, but it was hard to ignore empty bunks!

Early in the war air-crew members had only a thirty percent chance of completing their twenty-five mission tour of duty. That was increased to thirty-five missions in the summer of 1944. Statistics report that a total of 350,000 men served in the Mighty Eighth during World War II. Approximately 120,000 were air crew members and only one crew in five completed their tour of duty. A total of 26,000 airmen were killed in action (KIA), thousands were wounded in crashes and 28,000 bailed out of disabled planes to be listed as MIA (missing in action.) Thousands of those guys served time in German prisoner of war (POW) camps, but many men were never located.

German Archives photo

Ten man German anti-aircraft crew of an 88 mm flak gun (Flugzeugabwehr-Kanone)

T/Sgt. James Lee Hutchinson, Ed.S.

Flak - Airman's Nightmare

The 88mm anti-aircraft gun, the Flugzeugabwehr-Kanone (flak-gun) was one of Germany's most effective weapons. Eighth Air Force daylight bombing missions and the RAF at night kept Germany's flak guns busy. They were equipped with radar sights and could reach a height of 35,000 feet with fused fragmentation shells timed to explode amid tight bomber formations and long bomb runs when pilots were unable to take evasive action. The gunners could set the shells to explode at our altitude and fill the sky with metal slugs. When used as an anti-aircraft gun, with a ten man crew, it could fire up to twenty shells per minute to a height of 35,000 feet. Nazi gunners used two tactics to bring us down. They could lay down a "box- barrage" over the target for bomb formations to fly into ---- or "track" us on the bomb-run. Bombers could not take "evasive action" during the bomb-run with bomb-bay doors open. The plane had to be level for the bombsight to work accurately. All we could do was hunker down and trust God, our steel helmet and forty-five pound flak jacket to protect us as we flew into a sky blackened with exploding shells. We were "sitting ducks" and it was a perfect time to have a chest-pack parachute hooked to your harness, there were some cases when a plane exploded from a direct hit and propelled airmen into space!

The 88 mm cannon was a triple threat, it had two types of shells and could be used against planes, tanks and troops. German troops used it with an armor-piercing shell could knock out a tank at 2000 yards and shrapnel shells were used against ground troops and aircraft. s.

Bomber crews flying missions quickly learn the basic information about flak. I was scared to death every time we had to fly into the deadly stuff. Exploding shells filled the sky with harmless looking puffs of black smoke that drifted away in the wind. The 88 mm shells casings were grooved inside and filled with pellets which filled the sky with slugs to riddle planes and wound airmen. The anti-aircraft shell was just like giant shotgun shell that exploded in black smoke and filled the sky with iron slugs to get a rabbit -- only now our plane was the rabbit!

I often had nightmares about flak bursting around our bomber. On the close ones, you saw a dirty red flash in the center of the smoke and a "whump" sound as it shook the plane and showered it with hot shrapnel slugs that sliced into the thin aluminum body of the bomber. Flak often vital aircraft parts like control cables, gas or oxygen tanks, instruments and motors. Air-crew members feared flak more than enemy fighters because we could see fighters and fire back at them, but flak was a deadly "invisible enemy" which struck without warning. Bombers returning from missions often carried wounded airmen. Enemy flak and fighters damaged or shot down many planes. For example, November 1944, fifty-six bombers were lost on one raid in the Ruhr Valley.

The B-17G had armor plate around some positions and airmen wore steel helmets and forty-five pound flak jackets that saved many lives. The flak jacket made up of 1 ½ inch wide strips of steel layered and sewn into a canvas apron to cover front and back. Crewmembers usually scrounged around for extra jackets to place under them for extra protection of the family jewels. The plane's aluminum fuselage gave no protection against flak and bombers often returned to base riddled by slugs. Ground crew became adept at counting and patching holes before the next mission. We usually got a report of how many holes we brought home.

Germany's heaviest anti-aircraft batteries protected oil storage, airplane parts, airfields, and ammunition industries. Names like Regensburg, Schweinfurt, Hamburg, Munster, and Augsburg were really bad news at mission briefings because crewman knew there could be heavy losses. The industrial area of the Ruhr Valley was such a dangerous target that Eighth airmen sarcastically dubbed it "Happy Valley." RAF and Eighth formations had no option, but to fly 300 to 450 miles to a target covered by deadly fields of flak, drop their bombs and head for England! The 15th Air Force based in Foggia, Italy struck targets in Italy, southern Germany, Romania and Czechoslovakia. Heavy bomber defense was to fly at 25,000 feet, jam enemy radio signals and throw out aluminum strips of chaff to confuse enemy radar. Late in the war we could rely on the protection of our fighters. The Eighth now had fighters with long range fuel tanks to escort bombers to the target and back on every mission. The Luftwaffe was running low on planes and trained fighter pilots. However, there was still one "fly in the ointment", Germany had a new plane. It was the Messerschmitt 262 jet fighter which flew 500 MPH!

Flak gun towers with permanent installations were built in many areas. However, many were moveable and Germany mounted various models of anti-aircraft guns on trains and barges. I remember on a mission to Cologne we lost three planes when our 490th Group was hit hard by unexpected flak from river barges. During 1944, the Mighty Eighth lost 3,500 bombers shot down or destroyed by flak and 600 to enemy fighter attacks. Although, in fact, many or the Luftwaffe fighter "kills" were against bombers already crippled by flak.

Flak became heavier in 1944- 1945, because Hitler had less and less territory to protect. American and British Armies were advancing from the West and Russian troops from the East. Flak guns were very effective against tanks and ground troops. We always told the Army guys that we were doing them a favor by keeping all those cannons pointed up at the mighty Eighth! Targets were more heavily defended and Nazi anti-aircraft guns and fighter groups concentrated on protecting critical targets the Third Reich needed to continue fighting. Our job was to bomb them out of business

490th BG photo

One our 490th bombers in flak over the target – this was a visual bombing mission, note the smoke of bombs exploding on the target.

The Memphis Belle Story

Photo by Scott Maher

The above Memphis Belle B-17F is a replica of the famous Flying Fortress of WW II. This bomber was used in the 1990 movie and now tours the United States to provide flights and/or tours though the historic bomber. The educational tours are sponsored by the Liberty Belle Foundation. Check their website for information on tour schedules

The B-17F serial number 41-24485 began its journey to fame in Bangor, Maine in September, 1942 when it was assigned to the 2nd Lt. Robert Morgan crew. The pilot convinced his crew to name the plane *"Memphis Belle"* in honor of his girlfriend, Margaret Polk of Memphis, Tennessee. He then requested a copy of a Petty girl painting from the artist and the result was a glamorous redhead in an orange bathing on each side of the bomber's nose. Prior to flying the northern route across the Atlantic, Lt. Morgan flew his new plane on a "shakedown cruise" to Memphis, Tennessee where the new B-17F was christened *Memphis Belle* with a bottle of champagne by the pilot's wartime sweetheart.

The 91st Bomb Group made the North Atlantic flight to England in the final week of September, 1942 and was briefly assigned to the Kimbolton airfield before moving to a new base at Bassingbourn, station 121, just north of London. The *Memphis Belle* was assigned to squadron 324. The Group would eventually fly 340 missions and suffer the highest losses (197 bombers) of any of the 40 Eighth Bomb Groups!

It was early in the war and the Eighth was just beginning a long and costly campaign of daytime high altitude bombing to destroy the military bases, airfields and factories Germany had established in France. Brigadier General Ira C. Eaker was organizing the Eighth Air Force and his most important need was more bombers and some long range fighters the protect them. German submarines (U-Boats) were roaming the Atlantic and sinking many Allied ships bringing troops and supllies to aid the war. The submarine ports (pens) became top priority targets of the early missions of the RAF and Eighth Air Force. Meanwhile, Operation Torch was scheduled for the invasion of North Africa to establish heavy bomber bases for the Twelfth Air Force.

The *Memphis Belle* crew's first mission was November 7th to bomb a submarine base at Brest, France. They had very little enemy opposition and it was a "milk run" compared to what the future held. Their second mission to the St. Nazaire submarine pens farther down the coast of France was a different story. It was the crew's introduction to heavy flak and FW-190 fighters and the *Belle* came home with sixty holes! Four bombers were lost and several others heavily damaged. The balance of their tour was the same or worse. The *Memphis Belle's* tour of duty was during the worst days for crews of the Mighty Eighth. Losses were extremely high as planes flew long missions without fighter support. Bombers' gunners battled swarms of Luftwaffe fighters to make bomb-runs into heavy flak over the target and fight their way back to England.

It was estimated that the Eighth lost 75 % of its bombers and crews during those early bombing missions. The boys in the early bomb crews were pioneers in high altitude flights and precision bombing. Fighter escorts to distant targets were not possible until late 1943. Allied fighters could only escort bombers so far before they had to return to England before running out of fuel. Hordes of German Luftwaffe fighters would wait to attack bomber formations as soon as the Allied escort had to turn back. The extra long missions without fighter protection took a heavy toll on men and planes because the German Air Force, the Luftwaffe, had air superiority. It would be months before Allied P-51 Mustang fighters, fitted with long range fuel drop tanks, could escort our bombers to distant targets and back. Meanwhile, B-17 Flying Fortress and B-24 Liberator gunners had a hard time defending their planes against the machine gun, cannon and rocket fire of attacking Luftwaffe fighters. Air crew morale became so low that the Eighth Air Force command decided to put a limit on the number of missions airmen would be required to fly. Aircrews were encouraged to learn they would only have to survive twenty-five missions to complete their tour of duty.

The *Memphis Belle* bombed very tough targets and her gunners were given credit for shooting down eight enemy fighters with "probable hits" on five others. The bomber was shot up by fighter bullets and flak many times. On five separate missions, the Belle limped back to England with damaged or disabled engines and/or various parts which had to be replaced before it could fly again. Throughout her war-time service, the *Belle* was bullet-ridden, flak damaged, on five separate occasions had an engine shot out, and once returned to Bassingbourn with her tail almost shot off. Lt. Morgan once joked that his crew chief and ground crew had re-built his B-17 several times, but not one member of her crew sustained any major injuries. He said he stressed to his gunners and other crew members that they had to work as a crew with each man protecting the bomber and ready to take over another's position in a crisis.

Bombing results and severe losses were causing doubt about daytime missions and the Air Force was looking for ways to improve their success. The legendary WW II B-17 Flying Fortress with the Petty Girl redhead on the nose was the first Eighth Air Force bomber to complete twenty-five missions with its crew intact. In early 1943 Hollywood film Director, William Wyler, had come to Bassingbourn to film a documentary on the air war. He and his camera crew flew several missions on the *Belle* and other bombers and one of his cameramen was killed. The first plane to complete twenty-five missions was cause for celebration and Wyler completed his combat film called "*The Memphis*

Belle"; it was said that his documentary and the famous bomber's War Bond tour helped keep America in the war. Crewmembers were awarded a total of 60 medals which included the Distinguished Flying Cross. The story of their accomplishment has been told in a 1944 documentary and a popular movie in 1990.

The young men of the *Memphis Belle* crew received personal congratulations from King George VI and Queen Elizabeth of England who made a visit to the 91st Bomb Group to honor the crew that became America's heroes when our nation needed a morale builder. General Eaker then assigned the famous bombers and its ten man crew to do a special twenty-sixth mission. They were chosen to return to the United States for a three month tour of thirty large American cities to thank the public for supporting the war and promote the sale of War Bonds. The crew's mascot, Stuka, a black Scottish terrier, accompanied the crew back across the Atlantic and on the War Bond and Public relations tour. Washington, D.C. was their first stop, and as they approached the field, they received a radio message that General "Hap" Arnold ordered them to "buzz" the crowd at the reviewing stand. You can imagine the reactions of the crowd being buzzed by a Flying Fortress. The famous bomber visited thirty-two major cities before ending their tour. August 31, 1943 they said goodbye to the *Memphis Belle* at Washington National Airport and disbanded as a crew.

The legendary WW II B-17 Flying Fortress with the "Petty Girl on her nose dropped more than 60 tons of bombs over Germany, France and Belgium. During her 25 missions she flew 148 hours, 50 minutes, and covered more than 20,000 combat miles. The Belle flew ten months, from November 7, 1942 to May 17, 1943.

By war's end, the 91st Bomb Group had participated in 340 operational missions and dropped over 22,000 tons of bombs. 197 of its aircraft were lost. The Group's accomplishments show a total of 420 enemy aircraft destroyed, 238 probably destroyed, and 127 damaged. During its combat history the group's Force lost 1,010 combat crewman (887 killed and 123 missing in action) with more than 960 crewman to be held as prisoners of war. <u>The group's aircraft losses were the highest of any other 8th Air Force bomb group.</u>

USAAF Photo

The B-17F Flying Fortress "Memphis Belle" (Serial No. 41-24485) crew after completing their 25th mission. Captain Robert Morgan is in the back row, third from left. The famous bomber now has a permanent home at the U.S. Air Force Museum near Dayton, Ohio.

THE CREW

Capt. Robert K. Morgan - Pilot
Capt. James Verinis - Copilot
Capt. Vincent B. Evans - Bombardier
Capt. Charles B. Leighton - Navigator
T/Sgt. Harold P. Loch - Engineer/Top Gunner
T/Sgt. Robert Hanson - Radio Operator
S/Sgt. John P. Quinlan - Tail Gunner
S/Sgt. Cecil H. Scott - Ball Turret Gunner
S/Sgt. Clarence E. Winchell - L Waist Gunner
S/Sgt. Casimer "Tony" Nastal - R Waist Gunner
Joe Giambrone-Crew Chief replaced 9 engines, both wings, two tails and both main landing gears

T/Sgt. James Lee Hutchinson, Ed.S.

MEMPHIS BELLE MISSION SUMMARY

#	Location:	Date:	Target:
1	Brest, France	November 7, 1942	U-Boat Pens
2	St. Nazaire, France	November 9, 1942	U-Boat Pens
3	St. Nazaire, France	November 17, 1942	U-Boat Pens
4	Lille, France	December 6, 1942	Marshalling Yards
5	Rommily-Sur-Seine, France	December 20, 1942	German Aircraft Depot
6	St. Nazaire, France	January 1, 1943	U-Boat Pens
7	Lille, France	January 13, 1943	Marshalling Yards
8	Lorient, France	January 23, 1943	U-Boat Pens
9	Emden, Germany	February 4, 1943	War Plant (Ford Factory)
10	Hamm, Germany	February 14, 1943	Marshalling Yards
11	St. Nazaire, France	February 16, 1943	U-Boat Pens
12	Wilhelmshaven, Germany	February 26, 1943	Sea Port
13	Brest, France	February 29, 1943	U-Boat Pens
14	Lorient, France	March 6, 1943	U-Boat Pens
15	Roven, France	March 12, 1943	Marshalling Yards
16	Abbeville, France	March 13, 1943	German Fighters
17	Wilhelmshaven, Germany	March 22, 1943	Sea Port
18	Roven, France	March 28, 1943	Marshalling Yards
19	Antwerp, Belgium	April 5, 1943	War Plants
20	Lorient, France	April 16, 1943	U-Boat Pens
21	Bremen, Germany	April 17, 1943	War Plant (Focke-Wulf Factory)
22	St. Nazaire, France	May 1, 1943	U-Boat Pens
23	Antwerp, Belgium	May 4, 1943	War Plants
24	Lorient, France	May 15, 1943	U-Boat Pens
25	Wilhelmshaven, Germany	May 17, 1943	Sea Port

Captain Robert Morgan then volunteered to fly in the Pacific theater. He was assigned to command a B-29 Super Fortress bomb squadron with the 20th Air Force and flew another twenty-four missions. November 24, 1944, Major Morgan in his B-29 *"Dauntless Dottie,"* had the honor of leading the first B-29 mission to bomb Tokyo. Wing Commander General Emmett "Rosie" O'Donnell had selected him to lead and rode with him as command pilot. It was the first time Tokyo had been bombed since the Jimmy Doolittle B-25 raid in 1942. More than 100 Super Forts took off from Saipan for a thirteen hour round trip. Five months later, Morgan was promoted to Colonel and sent back to the USA. He said General O'Donnell told him that he was afraid his luck would run out.

Note - *My daughter Susan and I had the honor of boarding the famous Belle in 2002 while it was on display on Mud Island in Memphis and she took a photo of me at the radio operator's desk. In 2003 the plane was taken to the Millington Navy base and later it was dismantled and hauled to the National Museum of the United States Air Force near Dayton, Ohio for complete restoration. The Belle will never fly again, but the will always be on display to remind visitors of its role in World War II and of the young airmen who flew against overwhelming odds to save our nation's freedom! Susan, later attended a fund raising event in Memphis to hear Col. Morgan speak. Later at his book signing, she told him of my missions in the Mighty Eighth and he autographed his book to me! It simply said,*
   "To Lee, best wishes thanks for flying in combat in a B-17"

That autographed copy of his book, "The Man Who Flew the Memphis Belle" by Col. Robert Morgan USAFR, Ret. is one of my prize possessions. Colonel Morgan passed away in May 2004 at the age of 85 years. He was honored by a final 'flyover' of a B-52 bomber and a B-17 Flying Fortress with a P-51 escort fighter at his funeral in Asheville, North Carolina. The planes tipped their wings in a final salute to the famed bomber pilot.
   Today a B-17 named Memphis Belle B-17 which was used in the popular movie, *"The Memphis Belle,"* tours the U.S. offering flights to

those who want to experience the thrill of soaring in the sky in a WW II Flying Fortress or walking through the bomber. Check the Liberty Belle Foundation website or the educational tour schedule of the famous plane. 4

> *"History does not long entrust the care of freedom to the weak or the timid."*
>
> *- General Dwight D. Eisenhower*

The 95th Bomb Group

The 95th was based at Horham was less than 12 miles from my 490th base at Eye. Months after the war, I learned that three men from my hometown were with the 95th Bomb Group, but I knew none of them at that time. William "Ed" Charles, navigator, Doyle Byers, radio operator/gunner and Ralph Alexander, Crew Chief mechanic were members of the 95th Bomb Group. I knew none of them in 1944-45 when I was stationed a few miles away at Eye. We shared stories and friendship in Bedford, Indiana for many years and never forgot the days of our youth in the Mighty Eighth. Ed was my golfing buddy, Doyle became my brother-in-law and my oldest daughter married Ralph's son. The three 95th BG airmen, Ed, Doyle and Ralph became family men, friends and neighbors in Bedford until they passed. Ed Charles was very proud of his military service and often told stories of his days in the sky with the 95th Bomb Group especially about being on the basketball team and winning the Eighth Air Force Championship and several other titles. He remained active in the Air Force Reserve and retired with the rank of Lt. Colonel.

The 95th was first stationed at Alconbury to fly with the 92nd Bomb Group, but it had been operative only a few weeks when a bomb-loading accident caused a tragic explosion which disintegrated one bomber (the four motors were never found.) Four aircraft nearest the doomed plane were crumpled by shock waves and another eleven were declared no longer airworthy. The blast and shock waves killed nineteen members of the ground crew and injured twenty. They said shock waves killed several men standing in the area but spared those sitting or lying on the ground beside them. The Group was then transferred to a base at Framlingham, where they lost several crews and planes on the June 13th mission to the submarine pens at Keil. They were not flying in the usual Box Formation, but in a flattened formation devised by the new commander, Brigadier General Nathan Bedford Forrest, III. The new formation was swarmed by Luftwaffe fighters and the field of fire of formation gunners was limited. The FW-190 and ME 109 fighters attacked from the front and the General's B-17 was first to go down. The mission was a disaster as the 95th lost ten of their twenty-four bombers and twelve more from other groups were lost. A month later the 95th Bomb Group moved to a brand new field at Horham, Suffolk.

Lt. William "Ed" Charles

Lt. Charles was navigator on the Robert Kroeger crew when the 95th became the first group to bomb Berlin on March 4, 1944. Twenty-seven bombers, supported by a small group of P-51 Mustangs, refused to turn back and made history. He said the top brass and newsmen were waiting at the field when the group landed. Major General Curtis Le May, Third Division Commander, was on hand to congratulate the first group to bomb Berlin. Lt. Col. Mumford, mission commander, was awarded the Silver Star, and lead pilot, Lt. Al Brown received the Distinguished Service Cross. The 95th Bomb Group was awarded its third Presidential Unit Citation and Life Magazine featured pictures of the planes and crews who had survived the mission in its March 29, 1944 issue. It was a terrific mission which brought headline news and encouragement to every man in the Mighty Eighth. The 95th Bomb Group had proven that Berlin was no longer invincible and Luftwaffe fighters were weaker. (Berlin was the target of our Templeton crew's first mission nine months later on December 5, 1944)

Once Hitler came to power he began re-arming secretly for several years. He ignored the arms limitations placed on Germany after they lost WW I, and from 1936 on, especially during the Spanish Civil War

His air force, the Luftwaffe had developed rapidly and Messerschmitt Bf-109 were in production as early as 1937. Early in the air war, the German Luftwaffe ruled the skies. Germany had many experienced pilots, aces who had flown combat missions during the civil war in Spain. Hitler assured Germans that Berlin would never be bombed and his Hitler's right hand man, Reichsmarshall Hermann Goering once boasted of the ability of his Lufftwaffe fighters to protect Berlin.

"If Allied planes ever bomb Berlin, you can call me Meyer."

When our 95th BG bombers, escorted by P-51 Mustangs, bombed the German capital, Goering said, "When I saw Mustangs over Berlin, I knew the jig was up."

Early in the war, Eighth Air Force bombers were outnumbered and flew missions against heavy odds. Targets were often beyond the fuel range of escort fighters and Luftwaffe fighters waited to attack the bomber formations when U. S. fighters were forced to turn back due to fuel limitations. Combat formations sustained heavy losses and replacement crews were in great demand as few airmen completed their combat tour of twenty-five missions. However, as U. S. and RAF fighter groups grew stronger the Luftwaffe were losing pilots and planes they could not replace. German pilots were pushed to their limits and the Luftwaffe had a "fly till you die" policy. No rotation home and no limit on the number of missions or combat hours permitted those who excelled to rack up more missions and aerial victories.

Shuttle Missions

In 1944, Germany was still producing war materials and oil in areas out of a reasonable range of the Eighth or Fifteenth heavy bombers in England and Italy. The United States, Britain and Russia agreed on a plan to establish "shuttle mission bases" to reach those faraway critical targets. The first leg of these long-range missions allowed bombers to strike a German target, fly on past it to land at specified airbases. A day or so later, they refueled and loaded more bombs to fly another leg of their shuttle to blast more previously unreachable targets on a return flight.

The bases approved by Russia were farther away than the USAAF wanted, and despite the best efforts were barely adequate for handling heavy bombers. To set up the bases, all heavy equipment, oil, gasoline and ammo supplies had to go by sea to the ports of Murmansk and Archangelsk in the Arctic, and by train to the airfields in the Ukraine. Additional supplies and key personnel were flown in on Air Transport Command planes from an airbase in Iran. The logistical demands were enormous since almost everything had to be brought in from the United States, even the high-octane aviation fuel and the steel-plank runways. Delicate negotiations were required to allow a total of forty-two round-trip ATC flights to make the bases operational for the AAF, and allowed an additional rate of two weekly support missions to supply the U.S. airmen stationed in Russia. By the end of the operation, the ATC had delivered some 450 personnel and thirty-six thousand pounds of cargo to support these shuttle bases by June 1944.

Retreating German troops had destroyed most of the Soviet infrastructure and the spring season turned everything into a sea of mud. The program was a good idea but American officers found themselves dealing with an unfriendly and suspicious Soviet bureaucracy although U.S. pilots agreed that Red Air Force personnel at the bases were cooperative and eager to assist Allied airmen.

15th Air Force - 99th BG - The Fifteenth Air Force, of was first to carry out a "shuttle mission" on June 2, 1944, they bombed the railroad yards in Debrecen, Hungary and flew on to Poltava, Russia to earn the distinction of being the first U.S. bombers to land in Russia.

June 6th they took off to bomb a German airfield in Galati, Romania and returned to Poltava and first learned of D-Day.

June 11th The U.S. bombers left Poltava to complete the third leg of their mission to bomb a German airfield in Focsani, Romania and return to their home base in Tortorella, Italy.

The 15th did one more shuttle July 22 and later sent fighters to Poltava in support of an Eighth Air Force shuttle.

8th Air Force - 95th BG - The success of the Fifteenth's Air Force shuttle mission to Russia proved their value. The Eighth Air Force commanders also made plans to reach Germany's distant war factories, oil refineries and airfields. Arrangements had been made with Russia to prepare airfields and supply U.S. planes with bombs, ammo and fuel. Ed Charles said he volunteered to fly on that first shuttle mission to Russia because it was another first for the 95th Bomb Group and he wanted to be a part of it!

Lt. Ed Charles said, "Our 95th Bomb Group was one of several groups to do the first 8th AF shuttle mission to Russia. We prepared for a long flight and every B-17 carried a full bomb load, extra cans of gas and a ground crew mechanic. They gave us an escape kit with a compass, map, identification papers and a little plastic card with several phrases in the Russian language in case we had to jump or land in territory occupied by their troops. We practiced learning the most important phrase, "I am an American."

June 21 - Thirteen planes of our 95th Bomb Group took off on the first leg of the mission, bombed an oil refinery at Rhuland, Germany, we saw a few fighters and flew on into Russia. Some groups landed at the Poltava airfield but we landed on another field at Mirgorod. It was a long flight and we were in the air for almost twelve hours. The conditions at the field were primitive with only a few anti-aircraft guns for protection. Most of the buildings in the area were damaged and the people were walking or traveling by horse drawn carts. The Russian soldiers were very helpful and Russian interpreters were there to help our commanding officers with conversation. However, a German observation plane was spotted above the field and our Group Commander got leery of a German bomber raid. So we flew our planes back to another field at Kharkov. It was really a smart move, because in the middle of the night a German pathfinder plane dropped flares that lit up the Poltava field and an estimated seventy-five Nazi bombers blasted the airfield for almost two hours. Forty-seven of the seventy-three B-17s that landed at Poltava were destroyed and most of the remainder severely damaged. Even worse, the supplies of fuel and ammunition brought so laboriously from the United States were also destroyed.

The Russian soldiers were pretty somber and rugged, but were eager to help us, because they knew we were there to help them beat the Germans they hated. We were surprised that there were so many women working at the airfield. They said the Russian WACS were the ones who laid the metal strips to make the runways. Some of them were fairly good looking, but we couldn't talk with them without interpreters. It was one of those "look but don't touch" situations, although several did pose for pictures with us when they weren't working. One night I went to a Russian movie some other guys (officers) and some of the Russian WAC officers, but were we stumped by the language.

June 25 – We flew back to Mirgorod to load up with bombs and fuel for the second leg of the shuttle. This time, our target was an oil refinery at Drohobycz in southern Poland. We had no problems and completed a nine hour flight to a field near the Fifteenth Air Force base in Foggia, Italy. Everybody really enjoyed those sunny days and the Italian people. Our troops had chased the Germans north, Rome had been liberated and we enjoyed resting and touring in a safe relaxed area the days we were there.

July 2 – Shuttle planes loaded up again to fly a mission to Arad, Romania near the Black Sea. We bombed a power plant and railroad junction and were looking forward to more rest and relaxation in the sunny south when we returned to Foggia. However that didn't last long.

July 5 – We loaded again for the final leg of the shuttle and made a strike on the railyards at Beziers, France on our way to England. That ten hour flight ended for our 95th bombers when we touched down at Horham."

Note – *Thirteen B-17s of the 95th Bomb Group participated in a shuttle mission that bombed four distant targets in fifteen days with excellent results and no bombers lost! Eighth Air force bombers flew five shuttles until Russian troops advanced into Germany and those long missions to primitive airfields were no longer necessary.*

T/Sgt. James Lee Hutchinson, Ed.S.

The "Bloody Hundredth"

The 100th Bomb Group arrived in England in late May of 1943 to join the Eighth Air Force's strategic bombing effort to destroy German military targets. The B-17 Flying Fortress group was assigned to the Thorpe Abbotts RAF base, station 139. Early targets in France and Germany included airfields, submarine pens and wartime industries. The group's heavy losses during eight missions to strategic German targets in early June through October 1943 earned them the nickname of "The Bloody Hundredth". The group flew several missions in which a dozen or more bombers were lost. Three Flying Fortresses were lost on their very first mission June 25, 1943.

In less than four months the 100th earned the Distinguished Unit Citation for an August 17th raid on an aircraft factory at Regensberg. A second citation was awarded in March of 1944 for a series of raids on Berlin. Later Germany's oil supplies, airfields and transportation system became priority targets. The group bombed hitting railroads, bridges and gun positions in preparation for D-Day. As the war progressed, the 100th BG engaged in missions supporting ground forces at Saint-Lo, Brest and hitting oil depots, railroad marshalling yards and bridges during the Battle of The Bulge and the invasion of Germany.

The 100th Bomb Group suffered some of their heaviest losses during Black Week (Oct.8-14, 1943) in missions on some of the Germany's most protected targets. The group flew three days in a row to Bremen, Marienburg and Munster. They lost so many bombers and crews in those three days that they could only send up eight planes for the Oct. 14th mission to Schweinfurt. They flew with the 95th Bomb Group and Eighth Air Force losses were so heavy that it became "Black Friday"!

Air Force statistics show the 100th Bomb Group, based at Thorpe Abbotts, flew 306 missions between June 25, 1943 and April 20, 1945 with a loss of 177 bombers. The group arrived early in the war, earned two unit citations and stayed for the victory! The Bomb Group participated in six campaigns and dropped 19, 257 tons of bombs on enemy targets. The cost in aircrews and planes was high with a total of 177 planes MIA and lost 52 in operational losses. There were 184 Missing Air Crew Reports. (MARC) Casualties included 785 men killed or missing in action (KIA/MIA) and 894 Prisoners of War during the group's 306 missions from June 25, 1943 to April 20, 1945. In May, after the "cease fire," the group flew six Mercy missions to drop food cartons to the starving people in Holland.

The classic movie, "Twelve O' Clock High," tells the story of the Eighth Air Force and the stress and high losses of bomber crews in WW II. It was modeled after the Bloody Hundredth.

Sweater Girl of the 100th BG

The replacement crew of Lt. Richard B. Atchison arrived at the 100th Bomb Group at Thorpe Abbot's airbase August 25, 1943, and was assigned to squadron 418. The "Bloody Hundredth" had recently lost men and bombers to German fighters and flak in the August 17, 1943 missions when the Mighty Eighth attacked two high priority targets: a Messerschmitt aircraft factory at Regensburg and ball-bearing plants at Schweinfurt. Both targets were in the Ruhr Valley and heavily protected by fighters and anti-aircraft batteries. Bomber crews dreaded missions to this area, also known as "Flak Alley." That fear was well grounded because German fighters and flak brought down 60 of the 387 American planes that day! The "Bloody Hundredth" was in desperate need of replacement crews!

Heavy bombers flew long and often early in the war and were punished during long flights and flak over critical targets. Maintenance and repair were very important to keeping planes in the air. Bombers were in short supply and pilots were wary of engine problems which might keep them from returning home. Pilots had the option of "aborting" a mission after take-off if the plane developed problems, but they had better have a good reason for dropping out of the formation. The B-17F bomber, "Sweater Girl," had four REM s (returned for mechanical problems) and one failure to take off ranging from prop trouble to a booster pump failure between July and October 10, 1943.

The last failure was September 27th, two weeks before it was lost on a mission.

The Lt. Atchison crew was flying "Sweater Girl" instead of their own bomber, "Terry and Ten" when they went down on the mission to Munster, October 10, 1943. The official MACR lists four of the crew as killed in action and six as Prisoners of War. "Sweater Girl" had severe damage from flak and the fighters and before it went down. Two of the six airmen who survived, tell their stories. Navigator, 2nd Lt. Kenneth Baron and tail-gunner, S/Sgt. Van T. "Ike" Wright bailed out and were captured when they landed. Like many airmen who survived bailing out, both finished the war in a POW camp.

Lt. Kenneth Barron – POW – Lt. Barron said the formation was hit by heavy flak during the bomb-run on the target at Munster. After they had dropped their bombs and left the flak area, they were attacked by a large number of Luftwaffe fighters. During the running battle, Barron was hit in the right thigh which broke his femur. As the fighter attack continued, a damaged ME-109 crashed into left wing of the B-17 of the bomber flying beside them in the formation. The doomed plane burst into flames, went into a steep spiral and exploded in mid-air. Meanwhile, Lt. Atchison's aircraft suffered severe damage from the flak and fighter attacks. The wounded navigator said, "Our plane was hit in the # 2 engine, probably an oil line, and oil was pouring out. "Sweater Girl" was severely damaged before we were ordered to bail out. I was dazed and in great pain but I crawled to the lower nose exit, pulled the emergency release handle. I remember the bombardier was just behind me before I bailed out, but I never saw him again."

S/SGT. "Ike" Wright- POW - of Bloomfield, Indiana was tail gunner on the Lt. Richard Atchison crew when the "Sweater Girl", was shot down over Munster on his eighth mission, October 10, 1943. Ike bailed out and became a POW in Stalag 7A. He eventually ended up in Stalag 17 B at Krems, Austria. This was the same POW camp where T/Sgt Robert Stahlhut, engineer on the Lt. McMahon crew of the 384th Bomb Group and 2nd Lt. Corbin Willis, Jr., co-pilot with the 486th Bomb

Group were also prisoners of war! Their stories, in previous books, report many of the same terrible treatment endured by prisoners of war.

Ike said the Lt. Atchison crew was approved for combat after only five training flights. Their first mission was to Paris on September 15th. The second was a low-level night raid on the La Pallice submarine pens followed by missions to Paris and Emden, Germany. Ike and his twin tail guns received credit for shooting down an ME-109 on their fifth mission. Missions six and seven were in heavy flack over Hanover and Mariensburg. Their plane had to abort the eighth mission to Bremen because of engine problems (the 100th lost eight planes on this raid). The next raid was to Munster, near the deadly Ruhr valley, it was the target for October 10th. The Lt. Atchison crew was flying its ninth mission in less than a month.

"At briefing, we were told that we were headed for Munster and we could expect at least 450 German fighters and very heavy flak. We took off late because of a heavy ground fog and met our British Spitfire fighter escort over the English Channel. We knew they could not take us all the way to the target. Sure enough, we were hit by swarms of Luftwaffe fighters as soon as our escort left us. Our formation flew on towards Munster. I could see bombers exploding and going down. Then we hit the flak area over our target, and, as the saying goes, the flak was so thick you could walk on it. At the time I didn't know if we had reached the assigned target and dropped our bombs. Later on, I learned we had fulfilled the mission. We had made it to the target and turned back north when we were hit by fighters again. The ME-109 Messerschmitts and JU 88 Junkers came at us high and low from all directions. The Junkers stayed out of the range of our 50 caliber machine guns and fired rockets into the formation. One rocket exploded above my left shoulder. Someone must have been looking after me, because it created a hole I could have crawled through. I knew we were in deep trouble, the intercom was gone and our guns had quit firing. I crawled from my tail-gun position up to the waist. I saw both our waist gunners, Fields and Preble, were down. Fields was not moving. Preble got to his feet and he was bleeding at the mouth. I crawled on to the ball turret gunner's position, but it was not moving. The B-17 began to lurch and weave.

I opened the waist door and motioned to Preble that we had to jump. He nodded and pointed for me to go ahead. I jumped, but never saw him leave the plane.

I was very dizzy and light headed (off of oxygen too long), but I counted to 100 to get out of the flak area before I opened my chute. I figured I had left the plane at 20,000 feet. I saw our bomber dive, level off and dive again. I saw no chutes of my crew members. On my way down, I was buzzed by two ME-109 fighters. One came close enough to almost collapse my chute before he went back up to the battle.

I hit the ground safely, gathered up my chute and concealed it as quickly as possible. Then I hid in tall weeds in a ditch close to a road until dark. Five German soldiers passed, but didn't spot me. After dark, I moved out and headed north until almost dawn. It was cool so I found a haystack to sleep in, but not for long. Dogs found me and alerted two farmers who came running. Both had pitchforks. Soon, German soldiers on motorcycles came, handcuffed me and took me through Munster. The dirty looks and gestures I got from the civilians we had just bombed made me think this was it. An officer and soldier took me by train to an interrogation center at Frankfort on the Main. I saw other American prisoners at the train station, but we were forbidden to talk to each other.

They put me in a three by six foot cell overnight with a cot and bucket. The next morning I was taken before a German officer for interrogation by a German officer who spoke better English than I did. He said he was from Philadelphia. I only gave him my name, rank and serial number. I guess he must have thought I was too dumb to know anything else and he sent me back to my cell. The three days I was there, they gave me water, Black Bread and a small bowl of soup. The fourth day they took me to a "holding room" with seventy-five or more other prisoners. All had been shot down over Munster on the Oct. 10th or on the Schweinfurt raids on the 14th. I heard that the 100th had lost 13 bombers on our Munster mission.

Next, they took us down to the train station and loaded us into a boxcar. We were packed in so tightly that we could hardly sit down. There was no water or food until they made a stop. Then we got water, weak soup and the everlasting Black Bread. We were in that boxcar for the better part of three days until we arrived at Krems, Austria. From there, it was on to a fenced compound and barracks number 34 B in the prisoner of war camp, Stalag XVII-B. Prisoner of war camps for military prisoners were not the same as the Concentration Camps for Jews and political prisoners.

Our compound consisted of dozens of barracks surrounded by twin ten foot fences with a walkway between on all four sides and four guard towers. In front of the inside fence was a ten foot area known as the 'trip-wire area. The trip-wire was a knee-high wire inside of our compound to keep us away from the first ten foot fence.

We were warned this was "Verboten" territory and anyone crossing that trip-wire would be shot. During my stay, I saw a Russian and an Italian killed inside the trip-wire area. Later, one of the guys in our compound tried to escape. We heard him yelling "Kamerad", (I'm a friend), but he was inside the "Verboten" area and the German Kommandant showed him no mercy as he shot him in the head.

I estimate that we had at least 50 to 60 men cramped into our barracks. Our bunk bed consisted of wooden slats, a thin straw tick mattress or pad and one blanket. The barracks was unheated and cold all the time. Chilblains (itching on hands or feet due to prolonged exposure to cold) and frostbite were common, as were coughs and flu-like symptoms. They had taken away our shoes and given us wooden clogs; just wood soles with cloth straps. We stood roll call out in the exercise yard each morning and evening and were often made to stand in the snow, mud or rain until the guards saw fit to let us go inside. As I said, frostbite was very common.

Food was scarce, our menu consisted of "ersatz" coffee, barley soup (no meat) and Black Bread for about six months until the Red Cross parcels started arriving once a month. Each "one for two" package would serve two men. It contained crackers, jelly, cheese, a chocolate bar and cigarettes. A lot of the men didn't smoke so we played poker for the "cigs" or traded them for potatoes, onions or anything else available from the camp guards.

Stalag 17B was a big camp and had different area for its prisoners. There were men from Russia, Italy, Bulgaria, Romania, Albania, Serbia and a few English soldiers. Many of the English soldiers had been captured at Dunkirk early in the war. There were a large number of Russian prisoners and they fared very badly. They died daily and the wagon carrying the dead would pass our compound. The men in our compound were a tough lot and there was not a lot of complaining. We had been in the camp for over a year and a half when our guards told us we were going to move out. We knew something was going on because we had been hearing cannon fire in the east towards Vienna and Plauen. American fighter planes were sweeping the skies over our compound more often. Our bombers were hitting Krems, only a few miles from our camp and British RAF bombers were overhead every night. The allied armies were getting closer, so one day our guards herded us out of the POW camp and we started on a long march. There was little food. They fed us weak soup with Black Bread once a day. We stopped at farm houses each night and often slept in the barns with the cattle. We were "buzzed" by ME-262 jets a couple of time, but we didn't know what they were at that time.

One day on our march across Austria, we met a long column of Jewish prisoners, or slave laborers, headed in the opposite direction. They were so starved and emaciated I couldn't see how they kept going. The men in our group passed them what little food we had, which was mostly Black Bread. Their German guards were driving them on with bayonets and gun butts. They were in a hurry to take those poor souls somewhere. One prisoner fell and tried to rise, but a guard beat him to death with his gun butt and left him lying in the road. We saw more bodies as we moved on down the road they had just traveled, most were bloodied. It was evident that prisoners who couldn't keep up the pace were beaten to death. Our plight was very minor compared to those poor Jewish prisoners.

The long march was approximately 300 miles to Braunau Austria, where we were held in a forested area for two days. During this time, we heard gunfire in the distance and saw German soldiers retreating through the woods. Before long, our guards joined them. What a wonderful sight!

We stayed put and before long a group of American troops came along and told us we were free. They said to stay in a group until the army trucks picked us up and took us to a camp far behind the battle lines. Now we would be protected and transported by GI s of the U.S. Army. Once we got behind the lines and off those trucks, we were deloused. and issued new uniforms. Later we took showers, and ate real food. Of course, we couldn't eat too much at once. It took a while for our stomachs to come back from the edge of starvation. I had been a POW from October 10, 1943 to May 3, 1945. Germany surrendered five days later. At last, I was safe and free!"

Captain James R. Stout's Combat Log

Captain James R. Stout was a bomber pilot in the early years. His combat log is an amazing account of his Eighth Air Force B-17 bombing missions. As a veteran of 20 missions a year later, I can appreciate the flak, fighter attacks and engine problems they encountered in the early days. The fact that their missions were a year before mine when Germany's Air Force (Luftwaffe) was at its peak, awes me. The Stout crew survived practically every deadly situation experienced by thousands of WW II bomber crews.

James Rowland Stout, a fellow Hoosier, graduated from Shortridge High in Indianapolis, Indiana in 1934 and worked at the L.B. Price Company in Columbus, Indiana. Eight years later, he had a wife, Norma and a two year old daughter, Janet Rowlyn when he enlisted in the Air Cadet program at Bowman field, Kentucky in April 8, 1942.

He did pre-flight training at Maxwell Field, Alabama; primary flying training at Dorr field Florida; basic flying at Gunter Field, Alabama and advanced flying at BAAF, Blytheville, Arkansas. He completed pilot training with class 43D in May, 1943 at Hendricks Field, Sebring, FL. After thirteen months of intensive training, he was assigned to combat crew training at Moses Lake, Washington. Later, Second Lieutenant Stout and his crew were deployed to Kearny, Nebraska and prepared to fly the North Atlantic Route to join the Eighth Air Force in the European Theater of Operations.

The twenty-six year old pilot entered the combat zone October 15, 1943, completed thirty hazardous missions and attained the rank of

T/Sgt. James Lee Hutchinson, Ed.S.

Captain before he left the ETO, May 20, 1944. He remained in the service and volunteered as a test pilot in October. The veteran pilot was assigned to the Office of Flying Safety, Santa Anna, CA.

Captain James R. Stout was flying a B-25D test bomber when he was fatally injured in an emergency crash landing at Douglas Air Force Base in Douglas, Arizona on January 12, 1945. The engineer flying with him escaped with minor injuries. A second daughter, Joyce Rowjean was born after his death.

Note - *I wish to thank Captain Stout's daughter, Janet (Mrs. Tom Cotton) for allowing me to print her father's flight log. It is a very concise and informative set of notes written after he had completed each long, tiring and dangerous mission. This hero's story should be preserved to tell this and future generations of his Eighth Air Force combat experiences. Sit back and imagine you are the pilot of a B-17 Flying Fortress flying bombing missions over Europe in 1944.*

James R. Stout Crew (left to right)

Standing L to R: *Chester Polak, Bombardier; James Stout, Pilot; Robert Lunsford, Co-Pilot; Robert Nelson, Navigator;*

Kneeling: *Daniel Greene, Ball Turret gunner; Paul Calkin, Right Waist gunner; Bernard McDermott, Left Waist gunner; Wilbur Trembley, Radio operator gunner; Clarence Clegg, Engineer/Top Turret gunner; Charles Lynch, Tail gunner*

USAAF photo courtesy of Paul E. Calkin (Nov 2007)

The 2nd Lt. James R. Stout bomber crew arrived at the Bloody Hundredth October 15, 1943 and was assigned to the 349th Squadron. According to group procedure, they received training in formation flying and combat procedures before flying in tight formations. New pilots were required to fly their first mission as co-pilot with an experienced pilot. Lt. Stout's first mission was out over the North Sea and across Holland to Munster, Germany as co-pilot with the Lt. Donald H. Moede crew.

Munster Dec. 22, 1943 It was a rather uneventful trip except for moderate, but inaccurate flak. We sighted no enemy planes, but had plenty of P-47 escort fighters which certainly look good to a bomber pilot. We flew in the number two element of the lead squadron and used PFF radar to bomb through the clouds. Flying in the right hand seat as co-pilot was awkward. Mac came along too as waist gunner.

Ludwigshaven Dec. 30 This was our crew's first mission, our plane was "Dodie," # 783. There was no excitement on the way, except a continually "running away" propeller on engine # 4. We ran into flak at the IP (initial point to start the bomb run) but it was about 3000 yards to the left. However, it got very accurate and heavy over the target and afterward. We received a hole in the right wing; # 3 engine was smoking; Chet had holes in the plexi-glass nose; our astrodome was shattered and a piece of flak hit Nelson's desk, tearing his log. The main gas tank on # 2 was hit; the oil tank on # 1 was punctured and the prop on # 4 was still "running away." A flak burst exploded directly above us and stunned me for a second – so we were fairly busy for a while. After the flak finished with us, our leader, Captain Henry Henington dropped back with a feathered # 3 motor and Lt. Moede took over just before we were hit by the "Abbeville Boys", a Focke-Wulf-190 fighter group with a reputation for attacking in spite of Hell. They came in from out of the sun and clouds and got Lt. Marvin 'Pappy' Leininger's plane on the first pass. As the plane went down in flames (see Air Corps song) three chutes were seen to bail out, but one was on fire. They also got the Smith plane out of the low squadron and worked over George Brannan's plane until our P-47 fighters came in to chase them off. His bomber crashed out of control on our return to base, but no one was hurt. His bomber had been hit by a 20mm shell during the fighter attack: the ball turret gunner was shot through the ankle; the bombardier hit in the face; throat microphones were clipped off both waist gunners and one had five holes in his pants without a scratch!

Today we flew the # 2 position in the lead element of the High squadron and bombed by PFF through the clouds again. The crew performed very well, especially Charles Lynch, our tail gunner, a very good man. (Lt. Robert J. Digby co-pilot on the Lt. Dean Radtke crew was killed.)

Note – *Allied fighter and bomber pilots came to respect the "Abbeville Boys." The yellow nosed Messerschmitt-109 or Focke-Wulf- 190 fighters were flown by some of the best Luftwaffe pilots of the war. The JG26 (Jagdgeschwader Schlageter) fighter group was stationed at Abbeville, France. Bomber crews especially were respectful of them due to their ability to penetrate their escort fighter screen and shoot them down.*

Kiel Jan. 1, 1944 We flew #170 (Mikklesen's ship) in Purple Heart Corner with Lyons of the Morgan crew for ball turret gunner as our Danny Greene has the mumps now. Flight was all over water until we hit Denmark. Flak was heavy and accurate hitting our right wing. We got a hole in # 4 nacelle, behind the astrodome and a piece in my cockpit hit the oil gauges for # 3 and 4 engines. More worrisome was the erratic formation flying by our group leaders which finally broke up our element entirely. We straggled back alone, but finally picked up a B-24 and another B-17 as wingmen. We let # 4 run out of gas and feathered the prop before turning on our reserve fuel in the Tokyo tanks

We were very lucky that no enemy fighters came up for we were "duck soup." We came home alone behind the formation and had to crank the flaps down before landing. A ball turret gunner on another plane died of anoxia (lack of oxygen) and Mac's electric glove burned out, blistering his left hand. This was our second coldest mission. We had 45 below and the High squadron reported a low of 55. My crew's gunners made Staff Sergeant today and Clegg made Tech.

Ludwigshaven (again) Jan. 7 PFF Mission - We were pretty well frightened and worried when they uncovered the map at the briefing and showed us our target. We remembered the hell we caught at Ludwigshaven the last time, just eight days ago. S/Sgt Hopkins was our ball gunner this mission. It was an uneventful trip with light flak and the most beautiful fighter support I ever expect to see! We had P-4, P-51 and Spitfires protecting us. We saw no enemy aircraft, although we flew directly over the lair of the "Abbeville Boys." I saw one yellow nosed fighter leave the field, but he didn't come up after us. We flew plane # 972 and bombed PFF again. We were # 2 in the last element of the high squadron. Our most narrow escape of the day was during Group Assembly this morning, with B-17 and B-24 bombers whizzing every which way!

St. Omer Jan. 21 Visual mission to a Crossbow installation of V-1 and/or V-2 guided missile sites. We flew bomber # 783, now named "Call Her Savage," in the # 2 position of the second element with the High squadron. We went in over the target by squadrons at 20,000 feet. Bob put on his flak vest and flew the ship while I tried to put on mine. I couldn't get it on, got mad and threw it down in the hatchway. An action I regretted moments later when we flew into the most accurate flak we have seen. Something went wrong with the lead bomber's AFCE (automatic pilot) and we had to circle around and make a second pass through their defenses. This time it was "Bombs Away" and the ball turret gunner said our bombs went smack on the target. There were two flak holes in the leading edge of the left wing between engines # 1 and 2 visible from the cockpit. Radio operator called the Bombardier on the inter-com and said the bomb-bay door had a flak hole in it. We also got a piece through the # 1 nacelle and a piece through the bottom of the left wing outboard of the # 1 engine, which narrowly missed the fuel line. The piece through the bomb-bay door apparently went in on the first run when the doors were closed and our bombs were still in there! Bombardier says bombs wouldn't have exploded unless it had hit a fuse, but I wouldn't care to depend on them not going off! Seems like every time we fly bomber 783 we bring her home full of flak holes, but we <u>do</u>

come home. No enemy fighters today and good fighter support of P-38, P-51 and P-47 fighters, of which we saw forty. Putman bombardier was wounded. This was the third day we were briefed for this one.

Note – *Crossbow was the code name for Royal Air Force and Eighth Air Force bombing missions against all phases of the German long-range weapons program which was firing V-1 and V-2 rocket bombs into England. Crossbow missions were dedicated to destroying Germany's rocket launching sites and the manufacture and transportation of rockets. The target at Omer was La Coupole, a giant concrete bomb-proof rocket launching site under construction by prisoners/slaves from Poland and Russia. Crossbow missions had a high priority until the end of the war. The La Coupole launching site was never completed and today it a St. Omer tourist attraction as a WW II rocket museum.*

Heddernheim Jan. 21 Visual or PFF Recalled--- Well, we were awakened at 2:30 am for a 3:00 am breakfast and 4:00 am briefing for a target close to the heavily defended Frankfurt deep into Germany. We took off in pitch blackness at 7:00 am got into our # 3 position in the second element of the Lead squadron off Mik's wing. While circling, we saw a searing sheet of flames scud along the ground off to our right, which later turned out to be Drummond of the 351st. I was pretty well sickened by the thought of those poor devils dying horribly in that inferno. When we returned to the field we learned that he had dived into the ground to avoid another plane. The miracle was that there was only one man killed, the bombardier and one, the navigator, seriously injured. The rest of the crew exited under their own power. Well, after the Major dragging us and the low squadron through thick clouds, we hit for the enemy coast. We were past Brussels and making 258 knots with a strong tailwind when the "recall" came, only a few minutes from the target. We had marvelous fighter support of which we saw a hundred P-47s and 50 P-38s. Beautiful! Altogether there was to be 880 P-47, P-38 and P-51 fighters escorting us. No flak going in and only three, count 'em, weak bursts coming out near Dunkerque. BUT the bomb group ahead of us caught hell and the tail was shot off one plane, apparently scattering tail gunner all over Belgium. We dropped our "hot" bombs in the Channel and landed back at our field in the closing haze. Not bragging, but we were the second and only ship of my squadron to get in on the first pass at a badly obstructed field. This was our first trip in # 170 since it was assigned to us. Last night our crew and ground crew voted on a name and *"Pride of the Century"* placed first, "I'll Be Around" second and "Flak Foot Floogie" came in third.

Frankfort Jan. 29 Bombing PFF It was another repeat on the mission of January 24th. At 3:00 am, breakfast, 4:00 briefing and takeoff scheduled for 6:30 and as we taxied out to the runway (after the crew chief gave # 018 a quick pre-flight) we saw a $350,000 "bonfire" that one of our ships was making off the end of runway 28. It was Marks and his crew who were carrying ten 500 general purpose bombs which exploded on take-off. Three men were supposed to have survived. Nice repeat performance of January 24 and a very "encouraging" way to start off a draggy 8 hour mission. As we took off through the overcast and the thick black smoke from the early morning funeral pyre, Bob leaned over and said that he had something to tell me when we got back. As we cut the engines back at base, he told me that I had been taking off minus the supercharger, but he quickly turned on the electronic regulator to the correct setting and we lifted off, thereby he probably saved our lives. With a quick twist of the wrist and we live to take off another day. We had an uneventful climb and I found our formation over radio splasher # 6, however some of the boys never showed up and others aborted. It was generally screwed up. We crossed the enemy coast above a complete overcast and nothing unusual occurred on the way in. We got flak fairly heavy, but very inaccurate at the target and after turning to the formation rally point. Again, we had beautiful fighter support going in and coming out and saw no known enemy pursuits. However, somebody caught it as we could hear it over the UHF radio. Back at base we skipped down through the overcast as a group; a neat maneuver (Alexanders DeVore) As we circled to land, we got the "Bandits call" signifying enemy aircraft in the vicinity and we had to hurriedly re-load our guns. Mac, the left waist gunner, had a run-a-way gun, scaring us all and we found out later, the boys on the ground too. As we peeled off to land and tried to lower flaps. Clegg, the engineer went back to crank 'em down but had no crank extension; so I decided to make a no flap landing, a not too pleasant procedure. We were almost to the ground when I saw the plane in front of me on the runway was too close so we pulled up to go around on our fast-disappearing gas. Clegg found the trouble and changed the flap fuse so we had flaps. Bob called the tower to give us a clear priority on landing this time around as all the tanks were pumping empty. I had to cut out one man on the approach and another had to go around but we had to get in. Our actions were verified and justified. Moments later when the #1 motor coughed her last and ran out of gas as we taxied past the tower, we restarted 2 and 3 and taxied in on them.

As we were heading out this morning tail gunner, Lynch, again proved himself a real man by battling a leaky oxygen filler hose into submission in time to save us from aborting. Clegg, too had a busy day as he had to crank the bomb-bay doors down and up over the target, which at 25,000 feet is a superhuman task, standing there on a narrow catwalk with no chute doing a breath stealing, arm breaking job while staring into 25,000 feet of space, partially flak filled. Strong as he is, at that altitude he had to stop every few turns and rest, which was the smart thing to do. I'm pretty proud of my crew all the way around. Chet, our bombardier, had a sick headache on landing (I don't blame him.) We flew # 3 in the lead element Low squadron on Mik who scattered all over the sky both ways. We blasted I G Farber Industries. Nel came back from cleaning guns to say that we had only 20 gallons in motors # 2 and 3 but 1 and 4 were dry. All but Marks, Lundholm and the engineer died in the morning crash and only Lundholm is expected to live.

Brunswick Jan. 30 Mission Aborted 3:45 breakfast 5;00 am briefing for a repeat on Jan 11th "rough and tough" (59 bombers lost. We) took off at 8:15 and climbed right into position #3 lead element of high squadron (Moede.) Immediately after takeoff, oil poured 'up' over our #3 nacelle and the pressure dropped slightly. We stayed with formation, but it kept on and I aborted, intending to pickup # 347 and meet the formation at the last control point, but the left wheel would not extend so we went around. Going around, the oil pressure went out too quickly to feather the prop and the engineer reported that the wheel could not be cranked down.

We raised the other wheel and prepared for crash landing. We flew out over the Channel, dropped our bombs and flew back over the field and received instructions to go back out and jettison the ball turret. We did and had a hell of a time. The boys took off the necessary nuts and the ball slipped down and stuck at an angle. Clegg, Calkin and Trembly worked like beavers with Chet helping by battering at the hung part with a heavy sheet of armor plate. Everybody was holding on to everybody else and then Chet hit on the idea of using the armor plate as a crowbar and finally the ball went away with a great whooshing and the heavy armor plate actually floated in the hole for seconds before going down. All this time the # 3 engine was a molten mass with a windmilling prop. On our way back to the field it set up a great vibration and sparks showered back. Finally the prop broke down at an angle, still spinning and chewed our cowling and then flew off into space. We hoped it didn't kill anyone, but were very glad it was gone.

Coming back over the field, we circled 'til about 3:00 p.m. using up gas and then flew to Honington for the finale. I put the crew in the radio room, well padded and ready to set about setting her down. (# 972 Croft's ship.) My first pass was too high so I went around, taking more room next time, cut # 2 and dragged it in on # 1 and 4. It landed at 70 MPH very smoothly and I was able, to my surprise, to keep it straight with brakes. After stopping, before I could unbuckle my safety belt, co-pilot Lunds was out and jumping off the nose. I just sat there and had to laugh at his speed. I shut off the switches, climbed out and started collecting equipment. Met B. B. Smith of the 447th from Sebring there, he was sweating out a buddy who also had to belly land. They had our ship off the field in 45 minutes, very little damage was done to it. Flew back to base with Harrington. (On pass in London, we saw Murray make a belly landing in a newsreel.)

T/Sgt. James Lee Hutchinson, Ed.S.

Note - *Honington was a former RAF base used by the 8th Army Air Force as an Air Depot base to repair or modify B-17 Flying Fortresses of the 3rd Bomber Division. It was a designated site for bombers needing to make a belly landing.*

Wilhemshaven Feb. 3 PFF mission Just in off a pass and Whammy! It was a 3:30 breakfast, 4:30 briefing. Our boys got in at 3:30. Briefed for sub pens and repair docks with lots of P-51, P-47 and P-38 support which we got. Beautiful again today, semi-darkness at takeoff time, uneventful climb through it to altitude, got too high and had to come down as the formation formed between layers. Our # 2 and # 4 superchargers lagged badly from the start. Contrails were dense and lots of clouds. Finally at 28,500 feet and 46 below, we bombed as low group. The sky was filled with Eighth Air Force bombers being lead by our A group and Col. Harding in lead squadron. As far as you could see, planes carrying Hitler's medicine to him and fighters protecting them. (Blakely, now a Major and Lauro led B group.) We flew # 3 lead element off Moede's wing. The flak was moderate and not too accurate, although our left aileron was hit and a couple of holes outboard on our left wing. No enemy fighters were seen. On the way back, # 1 oil pressure started fluctuating, then the prop ran away and could not be feathered. It started vibrating and ran up to 3300 RPM. We were hoping for it to fly off, but "no soap:" we were 60 miles out over the North Sea with only one good engine, # 3, because 2 and 4 were still lagging. The prop acted like it would fly off at any minute, so I sent Chet and Mel back out of the nose. Finally, we reached the coast with # 1 still at it. Headed in calling "Clearup" and the Aylesworth base picked us up and said we could land there. Just then I spotted home and headed for it with gas dwindling. We got "Clear-up" and permission to come straight in. It was a nerve wracking, wobbly landing, but we got down okay and # 1 prop stopped at last and started belching smoke. We taxied back with the inboard engines. The firemen, complete with asbestos suits, followed us clear to our dispersal to the tower, at my suggestion that that it wouldn't hurt to be ready. Although I didn't think it would burn. Lost one plane on Monday, one today and many on the deck! Today, we carried ten 500 lb general purpose bombs.

Frankfort Feb. 4 Visual or PFF mission Here we go again at 4:15 breakfast - 5:15 briefing. It was eggs and lousy tasteless bacon for breakfast. Briefed for Frankfort and they announced that we had killed 5,000 and rendered 40,000 homeless on our last raid, which possibly was to boost our morale, but it just made me a little sick. Anyhow we were to fly our own ship #170 which was in the hanger where it had been for a while for repairs. When we were briefed they said to sweat it out as they didn't know if it was operational. While we waited, Capt. Herlihy came in and told us to take # 799, which Brown was going to fly but his crew was sick. I flatly refused 799 and said I would rather wait for # 170. We got off in our proper spot after a raunchy takeoff. We sweated it out because we aren't accustomed to flying a ship right out of the hanger loaded with ten 440 pound bundles of incendiary bombs. God himself must have been tapping me on the shoulder saying "uh huh" to # 799; because Bob Lunsford remarked about how insistent I was that I wouldn't take it. Brown got a new crew, took # 799 and did not come back! He was a hell of a swell guy. We can only hope he got out alive, if a prisoner.

We flew # 2 in the second element of low squadron. Mickleson led the squadron and did a p-- poor job. After the target, he passed out, dived and broke up the formation, which scattered. The flak was terrific, although our group was not hit hard, and ourselves not at all. B group had holes in every ship. We got in the edge of the Ruhr valley and it was the "walking on" type of flak for forty minutes straight. Before, at and after the target the flak was continuous. After Miks dive, the formation scattered and we went up to the diamond last element of the high squadron and then the pink Focke-Wulf-190s struck and I switched to the echelon off the # 2 man; however, they did not attack us. Three of our planes, Brown, Mc Phee and Green did not return. They must have been straggling behind as our waist gunner could see fighters swarming the stragglers. We don't know yet if flak or the 190s got them. Sweat (at 40 below mind you) popped out in the palm of my left hand gripping the wheel through two pair of gloves, wool and leather, so I must have been scared somewhat. After we crossed the Channel, we left the group, ducked under the clouds at 400 feet and came back alone. Number 2 and 3 superchargers lagged, but engines ran swell. Danny, in the ball turret, said Frankfort looked like peacetime Broadway at Christmas time from our bombs.

Note - *On visual bombing missions the ball turret gunner was a valuable observer. Hanging under the bomber, he could see how well bombs hit the target and report results to the pilot and intelligence officers at de-briefing.*

Villa Coublay (Paris Airdrome) Feb. 5 Visual mission Wow! Three in a row this is getting tiresome. Another 4:00 am breakfast and 5:00 am briefing for the Romilly Repair Airdrome but it was covered with clouds so we blasted the secondary target and I mean blasted. We were scheduled as a spare, but we took over a nice spot as # 3 in the lead element of High squadron. Col. Kidd led the group and Capt. Swarthout the squadron, very good lead today. Had our own plane, Pride of the Century, again today and her engines performed like a dream. Flak over Paris was moderate but accurate and we picked up holes in the wings. Saw FW - 190s but none attacked our group. We had P-51 and P-47 escorts all the way, mostly P-51s for a change. Made a bouncy landing back at base. It was a comparatively uneventful mission, for which I thank God.

Brunswick Feb. 10 Mission aborted Took off as a spare this morning. We had alternate snowstorms and clear weather all day. Altogether, ten planes were unable to get to home base (make the formation.) During the climb we were having low oil pressure on #3 and overheating (300°) on # 4 and we could not catch the 100th, so we filled in with the 96th at the # 2 slot in the second element of the High squadron. Got to the enemy coast and # 1 oil pressure plummeted down, but Bob punched the feathering button in time to feather the prop. We "aborted" the formation and a P-38 picked us up immediately. He took us all the way back to base. He dropped his wheels and flaps to slow down and flew formation with us. Took some pictures of him, hope they turn out okay. His number was 888 with R. L. C. on the side. One plane which looked like a P-51 came over, but the P-38 chased him off. We found a hole in the overcast muck and came down over Horsham St. Faith airdrome. Contacted them and requested a "Weather Clear-up." They advised us to land there, so we did, and it's a very nice Former RAF base built in 1938. The 458th Bomb Group of B-24 s had been there two weeks, but non-operational as yet. Had dinner and shot the bull with several P-51 and P-47 pilots who were also forced to land there (Maj. Irvine, Peterson and Christenson.) Rondo came over in a truck and took us back to base, after Col. Kidd refused to allow us to fly back on three engines. We were commended in a letter from the Armament officer to our C.O. for seeing that our plane and guns were properly cared for at a strange base. The fighter pilots said the Germans threw up everything today and that statement was later confirmed. We lost Croft and Scroggins today from the 100th. Flew ship 170 today. This was the third Brunswick raid we had missed, God is still taking care of us!

Bois Rempre Sunday Feb. 13 No ball mission Briefed at 12:00 for a no ball target (V-1 missile site) flew a 351st ship # 936 and filled the diamond in the second element of Low squadron. Took off at 1:15, made two bomb runs at 12,000 ft and knocked hell out of Adolf's secret weapons. No flak or enemy fighters. But the tail gunner saw a great explosion, thought to be a B-17 back of us.

Note - *The name "No Ball" identified the target as part of Hitler's unmanned rocket project. This target was a launching pad for V-1 flying bombs bombarding England. No Ball missions were special targets of the Royal Air Force "Crossbow" operation to destroy the deadly missiles.*

Brunswick (Vorden Drome) Mon. Feb. 21 PFF or Visual Breakfast at 4:45 am, briefed for Brunswick as the primary target PFF or visual at 5:45. We flew # 2 in the lead element of the Low squadron lead by Capt. Moede who finished his 25th mission today. (Went to Munster as Co-Pilot with him on my first raid.) Normal assembly led by Reeder, 100 B and Major Elton, 100 A. The formation got into the wrong Wing and ended up circling around and bombing the hell out of a Heinie airport. Saw scores of supporting fighters out of the 1,000 + promised in briefing. We saw a giant parachute-like explosion out over the Channel at 5:00 o'clock. Flak was present today, but none close. One plane, "Fletcher's Castoria" is missing.

Rostock, Germany Thurs. Feb. 24 PFF Mission Breakfast 3:30, briefing at 4:30 for Poznan, Poland. We flew # 347 as # 3 in the last element of the High squadron of Amiero until Gossage aborted then we moved up to # 3 off Harrison's second element. It was a long haul of 10.5 hours. Took off at 8:00 am and landed at 6:30 pm. Good formation, we had flak at the Danish coast, it knocked Gossage out. Then four Ju- 88s bounced our squadron with four passes coming in very close from 1:00 o'clock high. How in hell they missed us, and vice versa, I'll never know; they were so close I could see pimples on the pilot's nose. I think they were damaged by our gunners, only three came in on the second pass and two on the third and fourth. Got almost to primary target and it was overcast; we headed for Rostock and caught hell in flak on a half hour bomb run. More flak at the target, we bombed PFF. The group to the left and behind us caught hell from Fw -190 fighters and one ME- 109 came through from 10:00 o clock out of the sun to knock out one B-17 which peeled off to the left where the fighters bounced him. Back at base, we sneaked in and landed with the lead group 100 B because we had only 200 gallons of gas left!

Regensburg February 25 Visual mission Dear God, spare us another mission like this last one, Amen. Well, we took off in plane 018 flying # 2 in second element of the Lead squadron. We did individual climbs up through overcast to assemble on top. The group went in at 20,000 and caught hell all around us all the way. Saw plane after plane go down. Four Forts and a Liberator definitely exploded either on the ground or on the way down. There were some parachutes. Just prior to crossing a large river, we had 100 pound oil pressure on # 2 engine. She was smoking and we couldn't feather the prop. We dropped our bombs on Lowenstein and tried to keep up with the formation. Our tail gunner says we blasted hell out of the town we hit. We cut short of the target figuring to pick up with a formation heading home. We were circling all alone, but were not molested. We got in with the 95th formation and the leader slowed down so his men and we could keep up. All was okay until # 1 supercharger amplifier went out. Joe Daugherty (radio operator with 24 missions) changed the amplifier in the radio room and we got #

1 back. Of course we lost the formation and were once again all alone. Then # 1 ran out of gas and we transferred fuel from # 3, a little later # 3 went out and we only had engines # 1 and 4 left. I called a B-24 group behind us for fighter support, which we got. Meanwhile, we had thrown out all guns, ammo and flak jacket armor to lighten the load and save gas. Over France # 1 went out and we started down to ditch in the Channel. Flak from Abbeville laced us badly in the wings and beneath the radio room. We could not spare much evasive action and both the radio operator and I were sending out Mayday (SOS) calls. The Mayday station answered that they were getting us loud but garbled and that they had a fix (location) on us. Our last engine conked out and we started our last glide, calling Mayday. We hit the water about six miles from Dunkirk, France and Spitfires circled as we did. We hit hard and water rushed in immediately. Bob dived out his window head first and I thought he had fallen in so I went over the top to help him up. We went back to pull the raft from the outside as the inside handle failed. Our raft inflated okay but got away from us. Bob got in it and commenced to organize things. I had jumped in the water without inflating my Mae West and had to take care of that "toot sweet." Bob was in the raft with four of us hanging on the ropes around the side; Clegg with blood streaming from his head, Calkin, his hands frozen to the CO2 bottle and Mac, opposite from me. All of a sudden, Calkin screamed, "There's someone under the tail, get him!" I looked back and there was a bobbing human just out of my reach. It was Chuck, he had floated around from the other side of the plane. I got a hold on him and got him to hang on to the ropes. He was giving off the most pitiful gasps, but he obeyed instructions. Now we were all trying to get the raft away from the plane before it went down. It seemed that nobody could climb into the raft. Finally, I got both feet and one arm over the side (how, I don't know) and Bob pulled me in. Together we got Lynch, Mac and Calkin into the raft. Clegg was too heavy for us and although he must have realized he was doomed to die in the icy water, he was as calm as could be. There was one humorous moment, when Bob was bailing out water and throwing it out on Clegg, who said wearily,

"Throw it out on the other side Bob."

T/Sgt. James Lee Hutchinson, Ed.S.

Well just then the little rescue launches appeared over the horizon and I commenced selling Clegg on the idea of hanging on 'til they got to us. He did and the launch pulled the guys in our raft aboard. Those Air-sea rescue guys are wonderful. They got to us in less than a half hour and dived into the icy water to help us. Once inside the launch, I couldn't move and Lynch was actually green. I just sat there with my nose running while they got my clothes off and put on dry ones. They warmed us up and we headed back to Dover. The launch was # 186, commanded by a Lt. Jones.

Chet, Mel, Joe and Greene in the other raft were picked up by the second launch. Their raft had only partially inflated and was upside down in the water until Danny turned it upright; Chet was injured in the head and ribs. We were taken to RAF "Sick Quarters" in Dover where we received new Royal Air Force clothes, food and first aid for Chet and Clegg. I got two right foot boots which was comical. They took the officers to Lymone and enlisted men to Hawkings for the night. Lt. Sheen was swell to us at Lymone and there were also two rescued Liberator crews in there. One crew had bailed out and the other crash landed. Next day, we all met at Manston where a plane was to pick us up. Weather prevented that, so we all drew coats and took a train home. Our trip through London in boots and RAF Sergeant or Corporal uniforms was a panic.

Augsburg Fri. March 17th PFF Mission Breakfast at 3:00 and briefing at 4:00 am. We were starting all over again (after a three week rest) flying # 3 in the lead element of the high squadron. We had Me -109 and FW -190 fighters nearly all the way and near the I.P. there were 110s, 410s and Ju-88s in a groups of 21 firing rockets into the rear of our Fortress formation. We had our new silver ship # 607, "H for Harry." Saw two forts go down, one in flames and another smoking (both confirmed). Lynch got a twin engine fighter from the tail and Chet got an Me-109 flying 90 degrees across our nose. These were our first claims for kills of enemy fighters. Got the usual flak at the target and dropped our bombs on the PFF. About minutes after the target, we had to feather # 3 engine. Well, we sweated that one out remembering the last time. We stayed right in position and prayed. Coming back over the Channel, I listened in on an Air Sea Rescue frequency. Three ships had to ditch, one was a B-24 and only ONE man got out!

We left the formation and dodged barrage balloons all the way home, but we beat the group to land in the haze. The next day, they went to take #607 into the hanger to change engines and ran out of gas. That's how much we had to spare!

Note - *A major Messerschmitt factory was an important target at Augsburg, deep in the heart of Germany. It was a long mission almost out of range for bombers based in England.*

Augsburg (Lechfeld) Saturday, March 18 Breakfast at 4:00 am and a 5:00 briefing for the same vicinity as yesterday. Our 8:00 am takeoff was delayed one hour. We were leading the second element of the Low squadron. Corvans was squadron leader; Shaddix his right wing and Harte left wing. We had Horne as co-pilot and Myers in top turret (Luns and Clegg still in the hospital.) Uneventful flight to target and missed most of the flak. Then we caught it when Fw-190s passed on us twice from 2:00 o'clock high. Danny, in the ball turret, claimed a FW-190 skipped in from the front and killed Cowan's radio operator with a 20 mm in the back. One burst directly in front of Cowan's windshield (bullet proof) cutting his face severely. (For the last two days Joe has had no bullet proof glass.) Our # 2 engine ran rough all the way, but it's the first time I got back with all four props turning in a long time. Bad weather the whole trip.

Berlin Wednesday, March 22 Well, at 5;30 this am we were briefed for the big town, the first time for our crew 41. I led the High squadron in ship # 249 for my very first squadron lead. Kressling and Lauro were leading the group. We went the long way, across the North Sea and Denmark and south to Berlin. Saw no fighters in or out, except "friendlies" but my God the flak! The heaviest and most accurate in my 18 missions. What a big town Berlin is! We got at least 40 holes in our ship. All four engines were hit with holes in the bottom and sides of the bomb-bay, in the flaps and ailerons, the horizontal and vertical stabilizers and nose. Nelson's hand was scratched near the tail wheel. There were holes inches from Calkin, right waist gunner. Engine #3 exhaust was holed, # 4 throttle cables severed, and holes in gas tanks. Glad to get back "whole!"

Bordeaux (Merignac) Friday, March 24 Well, this was merely an eight and a half hour tour through France to bomb and airfield and assembly plant Merignac. Started out in # 607 leading the third element in the High squadron. Ended up over the target as # 2 in the second element of Lead squadron. Some flak no enemy fighters. One B-17 ahead of us turned left out of the formation slowly with # 2 engine smoking and four chutes came out. Our tailgunner reported it explodedd on the ground. We had excellent P-38 fighter support, especially at the target.

March 31 No mission Had a brush with an intruder(German bomber) who laid eggs on runway 28. We took off anyway, past the holes, but were recalled.

April 1 Recalled Flew # 607 as lead in second element of High squadron, but very bad haze forced us back.

Quackenbruch Saturday. April 8 Flew # 607 as lead of the third element, High squadron to hit an airfield. It was a nice "milk run" with lots of fighter support. Uneventful trip.

Lippstadt Wednesday, April 19 Flew # 607 as lead of the second squadron in the Low squadron, led by Morgan. Some flak, lots of P-38. P-47 and P-51 fighter support. We hit the target well. Unevental trip.

Marquisville Thursday, April 20 Flew # 710 in the # 2 slot off Mason, leading the group. No evasive action into the Noball target. Made a dry run the first time. On the second run we were hit by flak a couple of inches below my a____ setting the cockpit on fire. Clegg handed me a fire extinguisher and we got the fire out. The oil pressure on # 1 and 2 went out and I feathered # 1 but # 2 wouldn't feather and in the excitement, I pulled all four fuel shutoff switches off. Corrected it and came home on two engines later started # 3 again, I think the instruments were out. Landed and ran off the perimeter when the brakes failed. One landing gear collapsed on # 487 at the end of runway 28. Many men were injured.

Brunswick Wednesday, April 26 Flew # 607 leading the High squadron with Major Fitzgerald as co-pilot on a PFF milk run to dreaded Brunswick. Dense but in-accurate flak. No enemy fighters.

Berlin April 29 Stout flies the long ones! Flew # 607 again. We led the Low squadron. The Eighth lost 77 airplanes on this one, but our wing did not see an enemy plane. However, we did hit the famous Berlin flak and came home on three engines with # 4 having a flak hole that cut off our supercharger at 27,000 feet.

Sharguemines May 1 Flew # 723 and led third element in High squadron. Bob ended up leading the second element in the Low squadron as first pilot. Piss poor weather. Got attacked by four Me-109s but lost no one, although some came home alone on two engines. Blais-Moore co-pilot flew with us.

Berlin May 7 Today we led the Low squadron in # 607 on a milk run to "Big B." Had good fighter cover and saw no enemy fighters. Plenty of flak as usual, but got only one hole in a gas tank.

Berlin May 8 We were flying # 987 today in a screwed up deal. Started out leading the High squadron and the group leader never showed up, so we led the group. Horne was my co-pilot, because Lunsford was leading a High squadron after that until he too aborted. We flew on toward the I.P. and saw many "flamers" going down from other groups. We lost our # 4 engine just before we reached the I.P. and I aborted from the group to come home alone. Weather was lousy. Picked up four P-51 escorts and finally had nineteen altogether. Nelson did swell navigation on his last mission and we saw no flak on the way back. Flew at 28,000 feet today and had <u>eleven</u> abortions out of thirty one ships.

Liege Thursday, May 11 Flew plane # 607 and led the High squadron for 390 A. We had a good assembly. Flak at Antwerp got one ship out of the lead group and flak at the target got Hunter out of the 100th in A wing. Saw no enemy fighters and had plenty of fighter support. Herres and Roeder were exceptionally good wing men.

Brussels # 30 Saturday, May 20, 1944 **Fini! One Tour of Operations, USA here I come! (I hope)** Yesterday the group was hard hit. One ship limped back with its stabilizer "twenty milimetered" and all shot to hell. Another ditched and we lost Horne in our ship # 607. We took off in #806, a new ship on its first mission. Did an instrument take off and uneventful climb to assembly. Ran in to the target and out with little flak. We could not drop our bombs because clouds covered the target which was in country occupied by our ground troops.

Chet, Chuck, Mac and I finished our tours today, but could not buzz the field because of a 500 feet low ceiling and terrific haze. However, we shot off lots of flares to celebrate and we were damned happy!

War Department Telegrams

"Remember Pearl Harbor" became our battle cry as millions of men and women enlisted or were called for service; all males from ages 18-36 were subject to the draft (Selective Service Act.) Thousands of teenagers joined or were drafted. They were too young to drink or vote, but not too young to fight for their country. Often, there were two or more members from a family in the service. Sixteen million American men and women served in uniform during WW II. Millions came home with life-altering wounds and almost half million died. There are twenty-four American Cemeteries on foreign soil.

Blue Star banners (a small red and white banners with a blue star in the center) hung in windows to show they had family members in service. Many families had two or more members in the service. The blue star in the banners were replaced by gold stars as young men died serving our country. People supported the war and endured rationing of foods and materials needed for the war, but they lived in fear of those dreaded War Department telegrams.

Families were notified of their loved one's death or wounds by Western Union telegrams from the War Department. Those sad telegrams were delivered to thousands of homes as military casualties increased. One woman of the Greatest Generation told a story of one aspect of civilian life during the war. She said,

"We lived in a small town and our two sons were in the Army. Like us, most people in our neighborhood had family members in service. Husbands, fathers and teenagers had joined or been drafted into the military. Many parents had signed letters of permission papers for teenage sons to enlist before being drafted so they could choose the branch of service they wanted. Those dreaded War Department telegrams of tragic news were delivered day or night. Our local Western Union office delivery car was a black 1939 Ford. Everyone dreaded to see it driving through the neighborhood. That black car reminded me of a buzzard circling to find the right family to deliver the terrible news of another serviceman's death. I was scared to death every time I saw it and prayed it would pass by our house. Yet, I felt guilty knowing someone else's son had died."

The Armored New Testament

Millions of copies of the pocket sized Armored New Testament were carried by the sixteen million men and boys in World War II. Church membership soared as families sought the help and guidance of God. Families went to pray for the safety and life of their loved ones. Parents and wives sent the little 3x4 inch New Testament with a golden steel cover to servicemen around the world to read, obey and wear over their heart. I thought that was a very good idea and kept mine snug in my pocket on every mission. I still have my amored New Testament with the cover inscription:

May the Lord be With You

There are no records to show how many times that little piece of steel stopped a spent bullet or piece of flak. However, I know it gave aid and comfort to families and warriors seeking divine protection in World War II.

Note – *WW II stories illustrate two facts: the high loss of life in the Mighty Eighth and the terrible effect of war on families.*

Lt. John C. Walter, B-17 Pilot

A few years ago, I met John Walter a veteran WW II B-17 Pilot and the author of "My War," at the Indianapolis Air Show. John now lives in Columbus, Indiana, but spent his boyhood in Washington, a few miles south of Bedford. No doubt our high school basketball teams had a few clashes before we went to war. I spent all my missions at my radio operator desk behind the bomb-bay of the plane so I never knew what was happening up front. John's story presents a detailed description of a pilot's experience and activity in the cockpit during his first mission. He has generously given me permission to include a few pages of "My War" in this fourth book.

Lieutenant John C. Walter served with the 95th Bomb Group, squadron 412 and completed his thirty five mission tour of duty in March, 1945. No doubt our crews flew missions to some of the same targets. I heartily recommend his book, "My War," as an interesting account of the true experiences of a U.S. Army Air Force pilot in World War II.

Photo by Scott Maher

One look at the cockpit shows that B-17 pilots had complicated jobs. This is a photo of the Memphis Belle cockpit, owned by the Liberty Belle Foundation. The pilot sat on the left, co-pilot on the right; the flight engineer sat behind the co-pilot

Note – *John's crew members up front included: Tom, Co-pilot; John, Bombardier; "Columbus" Nelson, Navigator; and McCue, engineer/gunner.*

"Daylight was beginning to show in the East. As we settled into our seats and pulled our seat belts tight, it was time to check the rest of the crew. Through the intercom each position was called to make sure the intercom worked and everybody was on board. Then, Tom and I went through the checklist up to the point: "engine start". We had now to sit and wait until our watches indicated it was time to start engines.

The second hand on my watch passed twelve. I pointed the index finger of my right hand toward the instrument panel in front of Tom. He pushed the number one engine starter switch to the "energize" position. Slowly, the whine of the starter became louder as the inertia wheel gained speed. A few seconds later, I signaled Tom with a clenched fist, and he moved the starter switch to the "engage" position. The prop on number one engine started to turn and after several revolutions, I moved the number one engine magneto switch to the "on both" position. First, a single cylinder fired, then as the other cylinders joined in the chorus of power, the prop speed increased in little jumps and white smoke began to billow from under the engine nacelle. The engine speed accelerated, the firing smoothed out and the white smoke disappeared. With a little imagination you could feel that that collection of metal pieces out there on the wing sensed that something big was in store and it was ready to give the best it could. With the gentle vibration of number one engine, the whole airplane slowly stirred to life.

The starting procedure was repeated three more times. Now, all four engines were running. The engine and the flight instruments were now alive confirming the activity of the engines and signaling the aircraft's readiness for flight. The soft vibration and drumming of the fuselage made it seem as if the aircraft was quivering in eager anticipation of the upcoming flight.

The Ground Crew was signaled to pull the wheel chocks. In the dim light of dawn, they saluted and gave us the thumbs up sign. We were off to War.

Brakes were released and the outboard engine throttles opened slightly to start movement toward our position in the takeoff line. We moved out of the hard stand, paused at the taxiway entrance and, at the proper time, moved into the stream of airplanes.

Nose to tail, like a string of circus elephants, 36 bombers, some bright and shiny new and others in dull camouflage paint, purposefully proceeded along the taxi way.

Through the open cockpit windows came the very distinctive and almost intoxicating smell of burnt 100 octane aviation gas. The rumbling of 144 big round engines, with the potential of almost two hundred thousand horses, was punctuated with the squeal of brakes. Gentle application of the brakes served to hold the thrust of the engines in check and to maneuver the aircraft along the winding course of the taxi ways. Each brake application brought forth a squeal as brake blocks rubbed the brake drums.

Then it was time to run up and check the engines. Cockpit windows now closed to shut out the roar as each engine is checked to see if it performs as required. Everything checks out O.K.

The take off flare streaked upward from the control tower and lazily floated down. It was time to go. Soon came our turn to move into the runway behind the lead aircraft of our element. With partial power applied, the lead airplane brakes were released and it started the take off roll. For a few moments we were buffeted by the air hurtled back from the lead aircraft propellers. Our turn. We inched forward; waited the required 20 second interval; slowly advanced the throttles; released the brakes and began our roll down the runway.

After a short roll, the throttles were full open. Tom began to call off the airspeed as we seemed to move ever so slowly down the runway. This was the first time we had flown the airplane with a full load of fuel, ammunition and bombs. We had less than one mile to get 60,000 plus pounds of airplane, people, fuel and bombs up to flying speed. As the airspeed increased the rudder became effective, making it easier to keep the airplane going straight down the center of the runway. One third of the runway now lay behind. It was time to see if the tail could be brought up a little bit. Not yet.

Half way down the runway. She still hadn't made up her mind to fly.

Finally, with two thirds of the runway gone, Tom called out "120". A little back pressure on the control column. The bouncing caused by the unevenness of the runway ceased. We were flying, just as the end of the runway flashed by only a scant few feet below. A light touch on the brakes stopped the rotation and vibration of the main landing gear wheels. A thumbs up signal to Tom and the gear started up. Then the flaps were slowly raised. Our air speed crept up to 135. The throttles and prop settings were cut back to climb power as we started our ascent to assembly altitude.

What a sight! Hundreds of airplanes appeared to be milling about aimlessly in the early morning sky. Soon, out of this seeming chaos, orderly groups of aircraft began to form. Then, if by magic, the smaller groups merged into larger groups and the larger groups fell into trail and headed toward the rising sun.

T/Sgt. James Lee Hutchinson, Ed.S.

Our Group was a part of this, and we fell into our assigned position in the bomber stream. As we headed east toward the Continent, we continued in a gentle climb. A climb rate intended to get us to our penetration altitude before we reached the first line of anti-aircraft guns.

About midway across the Channel panic struck us. Something was wrong!! We were less than 1/4th of the way through the mission and we had used almost 1/2 of our fuel!! A quick check showed fuel mixtures and cowl flaps were set properly and cylinder head temperatures were on the money. After a little discussion, Tom and I concluded that this situation was normal. It just took a lot of fuel to lift 60,000 pounds of airplane, people, bombs, ammunition and fuel 25,000 feet into the air.

Soon, we crossed the Dutch coast and entered enemy territory. It was time to tuck up the formation to discourage the enemy fighters. And to hope they would leave us alone and go scouting for easier pickings. There were a few flak bursts every new and then. But nothing close. It looked just as menacing as we had been told it was.

Below us, some five miles, lay the enemy territory. However, it didn't appear threatening. In fact, it looked much the same as the friendly landscape of England. The bomber stream wove its way across the sky tracing the path which had been diagrammed on the briefing room map.

So far, the mission had been uneventful. Soon, we would be at the target. The I.P. (initial point) was just ahead. At that time, the Group formation would change from its defensive to its bombing configuration. From this point on it would be straight and level flying to the bomb release point. No evasive action would be permitted for the next 20 minutes. For the anti-aircraft gunners below, we were just like ducks moving across the target area in a carnival shooting gallery.

The flak from the target defenders began. A few bursts at first. A blink of dark red light followed by a vertical dumb bell shaped cloud of greasy black smoke. Then, the bursts became more numerous. The often made comment, "Flak so thick you could walk on it," was no longer a saying. It was reality!! The nearer we came to the target, the more intense the barrage became. Now, it was much closer. It could be heard above the sound of the engines. Near bursts bounced the aircraft about. Shrapnel rattled off the airplane like hail stones.

Then suddenly there was a very close burst. Just ahead of us. A little bit to the right. Slightly above our altitude. Pieces of shrapnel came through the windows in the top of the cockpit. One of them hit Tom on the left side just above the flak suit and above his collar bone. He straightened up briefly then slumped over.

I called McCue in the top turret to check Tom and help him. Mac came down out of the turret, looked at Tom and sat down on the base of the turret and stayed there as rigid as a stone statue. I leaned out of the seat and banged him on the head with the palm of my right hand thinking this might shake him out of his shock and into action. Instead, he just lowered his head and stayed put. I asked other crew members to help. Pat Murphy came forward from the radio room and, with the help from Columbus, got Tom out of the seat and down into the nose to see what could be done to help him.

During the time I was trying to get help for Tom, I had noticed number one engine must have taken a hit somewhere in the oil system as it was rapidly losing oil pressure. It was necessary to get it feathered before all the oil was lost. If all the oil were lost it would no longer be possible to stop the wind milling of the propeller. A wind milling propeller not only caused higher fuel consumption, but could also seize the reduction gearing and cause the propeller to twist off, endangering the whole aircraft. I was in time, there was enough oil left. The prop came to a stop.

The situation in the cockpit was now straightened out a bit. It was time for me to see where the rest of the formation was. Big surprise!! The only airplane in sight was another B-17 from the Group three or four hundred yards off our right wing. He, too, was in difficult straits. He had taken a flak burst just behind the tail gunner's turret. The burst had jammed the rudder forward into the vertical stabilizer and shredded all of the fabric from the elevators. Thus, he had no rudder to turn the aircraft and no elevator control to climb or dive. He was on a heading south in the direction towards Romania.

The formation was nowhere in sight. We were now all by ourselves deep in Germany with a wounded Co-Pilot and one engine out. I asked Columbus for a direct course home. I saw no purpose in trying to follow the zig-zag course of the group. We needed to get back as soon as possible to get help for Tom and reduce our exposure to further enemy action.

The next decision to be made was whether to call for friendly fighter escort or not. This was an option open to us. In the mission information sheet distributed in the briefing there were the codes to be used in just such a case as ours. However, in Officers' Club conversations it had been said the Germans listened to this frequency and, more often than not, beat the "Little Friends" to the bomber in distress. Taking our position deep in enemy territory into consideration, I figured there was a very high probability the enemy would be the first to answer our call. So, I opted not to call for help.

Columbus gave me the course for the base. I figured our best bet was to get out of enemy territory as fast as possible. Thus, it would be a good idea to trade our altitude for speed. Altitude was a defense against antiaircraft fire. However, it was doubtful the enemy would waste ammunition on a single aircraft. Altitude would be no deterrent for the enemy fighters.

I turned to the course Columbus had given me, lowered the nose of the airplane slightly and pushed the remaining three engine throttles to climb power. Losing about 100 feet per minute we literally streaked for home at more than 200 mph.

Information on Tom was not good. He had lost a lot of blood and was unconscious. McCue was inert. The rest of the crew was busy keeping an eye out for enemy fighters. Fortunately, none were seen nor did any of them see us.

The combination of our "straight for home" course and higher speed allowed us to beat the Group home. As we turned on final, we fired a red-red flare. We touched down and rolled to the end of the runway and pulled off onto the taxi way where the Medics were waiting. They quickly climbed into the nose to check Tom. Among the Medical personnel meeting us was Dr. Jack.

In a short time, Dr. Jack came to me and said Tom did not make it. The shrapnel had severed his carotid artery. Jack said that even if he had been on board, Tom probably could not have been saved. After Tom had been taken of the airplane, we started the engines and taxied back to the hard stand, shut the engines down and climbed out of the airplane. Still not believing what had happened, we spent time just walking around the airplane. Then, we saw how close we had all come. What must have been an 88 millimeter anti aircraft shell had gone through the left wing and left in its wake a hole about eight inches in diameter. It went through behind number 2 engine fuel tank and just ahead of the front edge of the left landing flap. Had the shell exploded either by its own fuse or by contact, the airplane would have been blown out of the sky in one fiery ball. Chance of survivors would have been nil.

When the shell passed through the wing, it cut away about half of the left flap torque tube. This is a cylindrical structural member about which the whole wing flap is constructed. This tube also carries the aerodynamic force when the flap is lowered. Given the severe damage inflicted upon the torque tube, it was amazing that it did not twist in two when we came in for our landing. Had that occurred, most of the left flap would have retracted and the aircraft most certainly would have slow rolled and gone in upside down on the final approach. Chance of survival? None.

We had been both very unlucky and very lucky that day, September 28, 1944. Thereafter, Thursdays would always be remembered by us as "Crash and Burn Day." We didn't; but we came mighty close. Debriefing was a detached experience. Once debriefing was finished, it was time to return to the hut. However, to put the return off as long as possible, John, Columbus and I stopped in at the Officers' Club. Finally, all the reasons not to go back to our quarters were gone.

We walked in the front door of the hut fully expecting to see Tom sitting on his bed. Of course, he was not there. Also not there were his belongings. In the time it took us to get back to our quarters, the Squadron orderlies had come in and collected and taken away all of his belongings. It was as if he had never existed. It was just like the World War aviation movies. Only this was not a movie it was for real.

That night, after a few more hours at the Officers' Club, fitful sleep was possible. The next morning I went down to the Squadron C.O.'s office to see what happened next. He said we had been removed from combat flight status for an indefinite time. This was no surprise. Tom would be buried at Cambridge American Military Cemetery within the next few days. We could attend if we wished. That was easy to answer. We would go even though it involved a long, bumpy and cold journey in the back of a 6 X 6.

To let us unwind, we were given a three day pass with the suggestion that after the funeral we all go to London and see the "sights" and try to forget. I told Major Pomeroy about McCue's behavior during the mission. Because of McCue's lack of response and action, which could have endangered the whole aircraft, I asked the Major to remove him immediately from the crew. To emphasize my feelings I told him I would not fly with McCue on the crew. Further, I recommended McCue be removed from flight status and grounded, permanently. The Major agreed immediately.

My concern now was that the crew might be broken up. After all, we didn't have a Copilot, an Engineer or a Radio Operator. The Major said Purdy would be put back on the crew to replace McCue. A fill-in Radio Operator would continue to cover until Hasselback was back on flight status. A Co-Pilot would be assigned soon. Until a permanent one could be found, we would fly using an available Co-Pilot.

We attended Tom's funeral. It was a dark and windy day with a fine mist falling. The size of the cemetery was hard to believe. It seemed to extend for acres and acres. And there were rows upon rows of white crosses. Sure a somber and sobering sight."

American Battle Monuments Commission photo

The Cambridge American Cemetery and Memorial site in England, 30.5 acres in total, was donated by the University of Cambridge. The cemetery contains the remains of 3,812 of our military dead; 5,127 names are recorded on the Tablets of the Missing. Most died in the Battle of the Atlantic or in the strategic air bombardment of northwest Europe. Almost three fourths of the graves and names on the Memorial Column are Eighth Air Force airmen.

Note - *The American Battle Monuments Commission (ABMC) was established by Congress in 1923, to commemorate the service, achievements, and sacrifice of members of the U.S. armed forces. There are twenty-four overseas military cemeteries, and 26 memorials, monuments, and markers managed by the Commission. Most are in European countries that have deeded land to the United States so the American flag flies over the graves of those who died for this nation. Nearly all the cemeteries and memorials specifically honor those who served in World War I or World War II. The sacrifice of more than 218,000 U.S. servicemen and women is memorialized at these locations. Nearly 125,000 American war dead are buried at these* *cemeteries, with an additional 94,000 individuals commemorated on Tablets of the Missing.*

Lt. Charles F. Miller, Bombardier

1st Lt. Miller arrived at the 303rd Bomb Group, "Hell's Angels" airbase in Molesworth, England on May 13, 1944. His crew was assigned to the 427th squadron and they flew twenty-two missions in a very short time. Sections of a short letter to his brother on June 9th, illustrate his situation and no doubt, his combat fatigue:

Dear Bud and Bette,

"There isn't much to write about because anything I would want to say is strictly illegal. There's no use in talking about the invasion (D-day) because by the time you get this letter, everything will be changed around anyway. Right now a good night's sleep is just a memory. Whether that will get better or worse, I don't know. It can't get much worse.

I guess Mom told you I met Margaret and we had a couple of Tom Collins ---- she was amazed that we have so much gin and scotch here at the base. I also got a couple of letters from her but haven't heard anything lately. I guess she's plenty busy right now. --------- I can't mention very much about my missions. In fact I can say practically nothing at all. I'm getting to be quite a veteran though and the biggest problem is sleep. I can see now why they kept us on the go during Cadet training. That just about covers everything I'm allowed to say so I might as well close, --------- Charlie"

Note - *This was about the same as thousands of other Eight Air Force crewmen. We flew missions but could never tell when, where or what happened. Our letters were censored and any war information or bad news was struck out. Mom said some of my V-mail letters looked like a crossword puzzle*

Lt. Miller was the bombardier on the B-17G, "*Blonde Buzz*" on a June 25th afternoon mission to take out the bridges at Sens and Coulange, France when he received flak wounds in the head and shoulders. He was hospitalized and not cleared to return to combat duty until August 8, after which he flew eleven more missions with three different pilots

That mission report said: Each B-17G carried two 2,000 pound bombs. Weather had little effect on the mission, but heavy 10/10 clouds and contrails over England resulted in assembly problems. However, it was clear in the target area. No enemy aircraft were seen and friendly fighter support was good. Moderate and accurate flak was encountered at Romilly-Sur-Seine and accurate fire at Londiniere. One man was wounded by flak and all aircraft returned safely to Molesworth.

By September 1944, First Lieutenant Miller had earned a Distinguished Flying Cross, a Purple Heart and the Air Medal with three oak leaf clusters. He had completed his tour of duty as a B-17 Bombardier in the Eighth Air Force and was slated to return to the States. He notified his mother and family of the estimated date he would be coming home. The Miller family was very proud of Charles, who had served in the army in 1938-39 and returned to serve in the tax department at the Elizabeth, New Jersey City Hall. He was the first City Hall employee to enlist after Pearl Harbor. His two sisters served as Army nurses and the Miller family became very involved in World War II. The war hero's homecoming was an event to celebrate and family members gathered at his mother's home at 518 Jackson Avenue for a welcome home celebration when they received a War Department telegram with the devastating news that Charles was "missing in action" over Germany. They later learned he had volunteered to fly one more mission as bombardier on a September 9th mission to the heavily protected I.G. Farben Plant at Ludwigshafen, Germany. It was his 33rd mission and their bomb-load was 12 x 500 lb M43 bombs. The flak, was intense and very accurate over the target and 1st Lt. Miller's bomber was shot down by two direct flak hits. Seven men died and two survived.

The Mission Report - There were 6/10 low clouds in the target area with tops ranging from 12,000 to 15,000 feet and dense, persistent contrails. The Group formation saw no enemy aircraft and our escort of 140 P-51s provided excellent support and thirty-five aircraft dropped 420 of the 500 pound bombs on the target. Meager to moderate flak was also encountered at Heidelberg, Germersheim, Luxembourg and Arlon. It was generally accurate.

Note - The MACR (missing aircraft report) stated: *Fortress #43-38323 of the 427 bomb squadron received a flak hit in the cockpit and another on the No. 1 engine. The entire nose section, left wing and No. 1 engine fell off and a burst of flame came out of the nose as it descended out of control. One man was seen to come out of the nose just after the B-17 was hit. He was followed down by observers in other aircrafts to 12,000 feet, but no parachute was seen before he became lost in the clouds. The Fortress crashed near Ludwigshafen.*

The tail-gunner on the crew of the doomed bomber was one of the two men able to bail out and finish the war in a POW camp. He later wrote:

"We were hit on my 28th mission and the ground fire blew the nose off and the left wing along with the No. 1 engine. It was like hitting a brick wall, and I wound up against the tail wheel trying to get out of my flak jacket. Luckily, I had seen the "tracking" flak overtaking us and reached for my parachute an instant before we were hit. I started for the escape hatch in the tail but looked forward to see what the rest of the crew was doing. I saw one gunner standing and on down. Getting back to the waist door was tough because of the dive and when I pulled the emergency handle nothing happened. So I hung on to the side of the ship and kicked the door until it let go. I waved the radioman and waist-gunner to jump and I went out ------- I saw the radio operator in a prison camp in Poland about two months later. The Germans reported that our waist gunner as "killed in fall," but at that time civilians were killing any crewmembers they caught, I was lucky that I came down in the center of town where German soldiers were waiting for me."

Three years ago the children of Charles' brother returned to find the plaque in a deplorable condition and barely readable. They requested the memorial to their heroic uncle be cleaned, but that request was delayed because no city employees knew the story behind the plaque or why it had been placed in such a prominent location. On a visit the following year nothing had been done and they again insisted the plaque honoring a man who died in the service of his country be cleaned. The third year the family returned, they were pleased to find the plaque cleaned and readable. Lt. Charles Miller's nephew who provided material for this story, said, "Ironically, the man who did the follow-through on the cleaning was raised on Jackson Avenue next door to the Miller family home; the house where the gathering took place in anticipation of my uncle's arrival from overseas."

USAAF Photo

B-17 G "Wee Willie" of the 91st Bomb Group squadron 322 was downed by a direct flak hit over Cratonburg, Germany in the last days of WW II. The pilot and a gunner were blown clear by the blast. The war weary bomber was on its 120th mission and was the second to the last plane lost by the 91st BG.

Chapter Three

490th Bomb Group (H) History

The 490th Bomb Group (H) station 134 trained as a B-24 Liberator outfit in Mountain Home, Idaho and flew the southern route to Trinidad, Brazil, Morroco and on to England. The group landed at the brand new Eye Airbase Station 134 H, (Brome Dome) April 28, 1944.

Lt. William E. Cranston, Co-Pilot

This story is adapted from portions of an interview of Bill Cranston, a Co-Pilot in the 490th Bomb Group. Lt. Cranston was an original member of the 490th at Eye and flew his missions in both the B-24 Liberator and the B-17 Flying Fortress heavy bombers. He completed his tour of duty December, 1944 at the rank of First Lieutenant with The Distinguished Flying Cross and the Air Medal with three oak leaf clusters. I thank his daughter, Sally Cranston for providing this information.

"I enlisted in the Air Cadet program of the Army Air Corps, but had to wait until there was an opening in the program February, 1943. We had three months of pre-flight training in math, science, weather, engines and many hours of physical training, we never got out of that. Pre-flight training was patterned after West Point or Annapolis with upper and lower classmen. We marched to classes in a formation and you didn't just saunter out the barracks to enter the formation, you hit the "rat line" at a trot and found your assigned place. The upper classmen had authority over the lower class and were always there haranguing us. They knew my name was Cranston so for me it was, "Who are you today? The Shadow! The Shadow knows! Heh Heh." They would also put you in a "brace" (a very strict attention position) and quiz you on regulations. Needless to say, training was more enjoyable when I became an upperclassman! Next, I was approved for primary flight training and sent to Parks Air College in Jackson, Tennessee where we flew the Stearman PT-17 bi-wing plane and PT-19 Fairchild low wing. Both were two seat open cockpit planes with 225 engines and dual controls. I sat in the front seat during training flights and the instructor taught me all the basics. My "solo flight" came as a surprise. One day we had been practicing landings and take offs on various airfields and before we landed at our home field, my instructor passed a completed A-1 Solo Form up to me. When we landed, he got out and said "There it is"! I was a little scared, I had to shoot three landings to pass my solo. I was glad to be finishing that first phase of my training and move on to complete Basic and Advanced flight training in a Beechcraft AT-10 with two engines. Flight training was like two months in every phase of instruction. I graduated in December as a 2nd Lieutenant, a "shave tail" and was given a ten delay en-route to my next assignment, so I came back home to Walton, New York.

I enjoyed my leave and reported to Salt Lake City. That's where I picked up my crew and was assigned to "heavy bombardment," multi-engine training at Tucson, Arizona for the first phase. After that, our crew was assigned to the newly formed 490th Bomb Group at Mountain, Idaho for combat crew training. I became a B-24 co-pilot on the Lt. Clifford T. Manlove crew. The 490th was ready to go overseas after we completed that phase of training. Our bomb group had about 2,000 men so the ground crew personnel went over on a troop ship, but our B-24 bombers were needed in England. We spent several days flying the southern route to England by way of Florida and Puerto Rico, where we had to stay overnight for an engine repair before going on to Forteleza, Brazil. Then we took off from Forteleza, and for this, planes always flew at night to cross the South Atlantic and land in Dakar, North Africa the next morning. We stayed the night and took off again the next day. We had a dangerous episode with the auto-pilot while flying from Dakar to Marrakech, Morocco. We flew out over the Sahara and when we got to the turning point we turned on the auto-pilot. Automatic pilots have little servo-motors that activate the plane's elevators and rudders up or down, but when they fail they wind up all one way up or down. When ours failed - it went down! Of course we were sitting there relaxing with no seatbelts and our feet up on the rudder bar. When the plane went down, we went to the top of the cockpit because of centrifugal force. Suddenly, we were clawing our way down to reach the auto-pilot release button on the pilot's wheel or another on the pedestal! We were lucky to scramble in time to take control. Then at Marrakech we had a supercharger out, so we had to stay there for two days. We were issued ammunition for our machine guns before we flew out to the 10th meridian to fly up the Atlantic Ocean. They put us out there because German JU-88 fighters were active off the coast of France. We had an engine go out three or four hours from England, but we finally got the prop "feathered" and came in on three engines. We had to land at a field in the western part of England to get the engine fixed. We then flew on to our base at Eye in East Anglia."

Later in the interview, Bill was asked which mission he especially remembered and he responded: "Oh, I guess probably the first, when we were bombing in France, most of the flak that we had was just four guns, and you didn't have that much flak. You could *see* flak. But the first mission in Germany was Hamburg. They had two different types of flak guns - one was operated by radar, usually there were four guns in a cluster and you could see the flakpattern. Near the big cities, like Berlin, Hamburg or Misberg, where they had a lot of industries and so on, they just put up what they call "barrage flak" – once they knew you were at a certain altitude, they would set the shells to go off over the target but they didn't follow (track) you like the radar. However, when you look out in front of you, and see that black flak, you wonder how in the Hell are you going to get through it! When we *first* went, the 8th Air Force didn't have enough fighter planes to over there to protect us, so the 9th Air Force gave us what they called fighter area coverage. You would see maybe 4, 5, 6 fighters way off on the horizon coming towards you, and you didn't really know until they got close enough whether they were your planes or German planes. They (fighters) never picked us up until we were quite a ways into France. But when the 8th Air Force got their own squadron of fighter planes, they would take off later than us, and pick us up on the enemy coast, and go with us. We usually had fighter planes above the bomber stream, and below the bomber stream. They would go with us to the target, and then they would leave and go back to England, and in the interim, more fighter planes would have taken off to pick us up on the RP (Rally Point.)

They called it the IP (the Initial Point,) when you started the bomb run in on the target. From there on in, the Bombardier had control of the plane and was steering the plane with the auto-pilot and bomb sight. You dropped the bombs and then standard procedure was you'd lose a thousand feet, and the flak would follow you right down! Then you would meet at the Rally Point to regroup the formation and take the prescribed course home. All of these different German cities had an area that their flak would cover, so you would take several different headings to get out of Germany and back to England. It was the same going in, so that you wouldn't fly over the flak of a city that you weren't going to bomb. Then usually, when you got back to the enemy coast, the escort fighter planes would leave us again. Of all the times, with our squadron, or our group, we never had fighter planes attack us.

May was organization month - The group lost three planes and attempted one mission which was "scrubbed" due to weather conditions.

May 16 – 848th plane, piloted by Lt. William Moss, crashed on take-off

May 28 – 851 bomber piloted by Lt. Riley F. Cavin was damaged beyond repair in a practice flight

May 29 – 851 aircraft piloted by Lt. Cavin crashed on a practice flight over Essex.– June 4th the group bombed an airfield in France and their D-Day assignment was to do three missions across the channel to support our invasion ground troops. June 6 - D-Day and missions to France. Targets were a transportation depot and two bridges, but all three missions were called back (aborted) due to a dense overcast.

One plane ditched in the Channel (four died) and two crashed on the runway at Eye.

June 7 – Two planes forced to land at another base collided on the ground

June 20 – Misburg oil refinery one bomber crashed on take-off (two died)

June 22 – Two railway yards in France – Lt. Richard W. Fellows plane shot down crew listed as missing in action (MIA) – Battle damaged plane of Lt. David P. Kilpatrick crashed near Dover – crew MIA

June 23 - Aircraft crashed on take-off – no injuries

June 24 - Two missions one to airfield another to a V-1 buzz bomb site

June 28 – Col. Frank P. Bostrom named Group Commander

July Acton – consisted of a series of support missions, bombing targets vital to aid our troops as they drove through Normandy and hitting Germany's supply lines. The group flew seventeen missions. The most important targets were on the 17th - a bridge near Sully- sur-Loire, France. The destruction of this bridge prevented Germans from moving troops and supplies between northern and southern France. Eighty tons of bombs were dropped and re-con photos showed that the bridge was rendered useless. On the 18th we aided ground troops with excellent strikes on enemy gun emplacements near Caen. Gen. Partridge sent letters of commendation to Col. Bostrom, congratulating the 490th for excellent results on destroying the important bridge. In regard to the Caen mission he said,

> *"I earnestly commend you and the members of your Group for the splendid bombing accomplished in the Caen area on 18th July. The precision results attained effectively eliminated enemy gun emplacements which could have exacted a heavy toll from our ground forces. This successful operation prepared the way for an important advance toward ultimate victory."* Major General Earle Partridge, Commanding General, Third Air Division.

July 29th – An 848 squadron aircraft was lost over foreign soil, *Pete the Pelican* made an emergency landing in Dubendorf, Switzerland. Lt. James R. Smith and his crew were interned until the end of the war.

The aircraft of Lt. Earlin H.W. Brunken, with a full load of gas and bombs, failed to get airborne on take-off and crashed 200 yards past the end of the runway, Most of the crew escaped before it exploded. The tail-gunner and radio operator were killed.

Lt. Wallace A. Johnson's aircraft, *My Mama Done Told Me* returning from the mission with a feathered prop failed to hold altitude on the landing approach, clipped some trees and crashed short of the runway near The Swan pub. The tail section of # 42-9495 landed on the Ipswich-Norwich road in front of The Swan. The crew escaped, but two men later died from injuries.

August – Say Hello to The B-17 – This month we said goodbye to our B-24 Liberators. They had done a good job but higher command decided the 93rd Wing should convert to the B-17 Flying Fortress for tactical reasons. This meant several bomb groups including the 490th would switch to the B-17s to standardize Third Division aircraft. The Group's last B-24 mission was August 6th to hit a V-I buzz- bomb site in France. The group had flown forty missions in the B-24H Liberator to bomb German rail transportation, heavily protected targets like oil refineries, rail yards and bridges. Many of the targets were in France to assist our ground troops.

The next two weeks were spent in the reorganization of the personnel of four squadrons; 848, 849, 850 and 851, and flying in war-weary B-17 bombers provided for the transition. Pilots and co-pilots practiced hours of take-offs and landings while crews became acquainted with new stations and equipment. The last phase was practice in group assembly, getting into combat formation and flying bomb runs on mock targets all over the United Kingdom. Sunday August 27th was the first 490th mission with the B-17. The target was a factory at Genshagen, Germany, but the second mission was a tough one: a Folke-Wolf aircraft factory at Bremen.

T/Sgt. James Lee Hutchinson, Ed.S.

September – Rough Duty - September Report – It was a month of heavy casualties for the 490th: Sixteen airmen died on the first mission this month. The target was a factory at Gustavsburg, Germany. The 848th squadron lost its commanding officer, Maj. Lamont D. Haas, in a mid-air collision over France while returning from the mission. The accident involved his lead plane, the Lt. John M. Kirklin's lead crew, and the Lt. Charles Frey crew. Maj. Francis H. Dresser, who had just arrived from the States, was also lost. It was his second mission. Other bombers lost in September included:

Sept 9 - Mannheim – Factory - the 1st Lt. John D. Beach crew

Sept. 13 – Ludwigshaven – IG Farben Chemical plant - The crews of Lt. Albert Davis and Lt. Robert W. Funk listed as MIA. Maj. Mitchell J. Mulholland, newly appointed 848th Squadron Commander to replace Maj. Haas, went down on a 96th BG plane.

Sept 27 – An aircraft piloted by Lt. Michael H. Primus crashed into a hill in western England during a night navigation training flight; twelve men died.

The 490th flew 18 missions, all but four in Germany and received some very good ratings on our strikes. Great improvement was noted in the formation and bombing patterns this month. Eight of the nine visual bombings this month were given ratings of good or better with only one poor. The PFF (radar bombing through the clouds) results were of course, unknown. The group experienced much heavier flak over targets like Ludwigshafen, Kassel and Meresburg!

Our War Bond drive exceeded its goal as the men on the base purchased $139,720 in bonds. Touch football teams were organized and goal posts were erected on the Yankee Stadium field between the 850th and 851st living areas. The group made a long mission to a synthetic oil plant in Brux, Czechoslovakia and sixteen other heavenly protected targets.

Bombardier Lt. Harry Lomicka

Lt. Lomicka recalls a flak hit on his second mission on September 9, "Our target was Dusseldorf but it was weathered in, so we went on to Mannheim and dropped our bombs visually. I was bombardier with Lt. Robert Gordon's crew and we were flying right wing of the middle-left element of the Low squadron. We were on the bomb run when a close flak burst exploded in front of our plane. A good-sized piece of jagged shell casing came through the sighting panel, glanced off the bombsight and caught me in the middle of the chest. Fortunately, my flak jacket stopped it and prevented any harm. However, in the same time frame, my flight googles had fogged up and I had pushed them up my head. The shattered plexiglass from the sighting panel hit me in the face and right eye. The force of the flak impact and plastic hit me at the same time, up-ended me off my seat and left me sprawled on the floor much to the surprise of the navigator. I knew I had been hit in the face and I could not see so I shouted over the intercom that I had been hit, but then realized that it was not too serious and I forced my eyes open by pushing up my eyelids. In the end, I managed to drop the bomb pattern with the lead plane's smoke trail when it began the bomb drop. When we returned to the base, I had to go to the hospital to get my eyes examined and washed out. They put a black patch over my right eye and I was grounded a few days until the irritation passed."

Sgt. Michael Walsh - POW

The Lt. John D. Beach 490th BG bomber was lost September 9, 1944 over Mannheim, Germany - Gunner Michael T. Walsh bailed out to survive the mission and wrote of his experiences as a prisoner of war for eight months.

"The targets for this mission, my 13th, were factories in Mannheim. We had just released our bombs when we were hit directly by flak and set on fire. The plane went into a steep dive and our pilot, Lt. John Beach, got the plane leveled off and ordered us to bail out. Bombardier,

Williamson and I were the last to jump. I later learned that both Lt. Beach and co-pilot John O. Terlecky, were killed by the flak, and tail-gunner, James. Vogt, was killed when he hit the tail assembly as he bailed out. I did not see Lt. Williamson again after leaving the plane, but our radio operator, Albert Ackerman, armor gunner Daniel B. Breckenridge, and I were picked by Germans soldiers along with men from other crews shot down that day. They showed us where our tail-gunner landed and told us that his chute never opened. We also saw the plane; it had crashed into a farmhouse.

We were all taken by truck to an interrogation center at Frankfort on the Main. There, I gave my flying boots to another crew's navigator who was shoeless after being blown out of his plane (another bomb group) when it exploded in mid-air. He said he was the only survivor of his crew and thought it was a piece of good fortune that he wore his chute on every mission. At Frankfort each of us was placed in a individual cell and interrogated alone. The interrogation was carried out by uniformed officers in a room lined with photographs of Allied planes, ships and submarines. They had more information than I was aware of and they knew the background of everyone on the crew. However, we prisoners gave only our name, rank and serial number. A couple of days later, we were loaded on trains and carried off to different POW camps. The enlisted men were taken to Stalag IV in northern Germany near the Polish border. The International Red Cross seemed to keep close tabs on this camp. Stalag IV was divided into separate compounds to separate prisoners by countries. Across the fence from us was a compound of British soldiers captured in the North African Campaign. The only doctor and minister was a British officer. Every week there was the Red Cross ritual distribution of parcels containing chocolate bars, cigarettes powdered coffee and powdered milk. It was really a welcome treat because the food supplied by our guards consisted of hard bread, a green soup called oleo and cold water. It was anything but appealing and many of the boys just could not eat it. Lice became a real problem because only cold water was available for washing and it was mighty cold at times. However, the Red Cross gave us razors and toothbrushes and the Germans gave us polishing powder to clean our teeth.

Our barracks were similar to one story CCC type barracks, each room housed 21 men and we had straw mats on the floor as beds. We had a small stove and guard rationed out bricks of a peat compound for fuel. Those bricks were used mighty sparingly as winter came on and we burned just enough peat to keep from freezing. They locked our barracks at night and armed guards patrolled the compound while large German shepherd dogs roamed the camp throughout the night. Our compound was surrounded by two ten foot wire fences with rolled barbed wire on top. The fences were between us and the guard towers which were manned all the time so escape was virtually impossible. We were called outside for roll call twice a day and if someone could not be accounted for, all the POWs had to stand in the snow and cold until that man was found. Guards constantly carried out raids in the barracks, looking for radios or anything else suspicious. The Russian forces were closing on the area in January and we could hear the cannons booming. At night, we could look through the cracks in the walls and see the flashes of the big guns. Our forced march in the dead of winter covered many miles and we endured plenty of hardships and food supplies diminished each day. We slept in any shelter our guards could find and usually put up in some abandoned building to sleep or rest. At one point we were in an abandoned factory when it was bombed by low-flying Allied medium bombers. Luckily, there were no casualties. We marched on for several days with nothing to eat and were nearly starving. Our march ended in May, 1945 when we were liberated by the Wolverine Division of the U.S. Army. Our liberators made the mistake of giving us their C-rations and too much food made most of us seriously ill for a couple of days. Later, we boarded C-47 cargo planes and were flown to Camp Lucky Strike in northern France for medical treatment and processing for a trip back to the USA."

Note - *Hitler had issued orders that concentration and/or POW camps were not to be captured. Prison guards were to move the camp or kill all prisoners as Allied troops advanced into Germany. Many prisons were evacuated and POWS were forced to make long marches in the snow and frigid weather. The weak and sick died during the trek as thousands were marched to Moosberg prison in Austria by the end of the war.*

T/Sgt. James Lee Hutchinson, Ed.S.

Lt. George B. Reeves

Squadron 851, a pilot close to finishing his thirty five missions, tells this story of the September 28th Merseburg mission

"Everything had gone smoothly on this mission until we had just finished the bomb run. Immediately after releasing our bombs there was a very close flak burst to the right and behind us. The plane, "Rugged But Right", lurched from the concussion. My first indication of the damage was the elevator control going limp and the plane starting a gradual decline. About the same time the tail gunner, John Volin, yelled over the intercom, "Help I'm hit!" and I ordered the engineer, Doc Cagle, to take a walk- around oxygen bottle and go to his aid."

Lt. Reeves said they were at about 23,000 feet when he discovered he could pull the stick back to his chest to level out and use the trim tab to maintain altitude. He then noticed that the right rudder pedal was all the way down to the stop and was useless. Meanwhile the other two bombers in the lead element abandoned them to return to their squadron location in the formation. The engineer had checked on the injured tail gunner and reported that he was unconscious with no pulse. Next, one of the waist gunners reported that the oxygen supply was gone, but crew members discovered that they still had oxygen in the front half of the plane, so they devised a system with walk- around bottles so everyone could re-fill them from the oxygen supply at the front of the plane. Lt. Reeves realized he had to drop to a lower altitude, even though they were still deep in Germany they had to take the chance. He checked with the navigator for the best heading to avoid flak guns according to the original flight plan at briefing that morning. They flew for some time before running into extremely heavy flak. Lt. Reeves said, "It was the heaviest I had seen but God was good to us and we suffered no more damage."

They had descended to 10,000 feet to solve the oxygen problem and allow the engineer and crew members to continue working to make repairs to the control cables. The tail elevators of a B-17 are controlled by two cables of seven strands of wire in each. They run overhead down each side of the plane. The engineer reported one of the cables was completely severed and all but one strand of the other cable was gone. The crew used what they had on board, including electric suit cord, to repair the cables and restore fairly good elevator control, but were still flying across Germany alone and a sitting duck for any Luftwaffe fighter that might come along. All the way back across enemy territory they kept a very close and nervous eye out for fighters, but thankfully the Luftwaffe pilots seemed to be taking a nap that afternoon. Finally, they crossed the Low Countries, reached the English Channel and it had never looked so good!

As they neared the airbase, Lt. Reeves warned the crew that the landing might be hazardous because of the damaged controls and maybe other unknown problems. He offered to maintain altitude if anyone wanted to bail out. The entire crew wanted to know what he was going to do. He told them he was going to take John Volin down, and everyone decided to stay with the bomber. The tower cleared them for an emergency landing and because the rudder pedal had been repaired they had a brake, but no rudder on the right side. Without that repair the plane would have spun out of control as soon as they touched down. However, by using left power and right rudder, the pilots were able to keep the plane straight in on the runway and hold it until they ran off the end. No farther damage was done and they were safe on the ground.

John Volin's body was removed from the plane, a piece of flak had severed a main artery below the heart and he had died shortly after he called for help. That piece of flak, the size of the end of your thumb, had gone through armor plate and a rack of 50 caliber ammo before it lodged in the tail gunner's chest. *Rugged But Right* had about thirty flak holes, but had proven to be a truly rugged B-17 and brought the crew back to Eye.

October – Bad Weather-Bad Flak - The weather took a turn for the worse making it harder to schedule missions and even harder to fly them. Runways were icy and visibility was very low making take-off and assembly more difficult. Aircrews who had been awake since two or three o'clock spent many mornings on stand-by in their bombers, waiting for the weather to clear for take-off only to learn the mission was scrubbed due to poor visibility over England or over the target. Of course the crews and flight-line boys were happy to go back to their huts for precious 'sack-time' before the next mission. They knew they might fly two or more mission in a row when the weather improved. In fact, twice this month, they did fly four in missions in five days.

The 490th flew fourteen missions this month bombing strategic targets to destroy Germany's ability to stop Allied troops advancing through France. Synthetic oil plants which provided fuel for Hitler's planes and tanks were prime targets. Bomb strikes on bridges and railroads to prevent movement of troops and equipment to the front were very important.

Berlin was the Groups's first mission to 'Big B' - Aircraft encountered intense flak on the October 6th mission to hit an ordnance depot. The Lt. William W. McLennan aircraft was lost - crew MIA. This month our B-17's came back with many holes from heavy flak from targets of railyards, tank factories and oil depots at Gustavsburg, Cologne, Merseburg and Hamburg. The PFF radar dome was used often because of the weather conditions.

October 17 - Cologne Marshalling yards – Lt. Wallace Johnson, who survived his B-24 crash of *My Mama Done Told Me,* near The Swan in July, was piloting a B-17 named *Big Poison* faced more problems on this trip. That mission his problem was a "feathered" engine, this time he had one he could not feather! Lt. Wallace received an almost direct flak hit that severed all oil lines on engine number two, including the one to the "feathering" pump. They were unable to feather the propeller which caused extreme over-speeding of the prop and with no oil to the engine it soon locked and caused the crankshaft to shear. This left Wallace with a propeller running wild (wind-milling) to drag down his speed. He could not keep up with the formation, even with the other three engines at full power. He said when they dropped out of the formation, they were picked up by two "little friends", P-51 fighters who escorted and protected them as they flew alone over enemy territory. As command pilot, Lt. Wallace had to decide whether to try to make it across the Channel or attempt landing on the Continent. There was a high risk that the run-a-way prop could break away at anytime and slice through the plane's nose and he would have to ditch in the Channel, so he chose to land at the Allied controlled airport in Brussels. It was a wise choice, because when the maintenance crew came out to inspect the aircraft they said the prop was ready to fall off at the touch of a finger. The Wallace hitched a ride back to Eye with another crew with a repaired plane. *Big Poison* was repaired and returned to Eye but later went down over England in a mid-air collision during an assembly.

November – Fog and Flak - Only ten missions were flown this month and most were PFF due to the weather. Many days the fog was so thick that all base activity ceased. Missions were scheduled at any chance of flying weather, but more missions were 'scrubbed' than flown. Ground crews worked long night hours to load bombs, guns and gas tanks for a mission. Aircrews also lost morale preparing mentally for missions which were scrubbed. Weather over Germany was often as bad as England's and several times clouds were so thick the Group had to abandon their primary and secondary target and bomb a target of opportunity. One mission was re-called without a bomb being dropped. The Group hit tactical targets including three strikes on oil targets at Hamburg and Merseburg.

Nov. 5 – Target was marshalling yards at Ludwigshaven, two aircraft were lost and the crews of Lt. Clarence Bridwell and Lt. Robert Jackson listed as MIA

Nov. 16 – Bombed at Duren, Germany in support of Allied ground troops breaking through at Aachen. Visibility was near zero at Eye when they returned and the formation was diverted to an RAF base at Carnaby, 134 miles north of Eye.

Nov. 25 – Target the synthetic oil plant at Merseburg. Lt. Frank Delmerico aircraft lost and crew listed as MIA. It was only their second mission.

Nov. 30 – Second mission to Merseburg

T/Sgt. James Lee Hutchinson, Ed.S.

We Arrive at Eye

The replacement air crews of Lt. William Templeton, Lt. Robert Tennenberg and Lt. Darrell Roufs had crossed the North Atlantic on a ship, traveled across the United Kingdom in a train. We were beginning to wonder if would ever see a B-17 again. Winter was setting in when our crews got off the train at the little town of Diss in East Anglia late that cold murky November day. The drivers of the canvas covered trucks waiting for the replacement air crews told us to toss our duffle bags in the back and crawl in behind them for a short ride to the 490th Bomb Group (H) base, station 134, (code name Hangstrap) in East Anglia. I still have a copy of General Order # 47 listing the enlisted men by rank, name, duty and serial numbers. The gist of the order said, "These men are assigned to the 490th Bomb group to participate in combat flights and operate planes or equipment until this order is cancelled."

We were the three new crews to arrive at Eye on November 14, 1944 and each man (boy) had completed the required Army Air Force training programs to prepare him as a B-17 aircrew member flying bombing missions. We were the rookies sent to replace 490th Bomb Group crews who had completed their tour of duty, been wounded or shot down. As I think back, I recall thirty tired young airmen standing in the cold damp evening waiting to be assigned to our barracks. The overcast sky wasn't fit for flying and the fog reminded me of a Sherlock Holmes movie. We knew we would soon be flying combat missions, but had no premonition that two of the thirty would be wounded and thirteen would die!

The three crews of Lt. William Templeton, Lt. Robert Tennenberg and Lt. Darrell Roufs were assigned to the in 848th squadron. It was almost dark when the officer-of- the- day escorted the pilots, co-pilots, bombardiers and navigators over to the Officers' Quarters. The squadron clerk, a feisty little sergeant, came out to guide enlisted crewmen to their assigned huts. We picked up our duffle bags and followed him through a group of steel huts. He dropped the other two six man crews at different huts and led us all the way to the rear of the compound to Quonset Hut # 29 and introduced us to the six other airmen living there. Evidently, it was standard procedure to place 'greenhorns' in with an experienced crew because we learned a lot from those veterans of several missions. Hut # 29 was our home for the next nine months.

Hut # 29 - The Brome Dome

Our base was one of the forty three Eighth Air Force heavy bomber bases built among the farms and parishes of East Anglia. They were concentrated in an area less than half the area of the state of Vermont. The 490th base provided living quarters for 420 officers and over 2,500 enlisted men, the majority were housed in steel Quonset huts on the east side of the field. Crew chiefs and mechanics usually chose to live in shacks near the flight line to be near their bombers. Our 848th huts actually extended into the community of Brome. The hut was a sixteen by thirty foot steel Quonset hut with a concrete floor. It looked like a giant steel trash can half buried in the ground with a brick wall in each end containing a door and two windows covered by blackout curtains. The furniture included foot lockers, clothes racks and metal double bunks for twelve men. Our bedding, neatly stacked on the empty bunks, included one pillow, two blankets and three biscuits or cushions

We soon discovered that the most important piece of equipment was a very small stove sitting in the center of the hut with a small stovepipe reaching up through the roof. That stovepipe was smoking most of our winter days at Eye. The gunners already living in the hut had taken the bunks nearest the stove to soak up what little heat that dinky stove put out. I soon discovered that my top bunk near the steel ceiling was a little warmer because of the rising heat. I kept that top bunk for two months, but moved down to a lower bunk next to the stove when our hut buddies completed their thirty-five missions and went home. By that time our crew had been named a 'lead crew' and a new replacement crew moved in to take the bunks farthest from the stove and we shared our mission experiences with the new boys. We gunners of the Lt. Bill Templeton crew spent many cold winter nights huddled around the stove or 'sacked out' in our cots to keep warm. Coke, a coal product for the stove was rationed. It was stored in a fenced area and each hut was allowed only one small bucket per day unless more was delivered to the squadron. This meant very small fires in a very small stove and lots of extra clothing all winter unless one of us got tired of being cold and sneaked out in the middle of the night to steal an extra supply of coke. Needless to say we made many of those "night missions" during that cold winter! Keeping warm was a constant battle, you almost had to sit on the stove to feel the heat. We needed to thaw out after flying missions at forty below zero were determined we weren't going to freeze our butt in our hut!

The second fly in the ointment was the fact our bunks had three sofa pillows instead of a mattress! The British called them "biscuits." The trick was to pull them together and cover them tightly with a sheet. However, they often separated in the dead of night and believe me, nothing wakes you quicker than a blast of cold air on your backside! The Supply Room eventually solved the "shifting biscuit" problem by giving us toasty warm sleeping bags.

The squadron latrine (showers and toilets) was located in the middle of the huts. The little brick building was not heated and hot water for showers was available for only a short time after supper. Otherwise the latrine was as cold as the outside temperature and a guy never tarried when answering nature's call. If we missed the hot water period, we skipped the showers and used a steel helmet to heat shaving water on the barracks stove. There were many adjustments to make in a combat, but they were minor compared to those of the ground troops fighting in foxholes in the mud and snow.

Our base was located in the agricultural area of Suffolk, eastern England. I could step out our back door and peer across the road at a red brick English manor house with a huge barnyard. A small pond just behind our hut and on our side of the road was a playground for farm ducks. I enjoyed watching their aquatic antics. It was a peaceful scene in contrast to the war. The Brome Dome was our home for the nine months we were stationed in England---from November 1944 through July 8, 1945.

We had arrived in time to get settled in before Thanksgiving and the big feast in the large Mess Hall featured turkey and chicken with all the trimmings. Winter had set in and the group had flown only six missions so far. Although two planes had already been lost earlier in the month, everyone was ready for a large meal and the 490th cooks didn't disappoint them. Our crew had flown no missions, but I had plenty to be thankful for; my family was healthy, I had survived the trip across the Atlantic on the Queen Mary and I was getting ready for duty at the 490th Bomb Group at Eye. Thanksgiving came and went and we were still training, but eager to get into the war. A crew had to survive thirty-five missions before going home and we wanted to get it done. However, we had to attend classes on aircraft recognition, operating our equipment at 40 below, conduct on base and interaction with our English hosts. The class that impressed us most was on "evasion and escape" in case we had to bail out into enemy territory. Avoiding capture was the duty of every airman forced to parachute into enemy territory. We learned there were men and women in enemy occupied countries who carried out underground activities and risked their lives hiding and helping downed airman to escape to fly again. Any day the weather was fit for flying, we practiced flying in combat formation. Base procedure required new pilots to be certified by the training officer as ready to fly in close combat formations. Our pilot Lt. Templeton reminded us the 490th sent out three squadrons on every mission, they flew very tight formations and they needed to make sure pilots and co-pilots, were ready for duty in a tight formation. Our crew was cleared for missions and we flew our first one in December. Four weeks later, January 5, 1945 we were involved in a mid-air collision during a training flight to help replacement crews switch from the B-24 to the B-17G. It was a day I'll not forget because pilot errors during careless formation flying took several lives quickly.

T/Sgt. James Lee Hutchinson, Ed.S.

The Swan Pub

Once we settled into Hut 29 some of the guys on the other crew took us up the road just off the base to the Swan Inn, Brome's only pub, for a drink or two. Sadly, England had no American beer. Pubs served only mild or bitters ale and it was warm. The red brick pub, The Swan on the Ipswich-Norwich road had been in business many years, but it was almost destroyed July 29, 1944 when a B-24 bomber was returning from a mission with one engine feathered failed. It came in too low on the landing approach, clipped some treetops and crashed just short of the runway across the road from the Swan. Eric Swain, 490th historian, recently sent a photograph in a local newspaper showing a scene of the black smoke from the crash near the pub and the tail section lying in the road in front of the building. Most of the crew survived, but two men later died from injuries.

Down through the past seventy years, many 490th veterans have returned to England to visit our old Eye airbase and include a stop at The Swan. Our 490th Group historian, Eric Swain, recently posted a photo of retired CMSgt. Wendell Lee standing in front of our old watering hole. Recently a British friend, Hannah Potter, sent a photo of The Swan Inn as it is today, the red brick inn is re-modeled and still in business. Hannah is involved in "Eighth in the East," a British organization doing in archeology and social history research on airmen and old airfields. Many cold evenings we sent out for a large order of hot Fish and Chips, which was the favorite English finger food. Everyone liked the deep fried chunks of fish and French fried potatoes. The fries were much bigger, softer and thicker than we buy today, the English called them chips. We often ordered Fish and Chips from the Swan in the evenings while sacking-out in the hut, especially if the mess hall chow hadn't been too satisfying. A local farm boy, Russell Etheridge, would go get them for a small fee and his fare share. Russell was a fourteen year old who couldn't wait until he was old enough to join the Royal Navy. His mother did our laundry each week for a small fee and he was our pick-up and delivery boy. He was also available in late evenings to run errands for a small fee. Fish and Chips were most delicious when sprinkled with vinegar, and we had many fine feasts in hut # 29. On cold winter nights, Yank crewmen and Russell could make a large package disappear quickly. I remember the cook at The Swan always wrapped the order in newspapers and Russell could make it back to the hut while it was still warm. One night, he proudly announced that his sister was getting married, so one of the guys managed to obtain a "damaged" parachute for her to make a wedding dress.

Merseburg Mission

We were not approved for combat missions, but we listened carefully to stories from our hut buddies who had flown several missions. They had a lot of good advice on ways to survive at high altitude. November 30, 1944, the Group flew into some of the heaviest flak ever sent up by German flak batteries. Intelligence reports said the number of flak guns had increased to 720. The number of anti-aircraft guns protecting critical targets increased as Allied troop victories forced Hitler's army to retreat into Germany. The 490th was leading the Eighth Air Force over the target when the PFF on our lead ship malfunctioned and another ship took over. Due to navigation errors over the clouds, the group missed the IP approached the Luena oil refinery from the wrong direction and for the next 17 minutes they struggled on through intense and accurate flak which ripped the squadrons apart. No one on that mission will ever forget it! We lost no aircraft over the target, but seventy-five percent had battle damage. Our planes that could not make it back to England were forced to make emergency landings on the continent. The Third Division lost seventeen bombers which was a great loss of planes over Germany due to flak.

We had taken advantage of the clear weather and got more flight training over England in mid-day while the formation was gone. Planes were allowed up for training or equipment checks on mission days, but all runways had to be cleared when at mission formation was due to return. Ground crews and aircrews not flying usually checked out the mission's return. Our Templeton crew was among the crowd on the flight line when the Group was due back from that Merseburg mission. We were completely awed by all the red flares and emergency landings.

Lt. Jules Berndt, Navigator - Information from the 490th Historical Record and an account by Lt. Jules Berndt, Navigator on the Lt. Rolland Peacock crew, provide memories of that day. His crew was on pass and another crew was flying their aircraft, *Magnificent Obsession,* so he and the co-pilot went down to see if it returned.

"About 4:30 the first ships began approaching from the east. The chaff ships, the first ships over the target, landed in good condition. We all knew thirty-six planes had been sent and we counted the rest of the planes for a total of twenty-four as the formation came closer. Four or five had feathered engines and several others fired red flares to request early landing. Red flares indicated wounded aboard or serious aircraft damage. Most planes had flak damage but the *Magnificent Obsession* received only two hits. The pilot said they flew thirteen minutes through the heaviest flak he had ever seen."

T/Sgt Frank McKinley's Story

T/Sgt. McKinley was the engineer and top turret gunner on the Lt. George Lyon crew of squadron 851. His story of the Merseburg mission is a perfect example of dangers faced by aircrews on thousands of combat missions.

"The other gunners and I were gathered round the little stove in our hut on the evening of the 29th discussing our mission that day to Hamm and congratulating ourselves that the bombing results had been assessed as 'good'. A messenger from the Orderly Room came in and told us that we would be flying the next day and we should hit the sack early. We were all up by 03:30 hrs on the 30th and the nervous chatter began as we entered the briefing room. The noise subsided when the briefing officer removed the curtain that was covering the large map at the back of the stage and we saw that we were in for a rough mission.

An audible groan filled the room at the sight of the red tape on the map that stretched from our base all the way to Merseberg in Germany. Today our base commander, Colonel Frank P. Bostrom flew the lead ship and the 490th Bomb Group led the other Groups of the 8th Air Force to Merseberg. It felt different without any bombers in front of us as we made our way into Germany. We were to be the first to face the Luftwaffe and first to test the accuracy of the flak gunners. I was quite comfortable in my top turret; my electrically heated suit kept me warm and the strong sun shining through the plexiglass of my turret felt good. I had my English candy bar, my cigarettes and a high altitude lighter. Our P-51 fighter escort was a welcome sight and the 851st Squadron was flying its usual perfect, tight grouping as the twin vapor trails of General Doolittle's P-38 passed overhead, checking our formations. The steady, synchronized drone of our four engines was soothing and almost put me to sleep. In my pocket was a government issue (GI) of a New Testament Bible. I would never fly without it because it had become my good luck charm.

There hadn't been any serious opposition on our flight over and we were now deep inside Germany. We were relaxed but always alert and ready for action. When we reached the area of the target, the refineries at Merseberg, there was no sign of the Luftwaffe and no flak. The sky was clear below and all around us but our navigator reported that the target was completely obscured by a smoke screen. We turned at the IP, the bomb doors swung open and we started on our bomb run. I heard the bombardier say to the pilot "No fighters, no flak - it looks as if we are going to get away with it". No sooner were the words out of his mouth then at 12 o'clock level, about 1,000 ft away, a huge box barrage exploded, filling the sky with thousands of deadly, jagged pieces of flak. The 490th flew right into it and it ripped us apart. The barrage continued, hammering us with intense, accurate flak. From my top turret I watched the red flashes of the 88 mm shells exploding all around and above us. I heard the muffled sound of the explosions and the pieces of flak ripping through our bomber; as I turned my turret I could see holes appearing all over the skin of the plane.

T/Sgt. James Lee Hutchinson, Ed.S.

The formation by now was widely scattered. Everyone was being buffeted by the shock waves of the bursting shells and we had not yet dropped our bombs. It seemed to me that we were making a large turn but the flak was following us. It was relentless and accurate. I began to think this could be the end for us and I remembered my New Testament in my pocket. I took it out and thumbed it open in my right hand, my left hand still on the turret control as I slowly turned to look for enemy fighters. The flak continued, brutally intense and accurate, and it seemed like we had been in it for 30 minutes. <u>I glanced down at my open bible and in bold, black letters the words Do not be afraid jumped out at me. I said "Thank you, God," and slipped the book back in my pocket.</u>

It seemed as though the flak would never stop and by now we were starting to experience malfunctions. Wires were short-circuiting and suddenly the landing gear dropped down and the bail-out bell started ringing. The pilot quickly got on the intercom, telling us to ignore the bail-out signal and to check in. Everyone did check in except Bolton in the tail, so the pilot ordered me to go back there and stop him from bailing out. I quickly scrambled out of my turret, snapped on a walk-round oxygen bottle and headed for the tail. Boy was I glad to see Bolton still sitting there; his intercom cord had been severed by flak. The walk through the plane was extremely cold and it was also difficult due to the buffeting from the shock waves of the exploding shells. I had to use caution coming through the open bomb bay; the bombs were still there but they could have been dropped at any moment. It's frightening to be looking down through an open bomb bay at fierce anti-aircraft fire. Back in my turret, I plugged back into my oxygen and electric outlets, reported to the pilot on the intercom that Bolton was still with us and gave him a brief report of the visible damage. Then came bombs-away and it looked as though it was going to be a poor strike pattern as the formation was widely scattered and the smoke-screen completely obscured the target; also, it was impossible to hold a steady course on the bomb run. I tried to count how many of our 490th were still with us; the terrifying 88 mm guns were still working us over and it was amazing that we seemed not to have caught a direct hit.

Finally we were out of it. The feeling of relief was tremendous but we were still aware that the Luftwaffe fighters could be waiting for us. Something seemed to have happened to our hydraulics because the landing gear had partially extended and the bomb bay doors wouldn't shut. The pilot gave me the OK to hand-crank them, so once again I was on a portable oxygen bottle and in the open bomb bay where the cranking handles are situated. It was so cold there that the vapors from my breath froze in the oxygen hose and I had to break the ice to get a breath.

Back up in my turret I watched other groups coming in over the target and the large explosions of B-17s as they took a direct hit and went down in flames, leaving nothing in the sky but a black smudge. Then the pilot ordered me up front immediately and as I approached the cockpit I could see it was filled with smoke. I checked the instrument panel and noticed that the hydraulic pressure reading was down to zero, so I shut off the pump, grabbed a fire extinguisher and gave the furiously smoking pump motor a blast. The co-pilot and I talked over the problem and worked out that when he had opened the # 4 engine cowl flaps to cool down that engine, we must have lost all our hydraulic fluid because that line had been damaged by the flak. Fortunately I had a spare can on board and when I filled the reservoir and turned on the pump the pressure came back up. We would be alright as long as the #4 cowl selector switch remained closed. The fact that we were able to deal with a major malfunction in such conditions was testimony to the quality of the engineering in the B-17. While I was talking to the pilot we noticed that the nacelle of #2 engine was turning a different color in one spot and the engine itself was showing a slight loss of power. I thought we had blown a cylinder head or flak had knocked a hole in it, but we decided not to feather it and to keep a close eye on it.

By now the 490th formation was back together again and we were heading for home. It was a miracle but a quick count revealed that none of our aircraft was missing. There was a long way to go before we would be out of Germany and we were all aware that anything could still happen. When the coast of England appeared it never looked better and we were thankful to have come through what we later learned was one of the fiercest attacks from the German 88 mm anti aircraft gunners of the entire war.

As we approached the field I had to crank down the landing gear and it was also necessary to crank the flaps down to 1/3 position as we were landing. While waiting for the truck to pick us up we started counting the holes in our plane; we got to a little over 100 on one side alone before the truck arrived. The coffee and doughnuts served by the Red Cross girls was very much appreciated and also that shot of whisky before inter-rogation. That night in our hut when the lights were out and I was in my bunk I began to re-live the mission. How lucky we were to get through that terrible barrage without anyone on board getting wounded. This was only our 7th mission - we had 28 more to go; what were the odds on our surviving another mission like this one had been? I decided to think about that one tomorrow, rolled over and went to sleep.

Visits to Diss

The road behind our barracks led to the Swan pub (public house) and on the way to Diss. I remember walking down the Oakley road past the big house up to the pub. An eight-foot brick wall bordered the road and the top of the wall had broken glass embedded in concrete to discourage trespassers. We visited the town many times when our crew wasn't on a mission alert. We had the choice of riding the pass truck, walking or biking. Diss was the railroad station for trains between Ipswich and Norwich. Anytime we received a three-day pass, we caught the base pass truck to Diss to board the train for London.

One of the first things we had to do was to learn the value of British money. They didn't even use U.S. money in the P.X. on base and we were going to be paid with English money. Things didn't cost too much on base, but everything was rationed. They gave us a PX ration card each month and punched off items we bought, like soap, candy, and such. I kept a US two dollar bill to add to my short-snorter. We didn't know a shilling from a quid and had a heck of a time adjusting to half-pennies, shillings, crowns and pound notes. Recently, I was sorting through my WW II files and found a yellowed piece of paper listing the value of British money. I had scribbled that valuable information to carry when

I went to town. The new money came in copper and silver coins of all sizes, shapes, and values. The paper money was very colorful and easier to remember.

Diary Notes From 1944

Copper Coins	Value	US value
½ d half penny	half penny - ha'pence	penny
1d Penny	penny	two cents
3d	three pence – thru'pence	nickel

Silver coins		
6d	six pence	dime
1s	shilling or bob	quarter
2s	florian	40 cents
2s 6d	half crown	50 cents
5s	crown 5 shillings	$1.00

Paper Money		
10s	10 schilling note	$2.00
Pound note	20 schillings	$4.00
Five pound note	100 schillings?	$20.00

Back in basic training down in Amarillo Texas we marched to an English song called "I've Got Sixpence," One line said, "I've got sixpence jolly, jolly sixpence -- I've got two pence to spend and two pence to lend and two pence to send home to me wife" --------- At last, I knew what a sixpence was worth.

    The town had a number of pubs and shops we could visit. The shops didn't have a lot of merchandise, but we went shopping as soon as we mastered the value of English money. First, Rod and I purchased ledgers from the stationer's shop for our diaries. I have included information from that faded old diary of combat memories in my books. After we made lead crew, Rod, Bert and I bought a small radio for Hut 29 and some of us bought new bicycles as soon as they became available. Bikes made transportation faster to the Mess Hall, around the airbase and to town. Used bikes were also available from guys who had finished their missions. I was also lucky enough to buy a 110 Kodak box camera which I still own. I got a lot of good snapshots and some are included in this book. The butcher shop always intrigued me, because of the lack of refrigeration the bodies of dead chickens, rabbits hung outside in their fur or feathers and didn't look too appetizing. I was reminded of a scene from an old Charles Dickens story. Diss also had a village green with a small lake and two swans that glided gracefully across the water. It was another peaceful scene in the middle of air raids and buzz bombs!

The Diss pubs (public houses) were neighborhood social centers and in the evening people would gather at their favorite pub for a pint of ale or a few games of darts. Food was also available although the menu was limited mostly to beans, bread or fish and chips. I was always amazed at the way they ate their beans by holding the fork upright and backward in their left hand and used a knife to mash the beans against the fork. My buddies and I tried it many times, but no one developed the art of eating beans backwards. People were very friendly and would often yell, "Ave a drink Yank" to welcome us as we entered the pub. One lesson we learned quickly was to never play darts with them! It was a favorite pub pastime and they were very good. We could go into town if we had a few free hours and weren't on alert for a mission the next morning. If the weather allowed, we sometime travelled by "shanks mare" or bicycle just for the exercise. We passed the Swan pub and went on down the narrow road covered by overhang limbs of giant trees. I wouldn't have been surprised if Robin Hood and his Merry Men had dropped out of those trees to demand our money. Then it was out of the trees and on the open road past a deserted golf course into town. There was little civilian automobile traffic because all petrol (gas) was needed for the war effort. Military vehicles, jeeps, buses and trucks were everywhere, but all traffic was on the wrong side of the road! Night driving was really perilous because all headlights were covered except for a small cross of light so the car could be seen by walkers. Blackout curtains were required on all buildings so the town disappeared into the darkness at night. The countryside was pitch-black on the way home. We sometimes saw flashes of the big guns on the coast in the distance or the flames of a V-1 rocket (doodlebug or buzz bomb) buzzing across the dark horizon to crash and explode in the countryside when it ran out of fuel.

English oldsters and youngsters were mostly the only Brits, we met because most of the young men and women were in the service or working away in the Home Guard, an organization made up of women, senior citizens and youngsters. They served as air raid wardens, or helped during emergencies and other catastrophes. Americans made up the bulk of the young male population in the country during these horrible war years. England had suffered through the Battle of Britain, German air raids and the threat of an invasion before the United States entered the war and turned the countryside into a giant airbase. The British were grateful for the assistance of our Armed Forces, Air Force and Naval operations on the seas surrounding the United Kingdom.

The U.S. Air Force occupied many airfields in the United Kingdom by 1944. There were 43 heavy bombers bases. Fourteen were for the B-24 Liberators, and twenty-nine were dedicated to the B-17 Flying Fortresses. England and the U.S. had off from various airfields to face fighters and flak protecting Third Reich military and industrial targets agreed to attack Germany with an around the clock bombing plan with Royal Air Force night missions and Eighth Air Force precision bombing raids each day. There were seventy-five Eighth Air Force fighter squadrons in addition to all the Royal Air Force bomber and fighter bases. Each heavy bomber base required about 500 acres of fertile East Anglia farmland and had to be nestled into very tight areas. One of our runways ran parallel to a row of houses. We were practically in their backyards. A loaded B-17 required a speed of 110 MPH and a long concrete runway to take off on a mission. Two of our Eye runways were only 4,200 feet long so the pilots had to power all four motors as to coax the 64,000 pounds of a loaded bomber into the air. The roaring of the 1200 horse powered motors of thirty or more bombers shook the countryside every morning we flew a mission, but it was a welcome wake-up call for area residents who knew we were fighting for peace. Eighth Air Force bombers took off every day the weather was fit and RAF bombers flew each night. Sadly, many never returned!

B-17G Flying Fortress

The Army Air Force used the B-17 E model of the B-17 Flying Fortress when the U.S. first joined the RAF in the air over Germany. Losses were especially heavy in 1943 – 44 when formations flew to face Luftwaffe fighters and flak with little or no fighter escort for protection. The Memphis Belle, a B-17E was one of the first B-17s to complete a tour of duty of twenty-five missions. The Flying Fortress was improved to the B-17F and B-17G models as the war progressed. Each change made the bomber a more effective weapon for delivering tons of bombs to German targets. The B-24 Liberator and RAF bombers were very effective, but the B-17 was more durable and often made it back to England with unimaginable combat damage.

The B-17G was powered by four 1,200 horsepower, radial air-cooled Wright Cyclone engines with three bladed propellers. That was enough power to lift a fully loaded B-17G weighing 65,000 pounds off those short runways thousands of times. Planes often made it to safety on two or three engines. I remember one day we were flight testing a lead plane and two engines conked out over Scotland. We prepared to bail out, and we sweated out the flight back to base. The Fortress carried an 8,000 pound bomb-load and 1,700 gallons of gas in the wings it could climb to 25,000 feet and cruise at around 170 MPH.

Our crew arrived late enough in the war to fly on the B-17G and reap the benefits of the improvements. The best one was a chin turret added just under the nose cone meant two more machine guns to increase the bomber's firepower. The addition of the Bendix two gun remote controlled gun turret gave the B-17G a total of thirteen Browning M-2 .50 caliber machine guns. The chin turret was operated by the bombardier or togglier. That addition, (added to the top turret) doubled a bomber's protection against head –on attacks by Luftwaffe fighters

The B-17G required a crew of ten men divided by the bomb-bay. The flight deck was occupied by the pilot and co-pilot at the controls and the flight engineer. The engineer, an enlisted man with a seat behind the co-pilot, helped with mechanical problems. He also manned the top turret to watch for fighters while in enemy territory. Two more officers: the navigator and bombardier had small desks down in the nose area (we called it the greenhouse) to plot our course and drop our bombs. They also manned the nose guns and chin turret during fighter attacks.

Five enlisted men (gunners) had positions behind the bomb-bay: the radio operator, ball turret gunner, two waist gunners and the tail-gunner. Bombardiers were sometimes re-placed by a nose gunner/togglier when the formation was doing saturation bombing. This enlisted man operated the chin-turret guns and dropped the plane's bombs at the same time the lead plane bombardier released his bomb-load.

The improved B-17G was armed with thirteen .50 caliber machine guns and each could spit out up to twelve bullets per second, but even at 40 below zero, gunners fired only short bursts to prevent burning out their gun barrels. The bomber was truly a flying fortress and Luftwaffe fighters spent many hours studying best angles to attack and escape a hail of heavy gunfire. They usually hunted for "loose" formations or lone crippled bombers.

The men (boys) who flew those daytime Eighth Air Force combat missions in WW II needed skill, nerves of steel and a faith that they would survive the hazards they faced in those deadly skies over Germany. A lot of thoughts go through your mind while you're plodding through the snow to a jeep or truck to take you out to your bomber. You've gone through briefing and you know the target. In a few hours you'll be soaring over the North Sea at 25,000 feet, at 40 below zero and on oxygen. You realize your life is going on the line and you may never see home again. With the optimism of youth you believe you'll make it, but you say a prayer to ask God's protection. Then, you toss your equipment into the truck and with a yell to the rest of the crew, "Let's get this show on the road!"

When you saw a swarm of Luftwaffe fighters swooping down on the formation you really learned how to pray! Their machine gun bullets, cannon fire or a direct hit by a rocket would send a bomber down in flames. There was a constant mental stress on aircrew members from the time they were alerted for a mission. We worried most of the night on the eve of a bombing raid, and sweated out every mission from take-off until landing. Most airmen feared flak worst of all because there was the reality of facing it over every target and at unexpected locations.

Briefing sessions before a mission always included information on the safest flak-free route to and from the target. Thirty or so bombers took off to rise up and assemble in formation, climb to 22,000 feet and head for enemy territory.

Aircrews relied on their pilot and navigator to avoid those hot spots, but many anti-aircraft guns were mounted on railroad cars, boats and river barges. Those mobile guns could raise havoc with a bomber formation. Flak was terrifying because there was no way of knowing when the sky would be filled with deadly exploding shells or who those iron slugs would strike. Flak was sneaky, especially if the anti-aircraft gunners were "tracking" us! By the time we saw the puffs of black smoke from exploding shells, the sky around us was full of iron slugs. It was even worse on the bomb-run to the target. We saw a sky full of flak that we had to fly into it to drop our bombs! That's when you learned to pray even harder!

Flak brought death and destruction to our bomber formation as we opened our bomb-bay doors and delivered the same to destroy Factories, railroads and other units of their war machine. We were always alert for an enemy fighter attack, but we could shoot back at them and our escort fighters could protect us. However, there was no defense against the flak barrage over the target. When you saw the air over the target filled with puffs of black smoke and knew you had to fly into it: that's when you learned to pray even harder! Flak shrapnel could wound or kill crew members, or bring down a plane and a direct hit by an anti-aircraft 88 mm shell meant disaster. Airmen knew that severe flak damage to a bomber's motor meant dropping out of the formation and losing of the protection of its guns. Lone flak-crippled bombers unable to maintain speed were prime targets for lurking Luftwaffe fighters armed with machine guns, cannon and rockets. A crippled bomber crew's best chance of surviving was to be picked up and protected by some of our escort fighters until they could make it out of enemy territory.

Each combat mission was a test of endurance with every crew member doing the best job possible at his position. The odds of a B-17 bomber completing a safe mission depended on luck, skill and the grace of God. There was no place for a crewman who was not in good mental condition. The crews on heavy bombers faced many hazards besides the actual mission. Examples include: crashes on take-off or landings, mid-air collisions, fire, engine or equipment failure, sub-zero temperature and anoxia (oxygen loss.) Combat fatigue was common and aircrew members sometimes '"snapped" under the constant fear of death. Crews often flew two or three days in a row. The common term was around the base was 'flak happy,' and we all sympathized, because we knew we might be the next victim of combat fatigue. Some crews endured unbelievable experiences in those dangerous skies of World War II. The Air Force recognized the fatigue problem and combat crews were given frequent three day passes to London or other recreational areas. Large R&R (rest and relaxation) centers were established in hotels or mansions for crews needing a week's vacation from the war! Numerous three day passes helped us keep our sanity. We were generally agreed that an airman who said he was not afraid, was either crazy as a loon or lying!

The Stars and Stripes, our armed forces newspaper, printed daily reports and results of the Mighty Eighth's bombing missions and fighter raids to show our successes in the war. We were always faced with the brutal statistics of the air war. Bombers that went down carried nine or ten men, so it was easy to count the casualties. Usually, the men (boys) listed as MIA (missing in action) were either dead or prisoners of war. War department telegrams went out to inform the family and bomb groups sent for more replacement crews. Airmen were keenly aware of the number of bombers and crews lost on each mission. Each bomber group kept a special clean-up squad go to the barracks of crews that were shot down and move out all property and traces of crews that were lost. This "sanitizing" prevented looting, and preserved the missing crew's personal property for relatives. Most of all, it helped surviving crews forget the fate of their unfortunate buddies, but it was hard to ignore empty bunks!

T/Sgt. James Lee Hutchinson, Ed.S.

490ᵀᴴ Bomb Group Bombers

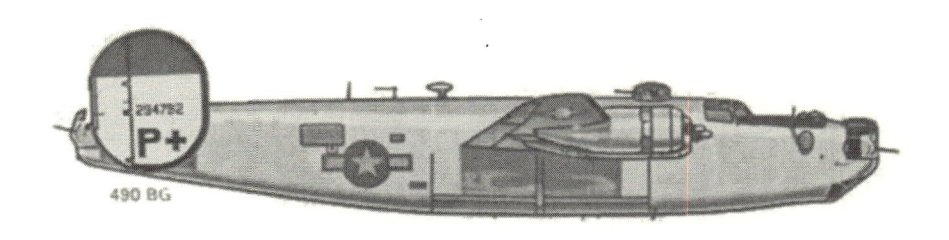

490th Memorial Plaques at Eighth Air force museum, Pooler, GA:
490th Bombardment Group (H)

Constituted as 490th Bombardment Group (Heavy) on 14 September 1943. Activated on 1 October 1943.

After training for combat in B-24 Liberators at Mountain Home AA Field, the 490th moved to England in April 1944 for operations with the Eighth Air Force, 3rd Air Division, 93rd Combat Wing. In England the 490th, composed of the 848th, 849th, 850th and 851st Squadrons, was stationed at the recently constructed air base at Eye, Station 134. The men of the 490th BG spent most of May preparing for their first combat mission. Meanwhile the 850th Squadron received transfer orders attaching it to the 801st BG to engage in Carpetbagger operations from 31 May to 12 August 1944. The remaining three Squadrons, 848th, 849th, and 851st, were combat ready by the end of May, and the 490th BG flew its first combat mission on 31 May 1944. More missions followed as the Group supported D-Day by bombing airfields and coastal defenses in France. Next the 490th bombed bridges, rail lines, road junctions, vehicles and troop concentrations in France. Its B-24s supported ground forces near Caen on 18 July 1944 by eliminating enemy gun emplacements. On 6 August 1944, the 490th flew its last mission as a B-24 Liberator Group and spent the next several weeks converting to B-17 Flying Fortresses. By 27 August 1944, the Group, once again with all four squadrons, resumed strategic bombing with its newly acquired B-17s. Additional missions to support ground forces by bombing harbor defenses near Brest occurred on 3 and 5 September 1944. Thereafter the Group concentrated on strategic targets, especially enemy oil plants, tank factories, marshaling yards, aircraft plants, and airfields.

During the Battle of the Bulge, December 1944 – January 1945, the 490th attacked supply lines and military installations. Missions in February 1945 resumed bombing strategic targets. In March 1945, the Group supported the advancing ground troops and attacked interdictory targets. The 490th flew its last operational mission on 20 April 1945. From 1 May – 6 May 1945, the Group airlifted food to Holland as part of Operation Chowhound. Following V-E Day, the 490th flew a series of Revival Missions from 15 May – 3 June to help evacuate the thousands of American, British, and French servicemen who had been held as prisoners of war by the Germans. During August and September 1945 the 490th returned to the United States and was inactivated on 7 November 1945.

In eleven months of operation from 31 May 1944 through 20 April 1945, the 490th Bombardment Group (H) completed 158 missions with 13,613 tons of bombs loaded and 459,139 rounds of .50 caliber ammunition expended. The Group participated in the Air Offensive, Europe; Normandy; Northern France; Rhineland; Ardennes-Alsace; and Central Europe Campaigns.

T/Sgt. James Lee Hutchinson, Ed.S.

S/Sgt. John Gann's Merseberg Mission

The Lt. Robert Tennenberg crew was the first of our group of replacement crews to fly a mission. They came back to Eye with two wounded men and 1000 flak holes in the bomber. Their experience on that combat mission did not encourage the rest of us, but at least we knew what we faced when our turn came up! John Gann recently gave the story of his first mission.

The target of this November 30, 1944 mission was a synthetic oil plant deep in Germany near Merseberg. The Luena refinery was generally considered one of the toughest targets in Germany with 750 flak guns protecting critical oil supplies. The 490th Bomb Group sent out 36 aircraft, led by our Base 490th Group Commander, Col. Frank P. Bostrom, was the group commander. The sky was clear a problem developed over the target because the group came in on their bomb run from the wrong direction. The mission leader decided to circle about to come in again. Thus, the group was in seventeen minutes of intense flak; the heaviest flak the group had seen. Seventy-five percent of the bombers sustained flak damage, none were lost over the target, but several were forced to land at Allied fields in Belgium or France.

Late in the war many bombers carried enlisted men trained as bombardiers. These men were called "toggliers." They were nose-gunners who operated the Bendix twin .50 caliber machine gun turret installed under the nose of the B-17G bomber. That remote controlled turret could spit out 750 to 1,000 rounds per minute. It was a great weapon against enemy fighters making frontal attacks out of the sun! Toggliers released their bombs when they saw the Lead plane bombs fall. Bombing missions started early in the morning as bombers assembled in group formation at 10,000 feet before flying out over the North Sea. At that time, the togglier entered the bomb-bay to remove a tagged safety cotter-pin from each bomb. The bombs were then "live" and he was required to save the pins in case he might need to use them, otherwise he was to give them to his de-briefing officer when the mission ended. During the long flight, he sat in the bombardier chair behind the bombsight in the plexi-glass nose cone to watch for enemy fighters. The controls for his machine guns in the turret below, swung down from his right any time they were needed. A long belt of 50 caliber shells hung down each side of the nose to the feed those guns.

The togglier opened the bomb-bay doors at the start of the bomb run and got ready to release his bombs. When he saw bombs drop from the lead plane, he then flipped the toggle micro switch which sent an impulse to release the bomb-load. Bombs were often released in salvo. At the beginning of the bomb-run, he fed data (altitude, airspeed, bomb size, etc.) into the intervalometer to set the timing of his bombs release pattern on the target, whether in salvo or spaced at intervals. There was also a mechanical salvo lever at his chair in case of an emergency.

Photo by Scott Maher

This photo shows the Memphis Belle's bombardier seat during the bomb-run. The bombardier also had a desk back on the right and the navigator's desk was on left. The Liberty Belle Foundation tours the nation providing flights and ground tours on this replica of the Memphis Belle.

Norden Bombsight - The top-secret bombsight used by bombardiers in the nose had twenty-four parts, but the two major parts were the stabilizer and the sighthead which was to be guarded at all times. The stabilizer was attached to the plane and connected to the auto-pilot, etc. while the bombardier removed the sighthead from the plane after a mission, stored it safely, protected it at all times and brought it to the plane for each mission. He was authorized to carry a .45 caliber side-arm and shoot anyone messing with the bombsight. The sighthead pivoted and was locked into the stabilizer and connected to the stabilizer and the directional gyro connecting rod and clutch.

Narrative by S/Sgt. John W. Gann, Togglier - "The event in question took place on the 30th of November, 1944. I had been nineteen for six weeks and this was our third mission. We flew our first three missions with pilot Lt. Harry Flook and co-pilot Lt. Joel Johnson because our pilot, Lt. Bob Tennenberg, had broken his foot. I was the nose gunner and togglier who dropped our bombs. Our bomb load was 100 pound bombs and the flak was very heavy. I opened the bomb-bay doors when we reached the target and started our bomb run. For reasons I did not understand, the lead bombardier did not drop his bombs, but instead the group made a big circle and went over the target again and the flak guns were shooting at us all the time. The engineer, Bob Hood, was hit in the right shoulder. He fell out of his top turret and some way he ended up down in my nose area. I put a pressure bandage on him and continued to watch the lead bomber. Then a piece of flak hit our navigator, Lt. Chet Deptula's, steel flak helmet and he dropped to the floor with a head wound. I put him next to Bob Hood. There was nothing more I could do, both boys had lost their oxygen masks and we were at 25,000 feet. I didn't know if they would live or die. Next, a piece of hot flak hit the "G box" on the navigator's desk and started an electrical fire. The nose was soon full of smoke and I had a problem locating the correct fire extinguisher. I put out the fire and hoped for the best, because I had to keep watch on the lead plane. I could tell by the actions of our bomber that some of our bombs had been dropped early as a result of flak hits.

The lead plane dropped their bombs, but when I hit the toggle switch to drop ours, nothing happened. I pulled the mechanical salvo lever but it still did not release our bombs. The radio operator always checked to see if the bomb-bay was clear. This time he was on the inter-com telling us we still had live bombs! We did not want to close the bomb bay doors with armed bombs hanging in there and the drag of the open doors was causing us to lose air speed and fall behind the formation. The pilot, Lt. Flook asked me to look in the bomb-bay to see what I could do. I put on a five minute portable oxygen bottle and climbed up out of the nose. I could not wear my chest-pack parachute in the bomb bay because I had to work from the narrow cat-walk. Some of our bombs had dropped, but the electric release solenoids on others had failed. The temperature was about 40 below zero, but with my heavy gloves I was able to drop all the bombs I could reach by pinching open their shackles. My hardest job was disarming those bombs I could not reach. It was a struggle and I used up several portable oxygen bottles before I managed to re-insert the safety cotter-pins into the bombs still hanging in their shackles.

When we were able to close the bomb bay doors, I went back to the nose, but I never did get oxygen to Hood or Deptula because I couldn't find their oxygen masks. They were two or three hours without oxygen. I have asked myself over the years if there was any more I could have done for them. Our plane caught up with the formation for the long trip home and dropped to a lower altitude over the North Sea.

We neared our base at Eye and our radio operator fired off red flares to show we had wounded aboard. The pilot gave the order to take up crash-landing positions as we went into the landing pattern. The boys in the back braced themselves in the radio room, but I decided to stay in the nose with the two wounded men. I am not sure why, because there was nothing I could do except to encourage them about the landing. When we hit the runway, we had a shot out tire and skidded off the runway and across an open field. I thought we were going to flip over or catch fire for sure. There was lots of snow, dirt and trash coming into the plane and the sunshine coming in made it look like the plane was on fire. The ambulances, fire trucks, etc. were there by the time the plane stopped. The rest of the boys got out of the waist door and stood around smiling. I knew that something happened and they couldn't wait to tell me about it. Ed Miller, our radio operator, the oldest and toughest man on the crew, had panicked when he thought the plane was on fire. He raced to the waist door and tried to get out, but in his haste, he pulled the ripcord on his chute and blocked the door. That caused a real panic in the rear of the plane. That was the finest thing that ever happened for me because I was the "baby" of the crew and Ed Miller was on my case on a regular basis. That event changed the "pecking order" on the crew. From then on, any time Ed said anything to me, I would tell him to be sure and get his parachute for he never knew when he might need it.

We were very lucky to walk away from that crash landing and the heavy flak over Merseberg. I have a copy of the damage report which says Lt. Flook and co-pilot Lt. Joel Johnson counted over 1,000 holes in our plane. I don't see how any of us survived that mission and landing! These things happened 70 years ago and I think I am the only surviving member of my crew. I have tried to forget that Merseberg mission, but I cannot. I have never considered that I was a hero. I always thought that as an American soldier, I should do the best that I could. However, I will go to my grave remembering looking down through the open bomb-bay doors at the snow covered ground and wondering how long it would take me to fall five miles.

John said, "They called me down to headquarters on the day after the mission and said I was going to get a medal. We went down to the flight line to take my photo next to the plane. Well, I never got the medal, but I did get the photo you see in this story!"

Note - *As told by former S/Sgt. John W. Gann, June, 2013*
S/Sgt. John Gann was later wounded but survived a mid-air collision over Germany on his twenty-third mission. See that story in 'The Boys in the B-17.'

Photo provided by Shari Garvin, daughter of Alvin Wilhelm

Lt. Tennenberg crew photo with Ground Crew chief before their mid-air collision. Standing L-R: Unknown, Lt Chester Deptula, navigator; Lt Robert Tennenberg, pilot; Lt Joel Johnson, co-pilot; T/Sgt Ed Miller, radio operator; Sitting L-R: S/Sgt Ray Janise, ball turret gunner; S/Sgt Alvin Wilhelm, tail gunner; S/Sgt John Gann, nose turret gunner/toggleer; S/Sgt Joseph Kennedy, waist gunner; unknown; T/Sgt Joe Poor, engineer/top turret gunner.

T/Sgt. James Lee Hutchinson, Ed.S.

490th BG Photo

The Templeton crew flew the Lead squadron (middle) to hit the Ansbach rail yards on February 22, 1945. This photo was taken after we completed our twelfth mission and earned a second Air Medal. Front row left to right: Sgt. Dwight H. Parrish, waist gunner; T/Sgt Ewing G. Roddy, engineer /top turret; T/Sgt James Lee Hutchinson, radio operator/gunner; S/Sgt Bert Allinder, armorer/ waist gunner. Standing L to R: 1st Lt. Bruno P. Conterato, navigator; 1st Lt William D. Templeton, pilot; 2nd Lt Dale F. Rector, co-pilot. Our tail gunner, S/Sgt Ralph Moore and ball turret gunner, S/Sgt Wilbur Lesh had been assigned to other crews. The Command pilot (mission leader), bombardier and radar operator are not shown.

    The Templeton crew flew eighteen combat missions, fourteen as lead crew and a prime target for fighters and flak! We earned a total of three Air Medals. also did two Mercy missions to Holland after the truce.

Hutch's Missions

I know I was lucky to serve on the B-17G bomber it was the latest of several models and contained all improvements made to the previous E and F models. Gas tanks in the wings held 1,700 gallons of gas to power the four Wright Cyclone 1200 HP radial engines and give the bomber a range of 1,850 miles. Air Crews flew long hours at a 150 to 170 mph cruising speed to hit targets deep in enemy territory. I have made an attempt to keep stories in the same time I was stationed at Eye

Hutch #1 - Berlin, Dec. 5, 1944 - Mission Commander Maj. Cochran; Capt. Gregory, was Deputy Commander. The mission alert came in the afternoon, so we hit the sack early, but our nerves didn't let us get much sleep! The CQ (charge of quarters) woke us up at 2:30 in the morning. The six of us put on our long- johns, electric suits and heavy flight clothing before hiking through the snow to the Mess Hall.

I was a scared nineteen year old plodding through the snow. I had said my prayers and was wearing all my 'lucky charms' for a safe mission. In addition to my GI dog-tags I wore my air cadet ring, a St. Christopher medallion and an ID bracelet. Like so many other men in war, I had an armor-plated New Testament snug in a pocket over my heart. Today's ACLU people would not approve, but I imagine very few of them have faced death in combat! I would soon board a bomber, with high odds that I might have a one-way ticket. I needed God' protection as I joined the brotherhood of young airmen who flew several hundred miles on B-17s to drop bombs on the enemy.

The Mess Hall gave us a great breakfast of bacon, eggs, toast and coffee, enough to last all day. The old-timers at the table laughed and advised us to eat up because it might be our last meal. Sometimes it was! They said a box of 'high energy' candy was all we would have on the plane. The 'old hands' were certain this would be a long mission because we were up so early, maybe Merseburg or Berlin. After breakfast, our crew followed the other guys out to catch a truck ride to the Briefing Room to learn where we were going to face death for the first time!

The scuttlebutt was still flying when the enlisted men of all crews were assembled for briefing. (officers had separate briefing) The room became very quiet as we nervously waited for the news. Our worst fears were confirmed when the briefing officer stepped up on the platform to pull back a long curtain to reveal a giant map of Germany with red thread showing our route to and from the target, which was <u>Berlin!</u> We all groaned when we got this news. Berlin had only been bombed a few times and was one of the most heavily defended areas in Germany. Our first mission was a long way from Eye! The Eighth was going to bomb Berlin for the first time since October, and the Lt. Bill Templeton crew had been invited to the party. We were briefed to expect 300 or more anti-aircraft guns and lots of Luftwaffe fighters. This was a raid on Hitler's capital and our formations would be protected by a large escort of P-51 and P-47 fighters equipped with extra fuel tanks for the long mission. The 490th was going to Berlin with twelve bomb groups, about 500 bombers, to strike technical buildings and labs in the northwest section of Hitler's capitol. However, a second purpose of the mission was to <u>draw up the Luftwaffe fighters for our fighters to destroy</u>. In other words, our bomber formations were fighter bait. To make it worse, we were flying in the rear of the Low squadron. This location was commonly known as the "Tail-end Charlie, "Purple Heart" or "Coffin Corner" position. It was the most dangerous position in a formation, because it did not have the full protection of gunners in other planes and was often the first plane to be picked off by Luftwaffe fighters attacking from the rear. New pilots were often given that position until they proved they could fly in a tight formation.

We were not "happy campers" as we moved on to the parachute hut for a chest pack parachute and harness, then on to the equipment hut before catching a truck ride out to the hardstand where our bomber was parked. A putt-putt generator hummed away to provide electricity in the plane so each man could climb aboard to check out equipment at his position. Ground crews had installed the guns, ammunition, helmets and flak jackets. We had drawn an older B-17G bomber, #44-6490 from the 849th squadron. It was a battle-scarred veteran with several patches from previous flak hits. One look told us that it had survived many missions, but the ground crew assured us she was ready to go, no worry. The officers arrived from their briefings where they received more detailed info about the mission. The pilots started the engines at 6:30, warmed them up and ran through their checklist. I checked out all the radios, got a radio check from the tower, tuned my Liaison transmitter units to assigned frequencies and checked the bomber code cards for the day.

The weatherman gave the OK, they fired a flare from the control tower and the mission was on. The deafening roar of four engines and the trembling plane told us we were ready to go. I said a little prayer as our ground crew gave us a "thumbs up" and we taxied out to line up on the runway where planes were taking off at three minute intervals. Our turn came up and our bomber, loaded with twenty 250 pound GP bombs, ammo and ten men, roared on full power down the runway to gain enough speed and power to lift the fully loaded bomber (64,000 pounds) up and over the trees just past the end of the runway.

On the snowy morning of December 5, 1944, the boys of the Lt. Bill Templeton crew took off on their first and climbed up through the dismal weather to assemble our formation at 12,000 feet on red and yellow flares. Our Bomb Group joined the bomber stream and we were soon over the North Sea and climbing to 25,000 feet before reaching enemy air space over Holland. Our pilot, Bill Templeton gave the order over the intercom:

"Pilot to crew, Pilot to crew --- man your guns, no chatting on the intercom --- keep checking your oxygen mask for icing ---- stay alert for flak or fighters. Call out the location of any plane you see!"

Ralph Moore had already crawled back past the tail wheel to his small space behind his twin tail guns and I saw our waist gunner, Orville Robinson, helping Wilbur Lesh slide down into the ball turret under his .50 caliber machine guns. My radio room in the middle of the plane gave me a good spot to see the guys behind me, but I had no vision of what the guys up ahead of the bomb-bay were doing. We were carrying twenty 250 pound general purpose bombs and headed for technical buildings on the outskirts of Berlin. I knew Lt. Bill Templeton and co-pilot Lt. Dale Rector were fighting the B-17 controls to keep a tight position in the formation. Flight engineer Ewing Roddy would be in the jump seat behind the Co-Pilot until he had to stand in the top turret on lookout for fighters. Down in the nose, Navigator Lt. Bruno Conterato would be at his desk and armorer, Bert Allinder had left his waist gun position and moved to the nose to occupy the Bombardier's seat to be our togglier. Co-pilot Lt. Dale Rector used the intercom to check that all were wearing their oxygen mask, flak jacket, steel flak helmet and had snapped on his chest-pack parachute.

Experienced pilots with Command Pilots aboard were leaders of the three squadrons in the tight box formation which required bombers to fly close together to prevent enemy fighters from diving through the formation. New pilots brought up the rear where they had a little more room to make mistakes. However, they also had less protection from the gunners other planes in the formation.

We were deep into enemy territory when our number three engine developed a problem and began losing power. We were losing air speed and lagging behind the formation. It was a sickening feeling to see the formation gradually pull away from us. It was too late to abort and we would soon be a sitting duck for enemy fighters! Templeton, Rector and Roddy worked like mad to correct the problem. Our only chance was to get that engine running or pray that one our own fighters would appear to escort us back to friendly territory, but there wasn't an escort fighter in sight. Luckily the engine regained power and we finally caught up and took our place in the formation. Later Bill Templeton said he didn't radio for escort fighter help because German fighters might intercept the call and get to us first. That battered war weary B-17 really gave us a real scare!

The 490th formation reached the Initial Point (IP) and because we were in the rear, it was my job to reel out my trailing wire radio antenna, (a long cable with an iron ball on the end) to send that information back to Eye. The formation started on the twenty mile bomb run to the target. It was our crew's first flight into a sky full of anti-aircraft fire with black smoke from the bursting 88 mm shells. We knew those flak shells were spewing thousands of jagged pieces of iron into the sky, like a shotgun shell shoots buckshot at a rabbit, only this time we were the rabbit! Our plane shook from close explosions, one right below us, and flak shrapnel hit our plane. Robinson and I had started feeding bundles of chaff into the chute two minutes before we reached the IP and he kept at it while I sent my IP report. The bundles of chaff separated into hundreds of 10 inch square aluminum sheets floating in the sky to mess up radar on the flak guns below. We threw out 336 bundles in 21 minutes. (I still have a sheet of chaff)

Pilots could not take evasive action to avoid flak during a bomb run. The bombardier used the auto-pilot to keep the bomber on a straight and level course to use his Norden bombsight correctly. The formation's B-17 opened bomb-bay doors and followed squadron leaders into the flak to drop their bombs. We bombed through clouds with the PFF radar dome and we did not see the results. After bombs away planes closed their bomb-bay doors and turned to the 'rally point,' tighten the formation and prepare for fighter attacks as they headed for England. I saw one Fortress peel off out of the High formation. Later reports said it was the Lt. Donald J. Kermode plane, the Lead of the High squadron, Capt Ralph E. Gregory was with them as Squadron leader.

The next day a Stars and Stripes article reported that Eighth bombers also blasted a big munitions plant northwest of Berlin. Dozens of Luftwaffe fighters came up after us as we left the target area and regrouped, but thank heavens they were intercepted by our escort fighters of more than 800 of our P-51 Mustang and P-47 Thunderbolt fighters. Bomber crews witnessed a terrific series of dogfights our and tail gunner, Ralph Moore, had a front row seat for all the action as we headed for England. He said it was an amazing series of diving and twisting fighters in dog-fights all over the sky behind us and he saw many planes go down in flames. Our mission had lured the Luftwaffe fighters into the range of our escorts fighters from the 357th, 479th and 355th Fighter Groups. The next day Stars and Stripes headlines reported that U.S. fighters shot down 80 German fighters. The Luftwaffe had suffered heavy losses which could not be replaced. Hitler was running out of fighter planes and experienced pilots. The Eighth lost 12 bombers and 22 fighters on this raid, but the Allies were on the way to gaining air superiority.

Our crew had an action-packed introduction to bombing missions over Germany! We landed at 3:30 p.m. and cleaned the machine guns, checked-in our chest pack parachutes and flight equipment and hitched a ride to the briefing room. The Templeton crew had survived its first mission --- only thirty-four more to go! The poor performance of our bomber on that day taught our pilots the importance of making sure that in the future we had a plane that could get us to the target and back. We didn't need another scare like the Berlin trip!

The de-briefing (interrogation) session was a welcome-home meeting where we were asked questions about anything we had seen on the mission (where we saw flak or fighters etc.) The Red Cross girls provided cookies and coffee. A shot of scotch was also available to help us relax. Sometimes guys managed to mooch several shots from non-drinkers and get so "relaxed" they could barely walk! The trip to the Mess Hall was a treat because we hadn't eaten since that early breakfast so many hours ago. Hut #29 was a welcome sight and we were happy to crawl into the bunks we had vacated fifteen hours ago.

B-17 MEMORIES

"Sack time was a precious necessity after a long mission!"

900 Heavies Hit Berlin, Hanover Plants

The 8th Air Force aimed twin blows yesterday at Germany's inner circle of war industry and what may be its last remaining industrial trump card when over 400 Fortresses bombed war plants in suburban Berlin and more than 500 ranged over Hanover to hit factories and railroad marshalling yards.

Significantly, ack-ack gunners in Berlin and Hanover yesterday threw up a stiff umbrella of flak, indicating that the Nazis, in expectation of savage attacks yet to come, may not yet have stripped their vital industries in central Germany.

Some fliers over Berlin, where tank, armored vehicle and weapons factories were attacked, reported particularly heavy barrages of ack-ack fire, besides thick clouds, which made bombing by instrument necessary in most cases. Clouds also covered Hanover, where the targets included plants making half-tracks and other armored vehicles.

Some 350 Mustangs shielded the bombers yesterday, but ran into no enemy fighters, a further gauge of the effectiveness of the 8th's and the 15th Air Force's recent saturation assaults on German airfields and plane factories.

Death Brings Fliers Top Awards

452ND BOMB GROUP, May 14—1/Lt. Donald J. Gott, 21-year-old Fortress pilot from Arnett, Okla., and 2/Lt. William E. Metzger, 22-year-old co-pilot from Lima, Ohio, who gave their lives in an unsuccessful attempt to save the life of a fellow-crewman, have been posthumously awarded the Congressional Medal of Honor, highest U.S. decoration.

Last Nov. 9 their Fortress Lady Jeannette was ripped by flak while over the target, a railroad yard at Saarbrucken, Germany. Two engines were set afire and disabled, a third damaged, and the plane's interphone and electrical systems destroyed.

Losing altitude rapidly and fully ablaze after being hit at low level by more German ack-ack, the Fort managed to get over friendly territory. With an emergency landing field in sight, Lady Jeannette slowly circled the clearing, but, when only whose sake they had remained with the bomber.

Fort Navigator Wins Congressional Medal

WASHINGTON, May 14 (ANS)—The Congressional Medal of Honor has been awarded posthumously to 2/Lt. Robert E. Femoyer, an 8th Air Force navigator of Huntington, W.Va., who, although mortally wounded, brought his Fortress safely back to its base, it was announced today.

Femoyer, assigned to the 447th Bomb Gp. (H), died last Nov. 2, shortly after his crippled B17 landed on its return from a raid near Merseburg, Germany. When three anti-aircraft shells struck the plane, wounding the navigator in the side and back, he refused morphine injections and remained for two and one-half hours

In the 490th Historical record, Navigator, Lt. Jule F. Brendt of the Lt. Rolland Peacock crew of squadron 850 told of the High squadron break-up: "Just a few minutes after bombs away the lead ship of the high squadron broke from the formation with a feathered engine and part of the squadron followed him while the rest followed the plane of the deputy leader. This split the squadron and we lost valuable time trying to reassemble. We were in the dangerous situation of lagging several miles behind the formation which could have been fatal, but for the protection of our fighters as we poured on every bit of power in our engines in an attempt to catch up. I was busy throwing out chaff and I didn't know about the break-up of the high squadron. I'm sure all pilots knew the situation and were glad when the high squadron caught up to regain its position and tighten the formation. Meantime dozens of Luftwaffe fighters came up to attack, but were intercepted by our escort fighters. Our plane had only four flak holes; two in a wing, one in the nacelle of engine # 3 and one in the nose.

Hutch - Lutzkendorf (Aborted) Dec. 6 - This was the second day we were alerted for another mission; arose at 3:30 and repeated the previous day's procedures. Once again the new kids were assigned an old bomber, #135-B from the 849th squadron. We hoped it would be in better condition than the last one. The target was a tough one, a synthetic oil plant heavily protected by flak and fighters. Only twelve of our 490th bombers were sent up to assemble with another group. **T**ake off was 8:53, we assembled and started for Germany in the Low squadron again with a bomb-load of twenty 250 pounders. Out over the North Sea, our luck turned sour when that old plane developed mechanical problems with the number four engine. The pilots decided to abort and we returned to base at 12:15. In the summer of 2013, I asked our engineer, Ewing Roddy if he remembered that aborted mission.

Rod was quick to respond,

"Heck yes I still remember. All four engines were running perfect during the hour or so we spent in assembly over England, but engine number four started losing power shortly after we left the coast. The pilot and co-pilot didn't have much time to decide to abort (turn back) before we were in enemy territory. They tried to get more power and I went through every item on my trouble-shoot chart. I was on my knees checking the generators when they decided the problem could not be corrected. Both Lt. Templeton and co-pilot Lt. Rector decided to "abort" the mission. They stressed the fact that it was a joint decision and asked if I agreed. I had heard aborting a mission was almost an act of desertion, but I didn't think that engine was going to run right. Of course I agreed, but I wondered why that was so important until I saw the "welcoming committee" waiting for the pilots when we landed. As soon as we dropped down out of the nose hatch, two MPs (military police) escorted the pilots over to a mad Major sitting in a jeep. That guy was all over Templeton and Rector about why they turned back. I couldn't hear much of it, but they really caught hell for a while. I was sure glad that Major didn't come after me."

Note - *An unnecessary abortion was a definite strike against future promotions for pilots, but when mechanics checked the engine, they verified that our pilots had made the right decision. Three hours was more than enough time to fly in that bucket of bolts. As far as our crew members were concerned, our pilots had learned a valuable lesson on the first mission and we were glad they had the guts to abort!*

Eyes of the Bomber

My radio desk was in the middle of the plane on the left behind the bomb-bay with small windows on each side and a plexi-glass escape hatch overhead. I often envied the ball turret gunner's view while hanging under the plane, but never enough to change with him. The guys up in the nose "greenhouse" saw all in front and below. The Pilot and co-pilot had a 180 degree view while the engineer in the top turret and the engineer could rotate his top turret for a 360 degree view of the sky. It paid to keep a close watch while flying in a tight formation. Pilot error, inclement weather or prop wash caused more than one mid-air collision.

T/Sgt. James Lee Hutchinson, Ed.S.

CREW POSITIONS ON THE B-17

FLYING FORTRESS

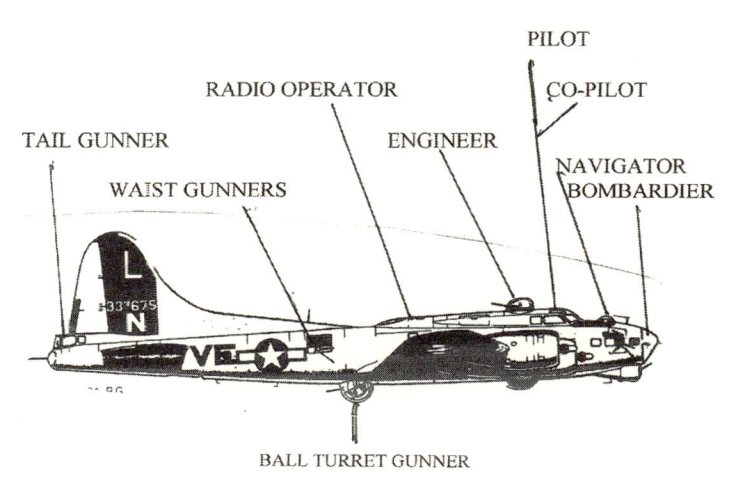

PILOT
RADIO OPERATOR
CO-PILOT
TAIL GUNNER
ENGINEER
NAVIGATOR
WAIST GUNNERS
BOMBARDIER

BALL TURRET GUNNER

Of our tail gunner had a great view to watch for trouble behind us. We searched the sky for Luftwaffe fighters at all times over enemy territory. Standard procedure was to imagine our plane was the center of a giant horizontal clock dial. Twelve o'clock was straight ahead three o'clock was on our right. Six o'clock area was the tail and my best view was at nine o'clock out my left window. I also had a great view of the sky above out the top hatch. We used the inter-com to report any sighting of any planes and used our "aircraft recognition classes" knowledge to determine if they were "bandits" or "Little Friends" who escorted our formation. Those aircraft recognition classes in gunnery school really paid off in combat when our lives depended on our ability to tell friend from foe!

Hutch # 2 – Hannover, Dec. 15 - Take-off was 8:50 – landed at 5:00 – our target was railroad marshalling yards. Snowstorms and fog had kept. Weather conditions were still bad, but we had 39 planes up today. The mission commander was Maj. Blum and Capt. Martin was deputy. Our crew was assigned to the Low squadron this time and our bomb-load was ten 500 pounder GPs and two M17s incendiary bundles. We were one of the chaff ships again and my radio room was crowded with boxes of chaff to toss out during the bomb-run to the target. Waist gunner Orville Robinson and I got rid of almost 300 bundles during the twelve minute bomb-run. We bombed by PFF (radar) at 25,000 feet. Hannover was in the center of north Germany and much closer than Berlin. The mission was five hours and 45 minutes and we were on oxygen four hours. The flak was moderate but we saw several rockets.

The next day's issue of the Stars and Stripes reported that the Eighth Air Force sent up 650 Flying Fortresses, escorted by 550 Mustang P-51 and P-47 Thunderbolt P-47 fighters, to hit rails and industrial plants. Fifteenth Air Force B-24 Liberators based in Italy pounded those targets in southern Germany and RAF bombers continued bombing every night the weather allowed. The Allied plan of bombing critical German targets 'around the clock' was in full force and ground troops were advancing.

Hutch # 3 – Stuttgart, Dec. 16 - We took off at 8:33 carrying the same bomb-load as yesterday, ten 500 pounders and two clusters of incendiary bombs. Our target was the Stuttgart rail yards in the Ruhr Valley; it was definitely going to be a tough mission. Maj. Gell and Capt. Martin led this mission of 36 bombers. Weather almost cancelled us out, but we climbed up through the overcast, joined the formation and hit the coast over Belgium. We had a few alerts of Luftwaffe fighters "bandits" in the area but saw none. The flak was light but accurate. We flew over the Ardennes area in Belgium on the way home, but had no idea this was the day Hitler had launched a massive full scale attack on our troops. The Battle of the Bulge was raging below us and our Army GIs were fighting desperately against overwhelming odds. The bad weather was closing in on us, so Major Gell decided we would drop down and go in under the clouds. Our formation did some low-level flying over the English Channel and landed safely at the Brome Dome. We had no holes in the plane when we landed at 4:16 after a flight of over seven hours; four of which were at 21,000 feet on oxygen.

December 16, all U.S. and RAF planes were grounded by heavy snows and bad flying weather. American troops were in deep trouble, but Allied bombers and fighters were prevented from supporting our men on the ground. December 22, 1944, we stepped out of the mess hall after breakfast, but the lead-colored sky showed no sign of clearing. In fact, there was the threat of another snowstorm. Our planes had now been grounded for five days. Ground crews continued working to clear the snow off the runways in case the weather cleared enough for a mission. The mechanics on the flight line said visibility was so bad that the pigeons were walking!

Meanwhile, Hitler's armies had launched a massive counter-attack. On the morning of December 16th, they broke through Allied lines along an eighty mile front. That area was protected by only six American divisions. In a short, time Hitler's twenty-eight German divisions, ten of which were Panzer Tiger tank units, re-captured much territory and created a large bulge in Allied battle lines. The Germans used captured American equipment and English speaking German soldiers in American uniforms to create havoc by changing road signs and giving false directions to American ground troops. Our troops desperately needed reinforcements and air support from bombers and fighters. Good weather was needed before Ninth Air Corps tactical bombers and fighters could fly to take out enemy artillery, tanks, supply trains and strafe German troops and convoys. The heavy bombers of the Eighth and Royal Air Force (RAF) could not fly to bomb train yards, oil dumps and railroad yards to prevent fuel and ammunition from reaching the German forces. But the weather was not cooperating visibility was near zero and Allied planes could not fly. The wintry weather was aiding the enemy.

The skies cleared on December 23rd and thousands of Allied planes flew missions day and night through January 16th to destroy all supply lines to German troops

Note - *Pvt. John Hill, from my area of Southern Indiana, joined the Ninth Division with a group of replacement troops just before the Battle of the Bulge. It was about the same time I came to Eye. I am fascinated by his combat experiences in the infantry while I was flying overhead. In an interview in the summer of 1212, John said he still remembers thousands of aircraft roaring overhead as he slogged through the snow and mud with a mortar crew of the 9th Division.*

Chapter Four

Hutch # 4 - **Frankfort on Christmas Eve** - Our bomb-load was thirty eight 100 pounders. Major Cochran was mission Commander, Capt. Wesson, Deputy Command and we flew Tail-end Charlie again In the High squadron. What a great Christmas Eve! The snowy weather was still with us and almost kept us taking off. We were up at 4:00am briefed at 5:30 and sat on the plane for two hours waiting for the weatherman to give us the OK. We didn't take off until 9:52 and returned at 6:11. Our target was a Luftwaffe airfield at Frankfurt in central Germany. We threw out chaff at two different places, once when we crossed the enemy lines in Belgium and again as we started the bomb-run at the IP (initial point). We bombed from 21,000 feet, caught the German fighters on the runway and plastered them with our load of thirty-eight 100 pounders. It was a very good strike! Flak was not heavy but we saw several rockets. Tail gunner, Ralph Moore, reported sighting jet fighters, but we had a good fighter escort so they chose other prey. This was the biggest mission ever launched by the Eighth. They sent up every airworthy bomber; as the ground crew said "Everything that had wings." The 490th sent out all four squadrons (50 planes) on this mission. By the time we returned to Eye, it was dark. We landed first, but after equipment check in and de-briefing it was late before we got to the Mess hall for a long awaited supper! We got back to Hut 29, built up the fire and crawled into our sacks about 8:00pm; happy that we had delivered Hitler's Christmas presents. Later the Crew Chief said we only had two holes in the plane but one was a big one in the tip of the left wing. I'm happy to say that our Lt. Bill Templeton crew went on to fly the Lead position on six of the thirteen 490th missions to support our ground troops in the Battle of the Bulge in December, 1944!

T/Sgt. James Lee Hutchinson, Ed.S.

There were only nine days out of the next twenty-seven that our 490th bombers were unable to fly to assist ground forces in pushing back Germany's last-ditch gamble to win the war. The Stars and Stripes reported that it was the biggest Eighth Air Force mission to that date. It was Christmas Eve, and the Mighty Eighth presented German targets with tons of bombs. The bad weather had broken at last and the Air Force could fly again. Our job was to continue pounding German targets to provide support for American forces at Bastogne!

Eighth Air force B-17 and B-24 bombers hit strategic targets all over Germany, while fighters and medium bombers strafed enemy troops, trains and supply convoys behind the German front. Over 2000 B-17 Flying Fortresses, B-24 Liberators and 900 escort fighters bombed airfields, communication centers, bridges and railroads to prevent German supplies and troops from reinforcing their position. Bombers were still taking off from England when the first groups were bombing their targets! I remember bombing our target and meeting bomber formations heading for Germany, as we were going home to England! Allied fighter escorts shot down seventy-six Luftwaffe fighters. The fighter planes and light bombers like the B-25 Mitchells and B-26 Marauders of the Ninth Air Force were flying low and blasting tanks, trucks, V-2 rockets and V-1 buzz bombs launching sites and railroad cars to hamstring German troops. The tactical bombers flew 1,175 missions in support of Allied ground forces. They destroyed 116 Nazi tanks, 778 armored vehicles and 56 railroad cars, according to reports in the Stars and Stripes. They also knocked out a major fuel dump and two important bridges. This Allied aerial offensive continued for three days, and the Eighth and Ninth Air Forces took out 218 Luftwaffe fighters in aerial combat while losing 38 bombers and 40 fighters. Eight of the eleven German airdromes attacked were put out of service. The cost was high but the offensive drive resulted in a greatly weakened Germany.

By mid January, Allied ground forces were advancing, and the Eighth Air Force was able to bomb visually because of better weather. Hitler's counter-offensive in Belgium was defeated by superior forces and a shortage of fuel for his tanks, armored vehicles and trucks. German troops had planned to capture Allied fuel supplies but failed and were forced to retreat. It was reported that some abandoned their vehicles as they were forced back across the Rhine to defend the Fatherland. The Eighth Air Force had flown through snow and bad weather to bomb those German oil dumps, marshalling yards and bridges to end Hitler's last big effort. The Templeton crew had flown four missions before Christmas.

GENERAL CASTLE'S MEDAL OF HONOR

Brigadier General Frederick Castle, the newly appointed commander of the Fourth Bomb Wing, was leading the Third Division on Christmas Eve. He was the command pilot in the pathfinder lead plane *"Treble Four"* of the 836th squadron of the 487th Bomb Group from Lavenham. He was leading the largest raid launched by the Mighty Eighth to that date. The mission of 2,046 bombers and 853 fighters was to bomb eleven German airfields, major communication centers, bridges and railroad yards west of the Rhine to prevent German troops and supplies from reaching the Battle of the Bulge area in Belgium. The 487th Bomb Group's target was the airfield at Babenhausen, Germany.

General Castle's B-17 developed a motor problem over Belgium and couldn't maintain enough speed to keep the Lead position. He could have dropped his 9,000 pound bomb-load to give his plane more power. However, they were flying over our front lines and he refused to drop his bombs on the American troops below. He dropped out of his lead position and lagged behind. The Luftwaffe knew that clear weather would bring the Mighty Eighth bombers to relieve the troops in the Bulge. German ME-109 and FW-190 fighters attacked the first formation (487th) near Liege, Belgium. The General's formation had no fighter protection because this was about 15-20 minutes before they were to rendezvous with their escort fighters. The Low squadron was attacked by ME-109 fighters. Later reports said German fighters shot out at least two engines on *"Treble Four"* and set the plane on fire. The

Flying Fortress was in danger of exploding when General Castle gave the bail-out order and remained at the controls to keep the doomed plane level until it went into a spin. The 487th formation and the Eighth bomber stream flew on to blast critical targets. Fifty-six bombers and over 500 airmen were lost on Christmas Eve, but the massive mission helped defeat Hitler's last major offensive of the war.

Brigadier General Frederick Walker Castle was awarded the Congressional Medal of Honor posthumously. He was the highest ranking officer and the last of seventeen Eighth Air Force members to receive the Medal of Honor. General Castle was buried in the American Cemetery at Henri-Chappelle, near Leige, Belgium; not far from the site of his crash on that cold Christmas Eve.

490ᵀᴴ BG December Report:

In East Anglia it rarely snows and some of the English found it hard to remember when they did have snow. This year snow and hoarfrost arrived with a vengeance and stayed all month. They base at Eye reminded many of New England snow scenes back home. Despite the weather the group managed to fly thirteen missions. The Battle of the Bulge developed in the latter half of the month and this threat had to be stopped. So the 490th flew in weather as bad as any of the locals could remember, to play our part in the counter-offensive. Much of the bombing was done by radar (PFF) for solid cloud coverage prevailed over Germany most of the month. December 5, the group bombed Berlin. There was considerable flak and the lead plane of the high squadron was severely hit. It was manned by Lt. Donald J. Kermode and Capt. Ralph E. Gregory was flying with them as command pilot and Squadron Leader. The seriously damaged plane fell behind the formation on the way home, near Dummer Lake, it was jumped by about thirty Focke- Wolfe-190 fighters and was seen to crash.

Some of the targets were bombed visually, such as Suttgart, Frankfort and Misburg. POW interrogations later revealed that on the Frankfort mission we had caught a squadron of German fighters about to take off to strike at our ground forces and completely ruined their plans. The group's second raid on Misburg had the same results as our B-24 raid back in June. The oil refinery was hit again and went up in smoke and flames. Maj. Cochran led the group with Capt. Martin and Capt. Valentine as squadron leaders. Credit for the bombing went to the lead crews of Lt. Evans and Lt. Cleaves. During the month Maj. Hoyt was relieved as Group Intelligence Officer and Capt. Reynard of the 848th squadron took over his duties.

Flak leave was enjoyed by many crews this month. A week off at a Red Cross flak shack was given to crews in need of Rest and Relaxation. R&R leave gave crew members a chance to forget the war and indulge in whatever pleased them most; hobbies – athletics – parties or just plain sleeping the week away in a comfortable bed. Ground crews were also given leaves to discover some of the things they had in common with our British allies. However, a curious mixture of beers called "mild and bitters" was not one of those things.

The third week the spirit of Christmas spread throughout the base as many packages arrived from the states. The Special services section and base Red Cross girls got together and planned a real Christmas party for the children of Eye and surrounding villages. The guys on the base contributed part of their PX rations in preparation for the gala event. The party was complete with a Santa Claus, movies, a fine Christmas tree and all the refreshments the young guests could eat. The children were thrilled beyond words and seeing their happiness was a morale booster for the enlisted men and officers. Many of whom had just flown in the Eighth Air Force's biggest mission of the war on Christmas Eve.

The base had other visitors for Christmas Eve when a bomb group from the First Air Division had found their base fog-bound after returning from a mission and had to divert to Eye. Extra beds were placed in all huts and the Officers' Lounge was full to overflowing. The 490th personnel felt sorry for them: spending Christmas away from home was bad enough, but spending it away from their own base without a change of clothing and the comfort of their own bed was really disheartening.

T/Sgt. James Lee Hutchinson, Ed.S.

Promoted to Lead Crew

The daytime strategic bombing ability of the Eighth Air Force was greatly improved when the PFF radar (Mickey) equipment was made available to our planes. The radar dome replaced the ball turret under the B-17G on lead planes. A radar officer replaced our ball turret gunner. This "Mickey" operator was seated across the aisle from me in the radio room. He operated the radar equipment with the aid of radar maps made from actual photos of German targets taken by USAAF planes. The Air Corps could now bomb through the clouds without seeing the targets! This made it possible to carry out more bombing missions in overcast skies when the target was invisible. This also meant more dangerous flying for the Flying Fortresses that took off and flew up through that "pea soup" and snow storms to rendezvous with the group over the channel and head for Germany to bomb through the clouds. Lead planes were equipped with a PFF (Pathfinder Force) radar domes which replaced the ball turrets. The PFF radar could penetrate clouds and pick out the target city outline of concrete and steel. The dome could be lowered when we neared the target and retracted for landing.

Switching to a squadron lead ship after four missions was a feather in our cap, but it also re-arranged the make-up of our crew. The average bomber carried a crew of four officers and six enlisted men. The formation was made up of three squadrons and each lead plane carried a command pilot, navigator, bombardier and radar (Mickey) operator. A lead crew's four enlisted men were engineer gunner, radio operator and two waist gunners.

Pilot Bill Templeton was joined in the cockpit by a "command pilot" and Co-pilot, Lt. Dale Rector, took the tail gunner position with the title of squadron gunnery fire control officer. He was also to report to the command pilot of any looseness or problems of planes maintaining a tight formation; Bruno Conterato, our original navigator remained with the crew for a while before being named a lead navigator. Operations officers assigned a lead bombardier and a Mickey (radar) operator for each mission. Our toggler, Bert Allinder returned to his waist gun position with Orville "Robby" Robinson, Ewing "Rod" Roddy was flight engineer and top turret gunner, and I monitored the radio in case of messages from the base. Tail gunner, Ralph Moore, and ball turret gunner, Wilbur Lesh, were taken off our crew and reassigned to the 490th Bomb Group gunnery pool to fly as substitute gunners until assigned to another crew. Flying lead plane position was an honor, but it also had a downside. As in all wars, the primary plan was to kill the enemy's leaders and win the battle. The lead planes carried the squadron or group commanders, therefore were now a more important target of flak and Luftwaffe fighters seeking to break up our formations. However, I liked the battle plan of the Army Air Corps. Everyone from Buck Sergeant gunners to high-ranking Staff officers and Group Commanders flew combat missions. Brig. Gen. Nathan Bedford Forrest and Brig. Gen. Frederick Castle died on combat missions. There were none of those pep talks saying, "Wish I could go with you boys, but I am needed here at the base." Everyone knew what B-17 bombing raids required of the crews who flew long hours through the flak and fighters. Everybody was in the same situation and rank was not so important as long as we did our jobs to the best of our abilities. Our group commanders had flown many missions. One guy said it best, "If you survive, you get promoted!" Our crew's goal was to fly safely and complete thirty-five missions alive!

Note - *Ralph Moore completed his missions and remained in the Air Force until his retirement. Wilbur Lesh became an ECM (electrical jammer) operator on another crew. He operated equipment to disrupt enemy radio and radar. His bomber was shot down and he and eight others were captured and killed by SS troops on the 490th mission to Prague, Czechoslovakia on April 19, 1945. It was the 490th's next to last mission. After his death, we learned that Wilbur had been volunteering for extra missions in order to finish his tour of duty and return to his wife, a beautiful girl we met briefly before leaving Sioux City.*

Test Flights - As a lead crew, the make-up of Lt. Bill Templeton's lead crew was just the reverse of a regular B-17 combat crew. We now had only four enlisted men aboard and six officers. My job as lead plane radio operator had suddenly become more important. We also spent many hours in test flights of lead planes. All equipment on lead planes needed to be in perfect shape. I remember when Templeton and Rector would put the plane in a 'stall' to check the engines. They would get up to top speed then put the B-17 into a steep climb until it shook like a wet dog! I was always relieved when they dropped the nose and the 'stall' ended! Then there was the time we flew under a large bridge up in Scotland! I don't know what test that was, maybe just nerves. However we did a lot off sightseeing over places like the Canterbury Cathedral, Cambridge, Oxford and Stratford-on-the-Avon. One of our most hazardous test flights happened over Scotland when # 1 engine conked out. We headed for home and the # 3 engine went out with oil was streaming across the wing. Templeton told us to be ready to bail out if it caught fire. I snapped on my chest-pack chute and joined the guys at the waist door. We finished the flight near the door with eyes glued on engine # 3.

Hutch # 5 - Bad Kreuznach, Jan. 2, 1945 - Take off: 7:36 and landed 2:36 Bomb-load of ten 500 GPs + 2M17s The 490th flew as deputy lead for the 3rd Division today. Col. Good was mission commander and Maj. Gell deputy.Our crew was a PFF ship in the Lead squadron and Lt. Dale Rector was co-pilot. Lt. Robert P. Russell was our bombardier, Lt. Oliver was Mickey operator again and we had our own navigator, Lt. Bruno Conterato. New Years Day had been a day off, but today it was back to work. The battle in Belgium's Ardennes Mountains was in full force and the Eighth needed to bomb critical targets to stop Hitler's supplies and reinforcements. The runway had been cleared by ground crews working all night to move the snow. This was our first mission of flying a lead crew B-17 with a PFF radar dome in place of the ball turret and sadly, it was our first mission without ball turret gunner Wilbur Lesh and tail-gunner Ralph Moore. Our target was at Bad-Kreuznach, a small town in western Germany, but an important bridge and railway junction for the enemy. The sky cleared and we were able to bomb visually. The Norden bombsight had again proven effective. The majority of the planes in our formation carried toggliers who released their plane's bombs when our lead bombardier dropped his. We were "pattern bombing" the target. We were also the camera ship, a camera to record bombing results was mounted in a compartment in the floor of the radio room. Luckily the sky was clear and we hit the target, better yet we had pictures to prove it! The 490th BG received an "excellent" rating for the raid which knocked out the railroad junction and the flow of German troops and equipment to the front.

Hutch # 6 – Aschaffenburg, Jan. 3 - The CQ (charge of quarters) rousted us out of our sacks at 3:15, briefed at 4:00 and took off at 7:30. We landed at 3:45. Another eight hour mission (three and a half on oxygen.) The Battle of the Bulge was still a toss-up and this time our target was a railroad yard at Aschaffenburg in southeast Germany. The previous day's raid on Bad Kreuznach's railroad junction had completely destroyed it and was another blockade to stop German military transportation of men and equipment to the front. That raid had earned another excellent rating for the Bomb Group and we were trying to duplicate it. Once we formed our group over England, we crossed the channel into liberated French territory and climbed to the specified height for the bombing mission. I was required to send back radio reports as our group passed certain checkpoints on our designated route to the target. More importantly, I had to keep those headsets on and monitor the assigned frequencies in case there were messages from our base in England.

This mission of 38 planes was led by Col. Good. It was our first mission with our co-pilot riding as tail gunner and squadron fire control officer. We were lead crew of the Lead squadron today with Capt. Earlin Brunkin as Command pilot; Lt. Robert P. Russell was bombardier; our own Lt. Bruno Conterrato as navigator and the Mickey (PFF) operator was Lt. Oliver. Our bomb-load was ten 500 pounders and two M17 incendiaries (fire bombs.) We bombed P.F.F. through the clouds to get the marshalling yard. The Command Pilot gave me information to send in a "strike report" back to Eye as we headed home. The mission was a "milk run" (easy mission) if there ever was one. We didn't see flak at all and only two rockets. However, combat fatigue hit us and we were really beat after two long high altitude missions on oxygen at 40 below zero (many crews flew three in a row). We were looking forward to a break and a lot of extra of sack time. We were really starting the New Year right this was our second mission in a row. This was our sixth mission, which earned us the Air Medal. It was presented later by our commanding officer Colonel Frank P. Bostrom at a base parade formation. Today, I have my Air Medal with two oak leaf clusters, Good Conduct and three campaign medals with my gunner and crewmember wings in a special display case hanging by my fireplace. The Air Medal was special, because many boys were wounded, prisoners of war or killed before they completed six missions.

Mid-Air Collision   Jan. 5

Thirteen replacement crews were assigned to our group in late December and they were as welcome as the flowers in May. However, these crews had only flown B-24 Liberators in their combat crew training in the states! Switching to the B-17 was a big challenge. They were allowed a few hours flying time to get acquainted with the Flying Fortress, but the final phase of the switch-over was learning to fly the tight box formations used on combat missions.

January 6th was the day selected for that event. Skeleton crews of combat veterans were selected to fly with the new crews as instructors. An experienced pilot, co-pilot, navigator, bombardier, engineer and radio operator was assigned to each of the thirteen bombers to help the new skeleton crew adapt to the B-17.

The weather cleared and thirteen B-17s roared down the runway and lifted into the skies in mid-morning. I hooked my chest-pack parachute to my harness and advised the trainee operator to do the same. The Assembly went fairly well and the formation with new crews formed up at 25,000 feet. The lessons began but the new pilots were doing a lot of dipping and dropping in and out of the formation. They seemed determined to show off their flying skills to their instructors. Lt. Bill

Templeton warned us to be alert, call out the location of planes too near and keep the intercom clear for emergency warnings. We were in the High group and didn't have to watch for a bomber dropping down from above, only those in our element or under us. The High and Low squadrons were 1000 feet above and/or below the Lead (middle) squadron in a close formation. I explained the radio equipment and mission procedures to the trainee who was seated at the radio desk. I was glad to be standing so I could watch for planes getting too close through the plexi-glass roof and side windows. It soon became evident that the new pilots were going to need a lot of coaching. They were very reckless in flying in and out of formation. A tight box formation was the best protection against fighter attack. The new pilots had to master this skill because they would soon be flying missions in our formations! The practice was completed after a few hours, the formation headed back to Eye. We were almost home when the deadly collision happened. I had stayed on watch on the trip home and saw the collision below and to our right. An aircraft stacked in the middle formation lost altitude and dropped down on top of a plane below. The lower bomber was cut in half but three of its crew parachuted to safety before both planes fell out of the sky near Bury St. Edmunds only twenty minutes from Eye.

T/Sgt Roger Coryell, radio operator of the 851st squadron Lt. Roy White crew and veteran of 34 missions, was not in either of the colliding aircraft, but like me, he was assigned to be an instructor we witnessed the collision because of our position in the formation. In the <u>Historical Record of the 490th Bomb Group H</u> wrote, Coryell said, it was my job to check-out their radio operator on United Kingdom radio procedures. I met the new crew and "instructors" at the plane -------- as soon as we were sure the mission was not going to be "scrubbed because of snow I got into the plane with the radio operator and started to show him how to tune the radio transmitter then branched out to a few things I had learned. I showed him how to hitch the "push- to- talk" button of his interphone so that he could still get at it while he was throwing out chaff on the bomb-run. ------- We tuned in to the 3rd Division frequency and listened to them sending to the mission that was out that day and then we shifted over to the local base frequency ---- I wasn't paying much attention to the planes in the formation until somebody up front said, 'Hey, watch this guy above you, he's kinda close.' I looked up and believe me he was too close. The ball turret of that plane was only about 15 feet above the plexi-glass hatch in the ceiling of my radio room! ---- I had assumed things were running smoothly with the instructor pilots in charge, but after that bomber scared us, I decided to take a longer look outside and saw the other two squadrons above me – I was in the number two ship of the lowest element."

T/Sgt. Coryell had a good view of the formation above and saw the reckless flying of bombers sliding in and out of the formation. He said he saw four near collisions in less than a minute so he stopped giving instructions and told the radio trainee to watch out the window while he watched through the top hatch.

Coryell said, "One of the objectives of this training exercise was to teach these guys how to fly our type of formation and how to open up and close in before and after a bombing run.----- They were also to practice flying a B-17 in a "stacked formation" for the first time. At one point we made three separate simulated bomb-runs. They all scared me because every one of them gave these junior birdmen a fresh chance to kill us all. Somehow we made it through. The boys were even being to fy pretty well and I was beginning to relax as we headed back to Eye. Then suddenly----- through the top hatch, I saw a bomber sliding past us from above. He was coming down fast. I called him out to pilot---got no answer and still the plane kept coming down. I began reaching for my parachute and then at last we dived—our pilot had seen him. It was about time, because that plane was about twenty feet above us when we <u>dived out of danger and out of the formation!</u> We even left the lead ship of our element! The trip home was made with a little more care by a bunch of 'jumpy' pilots, not to mention one jumpy radio instructor. I sweated out the procedure of landing right until we came to a stop and when it finally did, I blew my top heaping all the vile words I knew on the heads of those hadn't the sense to realize the danger they had placed us in.

We were lining up again in preparation to shoot some more landings when suddenly the instructor Navigator came charging through the radio room on his way out. I asked him if he was leaving. "Hell yes!" he replied, so we both got out as fast as we could, leaving our stuff on the plane to be picked up later"

Note - *My thoughts and actions were a lot like those of Sgt. Coryell. I felt lucky to have completed our sixth mission and sorry for the 'instructors' who were close to completing their tour of duty and leery of flying with a bunch of rookies. The odds were against us on every bombing mission and we dreaded any extra risks. It turned out that eighteen men died in the collision, some had only a few missions to complete their tour of duty.*

Major Edward F. Blum's Bail Out

Major Blum, 849th Operations Officer, was one of the instructor pilots helping to train the new pilots. They used a twelve ship formation to simulate a bombing mission. Blum was flying the 13th aircraft as a spare to replace any plane that failed to take off or had to abort. Maj. Blum wrote,

"Capt. Clarence J. Adams, the instructor pilot in the 12th bomber, said he would drop out of the formation half-way through the exercise and I should replace him to give my trainee pilot practice. After a couple of hours in formation at 25,000 feet, we began to descend. We were down to 16,000 feet and everything seemed to be going well when I heard a loud noise. I felt a heavy jolt on the aircraft and then it was very quiet. It was as if the plane had stopped flying and was just sitting there in air. As I looked back to the left, the engineer came out of his turret and went for his chest-pack parachute. The co-pilot, who had been standing between the trainee pilot and myself went for his chute and I turned around, looking forward, and opened my safety belt. I was wearing a back-pack chute. The plane immediately went into a violent spin to the right. I was thrown out of my seat and as I flipped over I remember seeing the autopilot controls which were under the throttle column between the pilot and co-pilot, appear to go behind me, upside down. I landed on my hands and knees in the crawlway to the nose of the plane. Realizing where I was, I started forward to the escape hatch which was about half- way up to the nose. I heard another loud noise and then I was knocked out.

When I came to, I was outside the aircraft. There was debris in the sky and I remember seeing sheets of aluminum and Vary pistol cartridge cases floating around me. It was a real mess. I reached down, pulled the D-ring and my parachute opened with a flurry, giving me a terrific jolt (my leg straps had been somewhat loose.) I was happy to be alive and started to look around. I drifted through a cloud bank and then saw an aircraft flying around below me. My hands and feet were getting cold. I had lost my outer gloves and both my outer boots. Fortunately, I still had my glove insert on and one electric boot insert on my right foot, but I still felt very cold."

Major Blum said he drifted a while, before landing in the middle of some woods with his 'chute caught in a tree. He was hanging in a tree with his feet barely touching the ground when a British soldier came to help him. The soldier took him to his home for a cup of tea, called the nearest American Air Force base to record his survival and drove him to it. The lucky pilot had a gash on his head and a deep cut on his chin.

Major Blum said, "Later we worked out how the accident had happened. We had been stacked down at the bottom of the formation and the aircraft above us on the left side had drifted back somewhat and dropped down. In the process, it had hit us, cutting off our tail in the region of the lower turret. Our bombardier had been sitting on the covering over the ball turret with his chest-pack between his legs when the collision occurred. He immediately grabbed his chute, clipped it on his harness and simply walked out of the hole. He told me later it was the only time a chest-pack parachute had ever clicked on the first time he tried it. Generally the clips are very strong and you have to work at them a bit to get the 'chute to hook on the harness. In the nose of the aircraft the trainee navigator and the instructor navigator had been keeping track of our flight path. When the accident happened the instructor navigator, who was wearing a back-pack chute, said he had also moved toward the escape hatch in the passage-way where I had been. He must have been close to me but I don't remember seeing him before the aircraft disintegrated."

Lt. Joseph F. Tighe's Cologne Mission

January 10, 1945 was the hundredth mission for the 490th Bomb group and the primary target was an important and long railroad bridge across the Rhine River. Germans were using it to move troops and supplies to beef up their forces the Battle of the Bulge area. Pilots were warned at briefing to expect more than 400 anti-aircraft guns. Each Fortress carried six 1000 pound bombs to destroy the bridge and railyards. Cologne was so important that 300 men had worked most of the night to clear the runways for a safe take-off. Bombing altitude was 27,000 feet at -53 degrees with deadly results. Three bombers in the Low squadron were reported missing in action on this mission: Lt. Walter A. McGrath, Lt. Edward F. Hodges and Lt. Charles W. Ward. The first two went down but Lt. Hodges' plane managed to limp out of Germany and land at an Allied airbase.

This was the tenth mission for the Lt. Joseph F. Tighe crew of the 849th squadron. The following is adapted from his recollections in the 490th BG Historical Record. The 490th flew south of the target area to approach the IP on a westerly heading. There was a predicted solid overcast over the city of Cologne but as soon as they arrived in the vicinity of the target, the skies cleared and the anti-aircraft fire from the 88 mm and 105 mm gun batteries around the city became quite intense. They approached the Initial Point to start the bomb-run, the bomb-bay doors were opened and they started the run on the target. Lt. Tighe said, "It was about this time when all hell broke loose." Two new factors had entered into the mission: one, the solid overcast over the city had broken up, the entire target area became wide open and the bomber formation became a visual target for the flak guns. Second, the Germans had towed barges up the Rhine River with 155 mm anti-aircraft guns mounted on the decks. Shortly after bombs away, the barges threw up a heavy barrage of 155 mm flak and wrecked havoc on the B-17s, especially on Lt. Tighe's squadron flying the Low position of the formation. In addition to the intense barrage of flak, the heavy caliber guns were "tracking" individual aircraft. It was impossible to avoid the heavy, accurate anti-aircraft fire. It was all around, over and under the bombers.

Lt. Tighe said, "Our squadron's Lead ship, flown by Lt. Walter McGrath, got a direct hit on the right wing which immediately caught fire. Within thirty seconds it was all over. I looked up to his position and saw the right wing of Mc Grath's B-17 rip off and almost instantly the aircraft flipped over on its back and went into a tight spin. Only four crew members were seen bailing from the doomed bomber. They survived and became prisoners of war in Germany until their release on VE- Day.

About a minute after Lt. McGrath went down, Lt. Ward's B-17 got hit in the # 4 engine and also started to go down. The aircraft was under control fairly well and seven chutes were seen leaving the stricken plane. Most of that crew ended up as POWs until the war ended, but Lt. Ward managed to evade capture and returned to England to fly more missions!

The next aircraft to get hit and fall out of formation was that of Lt. Eddy Hodges. In a matter of minutes, three planes had gone down, all from the 849th. This Cologne raid was only five and a half hours duration, but that was time enough for it to prove costly in terms of human casualties and aircraft. Within one week of combat during the first ten days of January, the 849th squadron had lost five aircraft and many crew members. Lt. McGrath had been shot down and killed on his thirty-third mission; after only two more he would have completed his combat tour and could have gone home. I remember he once told me that it was helpful to count the bursts of flak around your own aircraft. They usually came in bursts of three when you were being "tracked" by the anti-aircraft ground gunners: after two nearby bursts you could slip out of the formation slightly to avoid the third deadly explosion. Sometimes it worked, other times it didn't. As lead pilot on this particular mission, McGrath didn't have the option of doing that evasive maneuver on the bomb-run."

Sgt. Richard L. Lynde, Ball Turret Gunner

Sgt. Richard L. Lynde was the ball turret gunner on the Lt. McGrath lead crew on the Cologne mission. He managed to bail out of the doomed B-17. He recalled the formation had no problem going into the target area and no opposition directly over it, but after bombs –away when the bombers turned to reassemble at the "rally point" very heavy flak began coming up. Sgt. Linde said,

"It seemed like only a few seconds after I had reported the bomb-bay doors closed ---that we received a direct hit in the bomb-by area. Our aircraft, Old Patch just seemed to stand still. I listened for the bail-out alarm bell. My ball turret was still operating and realizing the plane was disabled, I rolled it down to prepare to get out and back into the waist. Then for some reason, I felt I did not have time, so I rolled the turret back up, opened the ball door and dropped out into the sky. How thankful I was that I had talked the supply guys into giving me a back-pack type parachute. I remembered how we had been cautioned to keep our hands off the rip-cord until we had cleared the plane. But I vividly recall thinking, 'What if I can't that handle after getting into the air?' So, against all advice, I made sure I had that handle right in my hand when I dropped out of the ball. (I was obviously very attached to that rip-cord handle for I still have it to this day!) The ship blew up as soon I left it. That's how close I came to being a fatality!"

Sgt. Lynde was the only crew member to bail, out his own. Three others from the front of the plane were blown out when the plane exploded. The navigator and, bombardier were wearing their chutes, but both were injured in the explosion. The engineer in the top turret had hooked only one ring of his chute to his harness and didn't remember pulling his rip-cord while flying through the air. The four were captured as soon as they landed. The wounded officers were taken to a hospital.

Sgt. Lynde said, "Chambers, the engineer, and I were taken to an interrogation center at Frankfort. We stayed together through a string of POW camps: Dulagfuft, Stalag 13 at Nurenberg and then on to Stalag 7a at Moosburg where we remained until liberated by the 14th Armored Division of Patton's Third Army on the 29th of April.

T/Sgt. James Lee Hutchinson, Ed.S.

S/Sgt. Richard T. Keough's Walk Out

This story illustrates one combat philosophy of never getting too close to other guys because they may die. Death was always waiting and nobody needed another tragedy to re-enforce that fact. S/Sgt. Keough was as member of my 490th Bomb Group, my 848th squadron and lived in a Quonset hut in my housing area. He arrived a month after I did and his B-24 crew flew on the January 5th training fight when they had to switch off from a B-24 Liberator to the B-17 Flying Fortress. No doubt both of our crews were flying in that formation and both witnessed the mid-air collision when two planes went down. We probably passed each other many times, ate in the Mess Hall, attended mail call and flew several of the same missions. We were in the training flight mid-air collision incident and flew on some of the same missions. But we never became acquainted!

S/Sgt. Keough followed the same path as I and thousands of other USAAF gunners. During basic training at the age of twenty, he volunteered to fly, entered the Air Cadet program and ended up as a ball turret gunner on a B-24 Liberator on the Lt. Roger Haendiges crew. They shipped out on the Queen Mary and arrived at the 490th BG as a replacement crew on Christmas Eve 1944.

Brad Keough, his son, is a veteran and "baby boomer" who decided to learn more about his father's Eighth Air Force service in World War II. Teenage talks with his Dad, photos and family records helped him learn stories he never heard as a youngster. The result of his research helped him better understand his father and preserved more stories which would have been lost. Brad's military record: a Turboprop mechanic, Flight Engineer/Door Gunner on HH-3E Jolly Green Giants, and an Army pilot flying CH-47 Chinooks. He retired as a CW3 Senior Instructor Pilot and Instrument Flight Examiner.

Brad said, "Dad never talked much about his Air Force combat days in WW II when I was a boy. He did say he requested to be switched from his crew to the gunnery pool after the "training flight" mid-air collision and a couple of close calls on his early missions. While in the pool, he flew a few missions as a replacement gunner with various crews. I believe the following event happened during that time.

Brad said his brother Scott was approached at a funeral for one of his Dad's brothers by their cousin Kathleen, a retired Air Force veteran, who asked him if he knew his Dad was a hero. (Brad confirmed this story with another cousin [John] who worked with his father after the war.) They told me a story that Dad had told his family soon after he came home from WW II. They said Dad's bomber was one of three planes shot down over Germany. He bailed out but not everybody made it out of the aircraft. Once on the ground those who survived the jump buried their chutes, linked up and hid in a barn. The German farmer and his wife befriended them and told them to stay hidden in the barn. However, the farmer then reported them to the German Red Cross who informed the local Nazi SS troops. The next day a small group of SS troops surrounded the barn and the survivors surrendered. The Nazis lined up them up, walked down the row behind them, stopped behind Dad and shot the guy standing next to him in the head. Dad and the other airmen overpowered and killed the SS soldiers and the farmer and his wife. Some airmen were killed during the struggle and the few remaining vowed to never surrender again. They used maps and compasses from the escape kits attached to their parachute harnesses and everything they learned in "evade and escape" classes to work their way toward American troops in France. They traveled only at night and killed any Germans who discovered them, regardless if they were civilian or military. Once they made it into France they found some parachutes to use for warmth and cover until they made it to American troops. (Brad's cousin John added that his Dad had an extremely hard time dealing with those memories after the war.)

They were sent back to the 490th Bomb Group and Dad was returned to flight status and flew several more missions. After hearing this story, I remembered seeing an old "V-mail" letter from Dad telling his parents he was still alive and to pay no attention to the "cause of death" telegram they received from Uncle Sam. I also remember comments Dad made when I was young and he talked about sleeping under parachutes to stay warm. One time I asked him what happened if a flyer was shot down. He looked at me and said very sternly that you only surrender to German soldiers, never to the S.S. or civilians because they would kill you for the sport. My Mother freaked out and Dad just clammed up.

I enlisted in the Air Force when I was seventeen and was scheduled to leave for basic training about a month after my eighteenth birthday. At that point Dad began to tell me more about his twenty-five B-17 missions and his assignment to the Lt. John N. Shirley crew in the 850th squadron. He said he had flown most of his missions with that crew as a ball turret/nose gunner and/or togglier. He said his worst experience in the ball turret happened when he was in his turret on a mission and his best friend was in the bomber next to his. He said he spun his turret around and they waved at each other then he did another 360 degree turn and his friend's bomber came back into view just before it exploded right in front of him.

Prior to the time I left for basic training, Dad took me to meet Mr. Shirley who had retired as a Colonel. He told me he felt bad for my Dad because the crew gave him a cold shoulder when he joined the crew. They thought Lt. Shirley and Dad plotted to get the original ball turret gunner kicked off the crew. Mr. Shirley said the real story was they lost an engine on a mission and had to fall out of formation. He told his ball turret gunner to scan below for possible fighters, but he refused to stay in his turret in case they had to bail out. They made it back to base and Lt. Shirley asked to have him transferred to another crew. The Squadron Commander removed that S/Sgt. from flight status, busted him to private and shipped him to the Infantry. Mr. Shirley said if he had known that would happen to him he would not had done it. He said he never felt closer to any other bunch of guys in the military as he did from WWII. He told about being on the April 7th mission to the Parchim airbase, the fighter attack and the German fighter crashing into Cagel's bomber. It was about the same story you wrote about in your book, "The Boys in the B-17." He also told me about a mission when they went out in small flights looking for targets of opportunity. He said they were leading a flight of three aircraft when they sighted a German flak train which they quickly over took and he had to make a 360 degree turn to make another run. Dad was the togglier and he said they were flying so low that he could see the gunners putting fuses in the rounds. Shirley said the first flak shell exploded a thousand feet or so above them, but the crew on his left wing was on their last mission and when the flak exploded overhead that pilot pulled up, dropped his bombs and broke for home. Shirley laughed and said he was glad the guy did it because he was thinking the same thing. Dad said they made the Yank magazine for taking out a rail bridge.

Mr. Shirley also told about the time they had a hung bomb and were going to drop it in the Channel before returning home. He told Dad to open the bomb-bay doors and jettison the bomb. However, Dad said when he looked down there was an American Navy convoy below them with every gun turned up toward them because of the open bomb-bay doors. Dad said he quickly closed the doors and went out on the catwalk to disarm that bomb.

Dad flew two low-level Chowhound missions after the truce in May when the 490th Bomb group was dropping food cartons for the starving people in Holland. His crew also made a POW Repatriation flight to Austria to bring French POWs back home. Mr. Shirley said the bomber was really packed with the free French prisoners (they even had platforms in the bomb-bay.) The crew was touched when the POWs started crying as their bomber took off for France. Dad said Lt. Shirley gave them a special treat when he circled the Eiffel Tower before landing near Paris."

A final coincidence: Richard Keough and I received our Honorable Discharge and $300 separation pay at Baer Field, FT. Wayne Indiana within a two weeks of each other in the fall of 1945.

Hutch #7   Derben   Jan. 14 - We took off at 8:00, our target was the underground oil storage tanks at Derben in the heart of Germany, almost to Berlin. It was an eight hour mission (five on oxygen.) We were flying Lead of the High Squadron with a load of ten 500 pounders. Captain Ray Pitman was our Command Pilot with officers of Russell, Dilts and Oliver as Bombardier, Navigator and Mickey. S/Sgt. Bert Allinder and Orville Robinson were waist gunners. Lt. Rector flew as tail-gunner. We had 38 bombers on this mission. We knew this mission would be rough because the oil dump would be heavily protected by flak guns and Luftwaffe fighters. The sky cleared over the target and we bombed visually to destroy more of Hitler's oil supply. Our P-51 fighter escorts had a busy day and did a great job protecting our formation

T/Sgt. James Lee Hutchinson, Ed.S.

The 490th BG Formation chart for the Derben mission shows us leading the High squadron.

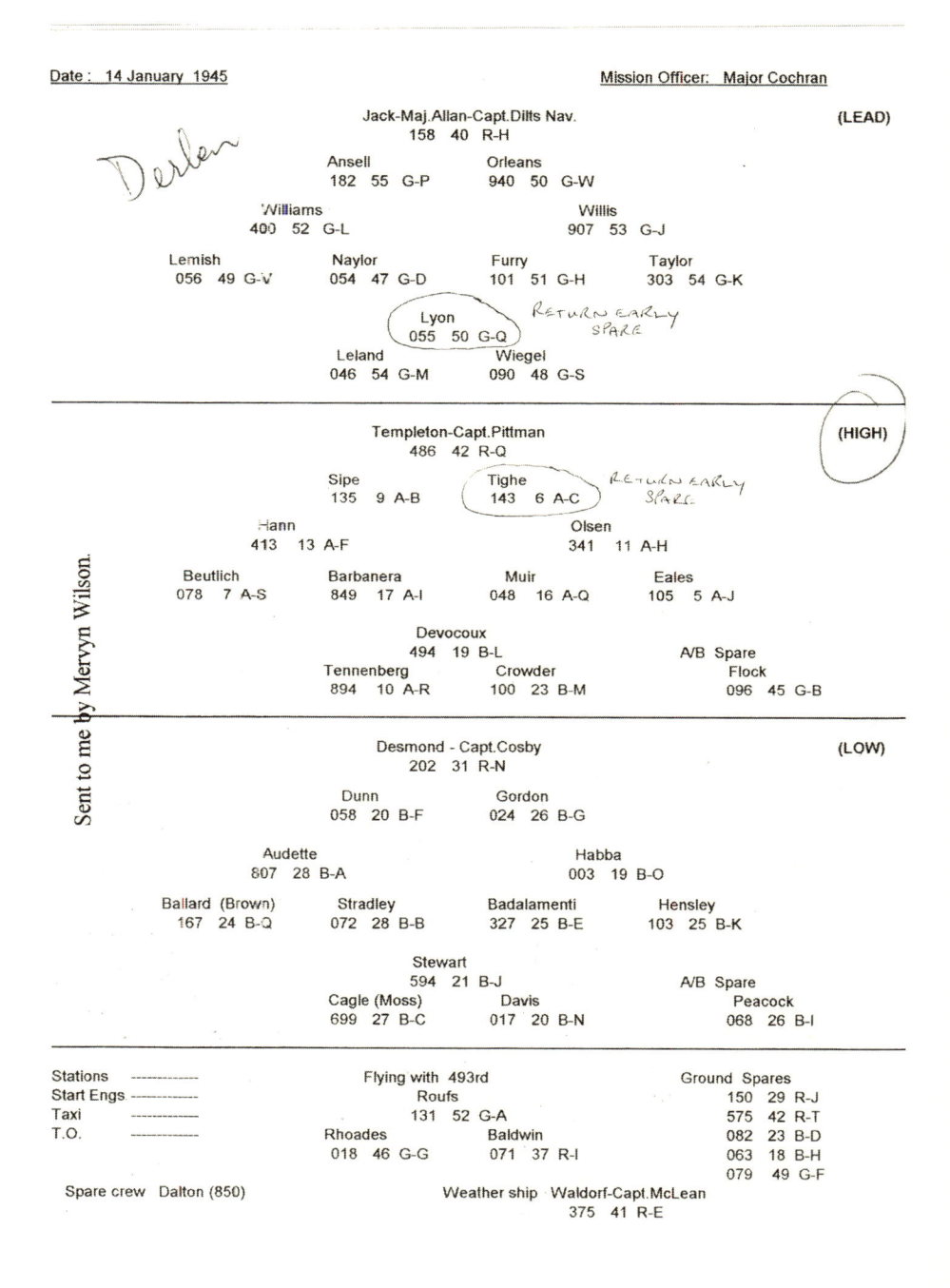

Derben

Date: 14 January 1945   Mission Officer: Major Cochran

```
                    Jack-Maj.Allan-Capt.Dilts Nav.                    (LEAD)
                           158   40  R-H
                  Ansell                 Orleans
                  182  55  G-P           940  50  G-W
            Williams                           Willis
            400  52  G-L                       907  53  G-J
      Lemish          Naylor         Furry            Taylor
      056  49 G-V     054  47  G-D   101  51  G-H     303  54  G-K
                              Lyon         RETURN EARLY
                              055  50 G-Q   SPARE
                      Leland              Wiegel
                      046  54  G-M        090  48  G-S
```
───
```
                    Templeton-Capt.Pittman                            (HIGH)
                           486   42  R-Q
                  Sipe                  Tighe       RETURN EARLY
                  135   9  A-B          143   6  A-C  SPARE
            Hann                            Olsen
            413  13  A-F                    341  11  A-H
      Beutlich         Barbanera      Muir             Eales
      078   7  A-S     849  17  A-I   048  16  A-Q     105   5  A-J
                           Devocoux
                           494  19  B-L
                  Tennenberg           Crowder               A/B Spare
                  894  10  A-R         100  23  B-M          Flock
                                                             096  45  G-B
```
───
```
                    Desmond - Capt.Cosby                              (LOW)
                           202  31  R-N
                  Dunn                  Gordon
                  058  20  B-F          024  26  B-G
            Audette                         Habba
            807  28  B-A                    003  19  B-O
      Ballard (Brown)  Stradley       Badalamenti       Hensley
      167  24  B-Q     072  28  B-B   327  25  B-E     103  25  B-K
                           Stewart
                           594  21  B-J
                  Cagle (Moss)         Davis                 A/B Spare
                  699  27  B-C         017  20  B-N          Peacock
                                                             068  26  B-I
```
───

Sent to me by Mervyn Wilson.

Stations   ----------   Flying with 493rd   Ground Spares
Start Engs.   ----------   Roufs   150 29 R-J
Taxi   ----------   131 52 G-A   575 42 R-T
T.O.   ----------   Rhoades   Baldwin   082 23 B-D
                                   018 46 G-G   071 37 R-I   063 18 B-H
                                                                  079 49 G-F

Spare crew   Dalton (850)   Weather ship Waldorf-Capt.McLean
                                            375 41 R-E

B-17 MEMORIES

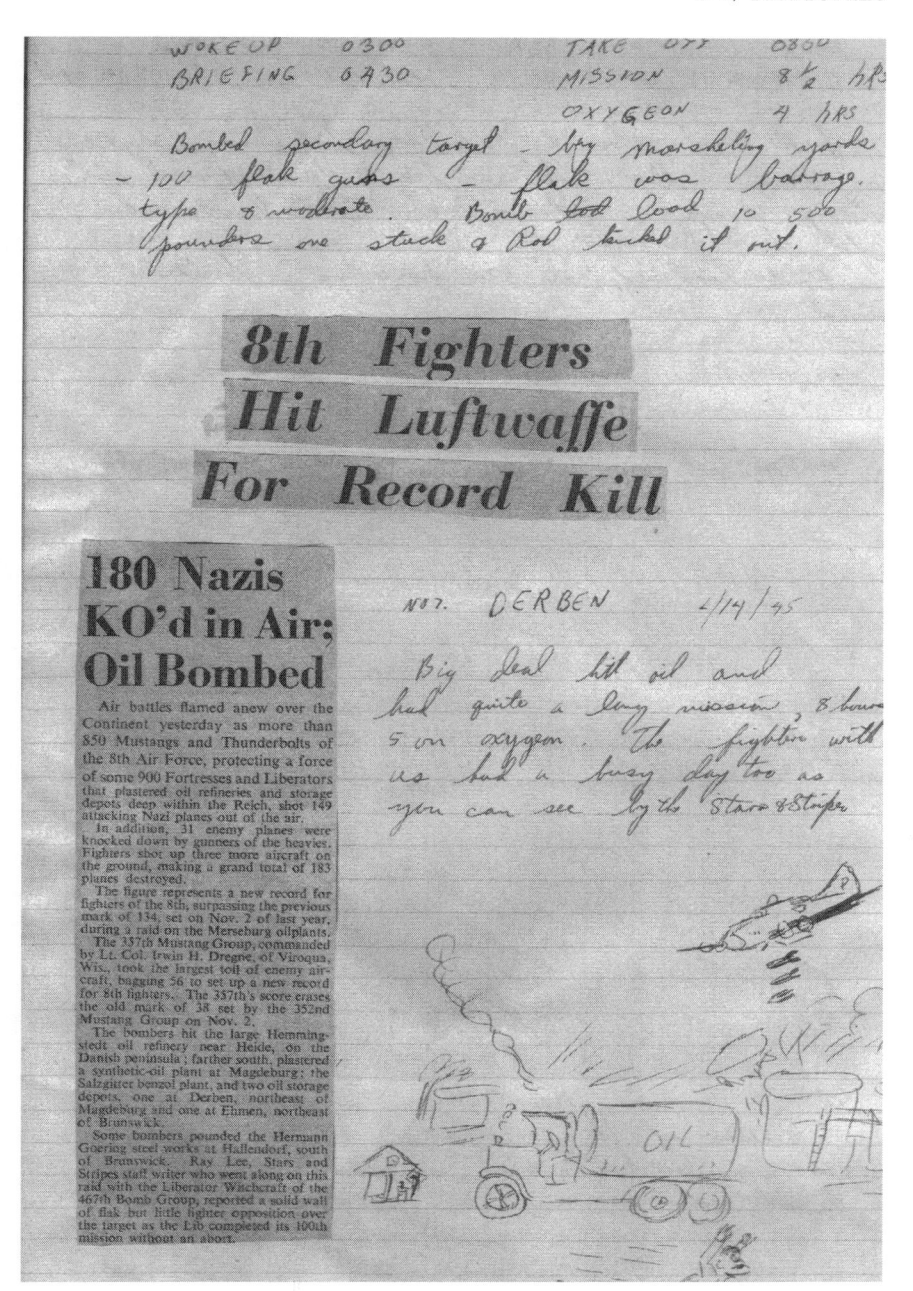

WOKE UP 0300   TAKE OFF 0800
BRIEFING 0430   MISSION 8½ hrs
                      OXYGEON 4 hrs

Bombed secondary target - by marsheling yards - 100 flak guns - flak was barrage type & moderate. Bomb load 10 500 pounders one stuck & Rob kicked it out.

8th Fighters Hit Luftwaffe For Record Kill

180 Nazis KO'd in Air; Oil Bombed

Air battles flamed anew over the Continent yesterday as more than 850 Mustangs and Thunderbolts of the 8th Air Force, protecting a force of some 900 Fortresses and Liberators that plastered oil refineries and storage depots deep within the Reich, shot 149 attacking Nazi planes out of the air.

In addition, 31 enemy planes were knocked down by gunners of the heavies. Fighters shot up three more aircraft on the ground, making a grand total of 183 planes destroyed.

The figure represents a new record for fighters of the 8th, surpassing the previous mark of 134, set on Nov. 2 of last year, during a raid on the Merseburg oilplants.

The 357th Mustang Group, commanded by Lt. Col. Irwin H. Dregne, of Viroqua, Wis., took the largest toll of enemy aircraft, bagging 56 to set up a new record for 8th fighters. The 357th's score erases the old mark of 38 set by the 352nd Mustang Group on Nov. 2.

The bombers hit the large Hemmingstedt oil refinery near Heide, on the Danish peninsula; farther south, plastered a synthetic-oil plant at Magdeburg; the Salzgitter benzol plant, and two oil storage depots, one at Derben, northeast of Magdeburg and one at Ehmen, northeast of Brunswick.

Some bombers pounded the Hermann Goering steel works at Hallendorf, south of Brunswick. Ray Lee, Stars and Stripes staff writer who went along on this raid with the Liberator Witchcraft of the 467th Bomb Group, reported a solid wall of flak but little fighter opposition over the target as the Lib completed its 100th mission without an abort.

NO 7.   DERBEN   1/14/45

Big deal hit oil and had quite a long mission, 8 hours 5 on oxygen. The fighters with us had a busy day too as you can see by the Stars & Stripes

T/Sgt. James Lee Hutchinson, Ed.S.

OUR LITTLE FRIENDS

U.S. fighter pilots were an elite group of young men who faced and defeated the German Luftwaffe. However, the Army Air Force was in its infancy in 1941 and had very few fighter squadrons at the start of World War II. Aircraft production and pilot training became a desperate need after Pearl Harbor. There were American pilots who joined the RAF (Royal Air Force) Eagle squadrons composed of U.S. pilots to fly British Spitfires against the Germans in the Battle of Britain. Once the U.S. entered the war and the Eighth Air Force was stationed in England, three RAF Eagle squadrons were transferred to U.S. groups. The Eighth had 96 fighter groups by 1943, many moved into captured enemy bases in France or Belgium in 1944 as our ground troops forced Hitler's forces back to Germany. They were our "Little Friends" who escorted us on bombing missions. They met and defeated Luftwaffe fighters determined to stop our bomber formations before we reached the target.

The Republic P-47D Thunderbolt A heavy-weight fighter-bomber with a more than 2,000 HP Whitney powerplant and a maximum speed of 435 MPH. It was armed with eight 50 caliber machine guns in the wings and exterior racks for rockets or bombs. The Thunderbolt was a great fighter, but also very effective in straffing and bombing troops and trains. More than 16,000 were produced.

The North American P-51 Mustang The P-51D with a 1500 HP Merlin or Rolls-Royce engine and a four-bladed paddle propeller could reach speeds of 450 mph. The "bubble" canopy gave pilots a 360 degree view of the sky, a distinct advantage in combat. Its gasoline drop tanks gave it a range of 1250 miles to escort bombing formations to Germany, jettison fuel tanks and engage Luftwaffe fighters in aerial combat. It was armed with three machine guns in each wing and racks to carry eight rockets or two 500-pound bombs in. Over 15,000 Mustangs were produced

The Lockheed P-38 Lightning The P-38 Lightning with its twin body was easily recognized. Germans called it "the fork-tailed devil". Powered by two 1300 HP engines with top speed of 414 miles per hour. Armed with a 20mm cannon and four machine guns, it could carry two bombs and was later adapted for rockets for air-to-ground raids.

B-17 MEMORIES

I shudder to think what my Eighth Air Force bombing missions would have been without the protection of the our "Little Friends" It was always a thrill on a bombing mission to look out and see those sleek fighter escorts flying on our wings. They often flew in close enough to exchange salutes or "thumbs up" signs and dart away. They reminded me of western gunfighters in the sky; protecting the good guys and ready to take down the bad ones!

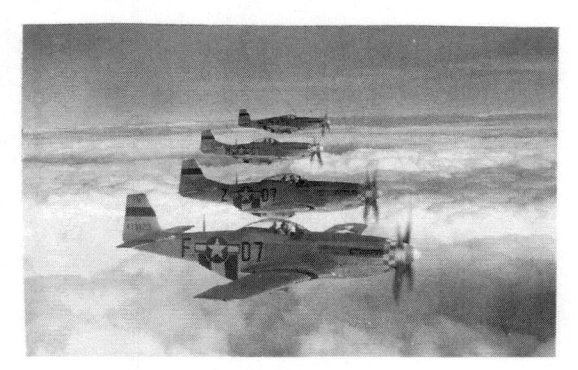

USAAF Photos

Top– P-47 Thunderbolt Bottom – P-51 Mustang.

T/Sgt. James Lee Hutchinson, Ed.S.

Bandits and Bogies

Luftwaffe pilots were very good in aerial combat (dogfights) and attacking bomber formations. We kept close watch on the sky to spot fighters and alert our pilot to notify to call our escort fighters. Enemy fighters were nicknamed "bandits or bogies" and crew members dreaded an inter-com warning of enemy fighters in the area. The ME 109 and FW 190 were deadly, but the ME 262 jet was very fast. It was easy to spot that sleek bullet-like body with a jet engine on each wing. Those Luftwaffe pilots were literally riding rockets! The one thing in our favor was the fact that jet fighters carried a limited amount of fuel and only flew for short periods. They came up, fought fast and furious and returned to their base. Our fighters tried to catch them when they were taking off or landing. German air bases soon became important targets for our fighters and heavy bombers. They were extremely fast and could out run our P-51 fighter, but they had their drawbacks. They were difficult to fly, slow to make turns, used too much fuel and could fly only a short time. Our P-51 pilots could make much tighter turns and loop to get behind a jet fighter chasing them. This maneuver was called "the Luftwaffe Stomp." By 1945, Allied bombing missions had created a severe fuel shortage in the Third Reich. It was reported that in the last months of the war, the German ME 282 jets were hidden in the woods and to save fuel, the ground crews used cows to tow them out to the runway for take-off. We were reaping the benefits of all those bombing missions to oil storage dumps and the 15th Air Force in Italy to the Ploesti oil fields and refineries in Romania.

B-17 MEMORIES

USAF Museum photo

Top *Focke-Wulf FW – 190F had a fourteen cylinder radial BMW engine with 395 MPH top speed. It was armed with two 20mm cannon in wings and two machine guns in nose with bomb racks under wings.*

Middle *Messerschmitt Bf – 10 9G Daimlier-Benz 1350 hp 12 clinder engine with 348 MPH top speed. Armed with 30 mm cannons in the in wings and two machine guns in nose. A Luftwaffe ME 109 fighter group hit our formation on the Parchim mission.*

Bottom *Messerschmitt Me -262A Jet at was powered by two Junker-Jumo turbo-jet engines with top speed of 540 MPH and armed with four 30 mm cannon in the nose.*

177

T/Sgt. James Lee Hutchinson, Ed.S.

Hutch # 8 Augsburg Jan. 15 - Wake-up 3:00 –briefing at 4:30 - take off 8:50 - landed 4:15, another long mission. Our Templeton crew led the Lead (middle) squadron with Command pilot, Captain Mc Clean and our own navigator, Lt. Bruno Conterato. Our bombardier was Lt. Robert P. Russell and the Mickey operator, Lt. Oliver The bomb-load was twelve 500 GPs and the formation bombed a big marshalling yard with 100 flak guns protecting it. Flak was a barrage over the target, but was moderate. We had feared the worse, because Augsburg, in Germany's heartland was an industrial area for military supplies. Mission of over eight hours and we were on oxygen half of that time.

The 490th sent up 38 bombers with Major Adams as mission commander. This, again, was two missions in a row. After we left the target, we discovered that one of the 500-pound bombs had failed to release and still hanging the bomb rack! Our engineer, T/Sgt. Ewing Roddy, volunteered to go into the bomb-bay and try to release the "hung bomb" from its shackles. He was not able wear his chest-pack a parachute and had to use a portable oxygen tank to get out on the catwalk with bomb bay doors open. He was able to free the bomb and get back to his regular oxygen hook-up as the bomb-bay doors closed. It was a brave thing to do, but we later teased Rod for bombing an "undesignated target" and gave him credit for a direct hit on a dangerous Nazi barn!

By this time, Hitler's attack into Belgium was failing and Nazi troops were retreating to the Fatherland for a last-ditch stand. However, this meant more anti-aircraft guns to protect remaining targets! The Luftwaffe prepared for a desperate defense against tactical and high-level bombers. Heavy losses reduced their ranks and high ranking pilots were flying combat planes to defend against Allied raids. We were constantly made aware of the fierce fighting we would meet before Germany was defeated. The Battle of the Bulge was the biggest and bloodiest battle of WW II, lasting slightly over six weeks. More than 76,000 Americans were killed, injured or reported missing. Hitler's army lost even more troops and equipment as they were driven back toward the Rhine.

Hutch # 9   Sterkade-Rheine   Jan. 20 - Take off 7:00 land: 12:20
The railroad marshalling yards at Sterkade-Reine was our target. The 490th sent up 34 aircraft today. Maj. Lightner was mission commander and our co-pilot Lt. Dale Rector regained his old seat for this mission. Severe weather had kept our bombers grounded for four days. The Eighth Air Force sent up 1,000 Fortresses and Liberators escorted by 250 P-51 Mustangs. Targets included synthetic oil plants, railroads and bridges. This raid came one day after the Eighth's third birthday.

Today the Templeton crew led a Chaff Squadron of twelve aircraft loaded to the roof with boxes of chaff (packages of 7" x 8" aluminum sheets) to foul up the radar on the German flak guns. Our squadron was the first into enemy territory and. Since we were leading and out by ourselves, we had our own escort of P-51 Mustangs for protection. Of course, they peeled off as we flew into flak over the target and waited at the "rally point." We were flying at 27,000 feet, it was 57 below zero and some of the guns froze because they had been oiled too heavily. Our B-17 was loaded with boxes of chaff piled high in the waist area and my radio room. It was so crowded I could barely move. We had been briefed to be aware of a heavy concentration of 300 anti-aircraft guns, or more, over the target. Our crew's former ball turret gunner, S/Sgt. Wlibur Lesh rode with us today to help me feed bundles of chaff, which resembled bundles of paper towels, into the a chute in my radio room while Robby and Bert threw from the waist gun positions. Needless to say, we threw out chaff like crazy on the bomb-run to fill the sky with thousands of sheets of fluttering chaff and fool the radar on those anti-aircraft guns. It was great to fly with Wilbur again, but it was the last mission he flew with our crew.

Our engineer, Ewing Roddy, had an eye injury on this mission. A small piece of metal hit him in the eye but he managed to apply a bandage as we continued on to the target. An ambulance took him to the hospital for treatment as soon as we landed and he was cleared to fly on our next mission. I knew Roddy was determined to fly with us, because it was bad luck to miss a few missions and have to finish up with a different crew. This was the reason crew members seldom reported for sick call I remember a few times when I flew with a sinus cold and clogged eustachian tube which hampered equalizing air pressure on my eardrum and caused extreme pain as we changed altitude. The immediate remedy was to scream and pound my desk. I knew the yelling would equalize the pressure until my ears popped. My ears still pop when I ride a fast elevator. Another morning, we were riding out to the plane in the back of a canvas-covered army truck and waist gunner, Dwight Parrish, was sitting on the tailgate. The truck hit a snow bank and he fell out onto the concrete runway! Luckily he was well-padded by his flight suit and he was determined to fly the mission in spite of a few bruises. This was a short mission and we were back by noon and through cleaning our machine guns by 3:00 pm.

Hutch – Jan.27 – Mission scrubbed

Chapter Five

Streets of London

Three-day passes were great. Whenever we were given a three day pass, the gunners usually opted for a train ride to London's Liverpool Station and a short ride on the Tube (subway) to Piccadilly Circus, the entertainment hub of London. The American Club dubbed the Rainbow Club on Shaftsbury Avenue, was just off Piccadilly Circus and usually the first destination for enlisted men. Our Templeton crew was never given a week-long "Rest and Relaxation flak leave," but we did get a lot of weekend passes. Flak leave and weekend passes were given to flight crews as rest and relaxation time from the stress of combat missions. It was a time to forget the war a few days and forget about mission alerts.

We would pack our overnight bags with the bare necessities and catch the 490th pass truck that met all trains at the Diss station. London was our usual destination because it was a magnet for U.S. servicemen on leave and you never knew when you might meet an old buddy. It was great to have a few days of free time even though German V-1 and V-2 bombs were still striking London especially at night. I sometimes I had an uneasy night's sleep while bomb explosions sounded in the distance. When you went to bed in London, you were never knew where or if you would wake up! Some guys wouldn't take a London pass! However, we figured it was as safe as our airfield and the attractions were worth the risk. Londoners used the tube as a bomb shelter. Families, especially those with children, moved into the underground each night. It was their routine and they simply packed up blankets and bed clothes and moved down into the subway (tube) to sleep in government provided steel bunk beds fastened along the walls.

T/Sgt. James Lee Hutchinson, Ed.S.

The American Club at Rainbow corner was a "canteen" was operated by the Red Cross to provide a home base for the thousands of Yankees who visited London. British Red Cross hostesses operated club's Doughnut Dugout snack bar and served sandwiches, doughnuts, coffee, tea and scones in this USO type club. The volunteers helped G.I.s with directions, letter writing and phone calls, welcomed us warmly and were always willing to help with questions or directions. Rainbow Corner's most important help to servicemen was providing rooms for American at YMCA type hotels and the cost of only two shillings six pence, about .50 cents a night. We always requested rooms at the Columbia Club just a couple of blocks down the street. This American oasis in the heart of London was a blessing for morale, we could sign and/or leaf through large registration and/or message books. We could also send cablegrams to the folks at home for a small fee. I never sent a cablegram because I didn't want my parents to go through the shock of having that black telegram delivery car pull up to their house.

A special hostess and a familiar face for many American service men was, Adele, a regular volunteer. She was Fred Astaire's older sister and first dancing partner. She and Fred had starred in several musicals and movies such as "Lady Be Good' and "Band Wagon" before she left the business to marry a member of the British aristocracy. Her formal title was Lady Cavendish.

Rainbow Corner was our headquarters anytime we were in London. It was a great place to watch for guys we had known in our stateside training days. I met a couple of fellows from my Air Cadet basic training in Amarillo! They knew of several gunners who had finished their missions and gone home. Unfortunately, there were others who didn't make it. We could also check the guest register and bulletin boards for names and addresses of buddies stationed at other airfields.

We ate at various London restaurants but their wartime menus were very limited: a few vegetables, sausages and lots of fish. I usually ordered the sausages. You can imagine my surprise when the "Stars and Stripes" later reported that the British meat supply was improving and they would put less <u>sawdust</u> in their sausages! The American Club at

Piccadilly Circus was within easy walking distance of Leicester Square, Marble Arch, Hyde Park, Trafalgar Square, Hyde Park and Buckingham Palace. The famous city offered movies, restaurants and historical places and we were attracted like moths to a candle. One guy in our hut was a great photographer who got some great shots and often shared his photos. The famous city offered movies, restaurants and historical places to visit. Wandering the streets of one of the oldest and largest cities in the world brought new meaning to our High School geography classes. We tried various eating places, window shopped, and took in movies. Leicester Square, the theater section, was also within walking distance of Piccadilly. It was eerie to sit in a beautiful theater and hear V-1 buzz bombs bursting in the area. Plaster and dust fell from the ceiling when the explosions were too close. At one theater a platform with the organ player would rise from the orchestra pit in front of the stage playing God Save the Queen. The organ lowered back into the pit before the movie began. Trafalgar Square was a great spot to sit in the plaza among the statues under Lord Nelson's column and feed the pigeons on a rare sunny day. At age nineteen, I knew my way around one of the world's largest cities. Buckingham Palace was just a short hike through Hyde Park. Sometimes, we all chipped in for a taxi tour around London. We were in one of the world's largest cities and the best and quickest way to see it was a taxicab tour in a little Model A Ford type sedan with a Harpo Marx bulb horn. Taxi drivers made a good income from conducting sight-seeing tours for their Yankee visitors. During one pass we took the grand tour and whizzed past Parliament, Big Ben, Tower of London, St. Paul Cathedral and Number 10 Downing Street. The tour included a brief stop with time to go inside Westminster Abbey, one of my favorites. We later went back to spend more time in the famous abbey. Three or four of us caught the subway and emerged in front of the historical building. That second visit was one I'll never forget. Visitors were welcome, so we entered and were awed by the eternal flame on the British Tomb of the Unknown Soldier. We turned to look down the aisle to the beautiful golden façade and altar in the front of the church. I went down the aisle for a closer look and was nearly run over by the large choir, quietly marching down the aisle toward the altar. I was unable to retreat back to a side aisle, so I stumbled into a pew as the somber choir members passed by without a glance in my direction. They were probably amused by the predicament of a green country boy from Indiana. Subway (tube) rides were a great way to visit interesting places.

Large areas of bombed out and/or damaged buildings showed the effects of Germany's bombings in the "Battle of Britain" during August and September of 1940 followed by Hitler's eight month "Blitz in 1940-41. London citizens were still enduring bombing raids in 1942 when the Eighth arrived to establish airfields. German bombs killed thousands of innocent London civilians and left a million homeless and damaged or destroyed many historic sites. The east wing of St. Paul's cathedral had severe bomb damage. Barrage balloons were anchored on cables above important targets to prevent low-level bombing. Giant spotlights were located at strategic spots in the city and brilliant beams of light swept the sky the nights when enemy bombers came over. In 1944, the V-1 or V-2 unguided missile strikes continued the German reign of terror.

A visit to London was always a treat, it let us get away from the stress of flying missions. We could sleep late, go to a movie, take sight-seeing hikes or just hang out at Rainbow Club and watch the girls go by! That traffic really picked up in the late afternoon when the Piccadilly Commandos (prostitutes) came out to roam the streets in search of clients. Some nights we hung around to let the "commandos" hit on us and bargain for prices just for the fun of it. They loved to bum cigarettes and proposition G.I.s, but they moved on to the next potential customer when they couldn't make a sale. The scuttlebutt was that the prostitutes were licensed and regularly inspected for diseases, so it was a legal profession! Never the less, our crew never gave in to temptation, as far as I know. We had seen a lot of films about venereal disease in training and those graphic pictures of guys with VD scared the devil out of us. Besides that, our crew had first-hand experience on the subject. We knew one gunner on the base who had caught it and had to visit the hospital regularly for treatments. They let him fly missions, but he couldn't leave the base until he was cured. However, on one pass, we joined Mac's Dance Club at Great Windmill Street, Piccadilly just to see what was in that upstairs room. It wasn't much of a club just a few pool tables, several G.I.s and lots of girls, but I still have my membership card in case I decide to go back!

London was the big attraction for guys on a pass, however, as our gunners became more familiar with the English transportation system, we made trips to other destinations. One was a trip to Norwich where we visited the Saturday Market Day and toured a castle converted to a museum. I ventured out on a few solo trips when the weather improved and each one lead to big adventure. My first trip first was a bus ride to visit Keen Umbehr, my old Sioux Falls Radio School buddy. He was a B-17 radio Operator stationed with at the 486th Bomb Group in Sudbury, a few miles east of Ipswich. I stayed overnight but there were no empty bunks in Keen's hut, so I slept in a strange hut in the bunk of a guy who's crew had not returned from that day's mission. I didn't sleep very well while surrounded by that kid's family photos. Later, Keen wrote that the kid was OK, his crew's plane had landed safely at an airfield in Belgium. Several weeks later, Keen returned the favor and visited me at the 490th. However, I was able to provide him with the bunk of a guy on leave.

On later trips to London, our Hut 29 buddies gave directions on how to take the Tube out to a couple of "black market" eating spots they had visited, both were located in bombed-out areas. One, down a deserted alley, was operated like a prohibition "speak easy." We had to knock on the door and wait until a guy peeked out a small window to look us over before he let us enter. It was a little scary, but that black market cafe served a great breakfast of sausage and fresh eggs. We later visited another cafe in the same neighborhood. It was on the second floor of a bombed-out furniture store and we had to climb a rickety flight of stairs up the side of the building to enter. We later visited another cafe in the same neighborhood. It was on the second floor of a bombed-out furniture store and we had to climb a rickety flight of stairs up the side of the building to enter. They served a delicious steak and baked potato lunch. Fresh eggs and fresh steak were definitely "black market" items. I'm sure those places were cooking "vittles" stolen from British or U.S. mess halls. We deduced this fact because the breakfast sausages were all meat while British wartime sausages contained a small amount of sawdust. The steaks were very good, but they never served steak at our Mess Hall. This led some gourmet critics to say we might be eating horsemeat!

Templeton Crew Flak Casualty

Hutch # 10 - Hohenbudberg Jan. 28 -Take off at 8:50 Landed 4:22 at Mendelsham airbase. Major Lawrence S. Lightner, mission commander, was our co-pilot and we led the Lead squadron. Capt. Everett H. Kallstrom was our lead navigator. Lt. Russell was bombardier again and the Mickey operator was Lt. Andrew Dorish. This one should have been a short mission but it sure didn't turn out that way! The target was the railroad marshalling yards at Hohenbudburg on Germany's western border. We carried twelve 500 pound GPs (general purpose) bombs. The heavy snow storms were still with us and the runways were barely clear. We took off in a snowstorm and only eighteen planes were able to get airborne before the storm closed the runway. However, our reduced squadron joined the bomber stream heading for Germany. In spite of the unusually heavy snow, at one point in January the ground crews were organized into a "snow shovel brigade" and worked several days and nights to clear runways. However, the weather caused several scrubbed (cancelled) missions after we were briefed, loaded, and ready to go. Some days the take-offs and landings were almost as dangerous as the missions.

The formation bombed at 27,000 feet. No planes were lost, but many received flak damage and several crew-members were wounded. We had heavy and accurate over the target when the 490th released their bombs at 27,000 feet and we were leaving the area when a piece of flak hit waist gunner S/Sgt. Orville Robby Robinson's steel flak helmet just above the rim and its jagged edge cut him above the eye. Waist gunner

S/Sgt. Bert Allinder said he knew Robby's head wound was serious, but the temperature was - 40 degrees, the blood was frozen and it was easy to apply a bandage. Roddy went back to help Bert and they gave him a morphine shot from the plane's First Aid kit. That steel flak helmet had saved Robby's life. The Templeton crew had its emergency on this tenth mission. We were on our way home but there was still the threat of flak and fighters. I sent the "strike report" back to our base and was ready to take over Robby's waist gun position if fighters were sighted in the area. The snowstorm beat us back to Eye and we couldn't land. It was eerie to watch that blizzard sweep over and blot out the runways below. We were directed to hurry to land at Mendelsham, home of the 34th BG, a B-17 field north of the storm. Robinson was wounded and we were low on gas, but we beat the storm. T/Sgt. Roddy fired the red flares from his top turret to indicate we had wounded and an ambulance met us to pick up Robinson. We later decided that snowstorm might have been a blessing because that field had a complete hospital!

Later, the snow storm had closed the Mendelsham base too, so next morning we left our planes buried in the snow and were treated to a chilly truck ride back to Eye. Two days later, the weather cleared and those same trucks took us back to pick up our planes. We were glad to have time for a visit with Robby in the hospital. Bert had found the piece of flak in our plane and gave it to Robby for a keepsake! His head injury resulted in the loss of an eye. Sadly, that was the last time we saw him before was awarded his Purple Heart and transferred back to the states. The ground crew later reported that our aircraft had a hundred holes. Other crews reported higher numbers. There was no doubt that some of those trains had anti-aircraft guns mounted on flatcars. The 490th flew only eleven missions in January and our crew flew six.

"It was ironic that Robby lost his eye while stationed at Eye."

Bert Allinder and I met at the 490th reunion in Branson, Missouri in May, 2003 to visit and talk about our WW II Eighth Air Force days. Bert reminded me that he found the piece of flak in our plane that day so long ago and gave it to Robinson at the hospital. He said that piece was shaped like it came from the top of an 88mm shell. We decided that the shell had barely missed our left wing and gas tanks before it exploded above us. We decided that if it had been a few feet either direction, it would have instantly destroyed our B-17! Far too many Eighth Air Force bombers received those direct hits and went down in flames. The London edition of the "Stars and Stripes" gave the Eighth bombers huge headlines for this raid. This was the second biggest bomber raid on Germany since the Normandy invasion on June 6, 1944. It pinpointed the German rail and canal systems. Generally, the weather had cleared and the Eighth Air Force, the Fifteenth Air Force and the RAF bombed targets around the clock. The Eighth Air Force sent out more than 1,400 B-24 and B-17 bombers escorted by 800 P-51 Mustang and P-38 Thunderbolt fighters to smash Nazi transportation. The heavy bombers used a new technique for the first time. Instead of bombing from their usual height of 25,000 feet, some of the big bombers swooped down to as low as 1,500 feet! Bombers blasted more than twenty-four marshalling yards over a 38,000 square mile area in the heart of the Third Reich.

February 3 - We Flew as Weather ship over England during Group Assembly. Took off at 6:11 and landed 10:00 a.m.

Feb. 10 - Another scrubbed mission -- sat on the runway for an hour.

T/Sgt. Howard Tuchin's Thirteenth Mission

The curse of the thirteenth mission was especially worrisome to the boys in heavy bombers. The guys on my crew were so superstitious that we didn't fly a thirteenth mission, we called it mission 12-B.

The following thirteenth mission story is adapted from a February, 1945 Stars and Stripes article preserved in the records of T/Sgt. Howard Tuchin. The veteran of 25 missions shares military experiences from his memoirs "Flashbacks and Memories of World War Two" which he wrote for family and friends. Like me, he was a B-17 radio operator in the Eighth Army Air Corps stationed at Deenethorpe air base with the

401 Bomb Group. Sixty-nine years later, we are e-mail buddies and two old veterans swapping combat stories.

The B-17 Flying Fortress crew of 1st Lt. David Stauffer (Highland Park, NJ) was stationed with the 401st Bomb Group at Deenethorpe, England. Their dreaded thirteenth mission was February 14, 1945. The bad news was delivered by the briefing officer; the mission of the 401st BG was to hit oil refineries at Harburg, Germany. The target in the Hamburg area, was one of the toughest and most protected. German oil supplies were a high priority for the Eighth Air Corps. Our ground troops had won the Battle of the Bulge and were chasing the enemy through the Ardennes Forest, back into the Third Reich. A successful bombing mission would destroy fuel supplies for German planes, tanks and armored vehicles. Lt. Stauffer's crew climbed aboard their bomber, *Chute the Works*," and took off to join hundreds of other heavy bombers flying out over the North Sea.

The 401st formation dropped their bombs on the target from an altitude of 26,000 feet, but the radar sights on the German flak guns below had been adjusted to that altitude and the formation was bombarded with heavy flak and one of the 88mm shells exploded directly under Lt. Stauffer's bomber! Flak riddled the plane, wounded several crew members and knocked out the number four engine, the rudder and elevator trim controls, automatic pilot and the oxygen systems of two crew members. The heavy flak damage forced Lt. Stauffer to peel out of the formation. He and Co-Pilot, 2nd Lt. Edward Haake (Richmond, VA.) managed to stabilize the crippled plane, despite the fact that Stauffer nearly lost consciousness, because his oxygen supply had been knocked out. Flight Engineer, Sgt. Howard Smith (Monroe, LA) saved the day by hooking the pilot to the engineer's oxygen outlet and switching himself to a portable bottle which could be recharged as needed.

An intercom check revealed two wounded crew members and more mechanical problems. Turbo chargers on the remaining three engines were out of commission, number two engine had a hole but was still giving some power, number one gas tank had been hit, the plexi-glass nose was full of holes, and the left landing wheel was punctured.

T/Sgt. James Lee Hutchinson, Ed.S.

However, the most pressing problem was the run-a-way propeller on engine number four. Pilots were finally able to "feather" the prop and stop the violent shaking.

The most seriously wounded was Navigator, 2nd Lt. Tom E. Burns (Tarentum, Pa.) Flak cut a gash in his knee, tore open his hand and mangled his little finger. Togglier and nose-gunner, Sgt. Wilmer Eidemiller, (Greensburg, PA) remained at his position in the nose to provide him with oxygen and first aid. Lt. Burns refused further aid (morphine for pain) and although his navigation instruments were destroyed by flak, he was determined to stay conscious and give the pilots correct headings for a <u>flight of more than 350 miles</u> out of enemy territory.

The pilots, using every ounce of their strength, dropped to a lower altitude using clouds to hide from fighters and flak on the long flight to safety. The crew knew the situation was desperate because a lone damaged bomber was a perfect target for prowling Luftwaffe fighters. Meanwhile, Sgt. Smith made sure portable oxygen bottles were available to all crew members.

Waist gunner, Sgt. Lee Laura (Winthrop, MA) was wounded in the foot when flak hit and exploded a box of .50 caliber ammo in the waist area between him and the tail-gunner. Ball turret gunner S/Sgt. Arthur Wright (Knoxville, TN) came up out of his turret to bandage Sgt. Laura. <u>He also used a portable oxygen</u> bottle to revive tail-gunner, Sgt. Bill Dobson (Atlanta, GA) who had passed out from anoxia (lack of oxygen.)

Radio operator/gunner, T/Sgt. Howard Tuchin (Gloversville, NY) miraculously escaped serious injury or death by being in the <u>right</u> place at the right time. He was standing to adjust a radio receiver when a large fragment of flak burst up through the bottom of the plane, through his empty swivel seat, and cut several control cables as it exited through the roof. T/Sgt. Tuchin said,

"If I had been sitting instead of standing, I would have had it!"

He remained at his radio position to monitor radio transmissions or to send an SOS if necessary. "Chute the Works" was very low on fuel when they finally flew out over the North Sea. Lt. Stauffer realized the possibility of having to "ditch" the plane in the freezing water.

He ordered the radio operator to send an SOS signal. T/Sgt. Tuchin's distress transmission was quickly acknowledged by an American ship which was prepared to stand by and assist. Moments later they saw the White Cliffs of Dover, cancelled the SOS and flew on to their home base. Sgt. Smith fired red flares to indicate wounded aboard before they landed and skidded off the runway. An ambulance rushed to the plane and took the wounded men to the hospital where Lt. Burns received eight stitches in his knee and his finger was amputated. He and Sgt. Laura later returned to the crew. Lt. Stauffer said, "Never has a Fortress crew done a more beautiful job than my crew at such a critical time. Mere words of praise fall short of telling the story."

Note: Few unescorted, crippled bombers made it back to England in World War II, but the crew of *"Chute the Works"* had survived their thirteenth mission with a few gallon of gas to spare!

Story from the memiors of Howard Tuchin, May, 2013

Hutch # 11 - Frankfort Feb. 17 - Pvt. Dwight Parrish from the gunnery pool flew as our waist gunner to replace Robinson. The former Sgt. Parrish said he had lost his stripes when he over-stayed his pass in London for a few days.

Major Lawrence Lightner was our command pilot and we were leading the Lead squadron again with Capt. Kallstrom, Navigator Lt. Campbell was our bombardier and Lt. Gould L. Klein, Mickey operator. Our target was the railroad marshalling yards at Frankfort. We flew a seven hour mission at 21,000 feet and were on oxygen for four hours. We led the High squadron today and I sent the report on reaching the Initial point and strike report radio reports back to base. Over Germany, I received a message to change the target to Plan B. I relayed it to the pilots, <u>but</u> forgot to send the base a receipt for it!

A short guy in fatigues was in the plane as soon as we parked on the hardstand. He tore me out for failing to receipt that 'change of target' message. After flying a combat mission for seven hours, I was in no mood to be 'chewed out' by some "ground pounder". I let him have it with both barrels, pointing out that we had bombed the right target and admitted that I had not sent a receipt. About that time I saw the gold leaf of a Major peeking from his shirt collar under the fatigues He was the group communications officer and I was a Staff Sergeant who wanted to keep his stripes. I stifled my outrage, listened carefully, admitted it was all my fault and said "Yes, sir" several times!

The twenty-four aircraft mission was led by Major W.C. Cochran. We broke the weather jinx today and got in another mission. We hadn't flown a mission since January 28th and bombers had been left on the hardstand for eleven days because of weather and cancelled missions. The Stars and Stripes ran an interesting article stating the aircrew chances of survival were now double those of crews in 1943!

The 490th had flown only six missions in the first two weeks of February because of snow. Five bombers and many crewmembers had been lost in that period. Another flak damaged B-17 made a forced landing in Poland on the February 3rd mission to Berlin but the crew returned to fly again. Three days later, four bombers were lost in mid-air collisions on the Chemnitz mission. The first bomber collided with a plane from another group during formation assembly over England. A second crashed due to engine failure and two others collided over France on the way home!

Hutch # 12 - Ansbach Feb. 22 We flew Lead plane of the High squadron. The mission lasted nine hours, but we were only on oxygen two hours. Our target was railroad yards again. We bombed the "target of opportunity" or practically "last resort" by PFF at 21,000 feet. The Public Relations department took several pictures when we landed. Later they gave us individual photos and one of our crew It was our second Air Medal mission (an Oak Leaf cluster on our ribbon.) The 490th Bomb Group put up 38 aircraft. MajorCochran was mission commander and Major Lightner was mission leader and our co-pilot. Lt. Cambell was lead bombardier. We flew Lead plane in the Lead (middle) squadron. Next day's Stars & Stripes said the Eighth Air Force put up 1,400 heavy bombers escorted by 800 Mustangs and Thunderbolts. The B-17 and B-24 bombers blasted more than twenty-four marshalling yards, bridges and highway. The headlines read, "Second Biggest Air Blitz Hits Nazis".

Germany's transportation system was greatly damaged. The Nazis were beginning to feel the full wrath of the "bomber war" as tons of bombs rained down on their cities and industries.

Lt. Ron Cargill - A Tiny Piece of Flak

Ron Cargill was a typical American young man in high school and college. At age twenty, he volunteered for the Army Air Corps Air Cadet program to become a fighter pilot. However, at sometime in his flight training bomber pilots were in great demand. Ron's program was changed and he was assigned as co-pilot of a B-24 Liberator at a Heavy Bomb Group at Gowen Field, Boise, Idaho.

He was enthusiastic about entering the final phase of training. September, 1944, Ron wrote his parents about the guys on his crew and how lucky he was to have Lt. John Dolloff as his pilot. The young gunners had just completed gunnery school, one was still eighteen. It was a young crew with an average age of twenty –one.

"Dear folks,

I have finished processing and ready for the first phase of my Overseas Training Unit. I've completed my physical, received more shots, got more flying equipment and straightened out all my files. At any other post, this would have taken many days but this place got in done in record time. Yesterday morning I had three hours of engineering, which is my most important subject. The co-pilot is also the engineering officer of the ship. I'll know the B-24 as well as anybody at the end of this course. We received our passes to go in town today so I guess I'll eat now and venture into the famed metropolis of Boise. Will write again soon folks, so until then ----I send loads of love---- Ron"

The Lt. Dollof crew completed their combat training flying the B-24 and arrived at The 490th Bomb Group base with twelve other crews on Christmas Day, 1944; five weeks after our Templeton crew arrived. The boys in those new replacement crews faced an immediate problem. The 490th was a B-17 Flying Fortress outfit, a bomber they had never flown. The thirteen crews flew in the B-17, weather permitting, for 10 days.

Then on January 6th a training exercise was held to give those thirteen replacement crews experience flying in combat formation. Two of the bombers and eighteen crew members were lost in a disastrous mid-air collision, so their training continued a few weeks.

The first mission of the Lt. John Dolloff crew was February 6th and it was a long one to Chemnitz, Germany. The 490th BG flew 15 missions in February and the Lt. John Dolloff crew flew eleven of those. The crew had a brutal schedule and twice they flew four missions in a row with only two days rest in between. After ten missions, Ron sent this letter to his parents to explain why he had not been writing:

"Dear Mom and Dad, "Sorry I have been very poor in writing, but it can't be helped. It has been a very heavy week ---- just get so tired I have no ambition to write to anybody. I simply eat my supper, what little I eat, come back to the barracks and hit the sack hard. Sometimes I get so terribly tired that I can't eat or sleep and when I sleep and I get nightmares night after night. -----------Because of the censor I cannot tell you about my missions --- I know you are sweating them out with me ------ Someday I will write and tell you my tour is completed and I'll be home soon. After every mission I cut the story out of the Stars & Stripes and number it. Then when I come home you'll be able to read about every mission.-----Mom, you asked if I ever get to fly the plane ----- wish the pilot flew it all the time, but no pilot could fly a heavy bomber in formation all the time because of fatigue. ---we take turns of fifteen minutes at a time! ---------- Well, better run I'll write again when possible. I send loads of love. Ron"

This was Ron's last letter it was dated February 24, 1945; the day before he died. Second Lieutenant Ronald A. Cargill was killed in action on his eleventh mission. The story of his death has been pieced together from information supplied by former members of his crew. Navigator Lt. Robert Osborn's letter to Ron's parents in April 1, 1945 expressed the crew's sympathy and gave details of Ron's death. Tail-gunner, Sgt. Robert Thomas shared his memories of the event in a letter to Bill Amberman on January 29, 1996. I personally enjoyed Mike Broderick's letter on his visit to my old 490th airbase in Eye, England in 1995.

Mission to Munich February 25, 1945

The goal of the Mighty Eighth was to destroy Germany's transportation system. This day the target for the 490th Bomb Group was another long one, the railroad yards in Munich. It was mission # 120 for the 490th and number # 11 for the Ron's crew. The Lt. John Dolloff crew took off that morning in their B-17 *"Lotta Stern"* loaded with twelve general purpose bombs to be delivered to the railroad yard at Munich in south Germany. It was a clear day, they were flying at 24,500 feet on the bomb-run and the flak was intense and accurate. They had just released their bombs when Pilot Dolloff called navigator, Lt. Bob Osborn down in the nose to say Ron had been wounded. Osborn later wrote,

"I crawled up out of the nose to help engineer, Mike Broderick. We attempted to get Ron out of his seat, but his foot was jammed under the rudder pedals. He was unconscious so we administered first aid to him in his seat. Then we managed to lift him out and drag him down to the nose area to lay him down. We wrapped him in the heated blanket and gave him pure oxygen. I felt his pulse to check his heartbeat about every five minutes, but the vibrations of the plane made it difficult to check his breathing."

The bombardier watched him on the flight out of Germany while Lt. Osborne navigated the pilot to an emergency landing. They were almost sure Ron was gone but still had hope and decided land at a fighter base in Nancy, France instead of going back to England. They radioed ahead and a Flight Surgeon boarded the bomber as soon as it stopped rolling. He said Ron had died instantly from a tiny piece of flak, the size of the tip of your finger. It entered the back of his neck just above the flak jacket cutting his jugular vein and windpipe. The crew of *"Lotta Stern"* was shaken by the death of a guy they all liked and respected. Sadly, because of a tiny piece of flak, it was the last mission for twenty year old co-pilot 2nd Lt. Ronald Ames Cargill. His crew was assigned a new co-pilot and went on to complete ten or more missions before the end of the war.

Ron's parents did not receive the War Department Telegram of Ron's death until March 10th and so his father requested more information.

Meanwhile, April 1, 1945 the crew navigator, Lt. Robert Osborne, sent a letter to Ron's parents on April 1, 1944 to express the crew's sympathy and give their account of how he died. Eventually, the parents also received a letter from the Air Force Deputy Chief of Staff dated May 25th which contained Second Lieutenant Ronald A. Cargill's cause of death and in a list of his missions with the 490th Bomb Group.

I wish to thank Bill Amberman who conducted a search for more information about his uncle's death and shared it with us.

Today a white cross in the Lorraine American Cemetery in St. Avold, France marks the grave of:

Ronald A Cargill
2nd Lt. 851 Bomb SD   490 bomb Group (H)
New York   Feb. 25, 1945

FEBRUARY - The 490th BG flew fifteen missions this month (eight in a row). We flew twice as lead crew and made several equipment test flights. Eleven of the group's missions were against railroads and bridges.

Hutch # 12-B   Ulm   Mar. 1 - Take-off at 9:00 with formation assembly (rendezvous) at 15,000 feet on red and yellow flares. We flew Lead in the High squadron today. Major Lightner was command pilot- Capt. Ellis Beymer, navigator – Lt. Russell, bombardier and Lt. Andrew Dorish, Mickey Operator. Our bomb-load was twelve 500 pounders. I sent strike reports, but no control points. The mission lasted seven hours, and we were on oxygen for three hours. Ulm was a long way into southern Germany. We hit a railroad yard—good job. I had trouble with my ears. I had a package from home when I got back to the barracks after debriefing and Mess Hall. Mom sent a Dr. Grabow pipe a can of Prince Albert tobacco and some candy bars. Keen Umbehr, my old buddy from radio school in Sioux Falls, South Dakota, was waiting for me. I had visited his base at the 486th Bomb Group near Sudbury earlier and he was returning the favor. We had a good time reliving the "good old days" and shared what we knew about former radio school classmates. Those guys were scattered all over the globe. A few were serving in the Eighth, others had been sent to Italy or the

South Pacific, and one guy was a "ground pounder" at a remote radio station in Alaska. We each had heard of a few guys who had died. We had climbed the ladder of success and were now Technical Sergeants. A Tech Sergeant's salary was the grand total of <u>$204 per month, which included extra money for overseas and flight pay.</u>

Our group sent 37 bombers on this raid as the Eighth Air Force continued the effort they began in the last half of February. "Stars and Stripes" reported that 1200 B-17 Fortresses and B-24 Liberators took part in the Eighth Air Force's <u>eighth consecutive</u> day's raid of German communications system. The bombers had an escort of 450 Mustang fighters as they hit eight targets around Stuttgart and Munich. A second article carried a report from prisoners of war who had been freed by American and British troops as they over-ran German concentration camps. The POW's said Allied bombings had been so effective that German rail and communications systems were "shot to hell", and there was a terrible food shortage. They had spent four to five days on a train to Switzerland and safety, for what was once an eight hour trip.

T/Sgt. Howard Tuchin Bails Out

This story is adapted from the memoirs of T/Sgt. Howard Tuchin, radio operator on the First Lieutenant David Stauffer air-crew, Squadron 614 of the 401st Bomb Group stationed at Deenethorpe, England. The veteran of 25 missions shares military experiences from "Flashbacks and Memories of World War Two" which he wrote for family and friends.

March 14, 1945 the Lt. David Stauffer crew boarded their bomber, "*Chute the Works*," for their 18th mission. It was one month and four missions after returning their unescorted, flak damaged B-17 from bombing an oil refinery near Hamburg, Germany.

"We were awakened at 1:00 a.m. and dressed. Getting up so early usually meant we were in for a long mission. We leaned into heavy winds, with traces of snow and hail on the walk from our barracks for breakfast at the Mess Hall for breakfast. Everyone agreed this was not a good day for flying. Briefing took place at 2:30 A.M. and our suspicions were correct, it was to be a long mission. The weather report was the most ominous news. We were advised of possible thunder clouds and powerful wind turbulence during our 4:30 a.m. take-off. However, they promised clear skies and better wind conditions when we reached our Group Assembly altitude of 9,000 feet. The trick was to get our 60,000 pound bomb-loaded B-17 up through the bad weather.

It was dark as hell at take-off and at 2,000 feet we were still surrounded by dark and turbulent clouds which seemed to multiply. Visibility was near zero and we were in a situation where any bomber flying dangerously close could cause a mid-air collision. Lt. Stauffer's order came over the inter-com:

"Everybody keep a close watch for planes. I need to know when and where, because if you see one, it will be too damned close! Stay off the inter-com except to answer oxygen checks!"

I'm sure every crew member, was peering out a window into the darkness, it was a matter of self preservation. We were still in the "soup" at 7,000 feet and I could barely see our wing tip from my small radio room window. Art Wright, our ball turret gunner was watching at a waist window. (Art didn't slide into his turret until we were above the North Sea) A few minutes after that warning, he was yelling on the inner-com,

"There's a plane below on the left --- coming up fast!"

That was the last inter-com message I heard. Our pilot immediately banked the Fortress to the right, causing it to violently sway out of control. I was seated at my radio desk when the centrifugal force took over. Suddenly, I was under a tremendous pressure, literally "nailed" to my swivel chair and unable to stand. At that instant, I had no idea if we were upside down or right side up. I only knew I could not move!

A minute later, the bomber leveled off and I was able to get up to grab my parachute from where it was stored above the radio receiver. I barely had time to hook it to my harness before the plane went into a steep dive. I was again under tremendous pressure and it took all my strength to drag myself out of the radio room back into the waist area. My goal was the waist exit door and possibly bailing out. Once I reached the waist, I could see and feel the tail section vibrating crazily. Our flight was unsteady and the plane was shaking and leaning from side to side. Meanwhile, three gunners and I were being thrown around in the waist area as we struggled to reach and hold on to a position near the escape door. The inter-com wasn't working so we had no communication from our pilot to inform us of the situation. There had been no bailout order or distress signal from anyone up front and we had no idea of what would happen next. Maybe the guys up front were incapacitated or worst of all, maybe they had bailed out and the plane was flying on auto-pilot. No one was about to crawl into the radio room and through the bomb-bay to get answers. It was apparent that we had to make our own decisions. It was still dark out there and we had no idea if we were flying over England or above the North Sea. We knew we had lost altitude, but weren't sure we were high enough to have time for our chutes to operate effectively. However, we knew we were doomed if the plane went into another dive. There was no choice but to try to bail out!

I was pressed against the wall of the aircraft, inches from the emergency door, when the replacement waist gunner (Lee Laura was ill) grabbed and pulled the door's emergency switch. The outside suction tore the door from its hinges, sucked it out into the darkness and I was sucked out with it. My decision had been made!

It was like being shot from a cannon. I was literally thrown space came to a sudden halt and I felt a tremendous physical shock from the parachute harness when my chute opened. It appeared that I was not moving, I was just hanging in the cold darkness in complete silence. A moment later, I heard a distant sound like a plane in trouble and assumed it was our Fortress. I continued my descent although I still had no sensation of falling. As I gazed through the darkness in all directions I saw a chute below and off to my right. I called out and asked who was down there! I didn't expect a reply, but I actually did hear him yell back to give his name and say he was OK. It was the replacement, gunner who had evidently bailed out immediately after my unexpected exit. There was less darkness now and I could see the ground far below. My sensation of falling came back and I realized I was going down rapidly. Next, I was startled by a huge blast that lit the sky from horizon to horizon and I knew *"Chute the Works"* had crashed! Seconds later, shock waves from the crash of our bomb-loaded Fortress hit me. My parachute shook violently and I feared it might collapse as I held on to those silk cords for dear life.

I was dropping rapidly and the ground was coming closer. I do not remember my feet touching the ground. I only remember being very cold, flat on the ground with my head aching and the left side of my body in severe pain. When I opened my eyes there was a big man with a pitchfork standing over me!

I had no idea how long I laid there or where I was. The man kept his pitchfork pointed in my direction. I pulled myself up very slowly for two reasons. I was so sore it was hard to stand and I didn't want to agitate a man with a pitchfork. I could tell that he wasn't sure if I was a Yank, a Brit or a German. l managed to stand and slowly remove my parachute harness and looked around to see the replacement gunner, who had landed before me, running in my direction. The man with the pitchfork escorted the two of us to a nearby farmhouse. The English farmer explained that our captor was an Italian Prisoner of War who was working on the farm. The farmer carefully looked us over and asked many questions before inviting us into his home. It was very relaxing to sit drinking a cup of hot tea while waiting for news of the rest of the crew. This was a welcome change from the terrifying experience I had endured. I was so thankful to be warm and alive.

An hour or so later, we experienced pure joy when a jeep pulled up and our pilot, Dave, jumped out to greet us with a big smile to ask how we were! He had been hurt when he slammed against metal while bailing out, but the three of us were thrilled to be alive and united. A few hours later our crew was together again except for Buss Eidemiller, our togglier and Howard Smith, the flight engineer. It wasn't long until a truck arrived to take us to a nearby RAF (Royal Air Force) field where we were welcomed with a good hot meal and cots to rest. Later in the day we were taken back to our base at Deenethorpe where I spent two days in the base hospital for observation. I learned I wasn't the only guy with a bad parachute landing. Our engineer, Howard Smith, was badly hurt when he smashed into tree branches as he landed. He spent several days in the hospital before he returned to our crew. Buss Eidemiller, nose-gunner and togglier, had a broken leg and was sent back to the states for further treatment.

They told us our bomber had become disabled in flight due to solid ice freezing all the vital moving controls and electrical systems. We were soon assigned another Fortress and flying missions to bomb and destroy German airfields, railroad marshalling yards and administrative buildings in the Rhine river area. We flew eight more missions for a total of twenty-five before the war ended May, 1945."

Howard says, "Today a Caterpillar Club Plaque hangs in my den. It has a black background, a drawing of a parachutist with my name, the original rip-cord metal D-ring and the date of my bailout. It is among the prize mementoes of twenty–five bombing missions as a B-17 Radio operator in the Eighth Army Air Corps so many years ago!"

The Caterpillar Club

The Switlik Parachute Company of Trenton, NJ, founded by parachute pioneer, Stanley Swhitlik is one of the sponsors of the Caterpillar Club, a non-military organization formed in Dayton, Ohio in 1922, when a test pilot bailed out and became the first flyer to be saved by a parachute. Various parachute companies have sponsored this world-wide club for military or commercial aviators who survived bailing from a plane. Flyers prize their Caterpillar Club Certificate and/or lapel pin as a reminder of the event which caused them to bail-out into the wild blue. Information from the Switlik Company says the club name was chosen because the silk for the parachute and shroud lines are provided by the lowly caterpillar worm that spins his cocoon and crawls out to fly away from certain death.

The Irvin Air Chute Company factory in Buffalo, NY opened a second factory in Letchworth, England prior to World War II. That plant produced 1,500 parachutes a week during the height the war. The Caterpillar Club formed by Leslie Irvin was named after the silk worm (caterpillar) that spins the silk from which parachutes were made. The Irvin company issued thousands of gold pins and/or certificates to men/

boys who could document that they were forced to "hit the silk" in an emergency situation during World War II. By late 1945 there were 34,000 Caterpillar Club members. The silk parachute saved many lives in World War II. Enemy anti-aircraft fire, mid-air collisions and mechanical failure made thousands of my generation eligible for membership!

The following poem was found in POW Leland Potter's journal.

Little Silk Worm
Little silk worm - so very small,
You saved me from an awful fall.
Tho' you're such an ugly thing,
I owe my life to your man- made wing

Regrettably, many lives were lost because bomber crewmembers, especially gunners, stored their chute near their position rather than hooking the chest-pack chutes onto their harness. There were many incidents of men dying without a chute in mid-air collisions or explosions. My chest-pack was heavy and bothersome, but I hooked it on as soon as we were airborne. Of course, being seated at the radio operator's desk was a distinct advantage. Bomber pilots and some officers up front often had seat or backpack parachutes like those worn by fighter pilots.

Parachute instructions for bomber crews:

1. Handle the parachute pack gently and do not allow it to get wet or greasy.
2. It is advisable to have one side of the parachute pack snapped to the harness when in immediate danger.
3. B-17 bomber crew jumping suggestions
    a. make a delayed jump
    b. Dampen oscillation (stop swinging)
    c. Face downwind
    d. Keep feet together
    e. Unhook snaps before descent over water
6. Use static lines to bail out wounded personnel.
7. Three short rings on alarm signal (bell) indicates 'prepare to bail out' One long ring is the signal to 'Bail Out'

A sign in our base parachute shack "If it doesn't work-- bring it back!"

Para-troopers in training were told a truck would be on hand near the jump area to pick them up. One sad-sack's parachute didn't work – he said, "Oh fine, and I bet that damned truck won't be there to pick me up either."

Chapter Six

Date With a Brit

We finished our thirteenth mission (we called it 12A) March 1st and I decided to leave early on a three day pass to London. This was my first solo trip to London, but I planned to meet the rest of my crew's gunners at the American Club in Piccadilly Circus later that day. This was the day I ended up in a train compartment with a Navy Commander, a French refugee woman and an English WAAF. That morning I caught the 490th "pass truck" to the railroad station in Diss. The small station platform was crowded with G.I.s from airbases around the area and local citizens waiting to welcome or say goodbye to family members. I knew I had to move fast to find a seat on the small train when it pulled in from Norwich. Passenger cars on England's small trains were not arranged like our coach cars with seats on each side of a center aisle. British trains separate compartments to seat six to eight passengers with outside doors. Passengers could enter or exit directly from the station platform. The train was on schedule and luck was with me as I moved beside the train. Two airmen stepped out of a compartment and I jumped in, stowed my overnight bag overhead and took a seat across from someone in a blue uniform. Three shrill whistles later, the train pulled out of the station. My fellow passengers included a U.S. Navy Commander, a brunette French girl, a teenage blond British WAAF, and me. Actually, we were a representative group of millions of youngsters involved in World War II and only one was in her home country.

The Navy man who was older (must have been at least twenty-five) carried the conversation. He said his ship was in for repair, he was on shore leave and headed for a sight-seeing tour of London. The French girl explained in very good English, that she was a refugee who had come to work in London shortly before Germany invaded France. Anne, the young English girl wore the British WAAF (Women's Auxiliary Air Force) uniform she told us she had volunteered and was stationed north of London.

Note - *The Women's Auxiliary Air Force (WAAF) was created as a volunteer service in July 1939 for women to enlist to help the war effort. Later all British women were required to register for draft at age eighteen to release men for combat. Thousands of young women assisted the Royal Air Force as drivers, typists and many other non- combat duties.*

The four of us became better acquainted as the train chugged toward London and each told a short story on why we were on the train. It was a sort of a 1945 Canterbury Tales event. Shortly before our journey ended, the Commander offered to treat the group to an early dinner at Maxims Chinese restaurant in London. Everyone accepted and we took a taxi from Liverpool Station directly to the famous restaurant where we were soon seated in elegant surroundings. I knew I was way out of my element, but there I was, a Hoosier teenager at a table in one of London's finest eating spots with three people I didn't know before I boarded the train. The menu wasn't in Chinese but it might as well have been, because I was so ignorant I wasn't sure what to order. The girls ordered first, I hesitated until the Commander ordered then wisely said,
"I'll have the same!"

I had no luck with chopsticks, except for providing amusement for the others, so I opted to switch to knife, fork and spoon. During the meal, the Commander and the French girl made plans for the remainder of the evening. The WAAF, Anne, had a train to catch, but suggested I might visit her at her post northwest of London. She gave me her address and phone number and I agreed to call when I got another pass. I had a great story to tell when met the guys at the American Club that night.

Three weekends later a three day pass came through and I caught an early train to London. That afternoon I was on a train headed for my date with a Brit. I arrived late in the afternoon and climbed a long flight of stairs leading up to the town's main street. There was a busy pub on the corner and a guy in front gave me directions. He said the

WAAF barracks were in two stone buildings just a bit down the street. His parting words were, "You caun't miss it."

He was right, I gave Anne's name to the guards at the gate and she soon came down the walk looking very sharp in her uniform. She exited the gate, snapped to attention and flipped me a salute. Well, that was a complete surprise to me and the gate guards. I laughed and reminded her that no one salutes Sergeants. She answered quickly,

"You fly bombing missions so you deserve a salute!"

That was a great way to start a date. I had no idea of the entertainment available, but I knew the blackout would soon go into effect. I was glad she suggested going to a nearby theater to see a new Humphrey Bogart-Lauren Bacall movie. The first sour note of the evening occurred when the old guy taking tickets in the lobby glowered at me and muttered, "You dammed Yank!"

I was mad as hell about that remark, but I held back a sharp answer. My date explained that some local citizens were still upset by the antics of some of the American troops who had trained in the area before D-Day. I decided to ignore the ingratitude of the old guy and enjoy the movie. It was a good movie and nice to be sitting in a movie holding hands with a good looking blonde. It was actually not much different from a high school date back home and for an hour or so the war seemed far away.

The black-out was in full effect when we left the theater but I figured I could find my way back down to the railroad station in the blackout. Anne's pass ended at 10:00 pm so we hurried back to the barracks gate. She said she had a great time on her first date with a Yank, gave me a peck on the cheek, flipped me a salute and disappeared through the gate into the darkness. Just like that, her date with a Yank and my date with a Brit ended. My next worry was finding my way back to the train station in a strange town as dark as Hitler's mustache. I was amazed at how an entire city could disappear into the night. The black-out was very effective and there was not a flicker of light as I worked my way down the dark street to the Pub on the corner where the customers were still whooping it up. From the top of the steps, I could barely make out the shape of the train station below. Half way down the stairs, I began to worry about the stark silence and it suddenly dawned on me that I had a big problem. The station was closed and I was up the creek without a paddle! That was the second sour note. I have felt stupid many times in my long life, but I think that situation was the tops. I was stuck in a town fifty miles from London with no way out and no place to sleep. Worst of all, I was facing the prospect of being AWOL and losing my stripes was staring me in the face!

My first plan was to go on down to see if there was a schedule for the time the morning train would leave for London. I hoped it would get me there in time to catch a train back to Eye and save my stripes. I was trying to make out the schedule on the station door when it cracked open and an old night watchmen with a covered lantern let me enter. I told him my problem and he was very willing to help. I was sure glad he didn't have the same opinion about Yanks as the old ticket taker at the theater. The station watchman answered my question by saying the timing for making train connections would be "very iffy" and he couldn't guarantee his train would leave on time. The good news was that he offered a couple of options: I could spend the night inside the station and sleep on a bench or I could go back up to the Pub to hitch a ride from the truck drivers who regularly gathered there for a pint or two before starting midnight runs into London. He suggested I go back up to the Pub and try to find a ride and if that didn't work out, I could come back down to sleep in the station. I thanked him for his help and climbed back up the long steps to the dark noisy Pub. I took a deep breath and pushed my way through the double set of blackout curtains covering the door and became the immediate center of attention as I entered the dimly lit room. An Eighth Air Force Yank in dress uniform seldom dropped in that late at night. Well, I had their attention, so I asked the big question.

"Can any of you guys give me a ride to London?" The room was silent for a minute and then a little old man seated at a table near the bar stood up and said,

"Sure Yank, I'll be glad to tyke ye in me lorry (truck). Come sit down, 'ave a pint and we'll be off soon."

I was more than eager to drink with him and pay his bill. That pint of "bitters" tasted like Champaign as I realized the odds of getting back the 490th base on time had just increased by leaps and bounds. A half hour later I followed my benefactor out to climb into his lorry and we were on our way. I never asked what he was hauling. I didn't care if it was dynamite, I just wanted to get back to London and catch the tube (subway) to Liverpool station. Like all vehicles in wartime England, the headlights were mere slits of light to warn pedestrians. Our speed was moderate, but the old man knew the road by heart. I dozed off a while and we were in London by morning. I have often wished I had taken down the names of the station watchmen and the lorry driver who gave a wandering Yankee airman help when he needed it.

Time passed as the war began to wind down and I wasn't about to go back to see Anne because of the transportation problem. However, fate decreed that we would meet one more time. It was late May, the war in Europe was over and our crew had a pass for London. We arrived early at the Diss railroad station and passengers from London were still on the platform. Suddenly, I saw Anne, my British date. She was startled to see me, then gave me an anxious glance with a pained expression that said,

"Please don't say anything."

I watched as she turned away and ran to greet her parents. I took the hint, and watched her well-to-do parents usher her to the family limo. Two things were clear: Anne didn't want her parents to know she had dated a Yank and she never wanted me to know that she lived near Diss. I felt a little down, but was glad I hadn't embarrassed her. However, all was forgiven when she turned, smiled and flipped me a salute before she entered the family car.

March 9 – The mission was to Frankfort railyards. The aircraft of Lt. Carl J. Fauster suffered a direct hit and exploded. Crew listed as MIA

Mid-Air Collision – March 17 - The Group was returning from a mission to the Bitterfeld rail-yards when two bombers collided on the flight home. Bombers piloted by Lt. Robert Tennenberg and Lt. Arthur Stern collided over enemy territory. Both planes dropped out of the formation; the Stern crew was lost, but the Tennenberg bomber managed to make an emergency landing in Belgium. For two days, we believed our buddies had died and were greatly relieved when they returned. They had escaped unharmed except for nose gunner, S/Sgt. John Gann was wounded but later re-joined the crew.

Note - *Read the complete story of the collision by Co-pilot Lt. Joel Johnson and S/Sgt.John Gann in "The Boys in the B-17"*

Jet Fighter Attack

Hutch #14 - Plauen   March 21 - Take-off at 6:00 with 36 planes in the formation and were flying at 21,000 feet carrying 1000 pound general purpose bombs. Our crew was flying the Lead position (middle squadron,) with Major Cochran as our command pilot and Major O'Dell as lead navigator. We were about twenty minutes from the IP for our target, the railroad yards at Plauen, when I heard the chilling message over the inter-com

"Bandits at Twelve O' Clock High!"

Twelve to fourteen ME-262 Schwalbe twin engine jet fighters hit the Low squadron of the formation. They were sweeping past us like bats out of hell and three bombers went down. From my small radio room window over the left wing, I saw a sky filled with tracer bullets and jets. I thought it was eerie that the markings on the jets were almost the same as ours; a red band around the wings and tail. Three bombers in the Low squadron were lost before we delivered our bombs. The aircraft of Lt. William I. Audette and Lt. Herman L. Ballard were shot down and the Lt. John J. Schultz plane went down when the ME 262 they shot down, crashed into it. Gunners in our 490th group were officially credited for downing one jet. It was another long mission and we were on oxygen for five hours. The command officers said our gunners were great and Pvt. Parrish earned back his S/Sgt. stripes. Believe me, a jet fighter attack made it hard for the atheists to maintain their non-belief. On the contrary, it was a perfect time to start praying for God's help in a hurry. I'm so thankful He answered mine!

Note (*See complete story of the Plauen mission in "The Boys in the B-17."*

T/Sgt. James Lee Hutchinson, Ed.S.

Plan Mission
Author's Diary 3-21-45

Stuttgart Rail Yards Bombed

Bad weather confined the weekend's activity by the Eighth Air Force to an attack Saturday by a small force of Fortresses, escorted by P51s, on the Kornwestheim railyards in the northern suburbs of Stuttgart. Three bombers were lost.

The Kornwestheim center is one of the two main marshalling yards in the Stuttgart area. The other, at Unterturkheim, just south of the city, was bombed and severely damaged Dec. 9.

Forts and Libs of the 15th Air Force Sunday carried out an assault on synthetic-oil plants at Blechhammer and near Odertal in Silesia. Escorting Mustangs and Lightnings encountered their first sizable formation of enemy fighters in weeks over northern Moravia, engaging in over 50 dogfights.

More Railyards Struck

Other B24s, ranging Austria, struck at rail yards at Salzburg and other targets at Wels, 15 miles southwest of Linz.

Mediterranean RAF heavies attacked motor transport in Jugoslavia, and others dropped supplies to British troops in Greece.

A Reuter dispatch said 300 German aircraft operated over the U.S. Ninth Army front Saturday night.

Meantime, it was announced that all of the tracks of the important Innsbruck railyards, at the head of the Brenner Pass, were cut and most of the sidings blocked in raids Friday and Saturday by Italy-based heavies.

Forts and Libs of the 15th Air Force Saturday also attacked synthetic-oil targets at Brux in Czechoslovakia.

Forts Batter Nazi Rail Points

In an effort to block choke-points on road and rail routes carrying supplies and reinforcements for counter-attacking German forces along the U.S. First Army front, more than 300 Fortresses of the Eighth Air Force attacked road and rail junctions in western Germany Tuesday.

FEB 17, 1945

FRANKFORT

210

Hutch #15 – Hannover, March 28, Took off 6:15 – Landed at 3:15 Led the High squadron with Command pilot, Major Wharton Cochran, Captain Edward O'Dell, lead navigator. The target for our 500 lb bombs was a tank factory and/or the central railroad station in the center of Hannover in middle Germany. On the way in, we flew over the front lines at 18,000 feet. The railroad station was well protected and heavy flak was right on us during the bomb-run. Or bomber shook and rocked as shells exploded under us. Lt. Jack Owen, Mickey Operator, and I had a regular sweat session when a <u>chunk of flak</u> came through the radio room just above our heads. The 490th Bomb Group flew 21 missions in March to carry out the Allies plan to aid ground forces by bombing railway centers and isolating the northern Rhur Valley.

March Report – The 490th flew twenty-one missions - a record for one month. Most targets were communication centers, airfields and railyards. The Eighth Air Force plan to isolate the Rhur Valley industrial area to assist our ground forces was working. However, it was not without costs as five aircraft were lost and several planes returned with wounded aboard and severe damage.

ME-109 Fighter Attack

Hutch #16 – Parchim, April 17 - Take-off 9:30, landed at 4:30. The target was a ME-262 jet airbase. We led the High squadron with Major Edward Blum as command pilot and Captain Sullivan, navigator. We were up at 4:00 o-clock and got delayed (Chicago-twelved) for an hour due to poor visibility. Sitting on the runway was boring, a ME-262 jet airfield was we really wanted to hit it as a matter of self-preservation. Destroying Luftwaffe jets and their fuel supply beats meeting them in aerial combat. It turned out to be the Templeton crew's most dangerous mission.

The entire Eighth Air Force went up today to go after jet bases in northern Germany. Bomber formations were tempting targets for the Luftwaffe pilots making last-ditch efforts to defend their country. We had a heavy P-51 fighter escort and we needed it! We were fighter bait again and our formation got hit by a couple of ME-109's just before we reached the IP (the start of our bombing run.) In spite of the fighter attack, the bombing results were excellent and our formation did lots of damage to that airfield. The flak was meager but accurate. We got about 25 holes in the plane. The Germans were using their flak trains. The 490th lost two aircraft and shot down an ME-109

Me-109 Rammer attack: The Schulungslehrgang Elbe was a Luftwaffe "rammer" fighter group organized late in the war. It was reported that they had 300 ME-109 pilots volunteer for this duty. The plan was for the pilot to fly straight at his target while firing. At the last minute he was to clip the tail or damage a wing of the bomber with his wing then bail out. If this wasn't a suicide group, it was awfully close! The Japanese had used suicide pilots since late 1944. The mission of the Kamikase (Divine Wind) group of young fliers was to crash their bomb-loaded plane into allied warships. They were successful in sinking more than 50 ships and damaging many others. However, by 1945, Luftwaffe pilots were generally not quite that fanatic.

The alarm came over the inter-com---Bandits at two o'clock high! This was the second time our crew had met fighters. Looking out my window, I could see two ME-109 fighters swooping down on our formation. The machine guns in their wings were blazing as they dived and our formation's B-17 gunners were sending a hail of .50 caliber slugs and tracers at the attackers. I stood to get a better view through the plexiglass roof of the radio room. Roddy's twin turret guns and Bert's waist gun jarred the plane as they blazed away. It was "fire at will" and we all knew which one was Will! This was the time for a lot of praying! Our tail gunner, Lt. Rector, and waist gunners, Lloyd Parrish and Bert Allinder, cut loose as the bandits swept over the formation.

One ME-109 pulled out about 250 yards behind us and came in on a pursuit curve. Our gunners had nailed him but he was determined to take out my Lead ship. His fighter was shot to pieces, flames were peeling the skin off the fuselage and its frame resembled a flaming orange crate as he dived down on the formation trying to ram our Fortress. I saw the pilot in his black leather jacket, slumped in his cockpit. He was dead or dying and did not attempt to bail-out. He meant to crash into us but missed and crashed into Lt. Cagle's bomber leading the element to our right. The fighter crashed just behind the B-17's left wing and ball turret and bounced off. Cagle's bomber managed to continue flying, drop out of the formation and land safely in northern France. The ball turret gunner was injured but survived. The second fighter circled and came back for another pass at our formation. Lt. Druhot's bomber, was hit. It was in the last element of our squadron, but I saw it from my radio room window. It was eerie to watch one of our bombers go down; everything seemed to be in slow motion. First, the B-17 dropped out of formation, drifted lazily into the open sky as the crew bailed out. I counted the white chutes popping open and drifting downward and thought most crewmembers had bailed safely out of the doomed plane before it went into a spin. Our group leader decided to bomb in formation in order to concentrate our fire power on the fighters. The Luftwaffe fighters had actually followed us into the flak during the bomb-run.

Interrogation Report: Landed at 4;00 p.m. Two planes from the 850 squadron went down on this raid. The Lt. Richard L. Druhot crew was lost in action and Lt. Carrol D. Cagle's bomber was rammed and badly damaged by a fighter, but managed to land in Belgium. Those ME-109 fighters were from the Schulungslehrgang Elbe, a special 'rammer squadron' formed in the last months of the war. Their suicidal tactics were a last ditch effort to prolong a lost cause. We had met the rammer squadron!

Hutch - #17   Roudnice, Czechoslovakia, April 17, Take off 9:14 Landed 6:30 We flew Lead today, our target was an underground oil storage depot at Roudnice, Czchechslovokia. Major Druehl J. Day was our command pilot. Mission was 8 hours, 20 minutes and we were on oxygen 3 hours. We led the bomb wing and went practically to Prague. I was busy as hell---sent six control point (location) reports. We were so far away that I had to send the strike report a four times before I got a receipt. We had 30 aircraft and many escort fighters. Gunners were very alert as we were back in ME-262 jet fighter territory and the Luftwaffe fighters were very protective of their dwindling fuel supplies. We blew it up O.K. and Stars and Stripes reported more than 850 Eighth Air

Force fighters covered 1,000 liberators and Fortresses on raids deep into Germany and Czechoslovakia. The U.S. fighters downed 200 Luftwaffe fighters and destroyed another 240 on the ground. This brought the U.S. total to over 941 German fighters destroyed in two days. Mighty Eighth bombers hit four targets near Prague deep into Nazi territory.

490TH BLACK THURSDAY

Aussig, the German name for Usti nad Labem, Czechoslovakia was a prime target because of the Skoda Arms Works which produced arms and munitions in Germany annexed and occupied the country in 1938 and converted the Czech steel center into a giant military industrial complex, much like the Ruhr Valley. The city was located on the Elbe river near Germany's southeast border. A large Skoda munitions factory was also established at Pilsen. The area was almost out of the range of Allied bombers, so it led a safe life until near the end of World War II. As early as April 16, 1943, an RAF night mission of than 300 Lancaster bombers made the long flight to Pilsen, Czechoslovakia, to hit the Skoda Arms Works. They blasted the area with 691 tons of bombs, but lost 36 aircraft. They tried again a month later and the 150 bombers correctly identified the target, but dropped most of their bombs in a field outside the plant. The huge loss of men and bombers made the raids too costly. It was many months before another attempt was made. The next mission was not until October, 1944, when the Fifteenth Air Force sent bombers to Czechoslovakia. They were successful in striking the Brux synthetic oil plant, Skoda Works at Pilsen, and rail yards.

Our 490th Bomb Group lost four aircraft to ME-262 jets when the Eighth Air Force made the Aussig raid April 19, 1945.

The Templeton crew did not fly the Aussig mission, but it was a very important one to us because Wilbur Lesh, who was our former ball turret gunner and a very good friend was operating an Electrical jammer on one those downed bombers. It would be years before I learned of Wilbur's fate. Our former tail-gunner, Ralph Moore flew and survived that mission.

The April 19, 1945 mission to Aussig, Czechoslovakia was the next to last mission of the 490th Bomb group. It was truly our Black Thursday, because of the loss of crewmen and bombers. It was reported that the group overshot the IP (initial point) to start the bombing run and flew too close to Prague. The formation then had to circle west and come back to the IP. The 490th formation was attacked by a group of Luftwaffe ME-262 twin-engine jet fighters before they got back to start the bomb run. Four of our B-17 bombers were shot out of the low formation in a very few minutes. The following stories are based on recollections as printed in the *History of the 490th Bomb Group* and/or interviews with others who have provided information about that fateful mission to Aussig. Stories may vary, but the reader should remember that they are based on memories of those who were there in the heat of battle and/ or did research on a tragic incident that happened more than sixty- eight years ago.

Lt. Lawrence J. (Larry) Bellarts, pilot in the 849th squadron, was flying in the low squadron on his 35th and final combat mission to complete his tour of duty:

"I was flying lead of the third 'V' with Lt. Buford E. Stovall on my right wing and Lt. William E. McAllister on my left. Lt. Robert A. Norvell was leading a diamond element below and behind me. Near the target an Me-262 came in from two o'clock high and Stoval went down. Norvell brought up his diamond to fill the empty position on my right wing. The jet came in again from ten o'clock high and Mc Allister on my left wing was hit and went down. The enemy fighter made another attack from two o'clock and the Norvell plane fell out of the formation. He came after us once more from behind (six o'clock,) but was hit before he could pick me off. I had told the all the gunners to start firing, even before he was in range. I think that might have saved us. The doomed fighter passed under us; close enough for me to see the shattered cockpit with the black-suited pilot hanging lifeless out the left side."

Lt. Buford E. Stovall was the pilot of one of the bombers shot down. His graphic account illustrates the perils of bailing out and surviving against the odds:

T/Sgt. James Lee Hutchinson, Ed.S.

"A swarm of ME-262 jets appeared without warning and swept through my low squadron formation. They missed our plane on the first two passes. The third time around we were hit between the two left engines and a quarter of the wing was blown off. That hit knocked us out of the formation. Flak began bursting all around us and the fighters made six or seven more passes. Our flight controls, automatic pilot radio and oxygen systems were all hit. The three of us around the cockpit-co-pilot, engineer and I were not wounded, but everybody else in the crew had at least five holes in them from flak or bullets. One man was hit forty-three times. I gave the order to bail out and held the controls while everybody jumped. When I went out, the left wing broke off where it had been hit between the two engines"

Lt. Stovall landed in a pine forest and injured his legs, but managed to avoid SS troops in the area. He made contact with a Czech forest ranger who helped him hide for a few days until Russian troops liberated the area. On his trip back to England, he met his ball turret gunner in Paris and learned that the rest of his crew had been captured, but were okay now. One crew member who had been wounded many times was left in a Czech hospital.

Sgt. Dennis M. Richardson a gunner on the Stovall bomber also gave an account of the mission:

"The mission was going fine until enemy fighters attacked us at about 11:30 a.m. that day. After a running battle that was pretty hot, we were shot up so badly that we had to bail out about half-way between Aussig and Prague. Every crew member was wounded to some degree, but we all lived through it except our radio operator, Frank Mateyka. He was killed some time after he reached the ground. I had about forty shrapnel wounds in me by the time I landed, but I kept moving until I came to the small town of Litzen. A Czech doctor dressed my leg and side and then directed me to a hospital. About midnight, only twelve hours after bailing out, I was captured by the Germans and held there until April 22 nd. They took me to Rucine, just outside of Prague where I was held until the 6th of May when the Czechs and Russians moved in and chased them out. The Germans moved back towards the western front and took me with them. We reached the American lines on May 9th and I was free."

Maj. Joel R. Johnson, Co- Pilot (Ret) - Joel and I met at the 490th reunion in Washington D.C. and exchanged several e-mails in the following years. During his tour, Joel was involved in a mid- air collision and several fighter attacks. He had an excellent memory and shared many experiences for my stories before he passed in 2013. Second Lt. Johnson was co-pilot on the Lt. Robert Tennenberg plane which was also flying in the low squadron on the Aussig mission. Joel shared some of his memories of that fateful day:

"We were flying right wing in the lowest element of the low squadron An element is made up of three planes. Number one is the element leader, his left wing is number two and his right wing is number three. I remember two or three ME-262 fighters coming in from two o'clock high. They hit the lead squadron first with cannon fire and one plane on the left side blew. (Snyder) The next attack was on our low squadron and we lost three bombers in a matter of minutes. I really had a front row seat flying in the right seat on the bottom right of the low squadron. I had a clear view of the lead squadron. The first plane to go down was in the lead squadron, then I would say our low element leader was second, the airborne spare was the third and the right wing in the element above us was the fourth. So in the low squadron, that would have been Stovall, Norvell and Mc Allister. But, I am not sure of the names or the order they went down. Only one ME- 262 jet flew through our squadron with all of our gunners firing at him. He was trailing black smoke and John Gann, our nose gunner, said he was going so fast that he could hardly get a bead on it. However, our crew got credit for a "probable" downed fighter. All this action transpired in a time frame of five minutes or less and we were busy trying to survive and deliver our bomb load. This was my last mission and the first time that the palms of my hands perspired. I believe that if there had been four or five German jets with enough fuel; they could have shot down the entire 490th Bomb Group that day!

Lt. McAllister's bomber was the second to fall out of the formation with the number two engine on fire. However, they were able to extinguish the fire, rejoin the group and bomb the target. Sadly, the plane exploded in mid-air shortly after leaving the target and there were few survivors. Co-pilot Lt. Glen Howard, on his thirty-third mission, bailed out just before the explosion and tail gunner, Sgt. Paul Webb was blown out of the plane by the explosion. This was Lt. McAllister's first mission and he carried it gallantly to the end. The fighter attack and loss of four bombers did not stop the 490th Bomb Group from completing their mission; they continued on to bomb the railroad yards at Aussig! It was the next-to-last mission flown by ME-262 jet fighters and also for the 490th Bomb Group. The following story tells of the sad fate of eight airmen taken prisoner by the SS Troops.

"We salute the men who flew the Aussig mission"

German SS Atrocity

The 157th mission of the 490th Bomb Group on April 19, 1945 sent thirty bombers to hit the railroad yards at Aussig, Czechoslovakia. The mission with a total of 500 bombers turned out to be the next-to-last raid our group would fly and one of the most disastrous. The 490th Bomb Group formation was attacked by ME-262 jet fighters as it made a 270 degree over Prague to get back to the IP (initial point) and start the bomb run. Four bombers in the low squadron were shot down or damaged minutes before they reached the target. Some crew members of the Lt. Buford E. Stovall, Lt Robert A. Norvell and Lt. Paul A. Snyder bailed out into enemy territory. A few escaped into the heavily forested countryside and were aided by sympathetic Czechs who realized the war was nearly over. Other men stayed with their plane, hoping they could stay airborne. Lt. McAllister managed to extinguish an engine fire and re-join the formation to bomb the target.

Much of the following information was pieced together through the research information of Andrew Grier Smith Brunson and Scot Lowry. Both have visited the site of the atrocity and the Memorial.

A garrison of German Waffen SS troops was stationed at Konopiste Castle near Benesov, Czechoslovakia. Ten of the parachuting airmen landed inside SS Training Grounds and the SS troopers had been waiting as they floated down. One man was instantly killed, one managed to escape into the forest and eight were taken prisoner and interrogated. The fact that the war was almost over did not deter the SS soldiers from murdering their eight prisoners of war. This all happened only eleven days before Germany asked for a truce! The Americans were prisoners of war and should have been treated as such. Their murder was an atrocity that reveals the brutality of Hitler's fanatical thugs. Germans in the SS (Schutzstaffel) wore their black uniforms with pride. They were Hitler's elite guard, and had been empowered to enforce Nazi policy without fear of prosecution. In short, they had a license to murder!

S/Sgt. Wilbur Lesh

Wilbur was a former member of our crew. He was eighteen and newly married when he joined us in Sioux City for aircrew training as our ball turret gunner. We flew together for three months in crew training, and on our first four combat missions. Then the Templeton crew was made "lead crew" and flew bombers with the PFF radar dome in the place of a ball turret. Wilbur and our tail gunner, Ralph Moore were transferred to the 490th gunnery pool to fly missions with crews needing replacements. They often came back to visit Hut 29 and share the "fish and chips" we ordered from the pub up the road. Wilbur flew with our crew again on the January 20th mission to Sterkade-Reine. He later trained to operate the ECM Jammer equipment, a device to "scramble" enemy radio and electrical signals. I believe he was flying that position on the Lt. Paul Snyder plane when it was shot down. Wilbur was a great friend and it was a shock to our crew when we heard that our buddy's plane had gone down. We could only hope that he bailed out and landed safely.

It was sixty years later before I learned the details of his murder. The information was first given me by Eric Swain of London, England, the 490th Bomb Group Historian and Archivist. I included it in my first book, Through These Eyes." I have since gained more detailed information on the tragedy from recollections in the 490th Historical, interviews and the records/ research of Grier Smith Brunson and Scot Lowery who had relatives on the Aussig mission.

The Lesh family had four sons. Wilbur and two others died in WW II. His body was recovered from the mass grave shortly after American troops arrived and he now lies in the Ardennes American Cemetery in Neupre, Belgium: Row 25, plot A, grave 7. He is one of 5,328 other young men buried there, three fifths of which were airmen. The majority of the others died in the Battle of the Bulge.

Sgt. Newton Parker

Newton Parker, tail-gunner on the Norvell plane, was the uncle of Scot Lowry. The stories Scot heard from his uncle as a young boy, encouraged him to do extensive research on the Aussig mission. I am indebted to Mr. Lowery for the information his research and interviews have provided for his story of his uncle's escape.

"The Norvell plane had lost its number two engine, dropped out of the group formation and the crew was ordered to bail out. However, Lt. Norvell and the engineer stayed with plane, jettisoned their bombs and flew eighty miles before they were shot down and became prisoners of war. Ten men who bailed out of the downed Fortresses landed in an SS training ground. One was killed while trying to surrender, one escaped and eight were captured and became prisoners of war. The eight captives were taken to the SS headquarters at Konopiste castle for interrogation. Shortly before midnight on April 19, 1945 the SS troopers took their bodies away from the castle in a truck. These men were prisoners of war and should have been protected under the rules of the Geneva Convention, but they were murdered and buried in a mass grave."

The airman who avoided capture was Sgt. Newton Parker, tail-gunner on the Norvell crew. Years later, he told the story of his miraculous survival to his nephew, Scot Lowry:

"A strong wind caught his parachute when he landed and it dragged him towards the woods and away from the German soldiers who were firing at him as he fled into the trees. Sgt. Parker slipped out of his chute harness and ran for his life. He hid in heavy briars thickets and burrowed into snow banks while the Germans searched for him. He heard shots fired by troops searching for other American airmen. Although it was April, the Czech mountains still had snow and freezing temperatures. Parker had lost his boots when he was dragged by the parachute. However, he knew he must run or be captured. For seven days, he hid during the day and traveled by night, barefoot without food or water. The gritty tail gunner traveled many miles with the aid of his compass before he collapsed from exhaustion. A Czech railroad worker found him lying near the railroad tracks and took him to his home. The Czech family lived in the small village of Tochovice, in the middle of the Czech countryside. They helped my uncle recover, dressed him in farm clothes and passed him off as a deaf-mute son. The family heroically hid an American airman, knowing they would be executed if they were found out. He was very fortunate to be have been kept safely by this family until the war ended."

Sgt. Newton Parker narrowly escaped from the murderous SS troopers, but he said he had nightmares for the rest of his life!

First Lt. Lorenzo G. Smith Jr.

Lt. Smith was the co-pilot on the Norvell plane,"*Little Red's Wagon*" and they were flying their twenty-seventh mission. The number two engine caught on fire during the Me-262 attack and most of the crew bailed out. Andrew Grier Smith Brunson, the son of Lt. Smith, was one month old at the time of the atrocity. Mr. Brunson has done extensive research on the Aussig mission, visited and the site of the murder of his father and the other seven prisoners in Czechoslovokia. The following information was provided by Mr. Brunson:

"The airmen were interrogated, robbed of their valuables and dog tags. (identification) Each man was executed by a pistol to the temple sometime after midnight, so there were no witnesses. The SS squad then placed the bodies in a wagon and drove to a field two miles away where they buried their victims in a common grave and covered it with a haystack. The unmarked grave was discovered a few months later by a Czech farmer. My father, Lt. Lorenzo G. Smith was identified by dental records and re-interred at Arlington National Cemetery in 1949.

The Commandant of the SS Garrison, General Otto Haupricht and the SS Commander, Albert Karasche were allegedly tried for war crimes at Nuremburg, but testified that the prisoners were shot while "trying to escape." They avoided punishment and survived in Germany for many years. Members of the execution squad were never tried for their crime. Mr. Andrew Grier Smith Brunson states: "My father was murdered at Konopiste castle and I have spent a great part of my life making sure this war crime is not forgotten."

Today, at Konopiste castle, near Benesov, Czech Republic, there is a monument to honor the memory of the nine U.S. bomber crew members who were captured and murdered by German SS troops eleven days before the end of the war. The Czech people suffered greatly during the Nazi occupation. They have always been grateful to the United States for freeing them from Germany. The mayor of Benesov sent a copy of the Memorial drawing to Mr. Brunson for suggestions regarding the design of a new memorial which was re-dedicated in 2005. Town officials and military personnel hold wreath-laying services at the monument every April 19th to honor the 490th Bomb Group airmen who died to free their country.

Mr. Brunson continues: "My hat is off permanently to you magnificent airmen who fought so nobly for the freedom your children enjoy, and I wanted to add my voice to the thousands of Americans (and Europeans)who thank you for your courage and sacrifice. We shall not see the like of your generation again."

Sincerely, Andrew Grier Smith Brunson (adopted)

The 490th Monument in Czechoslovakia

The following inscription is in Czech and English:

We honor the sacrifice of these nine American airmen who were murdered while prisoners of war on April 19, 1945."

849th Sqd.
B-17 #43-38078

Lorenzo G. Smith, Jr.	1st Lt.
Leo L. Borden	2nd Lt
Carl B. Johnson, Jr.	Sgt.
Gordon P. Lake	Sgt.
Robert A. Johnson	Sgt.
Peter Malires	Sgt.

850th Sqd.
B-17G #43-38701

Joseph A. Trojanowski	2nd Lt.
Wilbur L. Lesh	Sgt.
Lyle E. Dole	Sgt.

FREEDOM

Hutch # 18 Nauen - April 20 - Wake up 1:00 and take-off 6:00 Landed 5:15 for a 7 and ½ hour mission; we were on oxygen for three hours. This mission was to support our ground troops, earlier we had been named a Tactical Air Force. Our former crewmember, Wilbur Lesh was shot down yesterday when his formation had been hit by ME-262 jets over Benesov, Czechoslovakia. We were sad and nervous on this second Air Medal Oak Leaf cluster mission. Col. Bostrom was Group Commander and Maj. Lightener as our command pilot in the Lead squadron. Our formation of thirty bombers was loaded with ten 500 pounders. We bombed from 22,000 feet. Nauen was on the outskirts of Berlin but we encountered no flak or fighters. We dropped to 5,000 feet on our way home and saw some of the destruction of Germany. It was a mission to support our ground troops. It proved to be the last combat mission for the 490th Bomb Group. It was a coincidence that our crew's first and last combat missions were to the outskirts of Berlin! We took a couple of group pictures with our Mickey operator's camera when we landed, but I never got copies. We didn't realize that it was our last combat mission!

April 25, 1945 - five days before Germany asked for a truce, the Eighth Air Force launched their last heavy bomber combat mission of the European Theater and destroyed 75% of the Skoda Armaments at Pilsen, Czechoslovakia!

490th April Report – Group members were saddened when President Franklin D. Roosevelt died April 12, a few weeks before victory in Europe. This was a costly month - we lost ten planes and many men as we flew 15 missions in 18 days. April 9th, the Lt. William S. Schoenfield crew was shot down again on a mission to an airfield at Schliessheim. This was the second time that crew went down. We lost three planes on April 16th and nine of the men who bailed out over Benesov, were captured, murdered by German SS troops and buried in a mass grave. Our friend and former ball turret gunner, S/Sgt Wilber Lesh was one of those men. Their bodies were later recovered from and Wilbur lies in plot A - Row 25 - Grave 7 in the Ardennes American Cemetery in Belgium. The Lesh family had four sons in service in World War II, three died.

At the end of the month Germany asked for a truce and the 490th Bomb Group prepared for food drop flights to Holland.

Chapter Seven

The Twelfth and Fifteenth Air Forces

Early in the war Stalin complained that he was carrying too much of the war in the east which was beyond the range of Eighth Air Force. We could not help Russia because they were simply out of range of heavy bombers based in England. Allied leaders recognized the strategy of attacking from the south and Operation Torch (invasion of Africa) was launched to create the Mediterranean Theater of Operations The British and American invasion of North Africa November 8, 1942 gained enough territory to send Twelfth Air Force bombers to makeshift airfields in the desert to bomb German and Italian targets in North Africa, Sicily and Italy. The 97th Bomb Group was first stationed in England and was the first B-17 group sent to North Africa in November of 1942. The 301st was the second group transferred from England and the 99th Bomb Group arrived in March of 1943. It was the third B-17 Bomb Group assigned to the 12th Air Force early in the war. The 99th Bomb Group flew 395 combat missions.

The Twelfth Air Force operated from temporary airfields at Casablanca. Marakech, Tunis etc. to hit German and Italian troops and moved often as our troops advanced across North Africa. Bombers provided tactical support for Allied troops and made long range missions to attack Sicily and Italy. As the war progressed, the 15th Air force was created and absorbed the 12th Air Force as a tactical unit.

August 1, 1943 while Allied armies were invading Sicily, a daring bombing mission named "Operation Tidal Wave" was carried out against the Ploesti oil fields in Romania. A formation of 179 B-24 Liberator bombers took off from bases in Libya for a low level surprise raid on the Ploesti oil refineries in Romania. Planes from the 44th, 93rd, and 389th groups of the Eighth Air Force and the 98th and 367th groups of the Ninth Air Force were combined to create the mission. It was a long flight, but the heavily protected area was a prime target as it was producing more than half of Germany's oil supply. However, German radar detected the formation and the element of surprise was lost, but 174 of the B-24s that reached the target went in at treetop level. The losses were extremely high: 55 bombers were lost, 17 were downed by fighters and another 38 were lost to flak. MACR (missing aircraft reports) showed that of the 1,137 airmen on the mission: 308 were KIA and 208 were POWs or interned. Ploesti was well protected and many more missions were carried out before the area was eventually conquered by Russian troops. Over 300 bombers and 3,000 men were lost before Hitler's oil supplies were put out of business.

Those missions paved the way for Allied troops to conquer Italy and the airfields were moved across the Mediterranean to Foggia, Tortorella, Ramitelli and other bases in Italy. By mid 1944, all airfields were located in Italy. The Ploesti oil fields in Romania were the source for approximately 60% of Germany's oil and gas for their war machines. They were heavily protected and one of the most dangerous targets aircrews could pull, second only to the Schweinfurt ballbearing plant or Regensburg aircraft factories in Germany. Once the allies conquered southern Italy, the airfields in the Foggia area became available for allied bomber bases. By April 1944, the Fifteenth Air Force became a large and efficient force, composed of twenty-one bomb groups which were supported by seven fighter groups. It was second only to the Eighth Air Force in England. Hitler's Third Reich was now caught between two powerful forces. The Eighth pounded from the north while the Fifteenth flew over the Alps and blasted them from the south. The Commander of Air Corps in Europe, General Carl Spaatz, declared after D-Day that one of the primary tasks of heavy bomb groups was the destruction of Germany's oil supply. The Ploesti, Romania oilfields supplied the bulk of Hitler's oil and became a prime target of the Fifteenth Air Corps. Airmen referred to Ploesti as the "graveyard of the Fifteenth" because it was such a heavily defended target.

Ploesti was always a tough target but it became much closer after the invasion. It was not long before Allied aircraft ruled the air in the Mediterranean area and the Fifteenth Air Force concentrated on supporting our troops and hitting strategic targets in Austria, Romania and southern Germany. Fifteenth bombers flew over the Alps to hit targets in southern Axis territory. Their bombers could now reach targets out of range of the Eighth in England. The Fifteenth had both B-24 Liberator and B-17 Flying Fortress Bomb Groups and their missions were very effective as they hit strategic targets to stop Mussolini and Hitler's war. With additional bombers and fighter support, they were able to fly more missions to destroy Germany's oil supply with shorter raids on the Ploesti oil fields in Romania. The Eighth and the RAF (Royal Air Force) Lancaster and Halifax bombers from England continued their "around the clock" raids on transportation and industry in central Germany. Allied aircraft were blitzing Germany by air from all angles to bring an end to the war. August 1944 the 15th launched missions to assist in the Allied invasion of southern France.

S/Sgt. Harold Plunkett

Sgt. Plunkett started his is diary on the day he boarded a troopship for North Africa; April Fools Day 1943. This article is adapted from that diary and personal interviews. S/Sgt. Plunkett flew fifty-six bombing missions on a B-17 Flying Fortress in the very early days of WW II when the 12th Air force was still based in Africa. He flew on fifty six missions of those flights over North Africa, Sicily and Italy when the German and Italian Air Forces were strong. Some days they did two missions. He nearly died twice. Today, Harold says hanging under the bomber in the ball turret gave him a complete view of the sky and all the combat action. In short, it was truly "the best seat in the house."

He served in the 49th squadron of the Second Bomb Group of the 12th Air Force first based in Casablanca. He had been trained as a Radio Operator, but his five foot five inch height was a perfect fit for the ball turret. He weighed 125 pounds, soaking wet, and quickly adapted to his new position; hanging under the B-17 in a plexiglass bubble while curled up under two fifty caliber machine guns. The ball gunner did not enter the turret until the plane was in flight. I recently asked Harold about that procedure. He said he had to manually crank the turret until the guns were facing the tail and pointing straight down. This rotated the ball so the entry hatch could be opened inside the plane and a waist gunner would help him slip down into the turret until he was lying on his back under the guns with his feet fitted into metal stirrups and his head lined up with the Sperry gun sight so he could control the vertical line on his gun sight with his right foot. Two handles over his head held controls to allow him to rotate the turret, adjust the horizontal line in his gun sight and fire his guns. Once Harold was in position and his chest chute was hooked to his harness, the waist gunner closed the hatch and Harold had power to rotate the guns up and forward for a clear view of the sky. In an emergency, he could open the hatch, unhook his safety belt and bail (fall) out. The turret had an oxygen hook-up, intercom and a heat plug for the forty below zero temperature. His crew faced flak over the target and enemy fighters on most of their missions. The ball turret rotated full circle and the guns moved 90 degrees up or down. It was a very important gun position for the bomber's defense. The gunner could be in the ball for five to six hours. The inter-com was his only contact with the rest of the crew. A small window on top of the ball turret allowed waist-gunners to check on him in an emergency. The turret was crowded he had space for his chest-pack parachute and a box or two of K-rations. There was no room for claustrophobia! When the mission was over and they neared the airbase, Harold rotated the ball so the guns faced the tail and straight down. A waist gunner would open the hatch on the ball so he could climb back into the plane. He then turned off all switches in the ball, closed the hatch and hand-cranked the guns up before they landed. Harold said he cleaned and oiled his .50 caliber guns on days he was not scheduled for a mission. His gun barrels some time needed to be replaced when they burned out during heavy fire in a fighter attack.

Harold's Diary – "Back on Dec. 7, 1941, my family returned from Church, had our Sunday dinner and was listening to the "Walgreen Hit Parade" on the radio when the program was interrupted and they announced that Japan had attacked Pearl Harbor. I had a friend who was in the Navy at Pearl Harbor. So the next day, Monday, Dec. 8, 1941, I went to the recruiting office and enlisted. The Recruiting Sergeant saw me looking at the model airplanes hanging from the ceiling and told me to pick out the one I wanted to fly. So I picked out a fighter plane and he said, "OK, sign right here". (We all know how that worked out). It didn't and I was sent to Scott Field Illinois, to be trained as a radio operator/mechanic.

Late March, 1943 - We left or combat crew training airbase in Lewistown, Montana, knee deep in snow, with all the wool clothes we could put on, and boarded a troop train. We unloaded in New Brunswick, N.J. and were quarantined to our barracks until we received orders to board ship. We boarded the ship wearing the same clothes we had on when we left the snow in Lewistown, Montana. We were given a barracks bag to tag with our name and put in all of our possessions. It was then placed in the hold of the ship, with thousands of others. April Fools' Day, 1943, we sailed from New Brunswick, N. J. aboard the S. S. Monterey a beautiful touring ship, in peacetime but now a troop ship. We did not know where we were going. The only word we had was that we were going to Africa as part of a very large convoy, going to combat the Axis. When we landed in Casablanca, April 11, 1943, the temperature was 110 in the shade and we were wearing the same clothes we were wearing when we left Montana. Every man was issued a steel helmet, a 1920 Springfield rifle, a clip of live ammunition, (we were now in a combat zone). We marched down the gangplank past a mountain of barracks bags and were ordered to grab one and keep going. We marched (very loosely), until we came to a very large vacant field about five miles east of Casablanca We were told to find a friend because we each carried half of a "pup" tent and needed to join up with another guy to make a complete pup tent. We were all in dire need of a rest room, with none in sight, so we were given shovels to dig slit trenches to relieve ourselves. It was very humiliating to us, until we noticed that the people walking or traveling along the highway were doing the same thing in the tree row beside the highway. Then we were allowed to lie down inside our pup tents for some shade and rest. I was a Staff Sergeant, which made me one of the few Noncoms, among hundreds of other GIs. I was soon prodded awake by an MP (military policeman) and told to pick several men to do guard duty surrounding our camp site by sunset. I was very unhappy with the assignment, as were the men I picked to help.

We were very scared, not knowing what the enemy might look like at night and carrying guns that we had never fired. Every once in a while, one of the guards would hear something out in the darkness make a sound and BANG they would shoot towards the sound. The Officer of the night watch and I would get in a Jeep and go towards the sound of the shot and when we found the guard he would be standing there, his gun at the ready and shaking in his boots. When we asked him what he shot at, he said, "I don't know, but whatever made the noise has stopped". Neither the officer nor I was willing to go out into the dark to find out what had been hit, so we waited until daylight. The next morning, we discovered a few dogs and one camel shot had been shot.

April 12, 1943 - We finally started to get some order in our camp, had some sort of breakfast and started to put up canvas on each side of our slit trenches so we could have some kind of privacy. We spent the rest of the day trying to find the man that matched the name on the barracks bag that we had carried off the ship! The next day we finally felt rested and were issued summer uniforms fitting for the heat of North Africa. Everybody was glad to shed those winter uniforms we had been wearing since we left Lewistown. Then we started trying to get friendly with our weapons. We had been given a few more clips of ammunition, just in case they would be needed, because the French people were divided between their allegience. Some were for Petain, some were for DeGaulle; we didn't know who was for us or against us.

April 15, 1943 - We worked all day washing down the airplane, *"Peggy O'Neil"*, named after the Pilot's wife. We knew that a dirty plane would have a lot of "drag" and we wanted our plane to fly "Fast." The first physical labor I had done in eight months. I went to bed early with a broken heart. I had been transferred to the crew of Capt. Roscoe Johnson, Pilot of the *"Wiley Witch"*. He needed a ball turret gunner and since I was only 5'5" tall and weighed 125 pounds I would fit in the turret very well, or any place else on the airplane a person was needed. I did eventually fly in almost every position on the airplane. The radio operator didn't do much during combat, no transmissions made during combat, unless it was an S.O.S., but the ball turret was a very busy spot.

The captain said I couldn't kill anybody with a radio. I had never been in a ball turret until we got into combat, but I did fit very well in it. Most of the men wouldn't have any part of it because it was a very cramped position and it was the only position on the plane where you couldn't look around and see somebody. In the ball turret, you saw nothing but space.

April 22, 1943 - It rained again all day, so we hibernated in the planes. They brought supplies to us in jeeps; supplies which consisted of "C" & "K" rations, stationery, magazines. They had run out of cigarettes, so they brought pipes and tobacco in tins and pipes for those who wanted to smoke. I wrote four letters home. The ground crews came into St. Donat by cattle car. It's going to be good to have somebody to take care of our planes, they know what they are doing and can do the repair on our planes in a fourth of the time that it takes us.

April 23, 1943 - Didn't do too much today, washed down the "Wiley Witch" using undershirts and 110 octane gasoline. Did a real good job. We sure don't stay in one place very long. We moved east again. Flew over to Chateau dun, Algeria, which will be our new base, but who knows for how long.

April 24, 1943 - The ground crews came over in trucks today. For some reason it seems to take those big lumbering trucks a long time to move from place to place, compared to the time it takes us to fly from place to place. What a day we had, handshaking, hugging, pats on the back, yelling until we got to pitch camp. The flying officers slept in all kinds of tents, from pup tents to six man tents. The administration offices were in tents, the mess hall was a tent...everything was in tents. Those rocks sure made soft mattresses, but at least we didn't have to sleep in the planes. The sleeping tents were laid out in a square, about a quarter of a mile each side, with everything else inside the square. We even had a baseball diamond inside the square. Our planes were scattered out about a mile to a mile and a half away from our camping area. Another Sunday without any church.

May 18, 1943 - Our target was somewhere in Sicily today, and General Doolittle flew on this mission, but we couldn't find our target because of clouds, so we dropped our bombs into the Mt. Etna volcano, trying to get it to erupt. We did this more than once but it never erupted until after we had captured Sicily.

June 23, 1943 - The Arabs are supposed to revolt today, don't know what about, but we are on a close alert for any uprising. They aren't really for either side, the Axis or the Allies. But every time we move and get settled in, the German artillery are right on us, until our own artillery shuts them down. We often saw an Arab man sitting on top of a sand dune playing a little flute, but didn't give it any thought. We later found out they were sending messages from hilltop to hilltop, giving the Germans our location. That is how they were finding our location, so we began to shoot the Arab's we found on a hill playing their little flutes.

June 25 - Went to Messina, Sicily, again today. While on our bomb run, with bomb bay doors open, I was in my turret whenever I am not shooting at an enemy plane. I continually rotate my turret, counter clockwise, looking for enemy fighters. I saw Capt. Hinsey's plane off of our right wing. I kept on rotating but when I got back to where Capt. Hinsey's plane should be...it wasn't there! All I saw was a big black cloud fading away behind us. A German fighter had flown head-on right into him. It is just a miracle some of the pieces didn't hit our aircraft. Later that night we had a movie, "Syncopation" with Jackie Cooper and Bonita Granville. It was a good show, but we just didn't seem to enjoy it.

June 30 - The 49th Squadron went to Palermo, Sicily, again today, but our crew didn't get to go. Since our Pilot is the Squadron. C.O., he has a lot of other responsibilities to take care of so we went on an Arab raid today. Our camp has guards posted every night for our protection. But since we slept on the ground in our tents, we would place our clothes and other possessions beside our beds on the ground and many times we would wake up with our clothes and things gone. We had also been missing some food and other equipment. We went out with our Commander, two Jeeps, a big truck, our rifles, a couple of Tommy guns and our .45 caliber pistols to a neighboring Arab compound with a high stone wall surrounding it. We drove through the gate with our guns loaded and drawn; we went searching their tents. They turned a few vicious looking dogs loose on us which we quickly killed. We had no way of communicating with them, no one in our outfit could speak Arabic, but they seemed to have received the message when we drove out the gate with the truck and both Jeeps, loaded with our supplies they had stolen.

July 4 - We went to Catania, Sicily, today. Really was tough, a lot of flak and German fighter aircraft. I assisted in shooting down two of them. The 20th Squadron lost another plane. To date we have 55 men out of our group either lost or missing. Once in a while, after watching parachutes popping out of planes going down, some of them survive, but we would not know it for weeks or sometimes months later. What a 4th of July this has been. Lots of excitement but not the kind we liked. Our Crew flew a different plane today, ours was still under repair and we got this one shot full of holes. I got "Killed" today or so my crew thought. The oxygen that I breathed at high altitude is carried in an aluminum canister above my turret and a German fighter plane shot it away. When the other crew members noticed that I had quit shooting and my turret wasn't moving anymore, they just mentally marked me off the list. After they looked around and saw the holes around the turret and that my canister was gone, they knew I couldn't live without oxygen. Fortunately for me the Germans were running low on fuel and left us. So the crew members hurriedly pulled me out of the turret and got me into the radio room. I had already started to turn black, but they put me on raw oxygen and I soon started getting my color back. So, I lived to fly another day!

July 19 - They said this mission would be a BIG ONE, and it was! Sometimes we don't know what our target is until we are out over the Mediterranean, then the Pilot will open an envelope with the instructions. We were going to ROME! Rome was the central railroad hub for all of Italy, and we were to destroy it. There were B-17's as far as the eye could see in all directions, hundreds maybe thousands of them.

Leaflets by the millions had been dropped all over the area of Rome, warning the people we would be there today and what time. Wasn't that nice to tell them here we come, so be ready? The was the real purpose, was to tell the civilian population to get as far away from the railroads as possible and apparently they did, so we were told. There was a Cathedral close by and we never cracked a window, but we sure did destroy those railroad yards. We didn't see any fighter planes, nor any flak until the instant we got there. Then the flak became so thick it just looked like we could have lowered our landing gear and landed on it. That black cloud of flak just appeared ahead of us...and stayed there. I don't know how many planes we lost that day, but I saw several of them going down. The mission was declared a total success. We were in the air seven hours and ten minutes. This was the 32nd mission for our crew.

August 6 - Went to Messina, Sicily, for bridges again today. Flak was pretty hot but we made it back home safe...again. I always carry my New Testament in my left shirt pocket. After getting our equipment in order and test firing our guns, we usually have about an hour before getting into enemy territory, so I get my New Testament out and read a chapter. The Captain knew this, so today he asked me to read whatever I was reading over the intercom so the entire crew could hear it; which I was glad to do. The Pilot of the crew is usually called the Captain, regardless of his rating.

August 19 – We went to Foggia, Italy to knock 0ut a hydro-electric plant. We did a perfect bombing job, but we had a rough day. We counted 40 ME – 109 fighters. They were everywhere and we lost Lt. Carter's *"Geronimo'* crew. They were a good bunch of boys; the tent next to ours will be empty tonight. The 20th squadron lost four planes. I was "Killed" again today, or so my crew thought. While I was firing at a plane about my 7:00 position, a fighter was coming up at our 3:00 position, and he put several bullets through the middle of our plane. One 20 mm came into my turret and shattered everything, knocking me unconscious. When some of the other crew members noticed my turret go silent, they looked around and saw the holes in my area. One of the gunners looked into the inspection window on my turret and all he saw was blood and black powder, and that my heat suit was gone from around the left shoulder. He just mentally marked me off as done for. The German fighters were running low on fuel by this time and departed the fight. The crew came running and got me out of the turret and into the radio room, where they gave me oxygen and some heat and started cleaning me up. After they had cleaned off the black powder and blood and pulled all the shrapnel they could find, I wasn't in really too bad a shape. After we got back to base, the medics found some more shrapnel and taped me up. I wasn't so bad. We had another air raid on our base that night. Our fox holes were in better shape this time and we enjoyed their safety for about an hour.

August 21 – Mission to Aversa, Italy to hit railroad yards east of Naples. We had a lot of flak but no German fighters because we had 72 P-38s flying cover for our 200 bombers. This was our 42nd mission and I had 260 hours of flying time in combat!

August 30 - Joseph Obradovich, who went to radio school with me at Scott Field in 1943, WALKED into camp today and WHAT A STORY HE HAD TO TELL! Ernie Pyle, war correspondent of WW2, related his story in his book, "Here is Your War", published December 1943. Joe was the radio operator for The Lt. Harry Devers crew and they had just flown in to North Africa from the U.S. They hadn't even been assigned to a combat unit yet or not even put a name on their new plane. They were on a flight of three B-17's flying from West Africa to the east to be assigned, when some German fighters jumped them, shooting one of them down. The two other planes then turned south to get away. One of the two planes then crash-landed in the desert and Lt. Devers then climbed to 11,000 feet and flew until they ran out of fuel, then the Pilot told his men to bail out. There were nine crew members at that time. Two days later all nine men were together again....out in the dessert. (The plane that crash-landed was discovered, mostly buried in the sand, twenty five years ago by an oil exploring crew.) Joe said they were eventually captured by the Germans and put in a prison camp. While in

T/Sgt. James Lee Hutchinson, Ed.S.

the prison camp, they were bombed by our own planes. The ones who survived were put on a submarine, to be taken to Italy, but our planes then bombed the sub and sunk it. Still some of his crew survived....and here was Joe. He didn't know about the others of his crew at this time. He might have found them later, but I never did know.

September 4, 1943 – Our mission today was an airfield at Terracini, Italy. My ball turret finally wore out, guess it will take a new motor. I kept it in motion by manually cranking it around. That way, if the enemy came around, he wouldn't know it was out of service."

Other diary entries told of living in tents, poor food and diving into foxholes during enemy bombing raids on the base. Harold said he once met a few guys from his basic training days and got the bad news that three of his buddies had been killed in action and another severely wounded. A highlight was when Bob Hope and Francis Langford brought their USO Show to the base in August. But, they couldn't compete with the joy he got from reading letters from his wife, Betty.

September 14, 1943 was a happy day for S/Sgt W. Harold Plunkett. That was the day his crew completed their required fifty combat missions. However, his joy was short-lived. The next day his crew was re-activated to aid in the invasion of Italy. They flew six more missions in three days, dropping anti-personnel bombs on the Italian troops at Salerno. The invasion was a success and the crew of the "Wiley Witch" was finally free to return to the USA. They had served with honor and earned credit for shooting down five enemy fighters. S/Sgt. Harold Plunkett had finished his tour of duty in Africa two months before our Lt. Bill Templeton crew arrived in England. He was an instructor at Sioux Falls when I was there in school.

September 10-12, 2007 - Harold and I spent three days together, with another Flying Fortress when the EAA (Experimental Aircraft Association) B-17 the "Aluminum Overcast" visited the airport at Bloomington, Indiana. Harold served as a tour guide, explaining the ball turret to all visitors. I say he was definitely qualified for that job

(Betty was there too.) I did a radio interview to promote the plane's visit, took a ride as "honored guest" on the historic bomber, told visitors the history of the B-17 in WW II and sold copies of my book; "Through These Eyes." Since that time I have written three more books, "Bombs Away," and "The Boys in the B-17' which is sold by the Liberty Belle Foundation on tour with the Memphis Belle B-17 Flying Fortress. Check the Liberty Belle Foundation website to see when they be flying to your neck of the woods.

Harold and I still exchange emails he likes to speak to classroom groups, vist Air Shows and like me, he is sometimes interviewed on television. I tell Harold we are just two proud old veterans telling our stories to members of a generation with very little knowledge of what the boys in World War II did to protect our country's freedom. Today, we are relics of an ancient War!

February 2014 – *Harold sent this email – "I trained on the "Peggy O'Neil" for a year as the radio operator but when we landed in Casablanca, my squadron Commander needed a Ball Turret gunner. He told me that I couldn't kill any Germans with a radio, so he switched me into the Ball Turret.......overnight!!!*

The "Wiley Witch" was a B-17F. It is sitting the bottom of the Adriatic Sea, five miles off the coast of Bari, Italy. They were shot-up rather badly but they ditched because of the lack of fuel. They said the plane floated for 20 minutes and all boys on the crew survived and rowed their life rafts into Bari, headquarters of the 15th Air Force!

The "Peggy O'Neil", ditched beside the island of Corsica, out of fuel, in rough sea and disintegrated with no survivors.

This all happened after I had finished my 56 missions and had returned home."

S/Sgt. James Allinder - Ploesti Oil Raid

Much of this article is based on the story Jim Allinder told his son Tom, years later shortly before his death. It was D-Day, June 6, 1944 and Allied forces, Operation Overlord launched a massive invasion against Hitler's German forces in occupied France. Meanwhile, on the southern side of Europe in Italy, Gen. Mark Clark's Fifth Army had liberated Rome which was a great victory, but its importance was overshadowed by the D-Day invasion of France and combat on the beaches.

Bombers of the Fifteenth Air Force continued their missions to destroy Axis oil production in Ploesti, Romania and hasten Germany's defeat. The Ploesti oil fields and refineries provided the oil and gasoline for Germany's trucks, tanks and planes. Oil was the 'life blood' of Hitler's war machine. Allied strategy was simple; destroy the Axis oil supply and the war would grind to a halt in a very short time. Ploesti was one of the most heavily protected and dangerous Axis targets and the top priority target for the Fifteenth Air Force. It was a beautiful, hazy day in Panatella, Italy as the B-24 Liberator bomber crews of the 464th Bomb Group prepared for another mission to the Ploesti oil refinery on June 6, 1944. The most gigantic military invasion in history was under way up north and the US Army 15th Air force was sending out a major bombing raid to add to Hitler's woes on D-Day.

Sgt. James E. Allinder, brother of our waist gunner, Bert Allinder, was a tail-gunner who was assigned on the eleven man crew of Captain George W. Leggat in the 776th squadron. Allinder's bomber, 'Sleepy Time Gal' was under repair from battle damage and he and the other members of his crew were split up and assigned to various bombers for this all-out mission. It was Allinder's 17th combat mission and he was flying with a new crew. He was nervous about being a substitute ball-turret gunner instead of tail gunner. He was on a new plane, in a new position, on its first mission. Bomb crew members always wanted to fly all their missions with their own crew and worried about any change which might bring bad luck. He recalled his worst mission so far was a raid on the ball-bearing plants at WeinerNeustadt, Germany when then "the flak was so thick you could walk on it."

The B-24 formation flew out over the blue Mediterranean, climbed to an altitude of 20,000 feet and proceeded on their mission. Hours later, their formation flew into the heavy flak over the Ploesti oil fields, dropped their bomb-loads, circled over Bucharest and headed for home.

Disaster struck quickly when a swarm of ME-109 fighters (yellow noses) hit the Bomb Group about 10:00 a.m. over Bucharest as they turned for home. Bad luck had found the Lt. Leggat crew!

Sgt. Allinder had his ball turret guns blazing at the fighter that hit their bomber with a cannon shell. Suddenly the B-24 was on fire and the ball turret hydraulics were shot out. Allinder struggled to rotate the turret in position so he could open the hatch and climb back into the plane, but he was trapped. Luckily, the two waist gunners stayed behind long enough to crank the ball turret into a position to open the door and help him climb out of the turret. The radio operator was dead and the plane was on fire. Jim said he grabbed his parachute, snapped it on his harness and headed for the waist door. The waist gunners were right behind him as he bailed out of the doomed bomber. He later learned that only one crewman failed to bail out and the radio operator had died from a direct flak hit. Allinder landed safely and hid-out for two days before he was found by a group of angry farmers armed with pitch forks and shotguns yelling, 'boom boom Bucharest. They wanted to kill him, but he was rescued by Romanian soldiers who hauled him off to an interrogation office and on to a POW camp where the main diet was turnips and cabbage. The prisoners knew the camp was near an important target because they were always ducking bombs from Allied planes. His POW camp was liberated four months later by Russian troops. The hungry prisoners were free, but had no food. They had to forage for food as they walked their way back to American troops and safety. Jim said he was 30 pounds lighter by the time he reached American soldiers and was sent back to his airbase in Italy. Tom said his Dad never ate another turnip the rest of his life!

Oxygen Mask Troubles

One of the prime requirements of flying at high altitude was taking good care of your oxygen mask. Anoxia was the name of the silent death which came gently, but quickly if your mask failed to operate properly. Anoxia (lack of oxygen) sneaked up on you, leaving you feeling fine with no pain until you passed out. Crewmen were warned to squeeze their masks often to crush ice crystals which formed in the mask and clogged the regulator valve. Standard Operating Procedure (SOP) on every mission was for the pilot to appoint a crew member, often the co-pilot, the duty of doing an inter-com "oxygen check'" on every position at ten minute intervals. If an airman failed to answer, someone was sent to check on him, because if a mask fails, the airman seldom realizes that he is not getting oxygen. There are many tales of guys who passed out but were saved by a buddy with a walk-about oxygen bottle. Sadly, there were also cases of many being found too late.

T/Sgt. James S. Peters Sr. Served up front as a B-17 engineer and top turret gunner so I recently asked him this question. What happened if the pilot or co-pilot was having an oxygen mask problem? His answer was: "Bombers carried extra oxygen masks and if the pilot's oxygen mask failed or was destroyed by flak, he could use to the engineer's outlet. The engineer's oxygen hose was long enough to reach the cockpit because it had to be long enough for him to use in his top turret, work in the cockpit area and/or crank the bomb doors closed, if necessary. That job had to be done from the bomb-bay. I didn't have much room to work, so I could not wear my chest chute. I had to crank up the doors on two missions and looking down at the ground 27,000 ft below without a parachute was an unforgettable experience.

If the pilot did have to use his outlet, the engineer would need to fill a portable oxygen bottle at the recharge outlet location in the cockpit area and move to another oxygen outlet in the nose or waist. Luckily this never happened on our plane. There were several sizes of oxygen bottles, the shortest one, a foot long, was good for about five minutes, or just enough time to get a man from one recharge station to the next. However, someone had better be watching the user in case of a hang up or otherwise strenuous activity. A larger bottle was about two and half feet long and the time it would last, depended to a large degree of how strenuous the work to be performed. This bottle would last around fifteen minutes when used with normal breathing or exercise, again someone had better be observing any crewman moving about or doing strenuous work at high altitude.

Another consideration was the altitude of the bomber. The oxygen regulator at each station was a Diluter Demand type which means that at 10,000 ft, the flow of oxygen would not be 100%, but as the plane gained altitude, the regulator would change the mix of air with oxygen until crewmen at high altitude were breathing near 100% oxygen. This became a factor on long missions because the oxygen supply would be reduced faster.

According to the 1B-17G-2 Maintenance Technical Order, there were two main O2 (oxygen) systems and four independent systems to serve the various crew positions. This safety measure prevented a complete loss of oxygen if one or more distributor line is severed by flak.

Group one --- 5 - G-1 O2 Cylinders behind pilot
Group two---- 3 G-1 O2 cylinders behind copilot plus one under cockpit floor
Group three - 5 or 6 G-1 Cylinders all under the cockpit floor
Group four -- 3 or 4 G-1 O2 cylinders under the radio compartment floor with another under the cockpit floor

The O2 system was a 500lb pressure system, the minimum pressure was around 425 PSI. Walk around O2 bottles, and recharging stations were located at various stations throughout the aircraft.

The small O1 bottle was supposedly good for approximately 5 minutes and the supply of the oxygen was sufficient to move from one aircraft location to another. However, caution had to be observed if strenuous activity had to be accomplished.

On the B-17Gs that I flew on, both the top turret and ball turret were furnished O2, electrical power and intercom, through the swivel base of the top turret and the swivel top of the ball turret.

The main hydraulic reservoir was alongside the top turret on the aft side of the cockpit, and, one could only hope that there was no leakage, that would enter the swivel fitting under the top turret, as hydraulic fluid is oil and oil and oxygen if mixed will result in a fire. If this did occur, the top turret operator (flight Engineer) would be involved in a fire.

The Type B-8 winter helmet of 1944 showing attachment of the Type A-14 oxygen mask by means of snaps or studs along the front edge. (SI Photo A4855E)

USAF Museum Photo

S/Sgt. Harold Plunkett – Ball turret gunner in the Twelfth Air Force had his oxygen supply shot out by enemy fighters or flak hit the turret on two separate missions over Italy. He was lucky on both occasions because his alert crew members pulled him out of the ball, dragged him into the radio room and got him back on oxygen in time to save his life.

Lt. Jule F. Berndt, 490th Navigator, reported oxygen mask problems on his first mission on September 30, 1944. At briefing, they learned that their target was the railroad marshalling yards in Bielefeld, Germany guarded by forty flak guns. They were flying number the number two position in the low squadron with a bomb-load of five 1,000 pound GP bombs. Lt. Brendt said,

"We took off at 08:00 and climbed to 18,000 to assemble our formation. Then at 10:00 the Wing and Division assembly was complete and huge formations of planes started out over the Channel toward Germany. Landfall had to be made at a definite point to avoid flak guns along the coast of enemy-held territory in Holland, France and Germany. Everything was going along well until just a few minutes before the IP when the pilot made a crew check to determine who was holding down the push-to-talk button on his intercom mike (depressing the button causes a buzzing noise in the entire system.) All crew members checked in except the bombardier, so the pilot told me to take a look at him. The bombardier was slumped back in his seat against the side of the ship. He was breathing heavily, his face was discolored and covered with sweat, even though were flying at 25,000 feet and the temperature was -35 degrees. I grabbed an extra oxygen bottle and hooked the stricken man's hose to it. After a few minutes of breathing pure oxygen he was able to continue his duties although hindered by the after affects of anoxia,"

Lt. Brendt went on to say that about that same time the ball-turret gunner called for help. His regulator valve and mask had frozen. An oxygen mask from the plane's emergency kit was passed down to him and his frozen mask was taken to the radio room to thaw out. That was a smart idea because sometime later a waist gunner needed it when his mask filled with ice and became useless. The final incident occurred on the way home when the waist gunner got air-sick in his oxygen mask!

T/Sgt. Howard Tuchin – also related an incident - The heavy flak damage forced Lt. Stauffer to peel out of the formation. He and Co-Pilot, 2nd Lt. Edward Haake (Richmond, VA.) managed to stabilize the crippled plane, despite the fact that Stauffer nearly lost consciousness, because his oxygen supply had been knocked out. Flight Engineer, Sgt. Howard Smith (Monroe, LA) saved the day by hooking the pilot to the engineer's oxygen outlet and switching himself to a portable bottle which could be recharged as needed.

Lt. John C. Walter, B-17 Pilot - with the 95th Bomb Group, allowed me to adapt this story from an incident in his book, "My War."

"Although we were at 30,000 feet, the flak was as murderous as it had been the two previous times. However, this time we came through with all four engines still running and very little damage. As we headed for the Rally Point, Mac (co-pilot) made another oxygen check. Everyone reported O.K. except Nelson (navigator.) There was no response. Mac asked John (bombardier) to check him out. Shortly, John called back to say, "He seems to be passed out; however, I don't see any sign of a wound." A few moments, John said, "His oxygen hose isn't hooked up to the regulator!!" John got a walk-around oxygen bottle, turned the regulator to pure oxygen and tried to get the navigator breathing again. In the meantime, having completed the bomb run, we and the Group headed toward home. Mac joined John down in the nose compartment and both kept working on Nelson. But with no success. There was no question he was dead.

As we neared the halfway point on the way back, it became apparent that in trying to revive Nelson, our oxygen supply had been greatly reduced and was nearing depletion. We were going to be forced to leave the formation and go to a lower altitude and head for home alone. Which is what we did."

A few days later, Lt. Walter wrote, "For the second time in little over two months, we made the very sad journey to the American Military Cemetery at Cambridge.

T/Sgt. James Peters Sr.

T/Sgt. Peters was a B-17 flight engineer flying bombing missions with the 15th Air Force in Italy about the same time I was in with the Eighth in England. His story tells of WW II airmen flying missions from Italy to blast Axis targets which were out of the range of aircraft based in England.

"December 1944, my crew flew a new B-17 to Italy via the Northern Route from Grenier N.H. to Goose Bay Labrador, Iceland and landed in Valley Wales. The next leg was south to Marrakech, Morocco, Tunis, Tunisia, and Gioia del Colle, Italy. I flew with the

348th squadron of the 99th Bomb Group of the 15th Air Force stationed at Tortorella, eight and a half miles east of Foggia. We were in the Fifth Wing which was composed of six bomb groups of the 2nd, 97th, 99th, 301st 463 and 483rd.

Berlin was without a doubt the roughest target in the MTO and the second was the Ploesti oil refineries. My pilot was selected as a Lead pilot of the second element after only a few missions. We flew Lead for most of my twenty-seven missions and the 99th BG was known for its close formations. After Russian troops captured the Ploesti area, Vienna, Austria became our second toughest target. One day after three consecutive missions to Vienna, our crew chief called the pilot, co-pilot and me to one side and threatened to shoot all three of us because on all three of those missions he and his crew had to change the right outer wing panel because the top wing spar had been partially cut by flak. We promised to be more careful!

USAF Photo

One of my missions was to the ammunition dump at Prague. My group with the "Diamond Y" was featured in the Tuskegee Airmen film "Red Tails" on the Berlin Germany Daimler Benz Tank Factory, and again in the other Tuskegee Airmen film. All of the other enlisted men on my crew participated on that long Berlin Tank Factory mission, except me. Our crew was split-up and used as fill-ins to man other crews. No one needed a flight engineer, so I sat that one out. The Berlin raid was supposed to the longest 15th Air force mission, although that is in question as some of the missions early on in the war, flown from North Africa had to be flown in two stages of part way overnight and then on to the target. However, those were with the early B-17s without the extra 1,700 gallons in the Tokyo tanks. Later missions with the extra tanks gave us a total of 2,780 gallons. The 15th Air Force also did the first shuttle mission to Russia on June 2, 1944. It was rumored that the mission was designed to take Germany's attention away from the D-Day landings at Normandy four days later.

RDX Bombs - Sometimes we carried RDX bombs on missions and could not bomb our target because of weather and/or mechanical problems, but when we returned to base we could not take a chance of landing with them on board. The runways in Italy for the most part were paved with PSP or Pierced Planking, also known as Marston Planking, composed of ten feet long by one foot wide sections of metal with holes in them. The RDX bombs were extra sensitive because of their "acid fuse" which was small vial of nitric acid that would eat through an aluminum plate that separated the nitric acid from the Fulminate of Mercury. RDX bombs with or without fuses were too sensitive for a hard landing on those runways. A bomb could explode on its own or the small vial of nitric acid could break and it would explode later when the acid ate through the separator metal connected to the Fulminate of Mercury. In North Africa one of those bombs rolled off the bomb trailer at the bomb dump, exploded and killed twenty-two men. However, that explosion was second to the accident at the 95th Bomb Group during their first few weeks at England. The ground crew was loading a bomber when it exploded killing nineteen men, wounding twenty and destroying four nearby aircraft. They said the shock waves killed several men standing but spared those near them who were sitting or lying on the ground.

The RDX bombs were considered a danger to everyone on the base because of their time delayed fuses. If the acid bottle broke on landing, the bomb might go off anytime up to thirty-six hours later, depending on the thickness of the aluminum plate that separated the acid from the Fulminate of Mercury. This danger also applied to regular bombs with acid fuses. The 15th Air Force was known by some as the "Adriatic Fish Killers" as both B-17s and B-24s would salvo those RDX bombs into the Adriatic Sea, if they could not be dropped on targets. Italian and Yugoslavian fishing fleets would lie off the coast and wait for those bombs to go off and then scoop in the fish killed by the explosions.

During my missions, toward the end of the war, I never saw an enemy fighter and no one on our crew was wounded by flak on any of my missions. However, the flak and the threat of a fighter attack was always there. On one mission my right waist gunner, ball turret gunner and tail gunner observed a lone German ME-109 attempting to climb toward us. About the same time, two of our P-51 escort fighters went after the enemy fighter and he dived for the deck. About thirty minutes later our pilot announced that those P-51 pilots were claiming one ME-109 destroyed!"

Friend or Foe? --- August 11, 1943, the 15th Air force sent out seventy two bombers to plaster the rail yards at Terni, Italy with 200 tons of bombs. Forty of those bombers were B-17s of the 301st Bomb Group. As they left the target, they sighted twenty or so German ME-109 fighters and a P-38 was flying with them. Suddenly the P-38 broke away and dived through the 301st formation at high speed. The P-38 fighter "walked his rudders" and sprayed the B-17s with machine gun fire and 20mm shells. When he made the first pass there was no return fire from the stunned B-17 gunners. On his second pass a few gunners fired at him, but on the third attack every gunner in the formation blazed away at him. The enemy P-38 shot down First Lieutenant Albert Fensel's bomber flying in the "Tail-end Charlie" position at the rear of the formation. It was the first aircraft lost by the 419th in over a hundred missions. Seven parachutes were seen before the B-17 hit the water, but only three crewmembers were picked up by a Navy Catalina seaplane after spending many hours in the water. Another 301 bomber piloted by Lieutenant Silvestri crash-landed east of St. Donat and that crew survived."

Note - There is an official record (MACR) of a 301st BG B-17 shot down. It was number 42-30307 of the 301st Bomb Group, squadron 419. It was assigned July 1, 1943. The bomber was flying its 14th mission when attacked by an enemy P-38. It was listed MIA (missing in action) on August 11, 1943.

T/Sgt. James Lee Hutchinson, Ed.S.

"There was another story of a hostile P-38 attacking our bombers that said the Germans had captured one of our P-38 fighters and left the U.S. insignia intact. The story said the Italian pilot spoke excellent American and flew that fighter extremely well. He would encounter a lone bomber going to and returning from targets in Germany throwing everything possible overboard, as heavy bombers often had to do to gain altitude when crossing the Alps. They said the P-38 pilot would feather one of his engines and ask if he could fly along with them for protection. When it appeared the bomber had tossed out their guns and were defense-less, he would un-feather his shut down engine and shoot down the bomber. On one occasion a lone B-17 pilot trying to lighten his load, encountered a lone P-38 fighter flying with one engine who asked permission to accompany the bomber for protection. However, the pilot had heard the story, so he warned the crew and told his gunners to keep their machine guns and ammunition. Sure enough, a little later, the P-38 pilot restarted his shut down engine and made several attacking runs. The story had gone around that the Italian pilot's wife was living in the Allied section of Rome, so the B-17 pilot radioed the P-38 Italian pilot that his wife was sleeping around with the Allies. The enemy pilot got angry and vigorously attacked the B-17. At that point, the B-17 gunners opened fire, managed to cripple the P-38 and he had to pull away. According to the account, the two pilots became friends after the war.

Two weeks after the German Surrender in May of 1945, I was removed from my crew and sent back to the U.S. to crew a P-51 between VE and VJ Day. My home flight was from the 301st Bomb Group at Celone, Italy to Gioia del Colle, Italy, then as a passenger on a returning B-24 back to Marrakech, Morocco, then south to Dakar, French West Africa, across the south Atlantic to Fortaleza, Brazil. it took the B-24 doing 170 MPH an hour and fifteen minutes to cross the Amazon River Delta. They say that huge river pours fresh water 100 miles off shore. We flew on to Georgetown, BR Guiana, Puerto Rico, and finally Savannah, Georgia.

I was later stationed at Fairchild AFB, Spokane, Washington with the 92nd Bomb Group (B-29) and (B-36), in 1950-1952, when I was transferred to the 99th SRW, equipped with RB-36s on January 1, 1953.

My old squadron (348th) was the Bomb Group that was equipped with the GRB-36 FICON (Fighter conveyance) that had a GRF-84K fighter hookup to the mother ship GRB-36. The 99th SRW was re-designated 99th Bomb Wing, and I went with them to Westover AFB, Springfield, MA. The 99th Bomb Wing was the second to be equipped with the B-52 Stratofortress." I retired as M/Sgt with 20 years of service."

Tuskegee Airmen – Red Tails

United States armed forces were segregated prior to World War II but many of of our nation's leaders recognized the need to train many more airmen and build a stronger Army Air Force. President Franklin Roosevelt and Congress approved flight training of African Americans in 1941. We needed more men in our armed forces and many of our nation's leaders recognized the need to train many more airmen The War Department created a separate aviation squadron for pilots to be trained at the Tuskegee Institute in Alabama and nearby airbases. The Tuskegee program began on July 1941, with thirteen students, including West Point graduate Captain Benjamin O. Davis.

The Army Air Corps insisted that cadets be held to the highest standards and many candidates "washed out" as pilots. However, this policy assured top-notch graduates and skilled pilots. In the next four years, almost a thousand military pilots completed the Tuskegee program. Approximately 500 served overseas with the 15th Air Force in the Mediterranean Theater. Early graduates were members of the 99th Fighter Squadron flying P-39 and P-40 planes. They trained at Tuskegee as a complete and separate unit with ground crew, support personnel and pilots. Captain Benjamin O. Davis Jr., was in the first class to graduate and was appointed squadron commander. The squadron trained and waited almost a year before they were assigned to fly P-40 Warhawks with the 33rd Fighter Group, a tactical group in Morroco, North Africa. They were the first African American pilots to serve in WW II combat. The 99th squadron was later attached to the 79th Fighter Group in January 27th 1944. Combat was heavy and they shot down eight enemy fighters. Near the end of their first year they were transferred to the 332nd Fighter Group in southern Italy.

Lt. Col. Benjamin O. Davis Jr. was Commander of the newly formed 332nd Fighter Group composed of four squadrons; the 99th; 100th; 301st and 302nd at last, Tuskegee pilots, had their own Fighter Group. They flew P-47 Thunderbirds for a short time before switching to P-51 Mustang fighters. The new 332nd Fighter group was stationed at the Ramitelli, Italy air base and was assigned to escort and protect B-24 Liberator and B-17 Flying Fortress bombers of the 15th Air Force. The group built their reputation while flying missions to strategic targets in Germany and heavily protected oil refineries in Ploesti, Romania. The skilled pilots of the 332nd soon became known as the "Red Tails" because of the bright red tails identifying their P-51 Mustang fighters. However, their enemies, the Luftwaffe pilots, called them "Schwarze Vogelmenshen," (the Black Birdmen.)

Armour G. McDaniel of Martinsville, Virginia was one of those dedicated African Americans who enlisted to serve his country. He graduated from Tuskegee in January, 1943 as a fighter pilot. Second Lieutenant McDaniel trained until December when he was deployed to Italy with the 301st squadron which was attached to the 332 Fighter Group. His WW II tour of duty included strafing and/or bombing ground targets as well as escorting heavy bombers to enemy targets in Italy and Germany. Combat with enemy planes was always expected. Specific incidents include: July, 1944, twenty German planes attacked the B-24 bombers on a mission to Friedrichshafen, Germany. Captain McDaniel and three other pilots shot down four enemy fighters. He barely escaped crashing into a mountain during a deep dive firing at a Luftwaffe fighter which did crash. Later in October, on an escort mission to German oilfields, Capt. McDaniel strafed an oil barge and barely cleared the target when it exploded in a ball of fire. The blast destroyed his wing guns, but he managed to fly back to his base at Ramitelli, Italy. January, 1945, Capt. McDaniel became commanding officer of the 301st Fighter Squadron

March 24, 1945, Col. Davis led the 332nd Fighter Group on the longest escort mission ever flown by the Fifteenth Air Force, a 1600-mile round trip to the Daimler-Benz tank works in Berlin. On this mission, Roscoe C. Brown, Jr., Charles Brantly and Earl Lane, each shot down a German ME-262 jet fighter aircraft.

The Group received a Distinguished Unit Citation for their achievements that day.

Lt. Gen. Benjamin O. Davis Jr. also flew F-86 Sabre jets in Korea and served in several high level leadership positions in the Air Force before retiring. He became a full General in 2002 when President Clinton awarded him a fourth star. General Davis passed away in 2007 at the age of 89. He flew 60 combat missions in WW II and was awarded the Distinguished Flying Cross, Silver Star and Air Medal. Under his leadership, the Tuskegee Airmen flew more than 15,000 combat sorties, including 1578 missions and 200 bomber escort missions. The Red Tails were credited with shooting down 112 enemy fighters and earned an excellent record of escorting and protecting bombers. During tactical air-to-ground missions, they destroyed 150 planes on the ground and 950 rail cars, trucks, and an enemy destroyer! Approximately a thousand pilots were trained at Tuskegee Army Air Field; 445 airmen served overseas and 150 lost their lives. This total included 66 pilots killed in accidents or combat and 32 who became prisoners of war. A second group of pilots were assigned and trained as a B-25 medium bomber group, but were never deployed overseas.

Tuskegee Airmen in WW II were awarded three Distinguished Unit citations and numerous decorations including several Silver Stars, 150 Distinguished Flying Crosses, 14 Bronze Stars, 744 Air Medals and numerous Purple Hearts.

T/Sgt. James Lee Hutchinson, Ed.S.

USAAF photo Tuskegee graduates, Jan. 1943

L-R George T. McCrumby, Quitman C. Walker,

Andrew Maples Jr., Charles R. Stanton,

Clinton B. Mills and Armour G. McDaniel.

Story based on USAF Historical Research and information from Col. McDaniel's wife, Faye McDaniel of Indianapolis, Indiana

Chapter Eight

Salute to Ground Troops

WW II G.I Joes in Europe endured untold hardships and saw comrades wounded or killed in battle. They were the youngsters of the Infantry, Armored Divisions, Artillery, etc. who slogged through heat, rain, snow and mud to defeat enemy forces. Frozen feet and frostbite was a constant problem and a pair of dry socks a precious possession. They lived on cans of C rations, seldom enjoyed rest or hot meals and sought shelter in foxholes and destroyed buildings. Their duty was to gain and hold ground as the literally walked across Europe to victory.

Massacre at Oradour-Sur-Glane

This story illustrates the inhuman treatment inflicted on citizens of countries occupied by Nazi troops. All human rights were ignored and torture and death were administered by the conquerors without fear of retribution until D-Day!

On June 10, 1944, four days after the Allied D-Day landings in Normandy, German SS troops descended on a small, peaceful French village, Oradour-Sur-Glane, in which about 700 people lived. In a matter of a few hours, Oradour-Sur-Glane ceased to exist. Virtually every person who lived there was indiscriminately shot or burned alive. Every building was also destroyed. After the war, the French government decided to leave Oradour-Sur-Glane's ruins as they stood as a solemn reminder of the horrors of war.

In February 1944, the 2nd Panzer Division (Das Reich) was stationed in the Southern French town north of Toulouse waiting to be resupplied with new equipment and freshly trained troops. After the D-Day invasion of Normandy the division was ordered to make its way across the country to stop the Allied advance. One of the division's units was the 4th SS Panzer Grenadier Regiment ("Der Führer"). Sturmbannfuher Adolf Diekmann was commander of the regiment's 1st Battalion.

Early on the morning of 10 June 1944, Diekmann informed his commander at regimental headquarters that two members belonging to The Vichy Regime the (French traitors) claimed that an Waffen-SS officer was being held prisoner by a French Resistance group in Oradour-sur-Vavres in, a nearby village. The German officer was said to be *SturmbannführerHemut Kampfe*, commander of the 2nd SS Panzer Reconnaissance Battalion (another unit of the "Das Reich" division), who may have been captured the day before.

On 10 June, Diekmann's battalion became confused and sealed off Oradour-sur-Glane, instead of nearby Oradour-sur-Vayres, where the prisoner was said to be held. Diekmann ordered all the townspeople, and anyone who happened to be in or near the town, to assemble in the village square. The townspeople assumed it was, to have their identity papers checked. In addition to the residents of the village, the SS also apprehended six people who did not live there, but had the misfortune to be riding their bikes through the village when the Germans arrived.

All the men were led to six barns and sheds where machine guns were already in place. All the women and children were locked in the church while the village was looted. According to the account of one man who survived, the soldiers began shooting at them, aiming for their legs so that they would die more slowly. Once the victims were no longer able to move, the soldiers covered their bodies with fuel and set the barns on fire. Only six men escaped; one of them was later seen walking down a road heading for the cemetery and was shot dead. In all, 190 men perished.

The Waffen-SS soldiers then set the church on fire. Women and children tried to escape through the doors and windows of the church, but they were met with machine-gun fire. A total of 247 women and

205 children died in the carnage. Only two women and one child survived; one was 47-year-old Marguerite Rouffanche. She slid out by a rear sacristy window, followed by a young woman and child.[3] All three were shot; Marguerite Rouffanche was wounded and her companions were killed. She crawled to some pea bushes behind the church, where she remained hidden overnight until she was rescued the following morning. Another group of about twenty villagers had fled Oradour-sur-Glane as soon as the soldiers had appeared. That night, the village was partially destroyed.

A few days later, survivors were allowed to bury the dead: 642 inhabitants of Oradour-sur-Glane had been murdered in a matter of hours. Adolf Diekmann claimed that the episode was a just retaliation for partisan activity in the other town and the kidnapping of the Waffen-SS Commander, Helmut Kampfe. A few days after the atrocity, Diekmann and over half his regiment were killed by D-Day invasion troops.

After the war, General Charles de Gaulle, saw the remains of the original village with burned cars and buildings and decided it should never be rebuilt, but remain a memorial to the cruelty of the Nazi occupation. The city was rebuilt farther up the road and In 1999, French President Jacques Chirac dedicated a memorial museum, near the entrance to the *Village Martyr* ("martyred village").

Paratroops and Gliders

Carved in stone at the WW II Memorial in Washington, D.C. are the words of General Eisenhower spoke to the troops of the 502nd regiment of the 101st Airborne Infantry Division the eve of June 6, 1944.

> *"You are about to embark upon the great crusade toward which we have striven these many months. The eyes of the world are upon you...I have full confidence in your courage, devotion to duty and skill in battle."*
>
> *General Dwight D. Eisenhower*

T/Sgt. James Lee Hutchinson, Ed.S.

U.S. Archives

Shortly after midnight on June 6, 1944 Airborne troops boarded planes to jump into dark sky beyond the beaches of Normandy in the early morning hours of D-Day. Drop zones included places like Ste. Mere Eglise, where the French maintain a museum to commemorate the event. Many paratroopers landed in trees or power lines and were shot before they got free. A mannequin of a paratrooper in a parachute still hangs from a church steeple to commemorate the jump. The incident portrayed in the movie, "The Longest Day" by actor Red Buttons.

A Stars and Stripes article said about the 53rd Wing of the Troop Carrier Command: "At a still young in age as a tactical unit, the 53rd overnight became a veteran in achievement, successfully executing one of the most dramatic and most difficult assignments in aviation history by spearheading the invasion of Europe. Flying low, often at tree-top level, and braving the flak of anti-aircraft guns blazing away below, 629 unarmed and unarmored 53rd Wing Skytrains and 412 gliders were dispatched to Normandy between June 5-7, carrying nearly 6000 airborne troops, 256 jeeps, 107 pieces of artillery, 230 gallons of gasoline to refuel jeeps, 308,786 pounds of ammunition, 14,204 pounds of rations and nearly 2,000,000 pounds of other equipment. All but three tow-craft and three gliders completed their missions. The C-47 Skytrains made a round trip of more than 500 miles requiring about five hours of flying time at the rate prescribed by field orders. Towing a glider at little more than 100 miles per hour made gasoline consumption a major problem. One C-47 returned to base with only nine gallons of fuel left from the original 700 gallon tank-load."

U.S. Army Photo

C-47 Skytrains, note the invasion stripes, dropped paratroopers into France behind the lines on the night of June 5th to June 7th to capture or destroy critical German targets during the D-Day invasion! They also towed troop-carrying gliders, dropped paratroops into enemy territory, and air evacuated sick or wounded patients. A C-47 could carry 28 passengers, 18-22 fully equipped paratroopers, about 6,000 lbs. of cargo or 18 stretchers and three medical personnel. Few aircraft were as well known, so widely used or used as long as the C-47. Affectionately nicknamed the "Gooney Bird," this aircraft was adapted from the Douglas DC-3 commercial airliner.

T/Sgt. James Lee Hutchinson, Ed.S.

S/Sgt. Merrill St. John

S/Sgt. St. John's interview added valuable information to our Veteran History project. He served in the 441st Troop Carrier Group, Squadron 301 as a radio operator/mechanic and studied navigation and navigated small flights from England to France He also navigated the first mission to drop supplies for the 101st Airborne troops when they were surrounded at Bastonge. Merrill flew 100 missions trough enemy fire and fighters and received four Air Medals, seven campaign stars. Merrill said he was never wounded. His C-47 often had flak damage, but it was a tough plane and always brought them home; one of the best planes ever made. His unit was awarded two Presidential Citations. The stories of his combat experience in the Troop Carrier Command during and after D-Day are greatly appreciated.

"We were told of the mission several days before the actual invasion, but were put on hold because the weather over the Channel and France. We were under armed guard for security reasons and the waiting was pressing on everyone. There was nothing to do except read, write letters and listen to the radio. It was espcially tough on the paratroopers who packed and ready to go. Finally, it was decided there was a "window" in the weather pattern and we would go at midnight June 5, 1944. The weather was poor enough to catch the Germans unaware, but good enough to allow airplanes to fly. The 50th Wing of the Troop Carrier Command had four goups who dropped the 101st and 82nd Airborne Divisions. The operation amounted to more than 700 planes to transport 20,000 troopers. A C-47 could carry eighteen to twenty fully equiped troopers. An Airborne Company was composed of three rifle platoons and a headquarters section. Each platoon contained three twelve-man rifle squads and a six-man mortar team squad. Some also had a machine gun attached to each of its rifle squads, and a heavy 60mm mortar in each mortar team. Airborne training was not easy, besides attending the standard airborne school, the unit had to perform battle drills and endure excruciating amounts of physical training. The purpose of all paratrooper training was to push soldiers to their limits, and to teach them to work together as a combat team.

We were the 301st squadron of the 441st Troop Carrier Group, and we dropped the 506th parachute infantry of the of the 101st Airborne. In the early evening of June 5th we began loading the troopers. I can still see their painted faces and the heavy equipment packs. There was no chattering or joking, all were very somber in that time of anticipation and concentration. The troopers was so heavily loaded with parachutes, weapons and quipment packs that we had to help them up the ladder into the plane. Those who survived the jump were to assemble and carry out specific assignments of holding crossroads, destroying gun emplacements, bridges and other critical targets to clear the way for the troops storming Normandy's beaches a few hours later. Each man knew any that reinforcements or relief would depend on the landing of the glider troops following behind and a successful D-day landing. When our C-47 was loaded, the officer in charge of the "stick" gave his men a final briefing. He closed by saying that any man who refused to jump would be shot!

Taking off in the total darkness was the hard part for pilots and then flying in formation without lights. Even in darkness you can still see your wingman if he is in the right position. Navigators had the tough job of getting us the assigned drop zone. Our nerves were on edge as we crossed the English Channel in darkness. The first anti-aircraft fire began as we reached the Normandy coast, there was no choice for evasion tatics as we continued to the drop zone. There was no turning away and it was pure hell for the next half hour until we dropped our troops. We immediatlely went down to treetop level to avoid the planes still coming in from England. They told us that our missions were not to try for escape but to "hit the deck and get the hell home!"

We made our way back through the darkneass and flak over France at full throttle. It was the eve of D-Day and the English Channel was packed with ships as far as I could see. We crossed the dark beaches of England and went directly to an airstrip where gliders where waiting for a tow. Some were loaded with troops, some had a jeep and four men, others carried howitzers and mortars or supplies. Their landing zones were several hundred yards beyond the D-Day beaches. We re-fueled and hooked on to the nylon rope of a heavily loaded glider and towed it across the Channel and back through heavy flak to release the tow line over their landing area. It was dawn as we again crossed the Channel above the invasion forces at Omaha Beach. It was an unforgetable scene of men, ships and vehicles in mortal combat. D-Day had been launched."

Commanders Ridgway and Gavin officially commended the Troop Carrier Command. Gavin's commendation said in part:

> "The accomplishments of the parachute regiments are due to the conscientious and efficient tasks of delivery performed by your pilots and crews. I am aware, as we all are, that your wing suffered losses in carrying out its missions and that a very bad fog condition was encountered inside the west coast of the peninsula. Yet despite this every effort was made for an exact and precise delivery as planned. In most cases this was successful."

Note - During December 1944 and January 1945, the men of the 101st Airborne Division fought in Belgium in the Battle of the Bulge. The 101st was in Belgium in December when the Germans launched their offensive in the Ardennes. They were ordered to hold the vital crossroads at Bastogne. They were surrounded by the Germans, but fought in frigid weather and snow under German artillery fire with limited rations and ammunition until relieved by units of Gen. Patton's Third army. The Allies defeated the German offensive. The 101st Airborne Division was awarded a unit citation for holding the line against overwhelming odds at Bastogne.

D-Day, June 6, 1944

D-Day should never be forgotten. Sixty-nine years ago Navy guns bombarded the concrete German pillboxes and shore installations beyond the beaches in the early morning hours before the thousands of Allied troops went ashore in landing craft. Twelve thousand warships and six thousand other naval vessels participated in the invasion as

130,000 American and British troops stormed the beaches of Normandy, France in the most massive invasion in history. Operation Overlord was launched on D-Day to defeat Adolph Hitler's reign of terror and restore freedom to the people of Europe. Germany surrendered eleven months later, May 8, 1945.

The landing of troops on D-day began at 6:30 am June 6, 1944 on five different beaches. British and Canadian forces landed on the Gold, Sword and Juno beaches. United States troops hit Utah and Omaha beaches. More than 4,000 men died and thousands more were wounded on that first day! Allied planes dropped airborne divisions and glider troops behind enemy lines to capture key targets while the infantry climbed into LCT and LST's to reach the beaches and charge out of the landing crafts into the deadly bullets and shells of German guns. Many men drowned or died before they reached the beach. The Utah Beach landing went smoothly and our troops gained the first day's objective. Omaha beach had more casualties because our forces were pinned down by the heavy fire of German guns in concrete "pillboxes" and "bunkers" on the high cliffs beyond the beach. Men of a giant Navy armada, six infantry divisions and five airborne divisions trained in the United Kingdom for six months to prepare for D-Day. Eighth and Ninth Air Corps fighters chased enemy fighters from the sky and strafed enemy positions while Eighth Air Corps heavy bombers hit prime targets inland. Fighters and bombers flew over 2,300 missions to support the invasion. They destroyed bridges, railroads and highways to harass German troop movements.

T/Sgt. James Lee Hutchinson, Ed.S.

US Army photo

Brig. Gen. Theodore Roosevelt, Jr.

He was the first Allied General officer to wade ashore on the Normandy beachhead (not counting those who landed in the airborne assault beyond the beaches) and the only general in the first amphibious wave.

T/ Sgt. Tom "Dody' Newkirk - of Medora, Indiana hit Utah beach at the eighth hour when the large doors on his LCT landing craft dropped into the sand. He was driving a half-track and pulling a trailer, but became mired down on a sand bar before he reached the beach. General Roosevelt II yelled at him to get that half-track moving and ordered a tank to hook a chain to the vehicle and pull it to dry land. Sgt. Newkirk said the General was one of the bravest men he ever saw.

Although Gen. Roosevelt had a heart condition and used a cane because of arthritis, he had volunteered to serve on D-Day. He had served in WW I as a young man and he was determined to lead his boys. Due to a navigational error on the part of the landing craft crews, the first wave of the 4th Infantry Division landed on the wrong inlet on Utah Beach which, fortunately for them, was less heavily defended than their original objective.

"We'll start the war from here!" was Gen. Roosevelt's famous quote. Quickly assessing the situation and seizing the initiative and advantage, he re-routed the remainder of the division into the new sector. American troops overwhelmed the defenses and rapidly drove inland. His 4th Infantry Division then proceeded to outflank the Germans on their initial objective, clear the entire beachhead, and link up with the airborne assault forces with fewer casualties than the divisions on the other four beachheads. Armed only with a pistol and walking with a cane due to arthritis, Gen. Roosevelt led several assaults along the beachhead in what then-Lieutenant General Omar N. Bradley, commander of the US 1st Army and of the overall amphibious operation, later described as the single bravest act he witnessed in the entire war. Perhaps Gen. Roosevelt had the same thought as another officer who urged men forward with this statement,

"There are two types of people on this beach --- the dead and those who are going to die, so let's get the hell out of here!"

Brigadier General Theodore Roosevelt, Jr. died of a heart attack on the battlefield in Normandy a little over a month after D-Day, just before word arrived at his headquarters that he had been promoted to Major General and reassigned to the command of another division. He was fifty-six years of age. He was buried at the American cemetery in Normandy. Brigadier General Roosevelt was later awarded our nation's highest honor and was buried next to his younger brother, Lieutenant Quentin Roosevelt, a pilot, who was killed in France during World War I.

Medal of Honor Citation - For gallantry and intrepidity at the risk of his life above and beyond the call of duty on 6 June 1944, in France. After 2 verbal requests to accompany the leading assault elements in the Normandy invasion had been denied, Brig. Gen. Roosevelt's written request for this mission was approved and he landed with the first wave of the forces assaulting the enemy-held beaches. He repeatedly led groups from the beach, over the seawall and established them inland. His valor, courage, and presence in the very front of the attack and his complete unconcern at being under heavy fire inspired the troops to heights of enthusiasm and self-sacrifice. Although the enemy had the beach under constant direct fire, Brig. Gen. Roosevelt moved from one locality to another, rallying men around him, directed and personally led them against the enemy. Under his seasoned, precise, calm, and unfaltering leadership, assault troops reduced beach strong points and rapidly moved inland with minimum casualties. He thus contributed substantially to the successful establishment of the beachhead in France.

By the end of day five, 326,000 men and 54,000 vehicles had crossed the beaches and moved into France and by the first of July that number grew to a million Allied troops. D-day gave Allied Forces a foothold in France and eventually, Allied forces battled German troops across France all the way to Berlin. Many Lawrence County men participated in D-Day and/or were later "replacements" for Army units fighting in France and Belgium. Replacement troops were desperately needed to relieve battle- weary men and replace the dead and wounded on the front line. Many young men were sent overseas after eight weeks of basic training and to be shoved into the front lines to learn combat the hard way.

Operation Overlord (D-Day) was a costly operation; thousands died and many more were wounded. Some units of the first to land had ninety percent losses. The American Cemetery at Colleville-sur-Mer in Normandy holds row on row of white crosses and Stars of David to mark the graves of 9,387 men who fell on the first ten days of the invasion. In addition, the names of 1,557 soldiers and airmen, whose bodies were never recovered, are inscribed on a wall of honor.

Citizens of our country must never forget the sacrifices of those who stormed the beaches of Normandy on June 6, 1944.

> *"Germany surrendered May 8, 1945 --- eleven months and two days after D-Day*

D-Day was extremely costly, but brought hope for victory. Shortly after D-Day Gen. Dwight D. Eisenhower said,

> *"The tide has turned. The free men of the world are marching together for Victory!"*

Ninth Infantry Division World War II

39th Infantry Regiment 47th Infantry Regiment

60th Infantry Regiment

15th Engineer Combat Battalion

97th Reconnaissance Troop (Mechanized)

9th Division Artillery

26th Field Artillery Battalion (105mm Howitzer)

34th Field Artillery Battalion (155mm Howitzer)

60th Field Artillery Battalion (105mm Howitzer)

84th Field Artillery Battalion (105mm Howitzer)

42nd AAA Battalion

<u>Special Troops</u>
Band   9th Medical Battalion

9th Signal Company Military Police Platoon Headquarters Co.

9th Quartermaster Co.

709th Ordnance Light Maintenance Co.

746th Tank Battalion

61st Tank Battalion

899th Tank Destroyer Battalion

894th Tank Destroyer Battalion

Note - *Norm Taylor and I interviewed many veterans on the Bedford-North Lawrence Television Veterans' History Project, but one of the most memorable was the session we had with WW II veterans Tom "Dodie" Newkirk and John Hill. Dodie, age 91, wore his WW II uniform and John, age 92 came in with his cane and a printed copy of his memories. They were friends who spent their boyhood was in rural area of Leesville and Medora, Indiana. Transportation was provided by Dodie's son and John's caretaker. Their stories were so interesting that we had them return for a second session. Both of these men have passed, but my notes and material from the recorded program provide remarkable stories of their war experiences to share with this generation.*

T/Sgt. James Lee Hutchinson, Ed.S.

John Hill's Story

Based on information supplied by WW II veteran S/Sgt. John I. Hill, L Company 47th Regiment of 9th Infantry Division

John Hill of Medora, Indiana entered the army April 15, 1944 and did a few months of basic training at Ft. Wheeler, Georgia. His unit was shipped out to England in September where combat infantry training continued for several weeks before they crossed the Channel to France in November where they boarded a train to the front lines somewhere in France. The Ninth Infantry was one of nineteen U.S. Army divisions to take part in the D-day invasion, but John said he got there too late.

Long, tall John Hill, at age 26, was older than a lot of the guys in the infantry, but tough enough to survive seven months of combat in some of the worst fighting of the war in Europe. His company was involved in the re-taking of the Siegfried Line before moving to Belgium in early December. He had missed D-day but was just in time for the Battle of the Bulge. He fought in the harsh winter weather, moving in the snow from one foxhole to another. His Company L, of the 47th Regiment of the Ninth Army Infantry Division continued fighting in the snow in the Ardennes and the battles of the Rhur and Hurtegen Forest, capture of the Rhine River Bridge at Remagen and fought to war's end without a wound.

I interviewed John on the Bedford North Lawrence High School Indiana History television program and had his story, but I wanted to talk with him again to learn more about his WW II combat experiences which were so different from my own. We met again in October, 2012 in a meeting at the Community Center in Leesville, Indiana. We were both born in the Leesville area and had been invited to present a program. John and I entered combat in November, 1944. I was glad to learn more about his life as a combat infantryman on the ground at the same time I was flying bombing missions above his battlefield.

He was ninety-four and in a wheel chair, those long legs that carried him from Bastonge to the Rhine as a young mortar man had finally failed him. Arthritis had damaged the bony hand he offered for a handshake. His face was thinner and he had lost weight, but he was very alert and glad to see me again. He probably weighed about the same as when he was a young soldier in 1944-45.

President Roosevelt told the nation that we must build an Arsenal for Democracy. Factories making weapons, armament and ammunition were very important to a nation at war. The men went to war and women went to work in factories. A large naval ammunition depot and an army powder plant were built in Southern Indiana. Jobs became plentiful and "Praise the Lord and Pass the Ammunition" became a popular WW II song and slogan, especially in Southern Indiana. The twenty-four percent employment rate fell to four percent as production grew.

Food was also important for the war effort and exemptions from the draft (Selective Service) were given to farmers and defense plant workers critical to the war effort. John was exempted from military service to work long hours on farms in the fertile White River valley. He endured being stuck at home and his watching buddies go off to war for a few years before patriotism got the best of him and at age twenty-five he joined the Army April 15, 1944. His basic training was in Camp Wheeler, Georgia. Replacement troops were badly needed in Europe and September 15, 1944 Buck Private John I. Hill was on a troop ship sailing for England. Four weeks later, after a little more combat training, John boarded an LST landing craft and crossed the English Channel to France and the war.

Note - John and I were on the same WW II timetable; less than three weeks later, November 4, 1944. I boarded the Queen Mary for a bomber airfield in England.

John's Story Begins

"I remember the short ride across the channel on the LST, picking up our equipment and stepping into France. We were marched to the train and loaded into boxcars with all our equipment squeezed in with us. I don't know how many boys were in our boxcar, but it was so crowded there was no room to move around or sit down. We were later transferred to trucks, but it was a cold and miserable trip. We arrived at a German town (Aachen), on the French-German border that had just been captured. It was Thanksgiving Day and about four o'clock they brought us a big dinner. We had been eating hard crackers and Spam for the last six weeks or so and did that dinner taste good! There were two slices of bread with it and that was the first thing I ate. Not being accustomed to that rich food, some of the boys over-ate and had to be taken to the hospital that night. I remember that cold morning, because I knew that we were replacement troops assigned to the 47th Regiment of the 9th Division. Just one of "new boys" sent to replace the dead and wounded of earlier battles.

Next morning our group of forty boys walked about two miles up the road and were met by the Sergeant who told us we were going up to the front lines and German artillery shells might come in on us. He warned, "If you see me hit the dirt, you all do the same!" I expect we walked another two miles before shells were dropping on us, one hit fairly close. We hit the dirt with Sarge and if that shell had been any closer, several of us could have been hit. However, I can assure you, our 'hitting the dirt' was like slow motion compared to the speed we did it after we saw what shrapnel can do to one's body!

We arrived at L. Company and I was sent to the second platoon. The Sergeant there was a big rough talking fellow and his first words to me were, "You are my First Scout!" All I knew about that job was what I learned in basic training. I knew it was very dangerous and had a very short life expectancy. I thought I'll give it my best. I told him I didn't have any training as First Scout, but was trained for heavy weapons in mortars and machine guns. His reply was, "Up here, you will learn fast or else!" Well, I was sitting there thinking it over when I heard someone with a long Texas drawl say, "I'm looking for a Private Hill -- John I." I thought it can't get much worse, so I yelled "Here!" That Sergeant, (I later learned it was Sgt. Bell) told me to come with him, but my Sergeant said, "You can't have him, he's my new First Scout." Sgt. Bell drawled, "Well, I've got a piece of paper here that says he's mine!" He showed it to the Sergeant and I was more than happy to follow him out of there. He told me I would be in his 60mm mortar section of the 4th platoon of L. Company. We moved out and set up near the town of Eisenwaller. This was my first glimpse of war in the raw: frozen bodies of dead Jerries, farm animals and some American G.I.'s from a previous battle lay along the road and in the fields. It was here that I met Richard L. Stoltz, a nineteen year old veteran of the D-day landing at Utah Beach who been wounded by shrapnel, but was back on the front lines again. I was sure glad to have a job I was trained to do, but I noticed all the men were dirty. Their uniforms and faces were caked with mud. Their faces looked like masks that would crack if they smiled, which they didn't. They looked like walking dead men! Later, I found out that Stoltz was from Ohio and Riddle from Illinois, so we all became friends. Dick Stoltz, who was almost as tall as me and eight years younger, sat me down and gave me some life-saving advice. He said,

"We are walking through this war, so take good care of your feet. Try to keep one pair of socks dry and change when you get a chance. Keep your eyes open and always know where you are going to hit the dirt when shells come in. If there's a ditch or low place close, move fast and hit it!" I know his advice saved my life, because that same night there was an enemy night attack and we lost about half of the replacement boys who had come up with me. Some were captured, others wounded, killed or MIA. (Missing in Action)

L. Company had been on the front quite a while so we were pulled off the line and sent to Verviera, Belgium for a rest break. Next we moved to Elsenborne where we stayed a week in a barracks the Germans had used to keep prisoners. The night of December 7th we moved out to the town of Hammich, dug in and pitched our tents. Water filled our foxholes so our 4th platoon moved into an old barn with my mortar section downstairs and the machine gunners in the loft. We built a fire in an oil drum to keep warm, but the smoke was almost unbearable for the guys in the loft. The next week, the Germans attacked. We were highly outnumbered and fighting for our lives in heavy snow!"

T/Sgt. James Lee Hutchinson, Ed.S.

The Battle of the Bulge

December 16th, Hitler's army (Wehrmacht) launched a massive counter-attack and broke through Allied lines along an eighty mile front. That area was protected by only six American divisions. In a short, time Hitler's twenty-eight German divisions, (ten were Panzer Tiger tank units,) re-captured much territory and created a large bulge in Allied battle lines. American ground troops desperately needed reinforcements and air support from bombers and fighters. Good weather would have allowed Ninth Air Corps tactical bombers and fighters to take out enemy artillery, tanks and supply trains. Our fighters could have strafed (machine gunned) German troops and truck convoys. The heavy bombers of the Eighth and Royal Air Force (RAF) could have bombed train yards, oil dumps and railroad yards to prevent fuel and ammunition from reaching the German forces. But the weather was not cooperating visibility was near zero and Allied planes could not fly. The wintry weather was aiding the enemy.

Units of the German 1st SS Panzer Division captured a hundred and fifty American soldiers near Malmedy, Belgium on December 17th. The GI's were prisoners of war, but they were disarmed, stripped of watches and jewelry and marched to an open field. The defenseless men, including non-combatant Medics, were assembled in that field and machine-gunned as a convoy of twenty-five Tiger tanks passed by for almost thirty minutes. Eighty-six Americans died while they hugged the snow covered ground to avoid the bullets. Others suffered severe wounds, but 'played dead.' When the firing stopped, German officers wandered across the field, killing wounded survivors with their Luger pistols. Details of this atrocity were verified by the survivors and later by captured German soldiers. This massacre illustrated the Nazi tactic of creating terror among its enemies. Photos of the frozen bodies in the snow served as a warning to Allied troops; better to die fighting than to surrender to murderers who ignored rules of the Geneva Convention!

Brigadier General Anthony McAuliffe and his 101st airborne troops held the line at Bastonge, Belgium. They were surrounded after three days. However, when German forces demanded surrender, General McAuliffe turned them down with his now famous answer, "Nuts!" His Airborne troops continued to hold out against superior forces another four days until they were relieved by units of the 4th Armored Division. They had clearly earned the nickname; The Battered Bastards of Bastogne!

National Archives
Tank moves into combat in the Battle of the Bulge, December 18, 1944

Snow and near zero temperatures were added hazards for our troops in the Bulge. Keeping warm and dry was impossible and there were many cases of frozen feet, frostbite and death from freezing.

The Army set up area warming tents for soldiers to visit, warm up and dry out their clothing. Frozen weapons and vehicles were also problems. It was said that General George Patton became so frustrated that he told Chaplain James H. O'Neil to pray for clear weather. He said "Get God on our side for a change," The weather cleared and Chaplain O'Neil earned a medal. Thousands of Allied planes flew missions day and night through January 16th to destroy all supply lines to the German troops. Bastonge was relieved and U.S. troops began the Ardennes Forest Campaign.

John Hill's Story continues - "December 19 - We made a sudden move by truck. We wore heavy underwear, sweaters, under our uniform covered by field jackets and windbreaker pants. Our headgear was a knit cap and a helmet liner under a steel helmet. Every man hung a canteen, first aid kit and spade on his belt and carried a gas mask. Our heavy overshoes gave us a good foundation. We rolled our tent and blankets to make our bed rolls; some slipped in an axe or candles. We were dropped off a few miles past the town of Eupren and walked through woods and out into a field covered by about six inches of snow. The field had foxholes in it, but they were full of water. Some of the boys (Stoltz) fell in them, so we scrapped away snow and lay on top the ground the rest of the night. The next day we carried our supplies a mile farther where we dug in. It looked like more snow so we put tops over our foxholes. Little Joe and I hit a rock quarry, but at last we had a good hole before the Jerries threw in a few shells. Two or three hit very close and like rats, we all disappeared in our holes. Several boys in the rifle platoon were wounded. However, our morale was better because the snow had stopped and we could hear the Eighth Air Corps bombers flying over again.

New Year's morning we were standing around a fire when three German fighters came in low and bullets were snapping over our heads. A limb fell at our feet and we dived back into our foxholes like scared rabbits. Three days later we fought our way to middle of the town of Kalterherburg to relieve another outfit and set up a defensive position. Later we moved forward to the end of town and set up in a house. Our squad had two bedrooms a living room and kitchen. We stayed there fifteen days and boy did we live in style! We rummaged for flour, lard, baking powder and other food. We found a sausage grinder so we killed a cow for hamburger. Runion and I took charge of the two milk cows and a milk goat in the barn and our squad had milk. We even saved the cream and churned out some butter. Our lot had improved, we in were out of the snow, dry, warm and eating hot food. We had nice bedrooms with featherbeds and innerspring mattresses. Fuel was getting low by the time we left and I figure the cannon company that moved after us must have burned the furniture or part of the house. We made two more short moves and took our cows with us, but January 29th we jumped off to Haffen. A day later we took off on the attack in snow about two to five feet deep. The German shelling slowed up in the afternoon, but Lt. Hurtsburger was hit that day. At nightfall, Riddle and I shared a foxhole about two foot deep in the ground and six foot from the top of the snow. It was about three foot wide and less than six foot long. I don't know how we both managed to lay down in it. Boy, it was a job to crawl out for guard duty! Then it warmed up during the night and melting snow began to seep into our foxhole, but we went to sleep anyway, mainly from exhaustion. Our uniforms were wet the next morning, but we were not alone, as the rest were in the same predicament. It was truly a miserable night. It made one feel like --- if I could just get hit slightly so I could go back, all would be well. The next morning they brought several prisoners past us. We moved forward as Jerry threw more shells at us. The area was pock-marked with holes and treetops were in shreds.

We came to a crossroad that Germans had zeroed in. Shells came in as we hit the snow and started digging in; the concussion was terrific. A pine tree fell across the road and we took off across the road into the woods. We moved about a hundred yards when they started dropping shells right on the column. I heard groaning and cries of pain up ahead, a call came down for the Medics and two riflemen came back carrying a boy of about twenty-one who was hit in both legs. The right leg had a bad shrapnel wound at the knee and the other was at least half was cut off. Both the boys carrying him were crying. Later, I heard that their buddy died. We went on just a few yards and our Lt. Kinsey lay in the snow face down still grasping his M1 carbine. He was very dead! A few yards ahead a boy with shrapnel wound in his rear was writhing in the snow like a snake with a mashed head. He was waving his arms and yelling for help when more shells came in. I hit the ground next to him and tried to melt down in the snow. Three more shells hit close. I think our combined prayers pushed those shells on over us.

Our squad jumped up and moved on about a hundred yards and found a dugout with a dead Jerry in a trench outside. The dugout looked like heaven to us, but we took off again through the woods to Heartbreak Crossroads outside Haffen, Germany. The Second Division had taken the place once, but the Germans pushed them out during the Bulge. Our regiment's job was to push the Jerries out this time. The crossroads was really shot up. Shells had cut up the trees so badly that no limbs or foliage was left on them, they looked liked telephone poles. We saw a German pillbox ahead and our morale went up, maybe we could spend the night. We really felt bad when we moved on past, but we stopped in the remains of a large building farther on. Heartbreak Crossroads was ours, if we could just hold it. My mortar section set up in the basement. It was smelly, but good shelter from the cold wind and snow. We were so much better off than the machinegun section and riflemen who were hunkered in fox holes in the snow out front. A few shells came at us, but no one was hit. Guards were posted and we bedded down in the straw were the Germans had slept the night before. We didn't have much room, when one of us turned, all had to turn. I well remember Runion's remark,

"I was told when I came in the army that I was just a cog in a big wheel. I didn't know they really meant it!"

The next day we got about thirty Jerries out of a pillbox about thirty yards away. That day wore on into the next and suddenly we had visitors. Generals, Colonels, Newspaper reporters and photographers were there to witness German prisoners being brought in and hauled away by the truckloads. The afternoon of February 5th we took off in two feet of snow to attack again and stopped in the woods to clean our weapons and heat some C rations. We ate, got our first mail in a long time and got ready to move out to attack Einruhr the next day."

Note: *C Rations in box a little larger than a crackerjack box had processed food for men in combat zones. There were two types of tin cans 4 inches tall by 3 inch diameter for each meal with a can opener soldered to the bottom. One can (M) contained meat combinations for breakfast, lunch and supper. The other (B) held a bread product, powdered drink, sugar, cigarettes etc. Rations of three M and three B cans per day were periodically distributed to combat troops to store in backpacks or field jacket pockets.*

"The rifle platoons took off about an hour before dawn. We followed and visibility was fair even though there was a blizzard blowing, but by daylight you couldn't see twenty yards ahead. As the day got older, the snow turned to sleet so our mortar section set up in the cellar of a vacant house to await further instructions. The majority of riflemen had snowsuits, but there wasn't enough for the whole Company, so we found some sheets upstairs and made us some. We cut out head and armholes then wrapped some over our steel helmets and let it go at that. We heard small arms fire and knew they had contacted the enemy up ahead. That morning we learned there were three Jerry pillboxes and several dugouts in the area. We later found out those dugout were fixed up rather snug because the Jerries had been there a while. Most had a small heater, straw and blankets.

The Medics were bringing our wounded back on toboggans because snow was knee deep everywhere and much deeper in low spots. The Medics were having a tough day, it was impossible to carry a man on a stretcher. At 3:30 the Jerries moved back out of our range and we followed. I saw my first freshly captured prisoners in this village.

We moved pulling our mortars, guns and ammo on a toboggan, but it didn't work so hot. Soon, we threw the thing away and carried the load. The Germans threw in more shells and one guy panicked and left us. He ran back down the road, guess he just couldn't take it anymore. We moved on to set up the cellar of another ruined house. We had a crowd because forward Medics and the mortar sections of I. and K. Companies were already there. The Jerries fired shells into the area we had just vacated. If that barrage had been two minutes earlier, it would have surely gotten some of us.

The Ardennes Forest

Sergeant Bell came in about 8:30 that night and yelled "I need three men to go out after a wounded man, you, you and you go" and pointed to Runion, Schilling and me. Cardovia from the rifle squad guided us to a draw with about five foot of snow. We found the wounded man covered with snow and so stiff he could barely whisper. He said he had been shot about ten o'clock that morning and his wound wasn't serious, but he had lost too much blood and the suffering from the cold almost had him. I didn't know who the man was, but we had to get him out of the snow. Schilling was short and Cardovia had a back wound, neither could do much toward carrying him so it was up to me and Runion to haul him out of there. We decided to carry him, but had to take off our gloves to hold hands and make a 'saddle'. The snow was up to our waist and we couldn't make over ten steps before we had to put him down. Our hands were so cold we had to have Schilling put our gloves on for us at every rest stop. After what seemed endless hours, we had only moved him about 200 yards. As we wrestled the wounded man around, he got warmer and talked a little more. He swore because he couldn't help himself and he realized we were 'all in.' At one point, he begged us to go off and leave him. Runion got mad and said he was going to get the Medics and would bring them back at gunpoint if there was no other way. Well, he brought them back with a toboggan and we finally got our man to safety. Runion and I sat down in the cellar to rest and the perspiration seemed to freeze on us. Our jackets had blood all over our sleeves from his wound. We were beat, but it was a good feeling to know we had saved a G. I. buddy's life. The Medics got the guy's wet clothes off, wrapped him in a blanket and gave him some blood plasma. Later he was talking and smoking a cigarette. He turned out to be Private Rosengrant, a boy who joined L. Company the same time I did. He had been wounded high in the leg. I don't know if his feet were frozen or not, but he never did return to L. company. Needless to say, we had spent a miserable and sleepless night.

The next morning we had C rations for breakfast before we moved ahead about 1500 yards and captured a German pillbox which overlooked the spot where we rescued Rosengrant. Old Lady Luck had been with us that cloudy night; on a night with a full moon they would have seen us and opened fire!

Riddle and I started digging our foxhole by a fallen tree. We dug through four feet of snow and just hit dirt when Jerry started shelling the area with 305 and 88 mm shells. You could actually see the big 305's whizzing over us; they sounded like a freight train. A few landed nearby and the 88mm's were landing very close. A shell was coming in about every three minutes on the nose. We could dig for about two minutes, then get down into whatever shelter we had. The soil was stony, but we dug and ducked all day and had a three foot hole by dark. Shrapnel hit our hole a few times. One piece hit Riddle's steel helmet and helmet liner but stopped before it hit his head. His life was spared, but he had a big headache for a while. They managed to get C rations and a hot meal up to us that afternoon. We also got blankets, wind breaker pants and boots. We dried our wet feet by a small fire and put on our new boots before we moved out in the rain. The snow was melting and it went through my new boots like water through a sieve.

U.S. Army photo

Mortar team with mortar tripod and shells. The small shovel holster on the belt carried a folding shovel to dig a foxhole in a hurry. Mortar men carried the M1 carbine instead of a heavy M1 Garand rifle.

Our 60 mm mortar section was on the left flank when we turned off the road into the woods and the riflemen were running, yelling and shooting like a band of Indians and took several prisoners. We missed the bellowing and roaring of Lt. Brown who had gone back to Heartbreak Crossing because of his feet. In this advance we almost stepped on a Jerry soldier who had been dead only a few minutes. Sgt. Lanxter got his pistol and we ran on climbing over and under downed trees. The Germans were retreating and we were running to keep up with our riflemen chasing them. Each man was carrying about 45 pounds. Our load consisted of a heavy mortar or its shells, a carbine, extra socks and boots. Farther on we got to ride half-tracks and tanks. Needless to say, there was not enough room for all of us to get in or on a vehicle. There was hardly room to stand and we were hanging all over them. What a miserable ride, first one would get stuck and then another. We were six hours going 600 yards. We all sweated out an enemy shell barrage and about midnight we stopped for a few hours. It was pitch black in the woods, but we found a level spot, scrapped away the snow and spread our ponchos. We all lay close together to keep warm, of course our boots had turned to ice by now. It stopped raining and things looked a little better, but then shells began coming in. They were big shells and shrapnel was flying through the trees around us! Stoltz got hit but it didn't draw blood. Schilling and Hodge thought we should dig in. I told them, 'You guys can dig if you want to, but I'm not moving. If it hits me, I go back and get out of this mess. If it kills me, I'll still be out of it!'

They agreed, so despite the fact we were cold and miserable, we went to sleep At 4:00 am we were moving again down into the valley, crossed the Ruhr river on a footbridge and entered a small town. They left us standing by the side of the road, but Lt. Walker posted Stoltz near the road to tell us when L. Company moved out and led us over to a house. Riddle and I found some nice smoked ham. There were three cookstoves and we soon had fires in everyone. We couldn't find skillets, so we just threw slabs of ham on the hot stove. The barn was in was in the next room of the house and Runion and I milked a cow. It all tasted very good because we hadn't eaten since noon of the day before, but our meal was cut short when Stoltz came in to say we were moving. I had saved him a big slab of half-cooked ham to wolf down. It was raining when we loaded up to leave the valley and turned into a driving blizzard as we climbed the hill. Stoltz had lost his ammunition load, so he helped Little Joe as we climbed to the top. Two tanks and the jeeps went to the top with us. They sure can go places where you couldn't even think of driving a car. The blizzard got stronger and we had to lean into it at an almost 45 degree angle to walk, but we kept plodding on and passed some enemy pillboxes. Two Jerries ran out of one, but everyone was tuckered out and nobody fired a shot. We slogged on and everyone was about exhausted by the time we entered the town of Wollseifen February 9, 1945. We were beat, the sleepless nights, and the long march in the snow with inadequate food just about had us! Major Tanner had walked with us. He looked stooped, tired and old for a 28 year old man.

US Army photo

Ninth Infantry patrol, passes a disabled tank

We set up our mortars in the front yard of a house which had just been vacated by German troops. A light was still burning in the cellar. We decided the Jerries had gone out the back door while we were in the front yard. They had left their packs and their half-eaten meal of ration biscuits and canned meat was still on the table. Several replacement troops joined L. Company here and we had a few days to do a 'dry run' problem to give them an idea of what to expect. Of course they could do 'dry run' problems a lifetime and not know what actual combat was like! Dawn of the 18th, we boarded trucks and rode until we stopped for a hot noon meal at an old Jerry camp. It was cold and rainy when we took off on foot with a new supply of C rations to relieve the 82nd Airborne near Schmidt up the Ruhr. We had to carry our packs, but not the mortars and ammo. We followed a trial made by the jeeps taking in them in with other supplies. They had the mud well worked up and it was shoe-top deep in many places. We were wearing four buckle overshoes and walking was a chore, but finally found the place and Stoltz and I scouted around until we found a ready-made foxhole. We found a super duper one lined with cardboard and had logs over the top. A few shells were coming in; one fairly close. It was pitch dark and raining, but we were snug as a bug in a rug. Little Joe and Triago couldn't find a hole, so we invited them in. We all managed to crowd in with a blanket over us and got to sleep about midnight. Four hours later we had a breakfast of C rations and the C. O. (Commanding Officer) told us to pull back 800 yards. Stoltz and I dug another foxhole covered it and then dug one for our mortar.

We were on the banks of the Ruhr again and our big guns were constantly shelling the German defense across the river. Sammy, who had been on rest leave, came back to our squad as a gunner. He had spent Christmas in England and was very nervous. One has to go through a few shellings (artillery barrages) before he really knows how to sympathize with a man in Sammy's condition.

The next afternoon another company came in to relieve us. We loaded our mortars and ammo in jeeps and walked out a different way than we came. We went through the woods, down a cliff that a goat would have killed himself going down and across a narrow valley. We had to climb a young mountain to get to the new position and some boys in the rifle platoon passed out before they reached the top. Stoltz and I dug another foxhole because we knew that laziness has been the death of many men. The woods on was cut up by shells and our 105 cannons were setting up about 300 yards behind us and firing over our heads. The jeeps brought in our equipment and we set up a tent next to our foxhole. At night, the muzzle blast from the guns would almost turn us over in bed, but we slept. One night Sammy crawled into our foxhole. It was cold and he didn't have any blankets, but he stayed most of the night. We all got a treat the next day. The hot- meals truck came in and they issued four cokes to each man; the first we had since coming overseas and they sure were good. That night the cannons boomed all night!

February 23rd near Schmidt, Germany

Lt. Walker called us together that afternoon to tell us L. Company was going to cross the Ruhr. He said, "Tonight is it men. It's going to be rough and it will be tough and there's no use saying otherwise."

He pulled out a map and we gathered around while he pointed out where we would cross the river. We were to cross in assault boats or by a pontoon bridge if the engineers could build it. On the other side was a castle sitting on a cliff which we would have to climb. It all looked possible on paper, even might work, but having been through actual warfare; we began to sweat!

He told us where we would go, what to do and how to pack so nothing rattled. We would carry our mortar, ammo, gun and pack with sleeping bag, personal items and C rations. We wore heavy underwear, sweaters, under our uniform covered by field jackets and windbreaker pants. Our headgear was a knit cap and a helmet liner under a steel helmet. Every man hung a canteen, first aid kit and spade on his belt and carried a gas mask. Our heavy overshoes gave us a good foundation. We rolled our tent and blankets to make our bed rolls; some slipped in an axe or candles.

We were to leave at 6:30 pm and I heard platoon leader, Lt. Brown, tell his men that some of them would die, but what the hell, they couldn't live forever. I guess it sounded blunt to the replacement boys who didn't know him and hadn't seen combat. However, he was telling the truth. We packed and waiting for the word to move out. Just then, Lt. Walker came up and said,

"It's been called off!"

Boy, were we happy! We put up our tents and made ourselves at home and L. Company rested a few days. Stoltz and I got mail and packages from home. A few Jerry planes came over and our anti-aircraft guns fired at them, but as Little Joe said, "They just wasted a lot of ammunition!" Five days later, they brought in cigarettes, chocolate bars and C rations. We heard that some units had crossed the river and knew we would be pulling out soon, as we usually did after receiving rations. February 28th we moved back down the cliff, into a valley, through a destroyed village and crossed the Rhur on a bridge. That sure beat the original plan!

Note: L. Company moved forward to take objectives and fell back according to Army strategy and the use of heavy weapons. They were often ordered to fall back to allow heavy artillery to blast and 'soften up' enemy positions ahead of the infantry. Troops were also halted or moved back to allow our Air Force to strafe enemy troops and/or heavy bombers to destroy German oil dumps, railroads and airfields. In reality, the infantry's job was to gain and hold enemy territory as they moved from foxhole to foxhole.

"Once across the river, we began a steady climb up a rough and muddy trail. The artillery set up their 105's near the castle as we climbed to the summit where we found a slow moving column of trucks, jeeps and tanks. The Jerries were throwing in a few shells there seemed to be a traffic jam. I saw Col. Tanner's jeep head down the line and the vehicles began to disperse. We moved on about eight miles to our assigned position in the woods and dug in a short distance from the town of Roth. The shells from our 105 howitzer bombardment last night had really torn up the trees. I dug in several yards from the trees so a tree burst wouldn't be so deadly and got a peaceful night's sleep near my foxhole the night of February 28th. The next morning, a mobile kitchen came up and fixed us a hot breakfast and another at noon. A supply truck came in and we traded our overshoes for boots.

We were alerted to move out and about three o'clock, we walked down the road to Roth and mounted tanks and tank destroyers. There were about twenty guys hanging on every vehicle. It was cold and rainy, needless to say, it wasn't very comfortable. We rode several miles and passed through another outfit that had taken Fussenich. I was glad to start walking again, the new boots were fine and it was a lot easier to keep warm. We passed one of our tanks that had been knocked out by a mine. The bodies of three of the crew lay in the mud beside it. Seeing dead Jerries never bothered us, but when you see dead G.I. lying there, it has a different effect. Farther along there were dead Jerries laying along the road, some with their hands still clutching machine guns or rifles. We stopped and dug in before dark, but water kept seeping into our fox holes so we slept in a tent next to it in case shells came in during the night. A little thing like water wouldn't keep you from diving in our hole if necessary! Next morning a small arms battle was going on to our left. We had a hot meal and we were oriented by Lt. Walker and our squad leaders about where we were to go and how to get there. We were issued the usual C rations and pulled out for Fussench at 2:00 a.m. carrying our mortars and ammunition. We had a full moon in a cloudless sky and it was almost as light as day, which made it worse for us. We passed through a destroyed village and passed two dead G.I.s in a ditch. Our unit was traveling in the open and might be seen from quite a distance. We walked at ten yard intervals, with no talking or smoking. You would be surprised how quietly a group of men can travel. We would walk a ways then stop while the scouts checked up ahead to see if the way was clear. Consequently, we sweated while moving and froze while waiting.

We had traveled nine miles cross-country and came to the outer defenses of the town about daylight. The Jerries were not manning the outer defenses because their trenches were full of water and L. Company never fired a shot going in. The Germans were not expecting us, some were still sleeping or having morning coffee. We set up in our mortars in the city court yard. Our boys rounded up about seventy prisoners and all went well until about 9:00 a.m. when snipers started firing from buildings we had not searched and then the Jerry artillery woke up and started shelling the town.

The civilians, young and old, hid in a concrete bunker next to the house we occupied. This was the first town where I saw underfed civilians. At first they were scared stiff, they thought we were paratroopers and going to kill them. They didn't know our infantry was in the area. Jerry artillery shells hit one of the cows in the hind legs and she couldn't get up. I wanted to put the poor thing out of her misery, but they had been told they could not kill one without permission of an officer. Stoltz and I convinced them it would be OK to kill an old crippled cow so they drug her around and I shot her. The townspeople were more than happy to butcher her for the meat.

We pulled out about three a.m. that night for Eldenich. It was March 3rd and by now, the Germans knew we were in the area. We walked about five miles in another moonlit night and were near the town when a Jerry machine gunner opened up in our direction. We had been ordered to hold our fire, we kept advancing and getting closer to that machine gun nest. Then the machine-gunner spotted us, his bullets came snapping close and we hit the ground to crawl into a plow furrow. Several bullets passed over me as he raked his fire up and down the line. That furrow was a lifesaver, but we were pinned down until help arrived. We were dead on our feet and chilling from lying on the cold ground. I almost dozed off a time or two, but that was no time to take a nap but some of the guys did sleep. At last our battalion tanks came up and we got ready to move out. Each man passed the word to those around him and we started running across the field carrying our mortar and ammo with Germans firing at us. We passed a dead G.I. and another badly wounded that the medics were treating and went into Eldenich. One of the boys shot the lock of the door of a house, we set up the mortar, posted a guard and tried to get some sleep. We were in out of the cold for the first time in twenty-two hours! There were enough beds for some of us; the rest slept on the floor. The townspeople came out of their shelters to start their day. They were not afraid and shared what food they had. One woman who spoke some English, showed us photos of her children. She said her son was a POW in the U.S. and her young daughter wore a German uniform, but she had no idea where she was.

We were sharing their house like relatives and the woman was glad to cook for us and we had hot meal March 3rd and 4th before pulling out about 4:30 p.m. to take another town. We got there to learn the 60th Regiment had already taken it. Lt. Walker returned to us, we had another hot meal and pulled out about 8:30 p.m. to head for Memmerich. I well remember that night; it was a long one. We walked, rode trucks for a while then walked again. We were on the Cologne Plains with no hills to slow us down. We set up our in Memmerich and the rifle platoons and machine gunners were sent across the Uft river to attack Muggenhausen. There was no battle, the Engineers had built a footbridge across the river, but knee-deep water was running over it. Runion and I decided to raise it, we got our feet wet and he injured a finger, but the others crossed with dry feet. We moved into town, we ate a few cans of cherries with C rations and just got bedded down for a rest when all of a sudden we had to pull out again. I. Company was having trouble and needed our help. We pulled out on the plains about four p.m. and Jerry began throwing shells at us, just as they had at I. Company. We ran to a building then moved up to another past one of our knocked out US tanks, a dead G.I. (a Company I. B.A.R. man) and four dead Jerries. There was another Jerry with a stomach wound, but our Medics were so busy with our own wounded; they left him there.

Our squad set up the mortars in the town courtyard, piled straw in a house and stable and bedded down for some much needed sleep. We were awakened in a few hours and were ready to pull out before midnight. We traveled sixteen hours to Heimerzheim, stopped in a house long enough to eat our C rations and some canned plums and cherries we found in the kitchen. Got a little sleep, but walked out again at 2:40 am. March 6th. We walked into Schourzenoor at dawn. A delirious girl came walking down the column, fainted and fell in the mud near us. Runion dragged her out of the mud and caught up with us at the house where we set up our mortars. It was just getting light when two American tanks and jeeps came up to our roadblock. We thought it strange that one of our tanks would arrive so soon. They were wearing G.I. uniforms, but Germans had used that trick before, Pat Moriority, who could speak German, asked them what outfit they belonged to and they tore off down the road. Pat told Lt. Brown and he yelled for our bazooka men loud enough to be heard in Berlin! The bazookas got off a few got a few shots at the tank. They didn't knock it out, but they did get one of the jeeps.

Note: A bazooka was a one man anti-tank weapon with a 300 yard range. It fired an armor piercing self-propelled rocket. It was much more effective than Germany's Panzerfaust, a recoilless, one-man anti-tank grenade launcher with a 33 yard range.

"Things were pretty exciting that morning. Some enemy action, mostly sniper fire, continued until noon. Hodge and Schilling were upstairs in the window of our house that morning when our bazookas went off just below. It nearly blew them out of the window, later we saw a G.I hit in the head by a sniper. The town had been bombed unmercifully the day before, killing and wounding many of its citizens. It was the worst bombed town I had seen with people still living in it, which was probably the reason of that girl's condition. People were out poking around in the rubble for missing persons or lost possessions. There were dead still lying in the streets and doorways. The body of one man, with his head, arms and legs missing, lay in the street in front of our building.

We fried some potatoes and fixed our beds for a little sleep, later our field kitchen came up to give us a hot supper, but we were issued C rations again which meant we would soon be moving out. Meanwhile, Runion and several others raided a wine cellar and got drunk. However, he did get a woman to dress his finger, which had become infected. Sgt. Chilek and the rest just got to sleep when the order came to move out. If you remember, this was the first time we had slept since crossing the Ruhr. It was March 6th and we hadn't had six hours of uninterrupted sleep since February 27th. Sarge griped as loud as the rest of us, but our griping just helped get rid of the steam.

We left about 1:00 pm on a dangerous mission to the infiltrate German lines and attack from the rear. The distance was only three miles, but knowing the army, we knew we would be walking a lot farther. Many of the boys were staggering but happy. Runion was becoming "slap happy" and the Medic told him to go back on account of his infected finger. He refused and began raising such a fuss that Lt. Walker came back and told him to go back to the Medics. Runion cried and begged to stay, but the Lieutenant ordered him to go. We all knew he didn't have any business on the front with that finger. He sure was a dejected figure as he went back. His shoulders slumped and big sobs shook him. We circled a woods about dark and moved in to make sure there were no Jerries. There weren't any, except dead ones. As we moved on, the 1st Battalion was having a small arms battle on the left and German artillery started dropping in shells, some close to us. Now, it was dark and a misty began to fall. Our trail led us deeper into the woods and visibility was near zero. The Germans had retreated this way and we were on their supply road, which was little more than a trail full of deep ruts made by Jerry horses and wagons. Many places we stepped into water shoe top deep. Wading through the mud with the loads we carried was almost too much for our exhausted condition. Only the excitement of combat kept us going. On a night watch you stop every few yards for complete quiet. When we stopped, some of the boys would go to sleep standing others sat down in the mud and immediately went sleep. When we moved again, we had to be sure the guy behind was on his feet and awake. We passed so close to one German field gun, we could hear them giving the orders to fire. One time a Jerry sentry yelled "Halt," but we paid no attention and kept moving. We had orders not to fire. We didn't shoot anytime on the march nor were we not shot at. We reached our destination, ran some civilians out of a farm house and set up our mortars. The rifle section and headquarters got in out of the weather somewhere else. We were scattered all over the place; in a wood shed, chicken coop, cellar and every room of the house. It must have been midnight before we settled down. We pulled a two man guard for every squad. Little Joe and I pulled the first shift then woke up Stolz and Samuelson to relieve us. When we got up for our second shift, Little Joe fell through a trap door to the cellar. He wrenched his leg and couldn't walk. The Medics took him back to the aid station for treatment. It was weeks before he returned.

We had a hot meal while the riflemen rounded up several German prisoners, all artillery men. Later a civilian came in to say the people of Bonn were waving white flags and wanted to surrender. We were within a half mile walk, but we didn't go. Instead, they ordered L. Company back to join the battalion which was back about where we started from the day before. The long walk back in the dusk didn't appeal to any of us, but we had to do it. Along the way, someone suggested we throw away the heavy mortar ammo. We almost did it but a jeep came along and we loaded it full of our guns and the mortar ammo. Getting rid of all that weight was sure a relief! It was raining when we reached our destination about midnight. Just as we got ready to bed down on straw in a shed, we were told to be ready to move any minute. We said to hell with them, took out our sleeping bags, rolled up in our ponchos and were dead until next morning. Later we went down and filled our ammo bags with new shells. Lt. Walker asked were we got the order to do that. No one seemed to know, so he dropped the subject with a warning.

"Next time, be sure the order comes from me!" (Later, Stoltz told me he gave it.)

It was raining the next morning, so we had a hot breakfast and were told to move out at 10:30 a.m. We moved farther up into the castle, had another hot meal and waited until the trucks came in around 2:30. The truck drivers told us they hauled their first load of troops to the Rhine and they walked across a bridge. This sounded like a bunch of baloney to us, but how were we to know? The trucks moved us quickly through some beautiful country, marred by artillery and bombs. There was much abandoned German equipment, including vehicles and ammunition. At last, we rounded a curve and saw a silver ribbon in the valley below. It was the much talked about and most dreaded natural defense we had sweated out. It was the mighty Rhine River, which had protected Germany from invaders for centuries!

March 8, 1945 - The road wound down the hill and we could see the bridge. Our big guns, 240 mm and 155mm were set up and the 105mm guns were crossing the railroad bridge. Just as we got to the town of Remagen, three Jerry planes came over and we bailed out of the trucks while the .50 caliber machine guns on the trucks and tanks opened fire. The planes dropped their bombs before they were shot down (A tank gunner near us got one.) They had missed the bridge and tanks and trucks hurried across into Germany. L. Company moved about 200 yards into town before Jerry began throwing shells from across the Rhine. Our mortar squad took shelter in a big house for a few minutes. Stolz found some canned fruit, we ate some, put some in our pockets and moved on up the street. This was the last time I talked to Hammond who was now a squad leader and busy getting his men ready to move out. We had been buddies since our replacement days and shared fox holes all along the way.

The Company moved through Remagen fast, running most of the time and watching for snipers. Lt. Fuller tore a big swastika flag off a pole and dragged it down the street. We always kept ten yard intervals on such daylight moves. I looked back to see Stoltz running full speed with a can of cherries in one hand and eating with the other. (We always carried a spoon with us.) He handed it to me to share and I ate some. I think he knew I still had a can in my jacket!

We reached the railroad bridge and ran about half way across before stopping. There we were, standing in the middle of the bridge when two German planes came zooming up the river. They dropped their bombs, but missed the bridge. One hit 100 yards short and the other hit beyond us as we ran into the Third Reich.

We were across the Rhine, the problem was to stay there!"

Nat'l Archives

The Ludendorf railroad bridge at Remagen

Remagen Bridge - John Hill

Note: October 14, 2012 at a meeting of the Leesville Community Center, 92 year old John Hill gave us this second WW II story of the capture of the Remagen Bridge. John said the movie story was highly exaggerated. This is a story as recalled by a man who was there:

"Our L. Company wiped out a German artillery outfit with rifle and mortar fire in an early morning attack and we moved on to the top of a hill. The Rhine river flowed like a silver ribbon in the valley below and there was very little activity around the bridge. The scouts reported that the strategically important bridge was guarded by only two armed soldiers supervising a work gang of Polish prisoners of war. Our officers quickly ordered L. Company down the hill where we formed-up around an armored truck with a .50 caliber machine mounted on top. As we started up the road, a German fighter came roaring up the river road to strafe us. Everybody dived behind the rocks or under the truck, but our gunner stood his ground and hit that fighter. The last we saw, it was screaming up over the hill trailing a stream of smoke.

Headquarters had told our Captain that the bridge was loaded with explosive charges and the Germans planned to blow it up rather than have it captured. We charged up the road and the Captain heard a German tell his men to run and flip the detonator switch to set off the explosives. Only a few charges exploded; we shot the guards and were on the bridge when two enemy bombers came up the river at a very low level. The first bomb fell short and the second passed over the bridge. I guess they only carried one bomb, because they never came back.

March 8, 1945 about dark, the 160 men of L. Company were among the first U.S. troops to cross the Rhine into German on the Ludendorff railroad bridge at Remagen. We knew we were going to need a lot of help to hold it against German troops. Sometime later, vibrations from hundreds of men, tanks and other vehicles of our invading forces weakened bridge footings and it fell into the river. U.S. Engineers constructed a pontoon bridge and Allied forces continued flowing into Germany."

Note: *For centuries the Rhine River, from Switzerland to the North Sea, stood as a natural barrier to defend Germany. It's cold, wide and swift waters flowing down from the Alps, were a moat to enemies. Our Allied armies were nearing Germany and commanders knew the crossing of the*

Rhine would be a difficult and costly task because Hitler had ordered the destruction of all bridges across the Rhine.

March 7, 1945, shortly after noon an American reconnaissance patrol reached the wooded hills overlooking the river at Remagen, and discovered the two lane *Ludendorff* railroad bridge from Remagen to Erpel had not yet been destroyed!

Americans quickly launched a full-scale assault on the bridge while the defending Germans scrambled to detonate the explosive charges that had been set to destroy it that afternoon. The fighting was fierce as both sides realized what was at stake. American soldiers scrambled under withering gun fire from girder to girder returning fire and ripping explosives from the bridge's super structure. The Germans detonated some explosives, but not enough to destroy the bridge, and four minutes after the assault began, American troops reached the town of Erpel on other side of the river. They secured the bridge and set up a defense as American troops, trucks and tanks streamed across the mighty Rhine.

The Allied army's possession of the bridge allowed hundreds of U.S. armored divisions and troops to cross into German territory and take the ground war to the citizens of Hitler's Third Reich. Always before, German troops had invaded and fought in occupied countries. Bombers had blasted their cities, but they had never been invaded, now American troops were in Germany. American and British troops were attacking from the west and south and Russian armies from the east. The war had come home to the German people!

Gen. George Patton kept his promise to" pee" in the Rhine RiverWhen allied armies reached the Rhine, the first thing many men did was pee in it. This was pretty universal from the lowest private to Winston Churchill (who made a big show of it) and Gen. Patton (who had himself photographed in the act).

German Counter-Attack

"The company moved into Erpel, but moved out an hour later to a spot about 300 yards up a hill to wait for orders. The wind was blowing and it began to rain so we wrapped up in our ponchos and cussed the Army foe sticking us on a hillside when there was a town full of houses just below us. Late that night I shared my can of cherries with Stolz, Meadows and Espinosa. As the night wore on, we heard small arms fire and knew the Germans weren't far off.

The chilly dawn of March 9th finally came. We ate our C rations and moved up the river road past the bridge and lots of our heavy equipment. The artillery guns were set up and ready to protect the bridge from Jerry bombers. We were tired, hungry and exhausted, and loaded down with weapons and ammo, but we kept plodding on. We reached Ohlenberg about noon and set our mortars near a farmhouse with a connecting barn. The house had a big cellar, a ready-made foxhole! That night, we had a little time for food and rest before setting up our defense on the hilltop above us. The rifle and machine gun squads moved out the next day to move up the hill, leaving our mortar outfit set up to cover them in case they needed fire power moving up. We waited until they dug their foxholes and waved us on up to set up our mortars. The German counter-attack March 9th was one of the most desperate we had faced since Bastogne. Hitler had ordered an all out effort to chase us back across the Rhine. The German troops pinned us down in the barnyard and the planes strafed our position. I got behind a big oak tree and switched sides every time a plane came back at us. Their artillery was dropping shells in on us and every time a shell exploded this little red rooster would fly up on a fence post and crow. He did it several times, before shrapnel finally got him. Three good sized pigs in a barn were also killed. We were finally saved by our artillery guns that literally laid down a ring of steel around us and beat back the attackers.

Finally, L. Company was ordered off the frontlines for food, rest and to pick up replacement troops for our dead and wounded. We had won the battle, but we paid a high cost. Of the 160 men who went up the hill, only twenty-six came down. All officers were killed except our Captain and he came out as a shell–shock case.

We were to attack a small town the next afternoon, it was less than a mile down the road so Lt. Walker convinced our C.O, Lt. Fraeser, that our mortars would do more good where we were set up than going up with the riflemen and machine gunners. They left about 4 p.m. and Trigo went along as a runner. Shortly afterwards, shells began coming in on us. We stayed in the cellar with our walkie-talkie open to listen for orders to move up or start firing, but all we heard was German church music. The Jerries had "jammed" our radio frequency!

The riflemen and machine gunners began to come in after dark, most were wet and muddy. We knew something had gone haywire and little by little we got the full story about the shape and strength of L. Company: Tex Papron was shelled shocked; Lt. Fuller, Richardson, Sgt. Gaston, Trigo and several others were wounded. Lt. Broen and several other boys were missing. The dead included our Lt. Walker, Hampton, Hammond, and my buddy, Hammerstrom!

Our C.O. Lt. Fraeser, was the only officer left. We later learned that the action of our skeleton force had stopped a counter-attack that could have endangered our bridgehead across the Rhine. The shells kept coming and the next morning all hell broke loose as the Germans plastered us with an artillery barrage. A Headquarters runner came up and told us to fall back, but Lt. Fraeser yelled,

"Get those mortars ready to fire in this direction and for God's sake, hurry, it's a counter-attack!"

Jerry troops charged with rifles, burp guns and machine guns. We were firing our mortars at about 200 yards and our 81 mm mortars and artillery behind us were dropping shells on them. The attack was stopped after a few minutes that seemed like hours, but fifteen minutes later their artillery shells plastered us again.

March 12 - Another unit came up to relieve us. We moved back for hot chow and a rest, there was plenty of food because there weren't too many of us left! We pulled out again in the afternoon and two Jerry ME 109 fighters came over. One came back to strafe us, but we were off the road, hugging Mother Earth. No one was hit and he flew on toward the Remagen railroad bridge. The 78th outfit below us was taking a heavy beating and many wounded were carried out. We took heavy shelling the next two days and saw a lot of German planes. The jets were really fast. Our Ack Ack guns shot down several planes before K. Company came up to relieve us. We were pulled back off the line and several replacements came in to replace our losses. Our company commander, Lt. Walker, had been killed, so Captain Petty of I. Company, took over. We moved out at noon and it was dark when we set up in Notschied. The riflemen and machine gun squads took off to attack another small town and many of the new men were captured, killed or wounded in their first night of combat. Willie Mauldoon and I got minor wounds, he on a finger and me on the wrist. Willie went back to the Medics and I never did, so I lost a Purple Heart and five points. Ouch! Captain Kelly had been captured so we were without a company C.O. again, but a new officer, Lt. Inglheart took over the company, but our 4th Platoon didn't have an officer. We took a shelling for the next few days. March 18th, about 3:00 am, our mortar squad moved back over the spot the 78th had been shelled so heavily. Some of their bodies were lying where they fell among the equipment left by our G.I.'s who were captured.

March 19, we moved on to Kettlestross, and our Military Government people came to town, so we figured we were safe and practically in the rear ranks. The rifle and machine gun squads joined us. Several guys had been hit and we were down to one machinegun squad. L. Company sure needed those new replacement troops waiting to fill our thin ranks. Our morale was pretty low and we needed a break. Sgt. Manning, who had come back up with the new replacements said,

"The new boys didn't know what to expect when you old timers came in. It was their first day anywhere near the front and they had never seen combat. You guys all had long faces with a distant look, no one smiled and everyone was jumpy."

In brief, we were just walking dead people. I guess he was right! We had several days rest before pulling out again for a night attack on a town farther up the road. The new boys had never been in combat, let alone a night attack. They really made us nervous. They were constantly making some type of noise and we were moving through the woods as quietly as a circus coming to town! We were definitely not the same L. Company that fought from the Ardennes to the Rhine!

Happy Birthday

The morning of March 27, 1945 was a beautiful spring day. Wild flowers were blooming in the woods and the trees were budding. We lay in the sunshine and talked of the war; when it would end and how it was progressing. In general, I guess could of had a much worse birthday!"

The evening of John's birthday the weapons platoon were handed C rations as they piled on trucks and rode for 24 hours before stopping for food and sleep. They rode tanks and trucks another 70 miles to reach Lenne for a well deserved three day rest before traveling another 50 miles on March 31st. Easter Sunday morning they marched until midnight (they called it their Easter Parade.) They went into battle when it was so dark in the woods they couldn't see the man in front of them. They kept contact by holding on to the coat or pack of the man ahead. The artillery opened fire to clear a way into the town ahead. They dug in on top a hill and hunched under ponchos in the drizzling rain before moving forward the next morning. L. Company liberated a POW sub-camp camp with both men and women. They were Poles who did slave labor on farms and in a small arms factory hidden from bombers in the local mines. They said they had been bombed often, but continued to work hardly hearing the explosions. They were forced to do high quality work or die. Thousands died from overwork and starvation. These prisoners were forced to help and support the country which took away their freedom. Victorious Allied troops over-running German cities gave them back that freedom.

"We moved into town to set up in two large houses. Ours was a sportsman's lodge with a lot a fancy rifles and trophies hanging on the walls. I found a nice cane pole complete with hook, line and sinker. I went fishing in the river, caught a nice trout and fixed a nice hot meal of trout, eggs butter, bread topped off with real coffee with cream and sugar. The boys said it was a real treat and later we searched some of the other houses for food to supplement the meals in those C ration cans.

April 4 - We were relieved by the 99th Division. Our four day rest with hot meals and lots of sleep was great. We mounted trucks, half-tracks and tanks and took off, but the Jerries attacked the place the next morning and drove the 99th out! We traveled some thirty miles to Hildfeld that day; the next morning we were walking again. We captured about sixty Volkstrum (home guard) prisoners without firing a shot. They were a sorry looking sight, old men and boys. I was going to make one carry my ammo, but they all looked so pitiful that I didn't do it. We went on down the hill to Olsberg and another outfit came in from another direction. The headless body of a GI tanker was lying in the street. He had his head sticking out and a German Panzerfaust (shell) took his head off even with his shoulders. The tank crew had laid him on the ground, later the Colonel came along and had the body moved out of the way. We stayed in a big house; Stolz, Trindel, Johnson and I found a room with two nice beds. We climbed into beds, muddy boots and all, of course. We were really sleeping good when they woke us at 2;00 a.m. and we were on the road again at 2:30.

Note: *The Panzerfaust was a recoilless one-man anti-tank grenade launcher with about a 33 yard range. It was not as dangerous as the U.S. bazooka which was also a one man anti-tank weapon with a self-propelled rocket and a 300 yard range.*

April 7 – At dawn, we were nearing Gevelinghausen when a machine gunner got one of our men at close range, before we got him. Later in town, I found some big hams in a cellar and proceeded to fry some. I had three big pieces in a skillet and they were almost done when we got an order to move. I put them on a plate to cool, then, I grabbed them and took off with three pieces in one hand and the ham in the other. I divided the cooked ham with some of the boys while we running to another house. We found eggs there and I cooked ham and eggs for the boys. This with our C rations made a good meal.

April 8 - The riflemen and machine-gunners out in front, were taking lots of prisoners. In all, we took over a hundred to send back down the line that day. The First Battalion moved through us just before noon, so we went further into town to catch trucks and ride a few miles before Jerry began to shell us. We dismounted the trucks, which turned around and left. We began advancing on foot, about dark we were approaching Merthied. In the meantime, are artillery shells had hit an ammo dump and the fire was lighting up the whole countryside back of town. We had to cross an open field that was probably covered by German machinegun. We could have been easily knocked off so we took a detour, climbed a hill and went down through woods to get back to the road. We fell in behind our tanks, of course the infantry was out in front. We had casualties, but took many prisoners awhile moving on into town. I forgot to mention that Lt. Brown had returned to us and it was good to hear him yelling orders again. He and several of his platoon had been captured at the Remagen bridge, but were later freed by our troops.

April 9 - The 5th Division relieved us and about noon we piled back on trucks and passed through many towns before stopping at Seidlinghausen. We had traveled 143 miles but got a three day break. We didn't do much but rest up and eat the Germans' eggs and milk their cows. Several went fishing but none of us caught anything. We didn't know what was about to happen, but knew something must be in store for us or we wouldn't be resting for nothing!

April 12- We joined the 3rd Armored Division and pulled out on tanks and trucks, nobody walked. It was a spectacular affair, our column of tanks, trucks and jeeps was as long as the eye could see! We moved through nine towns that day before stopping for the night in Blankenheim. Next morning we cleared the woods past town before the tanks and armored vehicles came up, we found no Jerries so we mounted trucks and moved along a back road toward Ahlsdorf. It was little more than a trail and the Jerries ambushed us as we crossed a railroad track. They had been hiding behind the tracks and let the tanks pass. When we came along in the trucks, they let us know they were there and started shooting at us. Our truck driver stepped on the gas and we began shooting back. M. Company had machine guns mounted on their jeeps and were firing up a storm. Our fire kept the Jerries pinned down and no one in our truck was hit. However, several men in L. Company rifle platoons were wounded or killed. We sure did go tearing down that road, and made it into town to take cover behind some buildings. Our machine gun platoons set up and I saw them get one guy. A Jerry sniper in a rock pile up on a hill kept everyone cautious. I'll bet he was shot at us a thousand times before he stopped or one of our snipers got him. During this stop, we liberated some food: eggs and milk from a dairy and several loaves of bread, canned jellies and much wine before we moved out. The truck was not so crowded, about 18 men and it was a lot easier to get in or out a hurry. We traveled another 26 miles, met a little resistance, but it was nothing compared to the first town that morning.

We were traveling across plains and the prisoners (slave) farm workers doing spring planting would leave their oxen or horses and come running to wave to us. The people young and old were really happy to see us. Many cried because they knew we were bringing them freedom. We yelled, waved back and threw them cigarettes and gum. There wasn't a one that went back to work.

April 14 - We met tough resistance from an estimated two battalions of Jerries in Kothen and many guys were wounded and several killed. We captured a bunch of old guys who were Volkstrum (Home Guard) members. The townspeople were scared stiff, they thought we were going to kill them all. Practically every house had boiling water on the stove to throw in the faces of the barbaric Americans. They changed their minds when we didn't come in shooting and later became very cooperative in helping us find eggs or drinks. We stayed in an apartment house we called it "Hitler's Hatchery" because it was full of young mothers with three or four kids, but none were married.

April 16 - Some of our tanks and riflemen led the attack on Merzien today, we were bringing up the rear. The Jerries were dug in with well camouflaged foxholes in a wheat field. They opened fire and Trendel, Stolz and I dived into in ditch along the road to return fire. I heard a bullet crack and saw the back of Stoltz's field jacket puff up as he crumpled to the ground. The ditch was too narrow to lay beside him so I crawled past him and turned my head toward his. The sniper was still firing and to make matters worse, artillery shells were dropping around our position. Stoltz said he didn't know how bad he was hit. I got his jacket and shirt out of the way to see the wound. The bullet had gone in the side of his neck and come out his shoulder just above the bone. I bandaged the wound and convinced him that he would be OK. The sniper had given him a "million dollar" wound and a ticket home!

Meanwhile, the shells were dropping closer and we were trying to sink deeper into that ditch. I was giving Stoltz a drink and had my hand on his helmet when one exploded very close. Shrapnel flew all around us and I saw it tear up the sod right by his side and another piece hit his helmet. I asked him if he was hit and he said no, but I'm getting out of here. We crawled back about three hundred yards where he climbed into an ambulance and was on his way to a hospital. Stoltz had his second Purple Heart; he got the first on D-Day.

The Jerries were fighting desperately, they had been driven back across the Fatherland and had their backs to the wall. We had many casualties, I saw a tank officer who had been shot through the stomach, a radioman in the head and several G.I.s lay dead or wounded in the field. We didn't have many riflemen left, the battles had taken one here and there. All of us in the weapons platoon armed with a carbine or rifle were sent up to become riflemen.

The attack went on, they were on one side of the road in the wheat field and woods and we were on the other. Our tank guns were firing into the woods while the fire of the riflemen and machine gunners were raking the field. More and more Germans began coming out of their holes to surrender and we soon had a lot of prisoners. It was a sticky situation because we had more prisoners than we had men left in L. Company. There were a couple of problems:

One Jerry with a machine gun shot a final burst at us before he threw down his gun, sneered and raised his hands to surrender. Somehow one of our .45 automatics accidently went off and he died.

One sniper's foxhole was surrounded by four of our guys but he wouldn't come out, even when they threw in a grenade. Finally, they sent another Jerry to go up to talk him into surrendering. He finally crawled out, but it sure hated to surrender.

We started loading prisoners on trucks and tanks to take back to Kothen. Suddenly, that Jerry sniper who had been so stubborn about surrendering began ranting about how he wanted to die for Hitler. He was sitting on a tank with many others. He was told to get down. He got off; a machine-gun barked a few times and too late, he discovered a generous G.I. had given him just what he asked for!

One officer said," That bastard was more dangerous than a hand grenade. He was trying to stir up the others. He had to be shut up!"

We had a quiet trip back down the road. We hadn't eaten since early morning so Runion and I fixed up a hot supper. I was put in charge of our mortar squad, but only four of us were left. Later, some of the boys found some liquor and whooped it up. I turned in early for a good night's sleep.

April 17 - We piled on the trucks at 6:30 am and drove through several towns to help another company finish taking Aken. We didn't have any trouble getting into town, no shells were coming in, but several snipers were causing trouble. One civilian started to tell where one was and a sniper bullet him before he finished. We located the sniper and Trendel put a bullet between his eyes. Those of us without rifles were rear guard and the other boys moved forward to attack Jerries hiding in buildings farther into town. Our P-47 fighters were a great help and really gave us close support by strafing houses on one side of the street while our G.I.s were on the other! The battle was won and our boys continued searching houses, especially cellars, to flush out Jerry prisoners. Many were just kids, the kind that are either fanatics or scared to death, depending on their leader. That evening, we sent another gang of prisoners down the road and began searching houses for canned fruit and jellies to sweeten our K rations.

April 19 – We left Aken with the armored company and moved fast. We were to take the Agfa film and camera factory at Wolfen. We got there about noon. The P-47s began their strafing attacks and soon the black smoke was rolling from the fires they started. That P-47 is certainly the work horse of the Air Force. It made us feel good just to see them. Part of the field was newly plowed, but most was planted in wheat. The L. Company rifle platoons were to clear the field and make sure there were no Jerries to fire Panzerfausts at our tanks and armored vehicles. We had about 700 yards of open field to cross and then a high board fence. This was usually the duty of the riflemen, but our rifle platoons had so many casualties that we only had two instead if three. We, the weapons platoon were now acting as riflemen, so we left our mortars and machine-guns on the truck, drew our pistols and moved out. We knew enemy machine –guns could open up at any time. There were plenty of ideal positions. We advanced well dispersed and moving fast, but we combed every foot of ground and met no enemy. The tanks came up, we went through the fence and we began searching buildings. It was dangerous work, those Jerries were waiting for us to come after them. I knew Trindel had worked with the rifle platoon before, so I watched how he moved and always took cover when he stopped. It was almost dinner time when we went into one of the factory mess halls and a bunch of women slave workers, mostly Russian, were hiding. They were happy to see us and wanted us to know it. They invited us to share their dinner. It was a soup made of vegetables, chiefly potatoes, carrots and milk. It tasted flat, but we were hungry so we spent a few minutes visiting the girls before we took off to finish our job. By now the smoke was as dense as a cloudy day, but we went until we hit a railroad and were posted there as a rear security. We scattered and got low along the tracks and under the cars. Our bombers were hitting Wolfen and the explosions shook the ground like an earthquake. There was an explosion two cars from where I was squeezed in behind a car wheel. No one was hurt, there was no shrapnel. The guys decided it was a concussion bomb and started searching for the Jerry who threw it. A shell came in few minutes later and shrapnel rattled on the boxcar and on the wheel I was behind. That boxcar wheel saved me from being hit.

We moved forward to a three story concrete bunker with extra thick walls only one window on each floor. Slave laborers were hunkered an in mere dugouts out in the yard around the building. The bunker was a deluxe bomb shelter with its own power plant, air conditioners and lights. It was full of the factory's German managers, secretaries, inspectors and foremen. Most were scared stiff and watched us with wide eyes and complete silence as we searched the joint. However, one big shot said,

"The American soldiers have come and are looking for Nazis."

That gave us a laugh because we knew there were plenty of Nazis within arm's reach. We searched every room, cut all the telephone lines but found no Jerries. There were great pots of good food in the mess hall, food full of potatoes and carrots. The slave workers asked if they could have some and we said they could have it all and those pots emptied like magic. As far as we were concerned, the poor souls could have the whole damn country. The fighting let up, so our weapons platoon moved up the street into town to find a place to roost. Our mortar, rifle and machine-gun sections picked fine big houses to bed down for the night. The occupants of our house stayed down in the cellar. It was a luxurious house with easy chairs, super duper beds and a baby grand piano. We had a good supper, set up a guard (we all had a turn) and slept well all night. April 21 – Next morning, the girls from the factory came into town. They were free for the first time in years. The people in this section had plenty of nice clothes and those girls knew how to loot. By 10:30 there were plenty of pretty girls parading around town bedecked in nice clothes, eve to the make-up. For every one who knows G.I s, it's useless to say that about everyone had a girl. The one I met was a Czech who could speak a little English. She could really play that piano and also sing the classics, some American. The order came to move out in ten minutes and we threw our rations and belongings together to take off for the trucks. It was a miracle that we all made it on time. We waved goodbye to a group of surprised and bewildered girls as the column of trucks pulled out of town. Guess they were surprised that such a helter-skelter bunch of G.I.s could obey an order so fast and bewildered about what to do next! Sixteen miles later, we stopped and set up a defensive position in Chorau for a rest. Jerry shells were coming in so I found a cellar where my squad could sleep. Local civilians told us there many German SS and paratroopers in the woods between us and Dessau. We had a good supper and slept on straw in the cellar, but we knew we had a big day ahead.

> *We herd sheep, we drive cattle, we lead people. Lead me, follow me, or get out of my way General George S. Patton*

BATTLE AT DESSAU

Note: Dessau, is about 70 miles southeast of Berlin in the lowlands at the juncture of the Elbe and Mulde rivers. The city had been bombed severely because of the Junkers aircraft factory, which produced motors for many of Germany's best planes, including some models of ME 109 and Focke-Wulf 190 fighters. The city was a favorite target for Allied heavy bombers which had faced those fighters. There was also a prisoner of war camp (sub camp of Buchenwald) at Dessau to provide prisoners as slaves-workers for those war industries.

"At sunrise we climbed into trucks without breakfast. Our column of tanks and trucks followed a trail that led across a field through woods until we came out on the road to Dessau. It was another one of those mornings when your nerves are tense and you're looking for any movement that will give away the enemy's position. Later, shells began hitting closer so our column stopped while the riflemen moved forward and cleared the area so our tanks could advance. We were riding the last truck when our column started on toward town and a sniper opened up on us. We all melted into the bottom of the truckbed while bullets were snapping over us. The driver stepped on it and stopped at the first house. Everybody piled out and we located the sniper about 250 yards off. The light machine-gun squad set up, but we had to get our mortars and ammo out of the truck. This was done by bounding out, climbing in, lying flat and passing the weapons over the side. The sniper was still shooting high, but not too much. He was with a bunch of Jerry troops in the woods about 300 yards off and by now our machineguns were talking from windows above us while we set up our mortars. Schilling, Montes and I were the gunners. We were getting firing orders over a walkie-talkie. We fired something like 150 rounds and were dropping our shells right where they were needed. The Jerries started running and we called the artillery in on them. That night the C.O. (commanding officer) said the mortar section did such a good job that he gave us his liquor ration.

The riflemen and machine-gunners advanced about 600 yards. We got the orders to move up, so we loaded our mortars and ammo on the truck and walked about 300 yards before we began to see the effects of our mortar fire. There were mangled bodies all over the area. Arms here, a leg there, feet somewhere else, some of the bodies were so mangled you tell if they were men or hamburger meat. We went on by the mess of humanity.

It put a new fright in those who hadn't seen how shells can mess up a man. To me and the other combat veterans, it was just another a reminder that it could happen to us if a shell was to drop in the right place.

We came to another open space of about 500 yards. S/Sgt. Eschador knew and we knew we would be exposed to enemy fire, but we had to make mad dash to get to the first building. We ran at ten yard intervals. My squad was first, followed by those of Meadows and Riddle. About 75 yards out, a shell hit short and to our right and we kept running as only scared men can. When you're scared, you run until you feel you can't take another step. Then a shell hits close to remind you to run faster than you ever did! Another one came in and I hit the dirt until I heard shrapnel whistle by then I jumped up and took off. Two more hit close, but I kept running until I reached the house. Everybody was slumped down or leaning on the wall gasping for breath. You never realize how exhausted you are until you stop. There was no cellar, we knew we were not safe, but we felt better with four walls and a roof. The other squads came running in and we had lost only one man. Riddle said Pvt. Kelly, a young replacement, had been hit but the Medics picked him up when he fell. We all assumed he had a million dollar wound, it never entered our heads that his wound might be fatal.

We kept advancing from one house to another through the village before stopping at a big house to set up our mortars and wait for orders. We hadn't eaten since supper the day before, so we raided a chicken coop and searched the cellar for canned food. We fried potatoes and eggs for supper and caught a little sleep before moving out again, carrying our mortars and ammo on our backs. We heard a firefight and turned off the main road into a POW camp where Russians had been freed. A sniper was pinning us down, but he stopped after we set up the mortars and fired a few rounds into the woods. The newly released Russian prisoners were running around like crazy and laughing like nothing was going on!

April 23 – We moved through the outskirts of Dessau to an apartment house. The women were afraid of us, but were terrified when they learned Russian troops were a few miles away. K. Company was trying to take a Jerry installation near the Elbe. We rested while the battle went on all day. Schilling came back, his wound was healed. We laughed when he said the Medics had told him to go work in the kitchen a while, but he couldn't find it so he came up to join us.

Early the next morning the rumor was that K. company had only a 100 yards to go and needed help, so we were sent out. The Jerries were dug-in on the river bank. They had covered trenches about six feet deep that zig zagged and were protected by barbed wire entanglement about 40 yards in front. Their defensive position was strong and they made the most of it. Heavy firing went on all day. We set up the mortars and two companies of riflemen and our ten tanks advanced firing .30 and .50 caliber machine guns and their big guns. The Jerries were returning fire and using Panzerfausts against the tanks. Finally, they surrendered and our tanks stopped firing. There were a lot of dead and wounded Jerries lying around. Our boys went in and took about 40 prisoners. Later three wounded Germans came in to say they had more wounded and others who wanted to surrender if we promised not to kill them. Lt. Brown told them we never killed prisoners and their wounded would be treated after we took care of ours. He said they could surrender if they wanted, it didn't make a damn bit of difference to him! Our company went back to the house in town. We had not eaten all day so Cella and I combined all our rations into one big supper an everyone slept late.

April 25 – We said goodbye to the Third Armored boys. They were a swell bunch of guys and who really appreciated our infantry and we hated to lose their protection and the trucks. Their truck drivers said they hoped to meet us again, only next time they didn't want to be scared to death. We piled on trucks and rode almost five hours to Libehna where each platoon was assigned a house. We were pulling guard duty in surrounding towns to keep law and order and protect the German civilians from the free prisoners and misplaced persons running around the area. They held big parties to celebrate and some died from drinking rocket fuel. We called it 'V-2 juice.'

We were here on May 8th when the war ended. That was VE Day and the next day, they held a Battalion formation and the Seventh Corps commander told us how good we were. I remembered that at least 150 of us crossed the Rhine a few weeks ago on March 8th, but less than 30 made to the end on May 8th.

Note: May 8, 1945 Germany surrendered and S/Sgt. John Hill had survived six months of infantry combat in freezing weather, rain, mud and snow, moving from foxhole to foxhole and house to house with only a small unreported wound. He was involved in battles of the Siegfried Line, Battle of the Bulge, the Ardennes, Hurtegon Forrest and was in the first infantry to walk across the Remagen Bridge. His L. Company advanced across Germany to a final battle on the Elbe river. L. Company trained for duty in the Pacific until Japan was defeated. John drove a jeep and was made Sergeant of the 60 mm mortar section. He later became chief administrator of a kitchen at the Moosburg Prison which now housed German POWs instead of Allied troops. After three months he was transferred to Headquarters Command and assigned to the fiscal office of the Stars and Stripes military newspaper. Four and a half months later, he was the Chief Administrator of Accountants at Stars and Stripes.

S/Sgt. John I. Hill, L. Company, 47th Regiment of the 9th Infantry Division was discharged May 16, 1945. He had served his country well!

Infantry squad slogs through the street of a bombed-out town

Sgt. Arlie Propes' Re-con Duty

We interviewed ninety-seven year old Arlie Propes on the Bedford North Lawrence Oral History television program in May, 2010 for his WW II story. He passed away a few months later but his story has been recorded for future generations. The Bedford native served four and a half years in the Army, the majority of time in a combat zone.

The Fourth Armored Division remained in England on D-Day. They landed on the beaches on D-Day + 30 and moved inland behind our advancing troops. The dense hedge-rows surrounding the French farm fields forced military vehicles to travel the roads as they moved inland. Sgt. Arlie Propes was commander of an armored Reconnaissance car with a three man crew. The re-con's duty was to scout ahead of the main body of troops to report on the location and strength of enemy forces. They were always out front of the Division to count tanks, troops etc and radio that information back to headquarters. Propes said that when they drove out ahead and stopped for scouting, they always parked the armored car facing back toward U. S. troops. The driver stayed inside in case they were discovered and needed to make a quick get-a-way, something like a bank robbery.

Battle of Bulge --- The 16th of December 1944, fifty German divisions (ten of Panzer tanks) attacked and over-ran American lines in The Ardennes Mountains of east Belgium. This was Hitler's final effort to split Allied lines and capture the seaport at Antwerp. General Anthony McAuliffe's 101st Airborne U.S. troops, the "Screaming Eagles" were surrounded on December 20th. They were holding the important crossroads town of Bastogne and were under siege.

The Germans had demanded their surrender, but General McAuliffe sent back the famous answer of "Nuts" to that request! At that time, General Patton's Third Army was in France, 110 miles south of Bastogne. Allied headquarters immediately ordered Patton to stop fighting at that location and move his forces to Belgium as fast as possible to relieve Mc Auliffe's paratroopers and turn the tide in the Battle of the Bulge. Sgt. Propes' re-con car was one of many ordered to move ahead to scout

out roads and bridges for the quickest route. He said: "We made it in twelve hours, but the Fourth Armored Division took a little longer, nineteen hours. It is reported that General Patton's thirty-four ton Sherman tanks ran twenty-four hours with no rest stops. They said the tank crews poured fuel into the tanks on the run! " Elements of Patton's Fourth Armored Division under Lt. Col. Creighton Abrams and the 35th Infantry Division arrived in time to start a counter offense by December 22nd. Four days later, they relieved Bastogne! More than 75,000 American troops were killed or wounded in the Battle of the Bulge. The snow, frostbite and freezing weather of Europe's worst winter in decades took a heavy toll on soldiers fighting in the forests and mountains of the Ardennes in the winter of 1944.

Sgt. Propes told of an unusual battlefield Christmas dinner, "One day during a lull in the fighting we were forward on re-con duty and found a large farm house standing in the middle of an open spot in the war-torn forest. There were no enemy troops in the area and the deserted house had escaped major battle damage. The three of us decided to move in and enjoy a warm dry night for Christmas. It looked like a great place to cook up a hot meal. The owners had left in a hurry and we found a ham and some canned food in the pantry. Dry wood was piled near the big kitchen stove and we soon had a hot dinner cooking. The warmth in the kitchen was a welcome change from the freezing weather outside. The meal was about ready when a woman came into the house, she was the maid. Not much later, the house owner and his wife showed up. I think they had sent their maid in to check out the situation. We couldn't understand their Belgium language, but they spoke enough English to talk with us. It was house so we invited them to join us for dinner to help eat their food. The owner was so happy that his house had not been destroyed by the fighting that he 'liberated' several bottles of wine from his secret hiding place in the cellar. Dinner was about ready, but before our little group gathered around the table, there was a knock on the door. It was the local priest, just in time for dinner! We all sat down, the priest blessed the food and we enjoyed a hot meal in the middle a recent battlefield. The boys and I reckoned this was about as good as it gets in a war and this would be a Christmas to remember for a long time! We spent the night in the warm house, but drove out into the snow and frigid weather early the next morning. It was time to join our outfit which was camping a few miles back in the frozen forest. Sometimes it pays to be the re-con guys scouting in front of the troops."

Sgt. Propes recalled seeing Gen. George Patton several times. He said, "It was never a secret when "Old Blood and Guts" was in the area. You would hear the siren, his jeep roared up the road and there was Patton with his pearl handled pistols. One time I ducked down behind my re-con car to avoid saluting him. Another day a bunch of us were all beat up by combat and the weather so we pretended to be busy with our equipment and didn't come to attention and salute him as he whizzed past. Boy, his driver hit the brakes, backed up that jeep and "Old Blood and Guts" chewed us out for five minutes and then demanded his salute!

Corporal Ermy Bartlett in Italy

Like me, Ermy received his draft notice the day after he turned eighteen. He never got his diploma from Needmore High school and in less than two months he was Buck Private Ermy Bartlett. He says his friends and neighbors selected him to go into the Army, but he has never found those rascals! The new soldier completed his infantry basic training in Camp McClellan, Alabama in three months and his company was immediately shipped overseas. He remembers the long and dangerous voyage crossing the Atlantic in a large convoy of troop and supply ships. Pvt. Bartlett said when he was allowed up on deck there were ships as far as he could see. At one point, German U-boats (submarines) prowling the Atlantic managed to avoid the U.S. Navy ships escorting the Allied ships and attack the convoy. He remembers seeing the smoke from a ship that had been torpedoed.

The troopships landed in the port of Naples, Italy to join Gen. Mark Clark's Fifth Army and into combat in Italy. Bartlett's Infantry Company was ordered to the Replacement Pool for new troops. His outfit was soon assigned to a company that had just come in from the front. Only eleven of the 200 soldiers in that unit had survived their time in battle! Bartlett and his buddies replaced the dead and wounded of that company and marched bravely into combat. They quickly became veterans and one of Ermy's buddies was hit and lost his leg as the Fifth Army fought its way toward Rome.

The destruction in Italy was unbelievable; tanks, canons and bombs had destroyed forests, bridges, railroads and villages. Trees were blasted with dynamite to fall on American convoys and close roads. Allied armies were fighting Italian and German forces were ordered to defend Italy's dictator, Mussolini. Besides that, Hitler needed Italy as a buffer-zone to keep Allied forces from invading France and Germany from the south. Fighting in the mountains in the winter was difficult and the both sides suffered heavy losses

Ermy remembers, "One day we were marching toward Rome, when our company came under a barrage of German 88mm cannon fire and everyone hit the dirt. My platoon took cover behind a high bank along the road. Cannon shells were hitting all around and my buddy took a direct hit. He was killed instantly and later, we found his dog tags sixty feet away. That same explosion knocked me about twenty feet away from the road! Later, we moved out of there to march farther up the road. When we camped that time, a buddy and I dug a wide and deep two-man foxhole. We piled the dirt in front and threw our packs on top for more protection. Next morning after breakfast (K-rations) we were sitting beside our foxhole waiting for orders when enemy fire started coming in. We jumped back into the foxhole just in the nick of time, because a mortar shell hit the ground where I had been sitting! The shrapnel burst went above us and we escaped death by a few seconds! I had never been too religious back home, but I learned to pray a lot after that shell hit. God had spared me and that's when I became a Christian!"

Note - The 88 MM cannon used by the German army was the same one they used as an anti-aircraft gun to bring down bombers. The 88MM was a versatile weapon with shrapnel shells for use against ground troops or planes as well as armor-piercing shell for tanks. We men in the heavy bombers dreaded flying into the fields of flak the 88MM canon fired up over our targets. Shrapnel from that gun brought down many planes.

Soldiers of the American and British armys marched into Rome on June 4, 1944. This was a great victory, but the event was knocked out of the headlines because two days later was the D-Day invasion of France! PFC Bartlett said, "The people of Rome welcomed us as liberators. Mobs of people crowded the streets and it was hard to march. They waved American flags, threw flowers and offered us wine and food. The women threw kisses and ran out to hug us as we marched. Our outfit didn't stay in Rome very long. We moved out that same day because there was still a lot of fighting to be done. The enemy had retreated to the Apennine mountains and set up strong defenses. Snow, rain and mud made it much harder to fight in the mountains. Both sides wanted the high ground. In one battle we were under heavy attack and out-numbered! The German troops had the high ground and were swarming down on our position. I was a Corporal now and the company radio-telephone man and the Captain yelled for me to call for our artillery to lay down a heavy barrage on the attackers. These were the old short range radios with dry-cell batteries and I couldn't reach anyone. The Captain yelled 'Keep trying! Keep Trying! We've got to have help.'

Finally, I heard a calm voice say, "This is a ship off shore can we help you with artillery fire? Give us the coordinates of the target. The Captain grabbed my map and gave them the coordinates. That ship laid a heavy barrage right on the attacking Germans and wiped them out. I knew those guys were coming to kill us, but it was really hard to watch them die. I soon lost those feelings because our Captain was wounded by shrapnel and died that same day.

"Near the end of war, we had marched in the mountains all day. That night we set up our tents just off the road to catch some sleep. It was really dark and during the night we heard troops marching past. The next morning we discovered that German soldiers had camped down the road from us! We grabbed our guns to get ready for a fight. Our Lieutenant told the German officer to surrender, but the German said in perfect English, "No, we have your troops out-numbered and there is a Tiger tank is coming up the road. You will be the ones to surrender!"

"Our Lieutenant realized that we were finished. He told us to put down our guns and line up in formation and the Germans marched the thirty-four of us down the road with our hands on our heads. We were prisoners of war (POWs) and really worried that we were going to be killed. They marched us up into the mountains for about three days. About five of us rode on the hood of a German half-track part of the way. They met up with other German troops and stopped to dig in to prepare for an attack by our troops. We were kept prisoners in an abandoned building behind their lines for about three weeks. All that time, I never knew whether I would live or die. We never knew if the next day would be our last!

We weren't treated badly and they fed us the same food they ate; things like blood pudding and cold mush (grits.) I still remember the first day they dumped a blob of cold mush on our table. We knew what it was (we had all grown up in the depression), but we didn't know how to cut it up without a knife. Our guard pulled out a U shaped tool with taut string stretched across one side and sliced off a few slabs. Then, he laughed at our ignorance as he left our prison. One morning the English speaking officer came into our 'prison hut' to talk with us. This had not happened before and we expected the worst. He asked one question,

"Why are you fighting the Germans?'

Our Lieutenant answered, "Because we have been ordered to fight---the same as you and your soldiers have been ordered to fight."

That answer may have saved our lives! The German officer paused for a minute and quietly said, "We will be gone in the morning."

"He turned and left the building and we just stood there amazed, wondering what would happen next! Sure enough, the German troops marched out the next morning, but we weren't alone very long. Italian Partisan soldiers swarmed down to hurry us to safety in their camp on the high ground. We stayed with them until the surrender about a week later. Corporal Bartlett said, "I spent two winters in Italy and earned the Bronze Star medal and the Combat Infantryman badge. I thank God I survived the war and capture by the Germans. I was a POW for over two months, but I can't prove it!"

Note --- *After the fall of Rome there were many Italians who believed Italy should surrender. Bands of these Italian Partisan groups roamed the northern Apennine Mountains and harassed Germans troops with sabotage and sneak attacks. These Italian patriots were fighting to regain control of their country. In late April of '45, Partisan troops caught Mussolini and his mistress trying to escape to Switzerland. They killed them and hanged them by their heels in the public square of Milan to show the world they were tired of dictators and wanted peace! Italy surrendered April 29, 1945. The 275 day Italian Campaign (Sept, '43 –May,'45) was one of the most costly campaigns of WW II and both sides lost thousands of men.*

Chapter Nine

Sgt. Arlie Propes' Story Continued – "Near the end of the war our outfit captured the Ohrdruf Stalag (extermination camp.) We were too late to save most the prisoners. The German guards had followed Hitler's standing orders, which were to kill all prisoners before the prison was captured. It was evident that they had called all the men out of the barracks and shot them before they ran off into the woods. Some of those guards were later captured in civilian clothes. It was eerie that the only prisoners alive were the ones too weak to come out of the barracks. This camp had no furnaces for cremation, only makeshift fire-pits made of cross ties and train rails. Guards burned the bodies on grills over pits layered with rocks and dirt. They had buried the ashes and bones in a large pit 50 yards long. We could see they were behind in their work, because hundreds of bodies were stacked in sheds or near the fire pits. They said General Patton became sick at his stomach when he entered the camp and saw the murdered prisoners."

Ohrdruf Death Camp

Ohrdruf, near Gotha was liberated by troops of the 89th Infantry Division and Fourth Armored Division, April 4, 1945. This was the first Nazi death camp to be liberated by Allied soldiers and reveal the crimes of Hitler's Holocaust. It was a holding facility for over 11,000 prisoners on their way to the gas chambers and furnaces at Buchenwald. A few days before the Americans arrived to liberate Ohrdruf, the SS guards gathered all of the inmates able to walk and marched them off to Buchenwald. They turned machine guns on the sick and lame and left behind more than a thousand bodies dead from bullet wounds, torture, starvation, and disease. The scene was an indescribable horror even to the combat-hardened troops who liberated the camp. Bodies piled throughout the camp were mute evidence of systematic murder. Mounds of dead bodies were still smoldering in the fire pits.

General Eisenhower learned about the camp's barbaric scope of atrocities and ordered Generals Omar Bradley, George Patton, other command officers and reporters to tour the camp on April 12. They saw the results of Germany's "Final Solution or Holocaust," a carefully planned program of genocide carefully designed to exterminate Jews, political prisoners, Gypsies and homosexuals. There were many torture areas at the camp including whipping tables, gallows and a firing-squad wall. General Eisenhower talked with some of the starved survivors and ordered photographs of the entire camp including the freshly murdered prisoners lying in the yard and more than 3,000 corpses stacked like cord wood near the "fire pits" containing the ashes, bones and partially burned bodies. He ordered that all camp atrocities be filmed and documented to show the world Germany's inhumanity and genocide so it could never be denied! He also ordered his troops to get statements from witnesses and preserve all captured photographs, films and records. He knew these horrible crimes had to be documented for the War Crimes trials. He knew years in the future, there would be "idiots" who would say that the Holocaust never happened!

Supreme Allied Commander, General Dwight D. Eisenhower saw the conditions at the Ohrdruf concentration camp and became disgusted with the citizens of Gotha and nearby towns who claimed to be unaware of the concentration camp activities. So he decided to show them what they had missed and ordered that everyone in the area, including children, be forced to march through the camp to view the mass graves, bodies and starving slave laborers who had survived. It was fitting that they should witness the atrocities committed against innocent victims whose only crime was being a Jew! After the tour, Gotha's mayor and his wife went home and hanged themselves. Men in the surrounding area were made to bury the dead and to exhume bodies from the mass graves for identification.

Ohrdruf was just one of several sub-camps holding victims for the infamous Buchenwald extermination camp several miles north of Gotha.

T/Sgt. James Lee Hutchinson, Ed.S.

By that time, Buchenwald itself had been captured and General Eisenhower decided the group should also tour that large extermination camp. Last but not least, he also ordered that all American soldiers in the area, not serving on the front lines, visit a camp to see what they were fighting against.

General Eisenhower was determined to insure that inhumanity of the Holocaust be fully exposed and recorded for history! He issued orders that the details of the atrocities of the camp be recorded. Those photos provided information on the murder of millions of innocent victims. They were used in the Nuremberg War Crimes Trials after the war. Today, The photos and film are used as proof against those who try to deny it ever happened!

General Eisenhower

"I have never been able to describe my emotional reaction when I came face to face with indisputable evidence of Nazi brutality and ruthless disregard to every shred of human decency. I visited every nook and cranny of the camp and can testify first hand that the Nazi brutality was not mere propaganda. I want every American not actually in the front lines to see this place. We are told that the American soldier does not know what he is fighting for. Now at least, he will know what he is fighting against."

General Bradley

"The smell of death overwhelmed us even before we passed through the stockade. More than 3,200 naked emaciated bodies had been flung into shallow graves. Others lay on the ground where they had fallen. Lice crawled over the yellow skin of their sharp, bony features. A guard showed us how the blood had congealed in course black scabs where starving prisoners had torn out entrails of the dead for food. I was too revolted to speak, for here death had been so fouled by degradation that it both stunned and numbed us."

General Patton

"This is one of the most appalling sights I have ever seen. Honestly, words are inadequate to express the horror of these institutions. The scenes witnessed here are beyond the normal mind to believe. No race except by a people dominated by ideology (sic) of sadism could have committed such gruesome crimes. Inmates in this state of starvation, even those who live, in my opinion, will never recover mentally.

We had experienced seeing bodies but what was astonishing about Ohrdruf was the scale of the place. Bodies and parts of bodies everywhere, stacked like cordwood, doused with lime. The camp officials had behaved as barbarians, animals, because no humans treat other humans without dignity. In another section of the camp, the officials had made a crude incinerator and then loading the corpses on top, fueling them and igniting them. But combustion was incomplete and one could identify a leg here and an arm and hand there."

In his book, A Soldier's Story, General Omar Bradley reported that General Patton became physically ill when he viewed the massive proof of criminality.

Noted WW II radio commentator, Edward R. Murrow, in his broadcast from London in April, 1945 reported the atrocities:

> *"I pray you believe what I have said about Buchenwald. I have reported what I saw and heard, but only a part of it. For the most part, I have no words."*

MAUTHAUSEN EXTERMINATION COMPLEX

The Ohrdruf camp was only one of many a sub-camps of the massive Mauthausen Extermination Complex which was only one off many prisons built to carry out Nazi plans to kill all Jews, Gypsies, homosexuals and political prisoners.

Shortly after the Anschluss in Austria the small town of Mauthausen, about twelve miles east of the city of Linz was selected by Nazi leaders as the site of a giant Concentration Camp Complex. Mauthausen was to become the central camp for the entire country of Austria. On August 8, 1938 prisoners from the Dachau concentration camp near Munich, Germany were transported to this small town to be used as slave-labor to construct numerous buildings and from the moment it opened, thousands of Nazi victims were imprisoned. There were entire Jewish families that Hitler planned to exterminate simply because of their religion. There were also political prisoners; men and women from German occupied countries arrested because of the disagreements or differences with Nazi ideology and policies. Others among the desperate and confused captives were Gypsies, artists, scholars, teachers, intellectuals and priests mixed with French, Polish and Russian prisoners of war. Later, there were transfers of Concentration Camp victims, mostly Jewish people, from camps such as Auschwitz, Bergen-Belsen. Sachenhausen, Ransbruck and Gross-Rosen. These victims were forced into long hours of slave-labor. The purpose and perhaps the motto of the camp was "extermination through labor". Records show that between 123,000 and 320,000 were starved and literally worked to death in mines, munitions, arms factories and ME- 262 jet plane assembly plants throughout the region. They were starved and disciplined severely if they failed to follow directions. They were forced to work to help the very country that had stolen their freedom.

The Mauthausen Camp was overcrowded and filled beyond human limits. There were as many as five sick men to a narrow camp bed while others slept crowded on floors. The camp was always populated by more than sixty thousand human beings. The sanitary conditions were at the lowest imaginable level and prisoners were dying daily of hunger and mistreatment. It was reported that the Mauthausen Complex, with its four sub camps, had 85,000 inmates in January, 1945. It has been estimated that 1,300,000 human beings were processed at the Mauthausen Concentration Complex. The Third Army led by General George S. Patton Jr. liberated the prisoners in the Mauthausen Concentration Complex May 6, 1945 Six days after the truce. Today, it is a museum, to display the horrible crimes against humanity by the Nazi Party.

March 7, 1946 in Dachau, Germany, sixty-one former Mauthausen Concentration Complex personnel were brought before an American Military Tribunal. The defendants were charged with beating starving, gassing, shooting, and hanging countless inmates. The trial began on March 29th and lasted only six weeks with the court finding all sixty-one defendants guilty. The court sentenced fifty-eight to death and gave the other three life sentences. Those sentenced to death were hanged on May 27 and 28, 1947.

Note - *Major Concentration camps often sent small groups of model prisoners out to work in regional farms, mines and factories. John Hill's story relates instances when small groups of prisoners left their jobs in fields or factories and came running with joy to greet U.S. troops marching into the area and bringing freedom with them!*

The Holocaust

Hitler's Nazi (National Socialist German Workers) party needed a scapegoat, someone to blame for the Depression that followed the first World War. Jews, Gypsies and Slavic people were considered sub-human and undesirable citizens The Nazi government searched for a scapegoat. They decided to blame all Germany's poverty problems the Jewish race and by 1935 they began the persecution which ended in a drive to eliminate the entire race and create a pure Aryan "master race." The Nazi government used genocide to eliminate the undesirables" and confiscate the property and assets of the people they condemned to death. Entire neighborhoods of Jewish families, men women and children, were rounded up in the middle of the night and loaded onto cattle cars bound for the death and slave-labor camps. It has been estimated that six million Jews, political prisoners Gypsies and homosexuals were killed in Germany and conquered territories during Hitler's reign. Special German units were organized to follow victorious German troops into these countries and massacre innocent people. Hundreds of mass graves were later found to testify to the terrible effectiveness of those "Killer Troops." One captured German photo shows a large group of children and women with babies standing at the edge of a mass grave before execution in Babi Yar, a small community near Kiev, Russia. German officials documented the killings with photographs and kept detailed records of genocide activities. This was especially true of the inhumane "scientific medical experiments" carried out on prisoners by German doctors at Auschwitz. Captured records revealed that 2,600,000 men, women and children were killed at the Auschwitz-Birkenau camps between1940-45. Hitler's elite guard, the SS (Schutzstaffle) was in charge of those camps.

Dachau was one of the first so-called "work camps." The sick and old were slain and buried in mass graves. Healthy prisoners were tattooed with an identification number on his or her left arm. They became slave-laborers to work in the industries and military installations of the country that had condemned them. They were destined to work until they died of exhaustion or starvation. There were eventually thirty-nine such camps or sub-camps in Germany and conquered countries.

The killing and disposal of human bodies became a problem by 1942, but SS chief, Heinrich Himmler, developed "The Final Solution." This new plan, used poison gas and incinerator furnaces, and was soon put into operation. Several "extermination camps" such as Auschwtiz and Birkenau in Poland were "remodeled" to carry out "the Final Solution," Railroad tracks lead directly into their gates to speed up the process. They used "Zyklon B," a special gas invented to quickly suffocate those in the chambers designed to resemble showers. The unsuspecting victims were told they could take showers after their long trip in cattle cars. Photos taken by German officials depict long lines of naked prisoners waiting to enter the poison gas showers. The bodies were then removed by Jewish prisoners doing slave labor to stay alive. The bodies were stacked until they could be cremated in large gas furnaces. German officials bragged they could kill and destroy 2,000 bodies a day.

This was the Holocaust (destruction by fire) a diabolical system of killing human beings. An evil project that astounded civilized people when it was discovered! Allied troops who liberated these "extermination camps" could hardly believe the condition of the starving prisoners. Many were walking skeletons weak from starvation and malnutrition. Hundreds of photographs documented the horrible conditions of the camps and the mass graves. American G.I. s unveiled the true horror of the Nazi "Final Solution" near the end of the war. They liberated all those camps which were designed to murder men, women and children as efficiently as possible. Allied troops witnessed wagons and box cars stacked with human bodies that had not yet been incinerated in the gas furnaces containing the bones of earlier victims.

Post war estimates reveal the following numbers: six million Jews; 20 million Russians; ten million Christians and 2,000 catholic priests.

Note - *The extermination camps of Auschwitz, Berkenau, Treblinka, Belsen, Buchenwald and Dachau were the most infamous. The horror stories of survivors, German photographs and eyewitness accounts of soldiers who liberated the camps eliminated any regrets the Allies might have had about the destruction of Hitler's Germany and the Third Reich. In today's world, there is a generation unaware of the Holocaust and nations who say it never happened. I recommend that readers check the internet; Google the WW II Mauthausen Concentration Camp, Ohrdruf or one of the other Death Camps in this story to see horrible photos of unbelievable treatment of humans by supposedly civilized humans. Yet blatant genocide continues today in many Third World countries!*

The Auschwitz Album

Nazis always took detailed photos of all their torture and death work for evaluation by their superiors. One surviving photo album of Auschwitz exists because a young Hungarian Jewish woman who survived as a prisoner was cold when the Auschwitz camp was liberated by Russian troops January 27, 1945. She found a camp guard's coat which she put on to keep warm as she fled. Larer, she found a photo album in the coat pocket which contained pictures of what went on in the extermination camp. Imagine her reaction when she saw a photo of herself coming off the train as well her family who had been murdered.

Today, the Auschwitz extermination camp, in Poland and many other camps have been preserved as museums and are visited by thousands of tourists each year. These Death Camp Museums serve as memorials to the horrible deaths of six million victims of the Nazi genocide in WW II. They are maintained in order that the world may never forget the Holocaust. Google the Auschwitz Album for heart-breaking photos.

T/Sgt. James Lee Hutchinson, Ed.S.

> *"Man's inhumanity to man makes countless thousands mourn"*
> *Robert Burns*

Mercy Missions

April 30, 1945, Hitler had committed suicide and the German High Command agreed to a truce prior to a total surrender. They also agreed to provide a narrow air corridor for our bombers to fly in at 500 feet for Allied bombers the drop food to the starving people in Holland We called them "Chowhound" missions. Germany occupied the country in 1940, drafted most of the men to work in their factories, destroyed bridges, dikes and flooded rich farmlands. There was no means of transportation for food or supplies. Food had been rationed for four years, and toward the end the war many people were living on a diet of sugar beets and tulip bulbs. It was reported that more than 16,000 Dutch died of malnutrition during the harsh winter of 1944-45. The Allied High Command organized a plan for the "Mercy or Chowhound Missions" as a means of getting food to the Dutch quickly. That night, the men of the 490th went to work loading bombers with boxes of ten concentrated meals. Special flooring had been installed in the B-17 bomb bays to handle the waterproof food cartons. All Third Division and many RAF bombers were assigned the task of carrying out these food drops. The British dropped "compo rations" in burlap sacks. A total of 5,626 RAF and Third Division bombers participated in the five "chowhound missions". Only one plane was lost in the operation.

The planes dropped to 300 feet when they made landfall in Holland. The drop area was a mile square field, marked by a large white cross. The field was surrounded by hundreds of people waving flags and bed sheets. We so low I could see happy faces in the crowd. The field was alive with people scrambling to gather the food as we circled to turn for England.

Hutch Mission - 19 - Rotterdam Food Drop   May 1, 1945 ---- The first Mercy or Chowhound mission was flown May 1, 1945. Germany had designated specific flight corridors, altitudes and drop areas. Approximately 400 Flying Fortresses, with bomb-bays full of food cartons, flew in single file over enemy territory at only 300 feet and dropped more than 20,000 waterproof food cartons (700 tons) to the cheering Dutch. The drop zone was a square-mile area marked by a large white cross. We dropped our load of ninety boxes of Army 10 x 1 rations containing meals for ten people. The approximately 18x12x24 boxes could float in the flooded fields and canals until they could be retrieved. It was strange flying in at low-level over the airport where Luftwaffe fighters used to come up to attack our group. Thousands of men, women and children below were waving towels and sheets in gratitude. They were in the streets, in the fields and on rooftops. They were cheering the bomber crews as we dropped the food they needed so desperately. We saw armed German soldiers on guard at various checkpoints in the countryside below. It was the first time I had seen German soldiers in uniform. After all this, the war was over before I at last saw the enemy!

USSAF Photo

398th Bomber dropping food cartons at 500 feet

Hutch Mission 20 - Schipol Airport Food Drop   May 2, 1945 was the second of five food drop missions flown by the 490th bomb group. We loaded 40 aircraft again. This time we dropped food at the Schipol Airfield, a German fighter base used by fighters who came up to attack bombers. We hoped they honored the truce! The townspeople stood on the rooftops and in the streets and fields waving and cheering. A large sign made of sheets said, "Thank You Boys". The Food Drop missions are celebrated by the people of Netherlands every May.

> *"It was a great experience, and it was a very good feeling to be dropping food instead of bombs."* Hutch

VE- Day — Victory in Europe

VE- Day, May 8, 1945 meant the end of World War II in Europe and peace was returned to millions of people who had suffered years of death and destruction by the armies of Germany and Italy. United States citizens celebrated the victory and our Air Force reorganized to focus on the defeat of Japanese forces in the Pacific War zone.

Germany asked for a truce April 30 and signed the formal surrender on May 8, 1945. The Nazi dictator, Adolph Hitler, knew by mid April that his Third Reich was defeated. His troops were surrendering on all fronts and some Generals were committing suicide. The Yank and British armies were coming from the west and the Russians from the east. Hitler turned the government over to his second-in-command, Admiral Karl Doenitz, to negotiate Germany's surrender. Russian troops had surrounded Berlin and capture was certain. Hitler feared the Russians most of all. He knew they were seeking revenge for the thousands of German atrocities committed in their homeland. Now, the shoe was on the other foot and it was time to pay the piper!

General Mark Clark's Fifth Army had conquered most of Italy. The men in his army had literally marched and fought their way the length of Italy from the toe of the boot to the Alps Mountains. After many Allied victories, Italian partisan joined against the Axis forces, and fought to bring an end to Mussolini's dictatorship. German forces in Italy supported him until Allied armies and Italian partisan forces won. Retreating German soldiers helped Benito Mussolini and his mistress try to escape to safety in the neutral country of Switzerland. The attempt failed and they were caught and killed by Italian partisan forces on April 28, 1945. Their mutilated bodies were hung by their heels in the town square of Milan for public viewing. The Italian partisans wanted to prove to the people that the dictator was dead and Italians should help defeat Germans troops!

In Berlin, Adolph Hitler feared the same treatment and decided to take the coward's way out. He chose suicide rather than capture and left detailed instruction to his servants before retreating to his luxurious underground bunker in Berlin on April 29th to prepare for the end. He married his longtime mistress, Eva Braun, making an honest woman of her. The next day, they committed suicide, both took poison and then, Hitler shot his new wife and himself. Their bodies were carried out by the servants, doused with gasoline and cremated. (it was one of the shortest honeymoons on record!) One of the servants who helped carry out Hitler's wishes lived until 2013.

Hitler and Mussolini brought ruin and destruction to Europe and to their own countries. Millions died and millions of lives were ruined because of those dictators. It would take years to restore the destruction in their countries and those they conquered. Both dictators are examples of men who were elected by the citizens of their country, gained complete power and became madmen seeking more power. Each generation should know of their crimes against humanity and see that they are never forgotten. We should learn from history and protect our freedom. Today, many countries are ruled by dictators who are a threat to world peace!

T/Sgt. James Lee Hutchinson, Ed.S.

US Army Photo

May 8, 1945 - Stars & Stripes and newspapers of the free world printed Extra editions and people danced in the streets to celebrate Victory in Europe. The Japanese Empire surrendered three months later. Little did people realize that the peace would last only ten years until the Korean Police action! People of my generation remember WW II as the last war we won!

Victory Flight Tours

The next item on the agenda was to take all the base support personnel on "Sight-seeing Tours" of France and Germany. All 490th personnel from the mechanics to the cooks were offered a flight, if they wanted it. A B-17 could carry a load of thirty men. We flew at low level over former targets to give them a first-hand look at what they had helped aircrews accomplish in the bombing missions. It was an informative tour for the aircrew as well, because we had never been this close to the destruction our bombs had inflicted on the German cities. I really got a kick out of the low-level flights rather than the usual 25,000 feet on oxygen. It was great to be wearing fatigues and free to relax and enjoy the scenery. We also circled Paris and got close-ups of Notre Dame and the Eiffel Tower, two landmarks that both sides had been careful to preserve. Those guys of the ground crews and airfield support groups were really impressed with what they saw on those flights.

Those flights were revealing to air crews, as well as the ground crews because we always delivered our bombs from high altitude and never witnessed the terrible destruction our thousands of bombing raids had delivered. It was a sobering experience to see the cities, factories and bridges in ruins. Hitler had brought this catastrophe upon the German people who had elected him to office and given the Nazi Party complete power. The Allies had no choice but to respond to Hitler's plan to rule the world with all the power they could muster to protect their freedom.

One cook on our plane summed it up for all of us, "Man, you guys really bombed the hell out of them!"

T/Sgt. Howard Tuchin's Repatriation Flight

Hitler, the architect of the destruction of Germany, had committed suicide. The May first ceasefire had been honored, the Nazi leaders still alive had agreed to an unconditional surrender and there were no more bombing missions. Eighth Air Force and RAF bombers were flying Mercy or Chowhound missions to deliver food to Holland.

T/Sgt. James Lee Hutchinson, Ed.S.

Eighth Air Force bomb crews were expecting to fly back to the U.S.A. to join the war in the Pacific. However, there was one more task to help the people of war torn Europe. The very bombers which had delivered death and destruction would now fly to bring home prisoners freed from German Concentration Camps. These repatriation flights were a great morale builder and a truly humanitarian effort to aid our Allies and restore peace.

In his memoirs, "Flashbacks and Memories of World War II," T/Sgt. Howard Tuchin wrote of his experience when the Lt. Dave Stauffer crew of the 401st Bomb Group made a Repatriation flight to Linz, Austria on May 8, 1945. It was the day Germany formally surrendered. It was VE Day (Victory in Europe), the fighting had stopped and the war was over!

Their bomber rose above their field in darkness the early morning of May 8th and flew at a low altitude directly to Paris, France. As they circled over the Arch de Triumph, thousands of people were in the streets below, looking up at the plane, waving, shouting and throwing kisses. The Arch de Triumph was decorated with French, American and British flags. The people of France were celebrating their freedom and showing their thanks for our help in liberating them from the German occupation. The Flying Fortress then headed east still flying at low altitude as it crossed into Germany. Airmen could clearly view the total and unbelievable destruction of countless German cities. The wide devastation was due not only to day and night bombing by American and British planes, but the artillery of ground battles.

The crew saw partially destroyed roads and highways clogged with thousands of captured German soldiers plodding along slowly in defeat. The exhausted Third Reich troops were guided and guarded by Allied soldiers. Their dreams of world domination had become a nightmare. However, there was another group of miserable humans on those roads and highways. The airmen were amazed to see thousands of German civilians, adults and children, weighted down with all sorts of household goods and/or pushing carts or bicycles. Entire families were fleeing to the west to avoid being captured by the Russian troops rapidly advancing to the Berlin area. It was a mass exodus of desperate people fearing the retribution of one of the Third Reich's former victims."

Note - *This reminds me of story of a nine year old German boy and the ordeals of his family in Berlin. They attempted to escape in a truck loaded with family belongings, but were turned back by gunfire by Russian troops. The boy was trapped in a Berlin bunker with his mother and sisters when the Russians came into Berlin. They took thousands of men prisoners and marched them out of town toward Russia. His first-hand account of living through bombing raids and the fall of Berlin is included in my book, "Bombs Away."*

T/Sgt. Tuchin continues, "This mass movement of humanity, seen from above and stretching from horizon to horizon will never be forgotten. Little did we know when we landed at Linz, Austria to join dozens of B-17 and B-24 bombers waiting for passengers, that we had landed at one of the most notorious German concentration camps named Mauthausen! We waited until we saw men being led slowly toward the bombers. The former prisoners and slave-laborers were ushered to planes in groups of twenty. They we extremely thin, bent, exhausted and showed no expressions. The men assigned to our plane stood meekly silent as we were told they were French prisoners of war captured at the Battle of Dunkirk in France in May, 1940. Our assignment was to help them board the plane and get seated safely. The Fortress was tightly crowded, but we finally succeeded in getting all the Frenchmen and ourselves ready for take-off.

We headed west toward our destination, the Orleans airfield. As we gained altitude and the Danube river came into view, the twenty prisoners began clapping and for the first time displayed smiles of happiness and appreciation.

The rest of the flight they strained to gaze out of the plane's small windows and all had tears in their eyes. I found a pencil and some scrap paper and asked each Frenchman to write his name and address. I still have that list safely tucked away in a special album. This was all un-believable, however I now have proof that I actually experienced this drama. We flew back over Germany and France and brought our heavy load down safely at the Orleans airfield just south of Paris. As each Frenchman was helped slowly out of the plane, he kneeled down on his knees and kissed the ground of his homeland. Just three days ago, they had given up hope of ever returning. Medical units and Red Cross nurses were there to welcome them home. It was true justice that the prisoners were taken home on May 8, 1945. Exactly seven years from the day the first victims arrived to build the Mauthausen Death Camp we left France and flew over the North Sea. Our crew was basically silent on the trip back to our 401 Bomb Group base at Deenethorpe. We were so proud that we had been chosen to liberate those poor French prisoners who had suffered so much during their five years in a German Concentration Camp. I have often wondered if those poor, tortured young French soldiers and the countless others who survived were ever capable of climbing back into society and living a happy, healthy and normal life." T/Sgt. Howard Tuchin and I often exchange emails. Recently, he reminded me that one of the prisoners they returned home from the Mauthausen death camp that day was Simon Wiesenthal, who became the famous Nazi hunter.

SIMON WIESENTHAL

At the time he was returned home from the Mauthausen death camp, Simon Wiesenthal was a thirty-six year old man over six foot tall, reduced to ninety pounds. He had survived five Nazi concentration camps and lost ninety members of his family in the Holocaust. He was reunited with his wife Cyla late in 1945. It was a very emotional meeting for each had believed the other was dead. Wiesenthal became the famous Nazi Hunter who devoted his life to identifying and hunting down Nazi soldiers and officials who had escaped capture, relocated and changed identities. He began immediately by tracking down information to aid in prosecuting Nazi criminals in the Nuremburg War Crimes trials. Wiesenthal continued his mission into his nineties and his organization is known to have tracked down 1,100 Nazis criminals. One of his most noted accomplishments was the locating of former SS Lt. Col. Adolf Eichmann in Argentina in 1960!

Eichmann had been arrested by American troops in 1945, but escaped from prison with a forged identity and went into hiding. As a top Gestapo officer, he had organized and managed the Nazi plan of transporting millions of Jews from Nazi occupied sections of Europe to the 'final solution' system of poison gas and furnaces in the "extermination camps" used to kill six million Jews during the Holocaust.

Adolph Eichmann was kidnapped and smuggled out of Arentina by Israeli agents and taken to Israel, tried and found guilty of his war crimes. The man who had engineered the death of millions remained defiant until the end. During his trial he said,

"To sum it all up, I regret nothing!" He was hanged in 1962.

Simon Wiesenthal's organization also located the Gestapo agent who arrested Anne Frank In August of 1944 and sent her to the Auschwitz concentration camp. It is estimated she died in March of 1945. Each criminal he tracked down was a tribute to the millions of innocents who died in the Holocaust.

World War II Memorial

The National World War II Memorial is located in Washington, D.C. on the mall between the Washington and Lincoln Memorials. World War II, our nation's largest war, required the total effort of all Americans. Civilians sacrificed for the war effort as well as the men and women who served in the Armed Forces. The war was fought in the air, on and under the sea and battlegrounds around world. I am proud to be charter member of the group Bob Dole formed to help fund the memorial. Speaking at the dedication, National Chairman, Senator Bob Dole, stated, "The Memorial will ensure that this nation, indeed the entire world, can never forget the men and women who won the largest war of all time." The $170 million World War II Memorial was completed May 2004.

T/Sgt. James Lee Hutchinson, Ed.S.

The dedication plaque honors us all:

> "HERE IN THE PRESENCE OF
> WASHINGTON AND LINCOLN,
> ONE THE EIGHTEENTH CENTURY
> FATHER AND THE OTHER
> THE NINETEENTH PRESERVER
> OF OUR NATION.
> WE HONOR THOSE TWENTIETH
> CENTURY AMERICANS
> WHO
> TOOK UP THE STRUGGLE DURING
> THE SECOND WORLD
> WAR AND MADE THE SACRIFICES
> TO PERPETUATE
> THE GIFT OUR
> FOREFATHERS ENTRUSTED TO US:
> A NATION CONCEIVED IN
> LIBERTY AND JUSTICE."

My family and I visited the Memorial during our 490th Bomb Group reunion in September 2006 and re-united with our engineer gunner, Ewing Roddy for a tour. I donated to help build it and proudly carry a charter member card. Sadly, it was erected many years too late for millions of veterans to appreciate. Today, in 2014, WW II veterans are rapidly fading into History. <u>Only 1.5 million of the sixteen million who served are left to tell their story and we are dying at a rate of about 1,000 a day.</u>

WILLIE AND JOE

I got Joe's room number from the receptionist at the front desk, signed in and went down the hall past several wheelchair residents sitting outside their room before I found him. I had not seen my old buddy since his health failed and was not sure what to expect. I hoped his mind was clear enough to talk about our good old days in WW II when we fought side by side from Bastonge to the Rhine river. Life takes many turns when you're eighty-seven. You never know what to expect when you hunt up your old friends. However, Joe was a special friend and I was standing at his door. I had come too far to turn back.

The door was open so I peeked in to see if he was awake. I saw the silhouette of a very thin man in a red flannel shirt and blue jeans sitting in a wheelchair by the window. He was intently watching something going on outside his room. He was not only awake; he was laughing. This was something I had not expected from an active man restricted to a wheelchair, but I was glad that he was making the most of being a nursing home resident. I rapped on the door frame and as he wheeled his chair around, I greeted him with an old phrase from our WW II days.

"Hello Joe, what do you know?"

His face lit up with a big smile; he was truly elated to see me standing in his room! His voice trembled as he asked, "Willie, how in the Hell did you find me? I can't get up, so get over here and gim'me a hug, you old son of a gun!"

We hugged but his thin body was nothing like that of the strong kid I remembered when we marched across Germany. It was a great reunion after so many years and we spent several minutes getting our emotions under control. Joe and I were the original "G.I. Joes" of World War II. We had literally gone through hell in the US Infantry as we fought side by side in the last and biggest campaign of WW II. We took a lot of flak from our buddies because Stars & Stripes cartoonist, Bill Maudlin, used two fictional characters named Willie and Joe to portray US soldiers in Europe. Those two bedraggled infantrymen found themselves in as many dangerous situations as me and Joe. We were typical frontline soldiers surviving in the snow, rain and mud as 600,000 men of the U.S. Army chased Hitler's army out of Belgium. We sought safety in foxholes or bombed-out buildings and fought for every mile of ground from the Battle of the Bulge in December of '44 to the crossing of the Rhine and victory in May 1945. It was a bittersweet victory; 81,000 American boys died. However, that was 68 years ago and forgotten or unknown by most in this generation. Me and Joe had a lot of catching-up to do. He wheeled over to a small table and pointed to a chair saying,

"Holy Cow Willie, it's so good to see you again! Come on in here and park your old carcass over here and tell me what you've been up to for the past ten years. You can see what I've been doing, lately."

I took a seat and said, "OK, but now I have two questions; tell me what's so interesting outside that window? It looked like you were still looking for snipers!"

"Oh, I like to park my wheelchair here by the window," he said, "I get a kick out of watching a flock of sparrows fighting for a turn at the feeder or splashing in the birdbath. I even pay for the birdseed. It's about the most excitement I can get around this place"

"OK next question, so how can you afford a private room?"

He smiled as he said, "You paid for part of it old buddy. Remember how much money I won and how much you lost in those big poker games at the St. Louis reunion?

"Yes, I always suspected you were dealing from the bottom, you old buzzard."

Joe said, "Well I wasn't, but actually, I sold my hardware store six years ago and invested wisely. My wife died last year and my sons are financially well off and also far off, so when my legs gave out, I sold the house and moved in here. I have three square meals a day, medical care, new friends and a few old friends who visit, but I never expected to see you again!"

We visited and talked until suppertime and both agreed that it wasn't long enough. I knew Joe was tired, but he wanted me to visit longer. I had the time, so I agreed to get a motel room and stay over another day. The next morning we spent more time talking about our days in combat. The guys in our outfit we remembered; those who died and those who survived. It was great to recall those WW II days when we were scared teenage G.I.'s slogging through the battlefields and bombed-out towns of Belgium and Germany. Those were the terrible months in combat when we supported and protected each other twenty-four hours a day. Joe had arranged for me to have lunch with him before I had to leave. Saying goodbye was tough because each knew this would probably be our last meeting. We had a couple of hearty hugs and emotional goodbyes before I hit the road again. But, as we said our last goodbye, Joe had a final question.

"Joe, you old dogface, answer the really big question for me. Do you think people know or remember what we did in WW II to save this country?"

I knew he wanted me to say yes, I hesitated, then crossed my fingers and assured him that we had not been forgotten by this generation. That visit is one I'll never regret, because two months later, Joe passed away to join the millions of WW II veterans who have already faded into history.

The Mighty Eighth Museum

The 490th at the Museum - Like many other WW II Eighth Air Force units, the surviving members of my 490th Bomb Group have ceased holding annual reunions. However, they made a $10,000 donation to insure that sacrifices of young airmen of the Mighty Eighth will never be forgotten. Two plaques telling the story of the 490th Bomb Group (H) of the Third Division now have a prominent place in the museum.

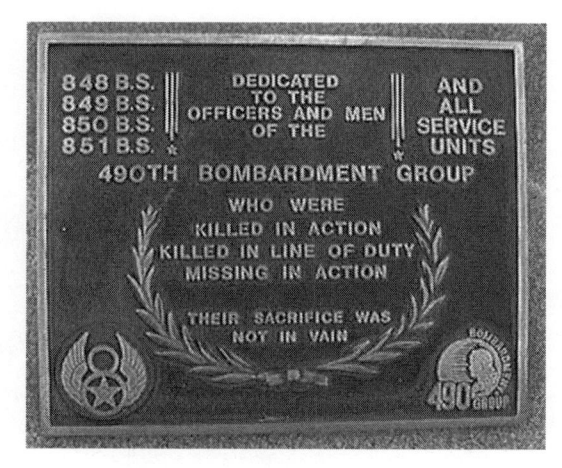

490th Bomb Group Plaque

T/Sgt. James Lee Hutchinson, Ed.S.

This plaque reminds me of guys I knew at Eye. Stories of their deaths mirror the terrible losses of twenty-six thousand men of the Mighty Eighth.

> *"Their golden youth blots out the sky, they let the comets plod.*
> *As each one flies to live or die for country and for God."*
>
> Grantland Rice

The mission of the museum: ***"To perpetuate the accomplishments and heritage of the 8th Air force for the present and future generations."*** In 1983, Major General Lewis E. Lyle, USAF Retired, a B-17 veteran of 70 combat missions during World War II, with the help of other veterans, began planning a museum. The museum would honor the men and women who helped defeat Nazi aggression by serving in or supporting the greatest air armada the world had ever seen—the 8th Air Force. These individuals pledged themselves to honor the courage and commitment of more than 350,000 members of the 8th Air Force. Of this number, 26,000 were killed in action and 28,000 became prisoners of war during World War II. Museum planners traveled throughout the United States and Europe, visiting museums and talking with staff from these institutions. The very best elements found among these facilities were then combined to create a dramatic 90,000-square foot museum complex. On May 14, 1996, to the applause of 5,000 8th Air Force veterans, their families, dignitaries, and supporters, the vision became a reality with the dedication of The National Museum of the Mighty Eighth Air Force in Pooler, Georgia, just west of Savannah.

On January 28, 1942, fifty-three days after the infamous attack on Pearl Harbor, the 8th Air Force was officially activated in the National Guard Armory on Bull Street in Savannah, Georgia. Today the Mighty Eighth Museum preserves our history and provides educational activities for thousands of students on school field trips each year. It has been officially certified by the state of Georgia as a Character Education Center.

The 90,000 square foot museum is located on thirteen acres at Pooler, Georgia on Interstate 95 near Savannah. It is a "must visit" destination for anyone interested in Eighth Air Force history. Hundreds of items and pieces of equipment are on display to provide a feel for the equipment used by crewmembers on WW II bombing missions. A library of WW II archives is available for those who research our accomplishments and food and drinks are served at the Crown and Eagle Pub a replica of an English pub. Visitors may experience a theater in the round type of a simulated bombing mission over Germany. The "mission" is complete from the briefing room to the target and back. It is a very realistic experience to aid visitors' understanding of bombing missions. I felt I was back on a mission!

North of the museum is the *Chapel of the Fallen Eagles*, designed to replicate a 16th century Old English village church. Its stained glass windows, like many in England, honor Eighth Air Force airman. The church presides over a reflection pool and the carillon chimes familiar hymns and melodies for visitors strolling through the Memorial Gardens. Families may arrange for plaques or markers to honor a veteran or crew. My daughter Susan donated to have my name placed on the wall. I hope to go back some day to find it.

Join the 8th Air Force Historical Society for $40.00 to receive the quarterly magazine, *The AF News,* a colorful publication full of Eighth Air Force information and history for history buffs. Visit the museum or check out the museum PX online for clothing, books and other memories of the Mighty Eighth at: WWW.MIGHTYEIGHTH.ORG

Salute to WW II Veterans

"Over the hill" or under the sod
Remembered only by family and God
Lie many who died in a foreign land
For God and country, they took a stand.

They fought a war to preserve our nation
Their battles un-known to this generation.
Few remember their victories or the terrible cost
Of thousands of patriots whose lives were lost.

T/Sgt. James Lee Hutchinson, Ed.S.

Don't ignore history to be politically correct
Remember the 16 million who stood to protect
Freedom of religion and democracy for the USA
Honor them all as they fade away!!!
James Lee Hutchinson 2012

Addenda

The Short Snorter

There are various stories on the origin and of the Short Snorter, a banknote inscribed by people traveling together on an aircraft. During World War II Short Snorters were signed by flight crews and conveyed good luck to soldiers crossing the Atlantic. Friends would take the local currency and sign each other's bills creating a "keepsake of their buddy's signature and/or address."

The tradition is believed to have been started by Bush pilots in Alaska, around 1925 to discourage others from drinking and flying. It was a reminder to restrict heavy drinking to "short snorts." Pilot who drank heavily didn't last long! The tradition spread to United States commercial and military pilots. When the Short Snorter was signed, the collector would have to produce it upon request, if not, they were bounded to give the signer a drink. Later, Short Snorters became not only a record of who a military-man had served with, but also a drinking game and a status symbol. The word 'snort' is derived from the slang for a stiff drink, and a "short" is less than a full measure. A pilot usually carried his Short Snorter in his billfold because when out drinking he might be challenged to show it. If he couldn't show it, he was obliged to hand over a dollar or buy a round of drinks.

The guys in our outfit adjusted the rules, because we didn't have access to liquor, except for a shot of Scotch they gave us at the debriefing session after a mission. So we collected banknotes from various countries, glued them together and asked buddies and crewmembers to sign it. The Snorter was a great way to get a souvenir. Optimistic signers often listed their home address in hope we would survive to exchange letters after the war. I recently discovered that short snorters have value. They are being sold on E bay as collector items, WW II memorabilia and to coin collectors. For instance, my five kroner note from Iceland is going for $75.00.

My Short Snorter is about a yard long with nine banknotes, it contains forty-nine signatures of my crew and other 490th BG airmen I served with during my six months at Eye Air Base, (AKA the Bromedome). I also found got signatures from ground crew guys who flew home across the Atlantic on our B-17 in July of 1945! I'm glad to have the signature of Russell Etheridge of Hall farm Road, the fourteen year old farm boy whose mother did our laundry. Russell delivered the laundry and often visited Hut 29 in the evenings. We paid him to run up the road to pick up orders of Fish and chips from the White Swan, our local pub. He spent a lot of time roaming the base, but his goal was to join Royal Navy and see the world!

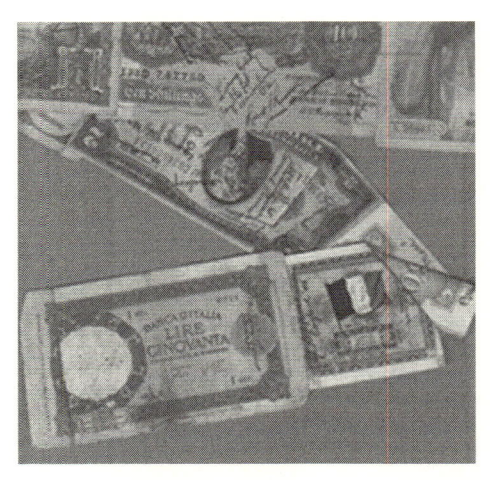

UK Ten schilling, USA two dollar bill, and France five francs

My Short Snorter banknotes with names still legible include:

United States two dollar bill series 1928D C93460463A <u>Hut crew</u> ---George Manthy --- Joseph Ricci --- Phillip Placentino --- Carson L. Perrin --- Howard Kirkland --- Vernon Anderson --- WC "Moe" Roberts --- Hal Kunzelman --- Al Ginsburg

Bank of England   10 shillings   J77D 747759

My crew --- Ewing Roddy --- engineer --- Robert Russell – Bombardier
Bruno Conterato --- navigator --- Dale Rector – Co-Pilot
William Templeton – Pilot --- Bert Allinder - Waist gun/armorer
James Campbell – Radar operator --- Dick Fleck
Walter Benedict – Bombardier --- Dwight Parish – Waist gunner
Ralph Moore - tail gunner --- Orville Robinson – waist gunner

Banque de France   100 francs A24396257   L.20865 049

Everette Bowman --- Guido Bucellini --- Paul Covington----Keen Umbehr Jr --- Russell Etheridge, Hall Farm Rd Brome NR Diss

Belgium: BANQUE NATIONALE DEBEGIQUE   5 FRANCS Z14 767104

Wm. L. Orsan --- K. D. Adcock --- B. U. Gallion --- Glen Peterson ---

EMIS EN FRANCE   CINO FRANCS   00454571

John W. Gann --- Carl Hultquist --- Joe Kennedy ---Raymond Lansford ---

Japanese Government   50 centavos   (Occupation script)

Alvin Wilhelm --- Dick Hine --- Allan Macdonald --- John Zinre Jules Blank --- Gerald "Monk" Monkman --- Bill Kuchauser --- Robert Merkel

Italy   BANCA D ITALIA   50 LIRE   I 631   6924   1940

Melvin Tyner --- E.J. Segura --- James Gardiner --- Stanley Fishfader --- Charles Chipple --- E.O. Qoulan

Reichsbanknote   50 reichmarks   1933   A-2439625

Ed Miller (lots of luck and no flak) ---Sam De Luca

Landsbanki Islands (Iceland)   5 kroner   A2206015   April 1928

Britain Says "Thanks Yanks"

The American Memorial Chapel in St Paul's Cathedral stands as proof that British people never forgot the young airmen who served there and the sacrifices of those 26,000 young American airmen who gave their lives to bring peace. Monuments, historical markers and stained-glass windows in churches are plentiful in the English countryside today. Great Britain deeded land for the Cambridge American Military Cemetery at Cambridge to the United States. Thus, Americans killed in action could be buried on American soil. There are 5,123 names on the Wall of Honor at the cemetery. One of those names is Spencer Flinn, a former classmate at Bedford High.

The Royal Air Force and the U.S. Army Air Force received much credit for turning the tide of the war. Many English citizens have compiled pictures and records and authored books on the men, planes and missions of the U.S. Eighth Air Force which helped them save England and destroy the Third Reich. The Mighty Eighth was in England from 1942 to 1945 but left a lasting impression. There are many excellent books complete with data on the planes, combat photos and information on the heavy bombers and fighters available in bookstores today. Some British authors have made the history of World War II their life's work. We were a long way from home and the English welcomed us into their country. Their friendship was evident in the pubs and shops of Eye and Diss as well as London.

It is estimated that 210,000 airmen flew out of England to carry the war to Germany. Twenty-eight thousand American airmen lost their lives. The "Brits" recognized the sacrifices made by the Yanks, and the government and citizens of Great Britain wished to honor their memory. A nationwide fund drive was initiated shortly after the end of the war. King George VI gave his blessing to the project. The "Jesus Chapel" in the east section of St. Paul's Cathedral in the center of London was destroyed in the 1941 German Blitz. It was decided to construct an American Memorial Chapel in this damaged area. The project would take several years but the people were determined to show their appreciation to the United States and those who perished in the victory over Germany.

The reconstruction proceeded, and a commemoration ceremony was held July 4, 1951. General Dwight Eisenhower formally presented the book entitled the "Roll of Honour" for display in the Memorial Chapel. The large red leather-bound book contains 473 pages listing the names of the 28,000 Americans who lost their lives while stationed in the British Isles. The project was completed in 1952. The chapel features stained glass windows with insignias from the forty-eight states, and a glass enclosed marble pedestal which holds the "Book of Honour." One page is turned each day. Copies of the book are available to visitors wishing to find names of relatives or friends.

English school children, grateful citizens and the British government were generous in contributions to the American Memorial Chapel. All wished to express gratitude to the "Yanks" who had perished in defense of freedom. It was decided to publish a hardback book to mail to the next-of-kin of the 28,000 U.S. dead. The informative book contains sixty-nine pages of information on the Memorial Chapel and photographs and stories about life in the British Isles during World War II. The book was a fine goodwill gesture to American families who had lost loved ones in Great Britain during World War II. The copy I reviewed carries the name of a friend, Staff Sergeant Spencer E. Flynn, USAAF. Spencer was the engineer/gunner on an Eighth Air Force B-17 and had flown several combat missions before he died in a mid-air collision over England November, 1943. He is buried in the American Cemetery in Cambridge.

Spencer's sister, Kathryn Henschen, recently allowed me to read the 8 by 10 book received by her family. Spencer was a year ahead of me in High School but we shared the same noontime duties of guarding the bicycle racks for 25 cents an hour. The book's title, "Britain's Homage to 28,000 American Dead" a drawing of St. Paul's Cathedral and the deceased airman's name is embossed in gold on the cover of the sky blue book.

The Queen's Letter

In 2005 I sent a copy of my first book "Through These Eyes," to the Queen and received this letter.

SANDRINGHAM HOUSE

17th January, 2006

Dear Mr. Hutchinson,

    The Queen wishes me to write and thank you for your letter, with which you enclosed a copy of your memoirs.

    Her Majesty was pleased to receive this record of your experiences as a young airman, serving in the Eighth Air Force during the Second World War, and was touched by your recollections of the months you spent stationed in this country.

    The Queen was interested to learn of your eighteen combat missions with the 490th Bomb Group based at Eye airfield, and thought it kind of you to pay tribute to the assistance you have received from Mr. Eric Swain in the preparation of your book.

    Her Majesty appreciated the thoughtful sentiments expressed in your letter and the good wishes you have conveyed, and I am to thank you again for your kind thought for The Queen.

Yours sincerely,

Annabel Whitehead

Lady-in-Waiting

The Boeing B-17G Specification

- DESIGNED BY: Boeing Company, Seattle, Wash.
- POWER: Four 1,200-horsepower Wright Cyclone Model R-1820-97 engines. These engines are nine cylinder, radial, air-cooled type with a 16:9 gear ratio. The propellers are three-bladed Hamilton Standard propellers, 11 feet, 7 inches in diameter.
- WEIGHTS: Basic empty weight is 34,000 lbs. Gross weight (wartime) is 65,500 lbs.
- FUEL CAPACITY: 1,700 gallons
- RANGE: 1,850 miles. Range could be extended when equipped with "Tokyo Tanks," (late model Fs) and bomb bay tanks which provide a total capacity of 3,630 gallons.
- WING SPAN: 103 feet, 9 inches
- LENGTH: 74 feet, 4 inches
- HEIGHT: 19 feet, 1 inch
- ARMAMENT: Thirteen Browning M-2 .50 caliber machine guns (G model). Fire rate approximately 13 rounds per second. No gun on a B-17 carried more than one minute's supply of ammunition next to it, but up to 14,000 rounds are known to have been carried at times. (the second Schweinfurt raid is one example when crews took that many, and one crew came back with 143 rounds total left on board.) The number of guns vary by model from 11 to 14 with custom field modifications.
- BOMB LOAD: Depending on types of bombs, maximum normal load could go to 8,000 pounds. If B-17 was fitted with special external racks, maximum normal short-range bomb load could go as high as 17,600 pounds.
- SPEEDS: Maximum 300 mph at 30,000 ft, maximum continuous 263 mph at 25,000 ft., cruising speed 170 mph, landing 74 mph, rate of climb 37 minutes to 20,000 ft. Formation speed of 155 mph.

B-17 Flying Fortress Possible Bomb Loads

B-17 Bomb load-outs showing quantity of bombs and weight of each bomb (in US pounds) of an iron bomb.

B-17 F & G: 2-2000, 2-1600, 2-1000, 12-500, 16-300, 16-250, 24-100 (from AN-01-1B-40 B-17 weight and balance, Army Manual 1943.

EIGHTH AIR FORCE BOMB GROUPS IN ENGLAND

Group	Station	Aircraft	Missions	Combat	Loss
34th	Mendelsham 156	B-17	170	34	
44th	Shipham 115	B-24	343	153	
91st	Bassingbourn 121	B-17	340	197	
92nd	Padington 109	B-17	308	154	
93rd	Hardwick	B-24	396	100	
94th	Bury St. Edmonds 468	B-17	324	153	
95th	Horham 119	B-17	320	157	
96th	Snetterton Heath 138	B-17	321	189	
100th	Thorpe Abbots 139	B-17	306	177	
303rd	Molesworth 107	B-17	364	165	
305th	Cheveston 105	B-17	337	154	
306th	Thurleigh 111	B-17	342	171	
351st	Polebrook 110	B-17	311	124	
379th	Kimbolton 117	B-17	330	141	
381st	Ridgewell 167	B-17	296	131	
384th	Grafton Underwood 106	B-17	314	159	
385th	Great Ashfield	B-17	296	129	
388th	Knettishall 136	**B**-17	306	142	
389th	Hethel 114	B-24	321	116	
390th	Framinham 153	B-17	300	144	
392nd	Wendling 118	B-24	285	127	
398th	Nuthampstead 131	B-17	195	58	

401st		Deenethorpe 128	B-17	256	95
445th	Tibenham 124		B-24	382	95
446th	Bungay 125		B-24	273	58
447th	Rattlesden 126		B-17	257	97
448th	Seething 146		B-24	262	101
452nd	Deopham Green 142		B-17	250	110
453rd	Old Buckenham 144		B-24	259	58
457th	Glatton 130		B-17	237	83
458th	Horsham St. Faith 123		B-24	240	47
466th	Attlebridge 120		B-24	232	47
467th	Rackheath 145		B-24	212	29
486th	Sudbury 174		B-17	188	33
487th	Lavenham 137		B-17	185	48
489th	Halesworth 365		B-24	106	29
490th	Eye 134		B-17	158	40
491st		Metfield 366	B-24	187	47
492nd	North Pickenkham 143	B-24	64	12	
493rd	Debach 152		B-17	158	41

Total Planes Lost

B-17s - 4,754   B-24s - 2,112

Hutch's WWII Books

Through These Eyes - 2005 - 114 stories of author's diary and bombing missions

Bombs Away! – 2008 - 70 combat stories & 24 of a boyhood in the Great Depression

Boys in the B-17 – 2011 - 90 stories – teenager's missions 1942-45; survivors, POWs and boys who died --- too young to vote, but old enough to fight!

B-17 Memories from Memphis Belle to Victory – 2014 – 97 memoirs memories and interviews of the heroes of the Eighth Air force, Fifteenth Air Force and the Infantry from D-day to victory.

The 88+ year old author WW II veteran earned three Air medals flying combat missions (14 as lead crew) as a teenage radio/gunner on an Eighth Air Force B-17 Flying Fortress. His combat diary, numerous photos and deeds of others tell of young airmen flying on oxygen at 25,000 feet and 40 degrees below zero. They faced enemy fighters and flak over the target! The black smoke of exploding 88 mm shells looked harmless, but filled the sky with chunks of iron like a giant shotgun shell. A direct hit knocked bombers out of the sky; a lost an engine or fire meant dropping out of formation to face enemy fighters alone or bailing out to become German prisoners of war (POW.) Hutch says, "My crew members, my lucky Air Cadet ring, thirteen .50 caliber machine guns and a tough B-17 Flying Fortress contributed to my survival. However, I'm sure my mother's prayers and God brought me through it all!"

Hutch interview --- Google "Wings Over Europe My Smithville"

Autographed copies at james_hutchinson_693@comcast.net or J.L. Hutchinson 331 Boyd Lane Bedford, IN 47421

Prices vary at Bookstores and internet: Amazon Authorhouse Barnes &Noble Liberty Belle and Kindle E-books

Autographed copies at: (james_hutchinson_693@comcast.net or JL Hutchinson 331 Boyd Lane Bedford, IN 47421 812-275- 4308

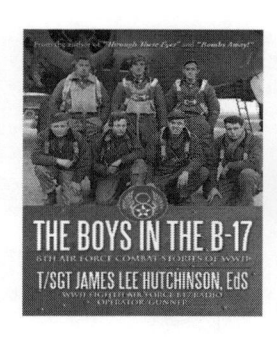

*Author honored before Indiana Senate and House February 2008

Hundreds of B-17 Flying Fortresses and B-24 Liberators filled the sky over England every clear day to assemble formations. They flew across the North Sea to blast industrial or military targets heavily protected by anti-aircraft guns. Luftwaffe fighters waited to attack the heavy bombers on their journey. Pilots tightened their formation and teenage gunners manned their 50 caliber machine guns to watch for the hell they knew was coming!

Missions in the 490th Bomb (14 as lead crew) provided the author with experiences to write of combat. Interviews of veterans and information from the 490th Historical Record provided stories of survival and/or death in the deadly skies due to fighter attacks, mid-air collisions, and being shot down to die or be imprisoned in POW camps. Mighty Eighth bomber formations fought of Luftwaffe fighters and flew into fields of anti-aircraft fire (flak) over the target to drop their bombs and battle their way out of enemy territory. They were never turned back by flak or fighters; 26,000 men (boys) of the Eighth Air Force bomber crews, fighter pilots and ground support units died and thousands were wounded in the WW II aerial crusade to destroy Hitler's Third Reich!

**See Hutch's DVD interview with WW II combat film:
Google "Wings Over Europe My Smithville**

USAAF Photo

Bibliography

1. *Historical Record of the 490th Bomb Group,* Lightner and Holland
2. *The Man Who Flew the Memphis Belle,* Robert Morgan and Ron Powers Dutton 2001
3. *Flashbacks and Memories of World War II,* T/Sgt. Howard Tuchin
4. *My War,* John C. Walter, Authorhouse, 2004
5. *The Mighty Eighth,* Gerald Astor, Dell Books, 1998
6. *High Noon Over Haseluenne,* Faley, M.P. and Luc Dewez, 2009
7. *Echoes of England,* Bowman M.W. Tempus Pub., 2006
8. *U.S. European Strategic Bombing Survey Summary Report, 1945*
9. *No Man's Sky,* Cline R. C. Authorhouse, 2014
10. *Aircraft of World War II,* Chris Chant. Metro Books
11. *Stars and Stripes,* News Items,1944-45
12. *B-17s over Berlin, 95th BG,* Hawkins, Ian, Brasseys, 1995
13. *Through These Eyes,* Hutchinson, J. L., Authorhouse, 2005
14. *Bombs Away,* Hutchinson, J. L., Authorhouse, 2008
15. *The Boys in the B-17* Hutchinson J.L. Authorhouse 2011
16. *WW II Duty Honor Country: The Memories of Those Who Were There,* Stephen Hardwick and Duane Hodgin, iUniverse, 2012
17. *They Served During America's Darkest and Finest Hours: The WW II Veterans of Wayne County, Indiana",* Duane Hodgin, Augustin, 2014
18. *Broken Wings,* Robert Kelly, Authorhouse
19. *The Mighty Eighth,* Roger Freeman,
20. *The View From the Bottom Up*, Robert Gilbert, Merriam Press, 2012

Films and Videos

1. Warbirds of WW II Tapes (www.timeless-video.com)
2. Twelve O'Clock High 1949
3. The Memphis Belle 1998
4. Red Tails, 1213
5. Hart's War 2002
6. Stalag 13 19536. The Great Escape
7. The Longest Day 1962
8. The Best Years of Our Lives 1946
9. Hope and Glory UK film
10. Hutch's DVD at: "Wings Over Europe My Smithville"